D0679667

EAT FISH, LIVE BETTER

Eat Fish, Live Better

How to Put More Fish and Omega-3
Fish Oils into Your Diet
for a Longer, Healthier Life

Anne M. Fletcher, M.S., R.D.

1817

HARPER & ROW, PUBLISHERS, New York
Cambridge, Philadelphia, San Francisco
London, Mexico City, São Paulo, Singapore, Sydney

Seasoning Mix for blackened redfish on p. 197 from *Chef Paul Prudhomme's Louisiana Kitchen* by Paul Prudhomme. Copyright © 1984 by Paul Prudhomme. Reprinted by permission of William Morrow and Company.

EAT FISH, LIVE BETTER. Copyright © 1989 by Anne M. Fletcher. All rights reserved. Printed in the United States of America. No part of this book may be used or reproduced in any manner whatsoever without written permission except in the case of brief quotations embodied in critical articles and reviews. For information address Harper & Row, Publishers, Inc., 10 E. 53rd Street, New York, N.Y. 10022. Published simultaneously in Canada by Fitzhenry & Whiteside Ltd., Toronto.

FIRST EDITION

Copyeditor: Nick Allison
Designer: Patricia Girvin Dunbar
Index by Rose Grant

Library of Congress Cataloging-in-Publication Data

Fletcher, Anne M.
　Eat fish, live better.

　Includes index.
　1. Fish as food. 　2. Fish oils in human nutrition.
3. Cookery (Fish)　I. Title.
QP144.F56F54　1989　　　613.2'6　　　88-45621
ISBN 0-06-015833-6

89　90　91　92　93　DT/HC　10　9　8　7　6　5　4　3　2　1

To my father, who inspired my love of science
and encouraged me to follow my instincts

Contents

List of Tables

Acknowledgments

I AM GRATEFUL to the many researchers and fish experts who were willing to be consulted for different sections of *Eat Fish, Live Better*. In particular, I would like to thank the following individuals who reviewed various parts of the book relating to their areas of expertise: Marc Fisher, M.D., a neurologist and cardiovascular disease researcher with the University of Massachusetts Medical School; my father, Alan M. Fletcher, a fish biologist, science editor and writer, and experienced angler; James Daniels, director of research and development at Mrs. Paul's Kitchens, Inc. in Philadelphia; Robert Learson with the National Marine Fisheries Service in Gloucester, MA; Anthony Guarino, Ph.D., Chief of the FDA's Fishery Research Branch; and my friend, Mary Kay Bedigian, M.S., R.D., a nutritionist with expertise in weight control. Thanks, also, to Jacob Exler, Ph.D., the principal investigator for the USDA's Handbook 8-15 on nutritional composition of fish, for his willingness to answer innumerable questions and share information. Similarly, research chemist Judith Krzynowek, with the National Marine Fisheries Service in Gloucester, MA, is always so agreeable about tracking down data and sharing her knowledge.

Linda and Mike Foley of the M. F. Foley Company in New Bedford, MA were kind enough to allow me to visit their facility for some first-hand exposure to the fishing industry. Mary Jane Laus and Eileen Atallah, nutritionists with the Massachusetts Nutrient Data Bank at the University of Massachusetts in Amherst, were infinitely patient and accommodating in providing nutritional analyses of the *Eat Fish* Recipes. I also used nutrition analysis software from N-Squared Computing Company in Silverton, Oregon; I appreciate their technical advice.

I am deeply grateful to Debby Fisher, a gourmet cook, who developed several of the *Eat Fish* Recipes and tested countless others. Her feedback as well as that of my friend Annie Tiberio was invaluable. My gratitude is also extended to the following friends who tested recipes and offered their suggestions: Karen Sabbath, Heidi Miller and Paul Adler, Karen Whitaker, and Monica Hottenstein. Of course, without the fish, where would I have been? For supplying me with both familiar and "new" fish, I thank Craig and Judi Strong of Wilbraham Seafoods, as well as Franz Stegbuchner of Atlantic Seafoods Fish Market and Restaurant.

Special thanks go to my husband, Steven, and my son, Wesley (and little Tyler, who had no choice in the matter)—who ate a lot of fish —for their love, patience, encouragement, and sacrifices. I also appreciate the support of all my other relatives and am particularly indebted to my sisters, Carol Daniels and Cynthia Rich (and Lois Fletcher, for her willingness), who helped me at a critical time. Thanks, too, to my parents, who encouraged me, and to my friend and mother-in-law, Ruth Keesing, whose phone calls kept me going. Likewise, I am grateful for the inspiration of two friends and respected colleagues: Larry Lindner, with the *Tufts University Diet & Nutrition Letter,* and Joan Fouhy, with Business Expressions.

I appreciate the flexibility, patience, and fine editing of my editors at Harper & Row. For the opportunities they've provided and for getting me over some rough spots, I thank Connie Clausen and Guy Kettelhack, my agents.

Foreword

THE ROLE OF diet in preventing heart disease is more important than ever at this time, a time when cardiovascular disease is overwhelmingly the largest cause of death in developed countries. Everything we know at present points to the beneficial effects of fish, a food high in protein and minerals, generally low in fat and calories, and rich in an unusual kind of fat of favorable composition. The unique fat tends to be highly polyunsaturated because of its omega-3 fatty acids, which appear to lower blood lipids and decrease the likelihood of forming blood clots that can cause heart attacks and strokes. This kind of fat is particularly rich in oilier fish such as mackerel and salmon.

Ms. Fletcher, an excellent nutrition writer, has produced an interesting, very well-researched book that offers an intelligent perspective on all of these favorable effects of fish as well as giving advice on how to procure, stock, and cook fish properly. She also provides appetizing and healthful recipes and tells how to incorporate fish into a reduced-fat, reduced-calorie eating plan. And for those who want to lose weight, *Eat Fish, Live Better* includes a sensible weight-loss diet that will not sacrifice good nutrition.

An extensive glossary describing less-common fish varieties makes this book so thorough a reference that no one who reads it need be intimidated by the idea of making fish a regular part of his diet. Guidelines are even offered for inland dwellers who want to eat more fish. And a thoughtful, reassuring discussion addresses the current concern with the safety of our fish supply.

Eat Fish, Live Better is a highly useful book that is both beneficial and enjoyable. It should be welcomed by those who want to do everything in their power to develop a more healthful, preventive lifestyle.

Jean Mayer
President,
Tufts University

As with all diets, the diets in this book should be followed under a physician's supervision. Before including the *Eat Fish* Recipes in your menu plan, it is recommended that you check with your doctor.

Every effort has been made to provide the most up-to-date information. Because the field of nutrition is changing rapidly, however, differing information may be currently available.

PART I

The Good News about
Fish and Health

CHAPTER ONE

Why Eat More Fish?

THE FISH FERVOR

Cardiovascular disease researcher Marc Fisher, M.D., calls it "the magic bullet of the eighties." "The gospel" is the reference used by William Lands, Ph.D., leading biochemist in fish-oil research. Artemis Simopoulos, M.D., chairman of the National Institutes of Health Nutrition Coordinating Committee, says, "Today, everyone is excited. . . ." Seafood nutrition expert Joyce Nettleton, D.Sc., R.D., proclaims, "Hopes and expectations are very high." They're all talking about the burgeoning field of fish* and health—one that is growing by leaps and bounds, with promise of uncovering means to prevent and treat a host of deadly and debilitating ailments.

As an experienced nutrition educator, writer, and registered dietitian, I am often asked what I view as the "hottest" topics in the world of food and nutrition. Without hesitation, I respond that fish as "health" food tops the list. The next decade will undoubtedly bring unprecedented findings about the benefits of fish and fish oils. In fact, the work is already well under way, as evidenced by keen enough concern on the part of the scientific community that the National Institutes of Health, along with the Alcohol, Drug Abuse and Mental Health Administration, are funding a nationwide research program to help determine how fish and its oils influence health, plus a number of diseases.

There's no reason, however, to wait around until all the facts are in —more and more experts are in accord that most of us should be eating more fish, starting today. Hence, the message of *Eat Fish, Live Better*: just about everyone should be eating fish three, four, or even more times a week.

Reputable nutrition scientists almost always use words of caution

* "Fish" refers to all edible fish—finfish, shellfish, seafood, and freshwater fish.

3

before making wide, sweeping recommendations to the general public to change the way it eats. Indeed, you're probably tired of the admonitions for "moderation" and "a balanced diet." Nevertheless, cautionary words usually *are* in order for a society hungry for dietary miracles—a society that sinks millions of dollars into bestsellers written by scantily credentialed or misled diet gurus.

When it comes to encouraging the public to eat more fish, however, the case is quite different; for even some of the most conservative nutritionists support a fish-rich diet—right now. *New York Times* health columnist Jane Brody aptly captures the feeling in the air with her statement, "We cannot afford to wait until every *i* is dotted and every *t* is crossed in nutrition research. . . . We really have to act on the basis of the best nutrition information currently available."

Another aspect of the good news is that, for once, instead of hearing that you should eat *less* of something—less sugar, fewer calories, smaller amounts of salt and fat—you're being told that fish is a good food you can eat *more* of. As with anything you eat, it's important to ask, "What's the right amount? Is it possible to overdo it? If so, how much is too much?" And, "If there are any risks, do the benefits outweigh them?" *Eat Fish, Live Better* will answer these questions as it gives you the facts behind the current fish fervor.

THE NEW FISH-HEALTH STORY

If you had grown up in a coastal fishing village in Greenland or Japan, not only would you have eaten fish every day, but you'd have a good chance of being spared from the number-one killer in this country: cardiovascular disease, the condition associated with high-fat diets that ultimately blocks blood vessels, resulting in heart attacks and strokes. For more than a decade, scientific investigators have known that certain groups of people who rely on fish as their dietary mainstay have a remarkably low rate of heart attacks. In one fish-eating community of 2,000 people, for instance, not a single death from cardiovascular disease was reported over a ten-year period. Contrasting sharply is the sad fact that two Americans die each minute as a result of cardiovascular disease (CVD).

When researchers looked at the diet of these "protected" people, they were at first confounded by the high total level of fat—amounting to about 40 percent of calorie intake, 10 percent higher than is currently recommended. They then began to suspect that it must be the unique type of oily fat in their fish-rich diets that actually confers the benefits. (As chapter 2 explains in further detail, fats include both oils and solid fats such as butter and shortening.) Fish oils are rich in what scientists call the "omega-3" fatty acids, which have a different chemical structure than the "omega-6" fatty acids of vegetable oils. The types of fish richest in the omega-3 fatty acids are formerly maligned oilier varieties, including mackerel and salmon; low-fat, white-fleshed fish and shellfish have lower amounts of the special oils. (For reasons that will become clear in a moment, I recommend eating more of *all* types of fresh fish.)

The observation that a high intake of omega-3 fatty acids correlates with a low risk of cardiovascular disease spawned a multitude of studies in which people were fed known amounts of fish and fish oils to see what the effects might be on their health. But the findings were not brought home to the general public until 1985, when one of the most prestigious of all medical journals, *The New England Journal of Medicine,* published three landmark studies indicating that fish is good for your circulatory system and, possibly, for your immune system. Here's what the medical evidence to date suggests fish and its omega-3 fatty acids have the potential to do:*

- *Protect against CVD,* even if relatively small amounts of fish are eaten. Researchers from the respected University of Leiden in the Netherlands reported that, compared to a group of men who ate no fish, "high" fish consumers—who ate one or more ounces a day on a regular basis—were two and a half times less likely to die from heart disease. Assuming portion sizes of three and a half ounces, just two small fish meals a week could make a difference! A diet rich in fish oil may also help lower blood pressure.
- *Favorably alter blood lipids,* namely, lowering triglycerides and cholesterol that are linked with CVD. Some people who have high blood levels of these lipids appear to benefit more from a diet rich in fish and fish oils than they do from traditional low-fat, low-cholesterol diets *or* diets suppplemented with the polyunsaturated vegetable oils so widely touted for the heart in recent years.
- *Bring about "thinner" blood,* rendering it less likely to clot and cause heart attacks or strokes. The omega-3 fatty acids can make blood platelet cells—cells involved in clotting—less "sticky," decreasing the likelihood that they'll clump together and form blockages in blood vessels leading to the heart and brain. Fish oils also appear to make blood more fluid, allowing it to squeeze through blood vessels that are already partially clogged.
- *Favorably alter the immune system* in such fashion that people with inflammatory ailments, including rheumatoid arthritis, may benefit. Harvard researchers observed favorable changes in certain white

* See chapters 3 and 4 for more details on fish and specific ailments.

blood cells—cells contributing to inflammation—in people consuming high levels of fish oils. There is also some evidence that omega-3 fatty acids have the potential to help people who have multiple sclerosis, lupus, psoriasis, asthma, and diabetes—all of which appear to be related to a faulty immune system.

· *Bring about cancer-preventing biochemical changes.* Not only do fish-eating societies have a lower incidence of CVD, but few of their females suffer from breast cancer, a major cause of death among American women. Findings of animal experiments indicate that fish oils may inhibit growth of breast, colon, pancreas, and prostate tumors.

· *Provide relief from migraine headaches.* Preliminary research suggests that certain people who are incapacitated by migraine headaches—finding no relief from other remedies—may experience remarkable improvement after taking fish-oil supplements.

THE DRUG VERSUS FOOD DISTINCTION

It may come as a bit of a disappointment to learn that, despite all the exciting talk about omega-3 fatty acids, I'm not about to tell you to rush out and buy fish-oil supplements at your local health-food store or pharmacy. Why? Because studies reporting the omega-3s' favorable effects are done under carefully controlled circumstances, with strict medical supervision to monitor potential side effects, such as bleeding tendencies. (See chapter 5 for more on fish-oil supplements.)

Here, it becomes important to make the distinction between a therapeutic or druglike effect of fish oils and a preventive or protective advantage. When used to treat people who already have ailments, such as elevated blood lipids or migraine headaches, the dosages of fish oils are high enough that their use is pharmaceutical and warranted only under the supervision of physicians and researchers who are familiar with omega-3 fatty acids. At this point, it is premature to suggest that most people start taking fish-oil supplements to ward off ailments.

It's not jumping the gun, however, to advise that adding more fish to your regular diet is a prudent gesture to help *keep* yourself healthy. The preventive advantage of fish is nicely summed up by fish-oil biochemist William E. M. Lands, Ph.D., from the University of Illinois at Chicago in his statement that having high amounts of omega-3 fatty acids "in our daily diets for decades represents a form of intervention that is unmatched by any drug research." Of course, the question here is, "How high?" The answer is that nobody knows the ideal minimum or maximum amount of dietary fish.

It *is* known, however, that it's possible to overdo it with fish, as demonstrated by a man who ate nothing but fish and seal meat for one hundred days: he experienced nosebleeds, developed anemia, bruised easily, and had a lowered sperm count. But there really is no reason to go to such extremes if you recall the Dutch study in which relatively small amounts of fish, eaten on a regular basis, seemingly conferred protection against CVD.

Weighing the evidence *for* eating more fish against the potential disadvantages of going overboard, the best advice is to up fish intake from the American average of six or seven times a month to a level somewhere between three and seven times a week.

THE OLD FISH-HEALTH STORY

Momentarily placing aside the *new* fish-health story, bear in mind that fish has many qualities other than omega-3 fatty acids that deserve honorable mention. Compared with other protein-rich foods, including red meat, pork, and cheese, most types of fish have a low-calorie, low-fat edge. In other words, fish is naturally "light."

If you're trying to lose weight or keep it down to a comfortable and healthy level, there's good reason to place fish at the top of the list as a low-calorie high-protein choice. Indeed, I often saw living proof of fish's value for dieters in my practice of counseling overweight individuals. People who were "stuck" at a certain weight often got the scales moving downward again simply by eating lean fish in place of red meat as frequently as possible. You can see why when a three-and-a-half-ounce serving of baked cod, at 105 calories, is half as fattening as the same amount of the leaner portion of sirloin steak and has *fewer* than half the calories of lean, broiled hamburger. Even so-called "oily" salmon has fewer calories per ounce than *lean* ground beef. (Chapter 6 tells you in detail how fish stacks up next to other protein foods.)

The reason why most types of fish are so low in calories is that they're low in fat. Fat is one of the three nutrients responsible for the caloric value of foods: unlike carbohydrate and protein at four calories per gram, fat provides nine calories in each gram. Since fat has more than double the calories of carbohydrate and protein, small amounts of fat in a food can substantially boost its total caloric value.

The low-fat nature of fish also lends itself well to the prescriptions of major health organizations, including the American Heart Association and the National Academy of Sciences, for lowering fat intake from the current American average—totaling close to 40 percent of calorie intake—to 30 percent or less. This guideline was set, in large part, because societies consuming high-fat diets tend to have a higher incidence of CVD, as well as more cancer of the breast, colon, and prostate.

Not only does meat usually contain *more* fat than fish, but the *type* of fat in meat is much more saturated. Saturated fats are the type of fats most likely to raise blood cholesterol, as you'll learn in chapter 2. Three and a half ounces of lean, broiled hamburger, for example, provides your arteries with 4 times as much saturated fat as the same amount of baked sockeye salmon and 25 times the saturated fat in boiled shrimp! Of course, the favorable numerical scores for fish can be wiped out if you're heavy-handed with fats and rich sauces in cooking. (Chapter 6 has more on saturated-fat values of protein foods and details the new cholesterol story for shellfish.)

Thus, the "old" fish-health story—extolling the lower calorie and fat virtues of fish—has preventive and therapeutic merit on its own, not considering the special oils in fish. In the *preventive* realm, fish helps to achieve the dietary recommendations to ward off CVD and cancer. If the low-calorie nature of fish helps you to keep your weight down, you're also lowering your chances of developing ailments associated with overweight, including hypertension, the adult-onset type of diabetes, and certain types of cancer. The *therapeutic* value enters if you already have heart disease, hypertension, diabetes, or elevated blood lipids because fish helps fill one prescription for each ailment—to eat a low-fat diet and keep your weight down.

FISH IS WHAT WE'RE LOOKING FOR

Healthful eating is "in." You can see it in the supermarket aisles just by scanning food-label enticements of "lite," "extra-lean," "less than 300 calories," and "low-fat." Traditionally targeted for people trying to lose weight, such products appear to be making their way into the kitchens of nondieters. People who define themselves as dieters— amounting to about one out of every three adults—use "light" or low-calorie foods and beverages as a primary means of controlling their food intake, according to a study conducted by an association of dietary product manufacturers, called the Calorie Control Council. Yet, a survey conducted by a marketing research company, the NPD Group, unexpectedly revealed that individuals who consider themselves nondieters actually use *more* "light" and low-calorie foods than do dieters. The implication is that a growing number of people are trying to adopt *permanently* a more healthful way of eating, as opposed to just when they're on a diet. Lower-fat, reduced-calorie foods have great appeal, for both the weight-conscious and the health-conscious.

Surely, fish fits the bill for the many people working toward a lifetime of health and fitness.

Another interesting trend is revealed by a poll on consumer attitudes toward nutrition conducted by the Food Marketing Institute, the major trade group representing supermarkets. FMI found that there seems to be a shift *away* from worrying about foods and ingredients perceived as harmful and *toward* selecting items believed to improve fitness, energy, and longevity. What better way to meet a desire for enhanced fitness and improving the odds of living longer than to make more fish part of your life?

Actually, government statistics suggest that increased fish intake has already become part of the nation's healthful eating trend; 1987 saw an all-time high for annual fish intake at 15.4 pounds (before cooking, waste removed) per person. Add to that the estimated per capita intake of recreationally caught fish—a surprisingly high 3 to 4 pounds—and you have an average of approximately 19 yearly pounds. Compared to 16 years earlier, annual fish intake has climbed nearly 4 pounds per person.

As favorable as these fish statistics sound, the average amount of fish we eat is meager next to the annual per capita intake of red meat and poultry. Yes, red meat consumption has taken a downward turn since the early 1970s, but the average American still eats well over 100 pounds a year. Poultry is on the increase at 50-plus pounds per capita. (While skinless poultry is certainly a healthful choice if cooked properly, it does not contain any omega-3 fatty acids to speak of.)

Moreover, the fish that *is* eaten in this country is not evenly distributed—well over half is consumed by about a quarter of the population. In other words, the bulk of fish is being eaten by a relatively small number of people. At that, the U.S. Department of Commerce estimates that almost two-thirds of fish eating goes on away from home, which tells you nothing about how the marine fare is prepared. It's not clear how much is slathered with butter and creamy sauces or what amount is subjected to deep-fat frying.

LET'S GET GOING

The statistics on fish intake make it obvious that neither the good "new" news nor the favorable "old" news about the health benefits of fish have gone far enough. The indications are clear, however, that many people would like to eat more healthfully prepared fish. Witness the proliferation of "light" batter and "less-than-300-calorie" frozen fish entrees in supermarket freezer cases. The problem is that many people don't know the proper ways to select, handle, and cook fish themselves, as indicated by a *Better Homes & Gardens*–National Fisheries Institute survey on consumer attitudes toward fish. Of the people who said they served fish "seldom" or "never," the top four reasons were *don't like smell, don't have good recipes, don't know how to cook it,* and *too expensive.* Here's how *Eat Fish, Live Better* lays to rest each excuse for not eating more fish.

Don't like smell. If an unpleasant fishy odor is part and parcel of serving fish in your home, then something is wrong at the market or in how you're storing your catch. The distasteful smell is a sign that the fish is not fresh. With a few simple guidelines, chapter 9— "Stocking the Best Fish the Right Way"—shows how to make certain that fish is fresh at point of purchase and kept fresh once you get it home. In addition, chapter 10—"Cook It Right"—offers aroma-enhancing techniques to spare your home from lingering essence of fish "the morning after."

Don't have good recipes. If Framingham Heart Study director William Castelli, M.D., is right in his opinion that the average American family eats from the same ten recipes over and over, then it's probably true that many people lack tasty, not to mention healthful, fish recipes. Chapter 12's *Eat Fish* Recipes fill the void, offering simple fare to add to your every-night repertoire, plus fancy, fit-for-company formulas.

If it's variety you're after, fish fits the bill far better than poultry or beef. After all, beef is beef and poultry amounts to chicken or turkey. But with finfish alone, you can choose from more than 100 different types, ranging from familiar swordfish, haddock, and sole to lesser-known mako shark, orange roughy, monkfish, and pollock, just to name a handful of the "new" fish varieties recently made available on a commercial scale. The choices grow exponentially when you consider the host of cooking methods chapter 10 gives you for cooking fish.

Don't know how to cook it. Next to smelly fish, the worst fish is overdone fish, as you'll also learn in chapter 10, "Cook It Right." Disappointing home fish-cookery results are almost invariably due to overcooking. The end product: a dry, leathery entrée. Chapter 10 guides you and offers you special tips to assure delectable results each time you serve fish.

If time is your master, tasty fish dishes need not be cumbersome to prepare. Actually, fish is nature's answer to fast food. Best-selling author, weekly columnist, and busy mother Jane Brody says it all: "Fish is what I buy when I know I've got only 15 or 20 minutes to get dinner on the table." If that conjures up images of boring broiled scrod or canned tuna on a bed of lettuce, picture Cheesy Fish Fillets, Broiled Basil Swordfish, Breaded Monkfish Medallions, and Shark with Crumbly Blue Cheese Topping—all prepared in less than half an hour.

Too expensive. This excuse is one that I have no time for in a society that, per person, manages to purchase between three and four meals a week away from home, a society that also finds twenty billion or more dollars a year to spend on diet foods and beverages, not to mention hundreds of millions of dollars on over-the-counter diet drugs and weight-loss gimmicks. I could certainly argue that some of these funds are misdirected and would better be spent on fish when you consider all its benefits.

Besides, have you ever really stopped and compared costs of various kinds of fish with meat and poultry to see if fish really *is* all that expensive? In chapter 9, I share the surprising findings of an informal before-and-after survey in which I compared the costs of certain types of fish, chicken, and beef. I also offer you some money-saving tips.

All told, fish has more bonuses than any other protein food: beneficial oils, a naturally "light" nature, an offering of unlimited choices, adaptability for quick and easy cooking, and affordability. When you carefully examine the reasons why people don't eat fish more regularly, it becomes clear that there really *are* no excuses for not making more fish part of your life, starting today.

CHAPTER TWO

What's So Special
about Fish Oils?

A PRIMER ON FATS

In order to understand the unique attributes of fish oils, you first need to learn a little something about their chemical family—the fats. To butter-fingered chefs, fats make for a messy cleanup, but are worth the travail for the rich taste and texture they impart to almost any food. Anyone who savors eating doughnuts or muffins at his desk knows fats as those indelible oily crumb marks left behind on important papers. But to dietitians, fats are the nutritional bad guys that add inches to your waist and raise the odds of developing cardiovascular disease and cancer. Similarly, physicians view fats as globules coursing through your bloodstream, waiting to lodge themselves in arteries and shut off the supply of blood to your heart or brain. Actually, fats are all of the above—the oils and solid fats in foods, as well as body fat and fatty particles floating in your bloodstream.

Food fats include greasy-to-the-touch ingredients: vegetable oil, butter, margarine, shortening, and lard, as well as the white fat bordering cuts of meat and the creamy fat deposits on poultry parts. Other foods which are so laden with fats that nutritionists "count" them as fats are mayonnaise, salad dressing, bacon, cream, and skins of poultry or fish. If you think, however, that what you see is what you get, then you're wrong about fats because the so-called "visible" fats, detectable by eye, account for only about 40 percent of the fat we eat. The rest is "invisible" fat dispersed through egg yolks, milk products, baked goods, and the fleshy parts of meat, poultry, and fish. Although too much dietary fat is undesirable, small amounts are needed to transport fat-soluble vitamins (A, D, E, and K) into the body. Polyunsaturated fats (see page 15) provide the body with lino-

12

leic acid, a fatty acid that the body requires to make its own fats properly. Fats also help you to feel full after eating a meal.

Body fats include the all-too-familiar storage fat depots—on hips, thighs, and bellies—that nearly everyone wants to minimize, plus fats traveling in the bloodstream. Also called adipose tissue, storage fat becomes excessive when you eat too much of any calorie-containing nutrient, be it carbohydrate, protein, or fat. Less simply stated is the effect of diet on blood fats—technically called *triglycerides*—and fat-like *cholesterol.* Collectively known as *lipids,* triglycerides and cholesterol are carried in the circulatory system in tiny protein-coated packets called lipoproteins. While some lipids are normally present in the blood at all times, high levels of either type are an ominous sign. Indeed, elevated blood cholesterol has long been known to significantly increase the odds of developing CVD. And, although the relationship between high blood triglycerides and CVD is less clear, the evidence in hand suggests that an elevation may also be some sort of danger signal for the nation's number-one killer. (For more on blood lipids, see "Close-Up on Blood Lipids" in chapter 3.)

Now that you know the basics about food and body fats, you can begin to come to terms with the more complicated impact that specific types of dietary fats—including fish oils—can have on your health. The unique effects of different food fats have to do with the types of building blocks, known as fatty acids, that compose them. Fatty acids are simply long chains of carbon atoms with varying amounts of hydrogen and oxygen atoms attached. These fatty acids can be saturated, monounsaturated, or polyunsaturated, depending on their number of what chemists term "double bonds." Saturated fatty acids have no double bonds; "monos" have one double bond; and "polys" have more than one double bond.

All foods containing fats have mixtures of the different types of fatty acids, but one type invariably predominates, determining the biological effect that that particular food fat will have. Following are the categories of fatty acids, their primary food sources, and descriptions of the impacts they can have on your health.

Saturated fatty acids. These predominate in most fats derived from animals. The richest sources are fats in whole milk, cream, ice cream, cheese, butter, lard, red meats, and poultry. Exceptions to the animal-fat rule are a few vegetable fats that are highly saturated: coconut oil, palm oil, palm kernel oil, and cocoa butter (the fat in chocolate). Countless studies of both individuals and large populations of people reveal that saturated fats are associated with high blood cholesterol—a leading risk factor for heart attacks and strokes. Societies that consume large amounts of saturated fats not only have a higher incidence of CVD, but they tend to have higher rates of certain cancers. Americans currently consume 15 to 20 percent of their calories as saturated fat, compared to the recommended healthful level of less than 10 percent. My personal feeling about saturated fats is: the lower, the better.

Cholesterol. While not truly a fat, cholesterol must be discussed in the same breath as saturated fats because many of their food sources—namely fatty red meats and whole-milk dairy products—are one and the same. Richer still in cholesterol are egg yolks and organ meats, such as liver. Poultry and fish contain cholesterol, too. But the amount in most types of fish varies from little to moderate. (See chapter 6 for good news on cholesterol in shellfish.) Although *dietary* cholesterol has been shown to increase *blood* cholesterol in some studies, the amount of cholesterol you eat is most likely to be harmful when your saturated-fat intake is also high. In other words, it's unlikely that cutting back on dietary cholesterol will appreciably lower your blood levels of the lipid unless you cut back on saturated fat (along with decreasing total fat) as well. The recommended upper limit for daily cholesterol intake is 300 milligrams. Here, a word of caution is in order because of confusing commercial messages boasting "no cholesterol" for food products. For a food without cholesterol can be high in saturated fat and could be more detrimental to your arteries than a cholesterol-containing item. Case in point: dairy substitutes, including dessert toppings and creamers, which are often loaded with highly saturated coconut and/or palm oils. My position on cholesterol: you shouldn't have to worry about it, as long as your total fat intake takes up no more than 30 percent of your calories and provided you eat egg yolks and liver no more than occasionally. Certainly, if you have a serious cholesterol problem, it would be wise to stay well below 300 daily milligrams.

Monounsaturated fatty acids. These are particularly rich in olive and peanut oils, as well as avocados, and some stick margarines. For years, the nutrition community told the public that "monos" had a neutral effect on cholesterol—neither raising nor lowering blood levels. Recent findings, however, indicate that the type of "monos" in olive oil may be at least as effective in lowering blood cholesterol as "polys" (see page 15). Moreover, there is evidence that a diet that includes a moderate amount of olive oil may lower blood cholesterol even more than a diet that severely limits total fat. My advice: as long as your total fat intake is curbed, there appears to be no reason to avoid olive oil. Incidentally, you can't extrapolate the olive-oil findings to the other "mono"-rich fats, peanut oil and stick margarine, because they have not been shown to have the same beneficial effects.

Polyunsaturated fatty acids. Predominating in corn, safflower, cottonseed, soybean, and sunflower oils, these have long been touted for their ability to lower blood cholesterol. Indeed, Dr. Castelli recalls his medical internship days when fellow classmates drank a shot of corn oil every day because "they knew they were going to go out to some hamburger heaven and pig out on saturated fat." But the long-term effects of consuming high amounts of polyunsaturated fats simply are not known. To be sure, some nutrition experts are nervous about animal studies in which polyunsaturated fats have been associated with the development of cancer, although this relationship has not been shown in people. I agree with the American Heart Association in its recommendation that polyunsaturated fats take up no more than 10 percent of your daily calories. You should also be aware that polyunsaturated fats can be "hydrogenated"—a commercial process in which vegetable oils are hardened to make such products as shortening. Unfortunately, hydrogenation renders the fatty acids in an oil more saturated.

Fish-oil fatty acids. These are also rich in polyunsaturates. But I consider fish oils to be in a class of their own because they contain a unique brand of polyunsaturated fatty acid—the omega-3 type mentioned in chapter 1—not found in significant quantities elsewhere in common foods. Compared to the omega-6 fatty acids in vegetable oils, which contain two or three double bonds, omega-3 fatty acids are even more highly polyunsaturated, with five or six double bonds. (The 3 and the 6 simply have to do with the placement of double bonds in a fatty acid.) The omega-3s are also made of longer carbon chains than the omega-6s.

There are about seven different omega-3 fatty acids in fish oils, but the two that are present in highest amounts are termed eicosapentaenoic acid (EPA) and docosahexaenoic acid (DHA). Soybean and walnut oils also contain appreciable amounts of omega-3 fatty acids, but they're not of the EPA and DHA variety. Leafy vegetables contain small amounts of omega-3 fatty acids, too.

Many fish attain their high levels of the special oils because they feed on zooplankton—tiny water animals that eat microscopic floating plants called phytoplankton. We can thank the phytoplankton for manufacturing the omega-3 fatty acids that ultimately become part of fish cells and tissue. Predators like tuna and cod attain their omega-3s by dining on smaller fish that consume zooplankton. Since the omega-3s act as a sort of biological antifreeze—remaining fluid even at frigid temperatures—the highest levels of EPA and DHA are generally found in fish that live in colder waters. Salmon and mackerel are good examples.

AN IMPORTANT WORD ABOUT TOTAL FAT INTAKE

Before going into more detail about the connections between fish and specific ailments, I'm compelled to reiterate the importance of decreasing total fat in your diet—not just to lower your chance of CVD, but to lower the risk of cancer of the colon, breast, and prostate. For all of these ailments are associated with high-fat diets. Moreover, since all fats have the same number of calories—nine in each gram or about a hundred per tablespoon—lowering your total fat intake will help to keep your weight down, another preventive move you can make against CVD and cancer.

You simply can't get away from the warning—be it issued by the American Heart Association, the American Cancer Society, the National Academy of Sciences, the Department of Agriculture, or the Department of Health and Human Services; Americans need to drop below their current fat level amounting to nearly 40 percent of calorie intake. That much fat adds up to eight tablespoons of butter or oil for someone who consumes 2,000 calories a day. (Remember, too, about the fat that's "hidden" away in foods.) The going recommendation for all Americans over the age of two is to drop down to 30 percent or less fat calories, at the same time avoiding saturated fat and cholesterol-rich foods. My bottom-line advice about fat is that it's to your advantage to use as little as possible. The fat that you do consume should come from a mix consisting mainly of fish and olive oils, with smaller amounts of polyunsaturated vegetable oils, and even less saturated fat. (Chapters 11 and 13 provide more details on implementing a low-fat diet.)

UNRAVELING A MEDICAL MYSTERY

In digging through the scientific archives on the relationship between fish and disease, I was surprised to discover that, at the very same time scientists discovered that vegetable oils can lower blood cholesterol (about thirty years ago), they also found that fish oils could do the same thing. Then I came across a somewhat obscure and unpublicized study, conducted by a Dr. Averly Nelson from the 1950s through the early 1970s, in which he placed people who already had heart disease on a low-fat diet that included fish (and emphasized oily fish) at least three times a week. Compared to a group of heart-disease patients who didn't follow the diet, the fish-eaters lived an average of four years longer. Over the course of the study, 36 percent of the group on the diet—but only 8 percent of the nondieters—remained alive.

Why, then, did the medical community encourage the general public to consume vegetable oils, saying little or nothing about fish oils, right up until the 1980s? In the first place, vegetable polyunsaturates have long been widely available in the form of oils and margarine. Other than in the vitamin supplement section (and that's a recent phenomenon), have you ever seen bottles of fish oil for sale in the supermarket? Fish oils likely got a bad rap because of their familiarity as grandmother's distasteful cod-liver-oil health tonic—foisted upon youngsters for decades. No one seemed to realize that just eating more fish (as opposed to using fish oil per se) could make a difference.

It wasn't until the early 1970s that the interest in fish and fish oils was rekindled. At that time two Danish physicians did some brilliant medical detective work that spurred the plethora of exciting research going on at this very moment. Their intriguing story is worth telling.

Clues from the Eskimos

Take a convoy of 10 dogsleds pulled by more than 100 huskies; plunge into Greenland's $-13°$ F coldness; and spend months analyzing the blood and dietary habits of a small community of Eskimos. Five such expeditions were led by Denmark's Hans Olaf Bang, M.D., Ph.D., and Jorn Dyerberg, M.D., Ph.D., in their search for an explanation for the near-absence of CVD in Eskimos.

Decades earlier, Danish explorers who studied the Greenland Eskimos never mentioned heart disease as a cause of death. More recently, hospital records kept on 1,800 Greenland Eskimos for a 25-year period revealed only three "possible" heart attacks. Compared to the Danes —considered a modern population of people, much like us—the Eskimos not only had much less heart disease, but they were also afflicted far less often with diabetes, bronchial asthma, and psoriasis. Even though today's Eskimos have adopted a more contemporary way of life, recent statistics reveal that heart disease accounts for just 3.5 percent of all deaths. For both the United States and Denmark, the heart-disease rate is at least ten times higher! In addition, breast and colon cancer, which are quite common in our nation, are rarities among the Eskimos.

How can so many Eskimos be spared from the ailments that plague us when, in fact, their very name was long thought to mean "people eating raw meat"? To be sure, the traditional Eskimo diet consists almost entirely of fish and fatty animals that eat fish—namely seals and whales. In addition, Eskimo fruit and vegetable intake is minimal because the environment is too frigid to support much plant life. It all amounts to a high-fat, low-carbohydrate, practically fiber-free diet for the Eskimos—quite the antithesis of the going dietary recommendations for preventing heart disease and cancer.

Intrigued by the discrepancy between the traditional Eskimo diet —which has about 40 percent fat calories, similar to the level in Danish diets—and the low incidence of CVD, Drs. Bang and Dyerberg set out on their first expedition to Greenland (a province of Denmark) in 1970. Their destination was a carefully chosen, somewhat primitive area called the Umanak district on the northwest coast of the island. Here, Eskimos held to old ways, with most adults earning a living as seal, whale, and fish hunters. The doctors drew samples of the Eskimos' blood in order to compare cholesterol and triglyceride levels with those of a group of Danes to see if therein lay the explanation for the difference in heart disease rates. The findings: both lipids were significantly lower in the Eskimos' blood.

It came as no surprise that a group of people protected against CVD had lower blood lipids than a population riddled with heart attacks; for the connection between high blood-lipid levels, cholesterol in particular, and CVD was already well established. What didn't make sense was the knowledge that people who eat a lot of fat commonly have *high* blood lipids. Conversely, low cholesterol and triglyceride values are usually found in individuals who eat very lean fare.

Could it be that the Eskimos are just born with a genetic predisposition for lower blood cholesterol and triglycerides which spares them from CVD? Not so, Drs. Bang and Dyerberg concluded, because, when they analyzed the blood lipids of a group of Eskimos expatriated to Denmark, their values were similar to those of the Danes—not those of the traditional Eskimos. That pointed to an environmental explanation for the lower blood-lipid levels in the Eskimos.

What stuck out like a sore thumb was, of course, the Eskimo diet. How could Drs. Bang and Dyerberg not be struck by the typical individual's daily fare, consisting of about 14 ounces of seal and whale meat, not even counting fish? Exactly what it was about this unusual subsistence that might confer protective benefits was unclear at the time, but the Danish researchers recalled earlier studies showing that fish and whale oil were full of polyunsaturated fatty acids. Knowing that polyunsaturates could lower blood cholesterol, the doctors put two and two together and surmised that the Eskimos must have lower lipids because their intake of polyunsaturates is higher than that of the Danes.

That was an easy hypothesis to put to the test because the level of polyunsaturated fatty acids in both food and blood lipids can be measured in the laboratory. (The more polyunsaturates you eat, the more polyunsaturated your blood lipids become.) On two separate expeditions, Drs. Bang and Dyerberg collected blood and a week's worth of food samples from their Umanak subjects. Surprisingly, the Eskimo diet was found to be *lower* in polyunsaturates, as was their blood.

The traditional Eskimo diet did, however, turn out to have something curious that Danish food didn't—16-fold greater amounts of unusual long-chain fatty acids known to be present in marine animal fat. Eskimos also had much higher blood levels of these fatty acids (that we now know as the omega-3s) than did the Danes, who carried more omega-6s in their blood lipids. Thus, Drs. Bang and Dyerberg hypothesized that the omega-3s from fish oils must be more potent than the omega-6s from vegetable oils in lowering blood cholesterol and triglycerides. (They were on the right track, as you'll see in chapter 3.)

At this point the doctors' research took a different turn because they knew that, although the Eskimos had lower blood lipids than the Danes, the levels were only different enough to explain a *delay* of CVD in the Eskimos, not the virtual *absence* of sudden heart attacks. (Middle-aged Eskimo men, for example, had cholesterol levels of about 247 milligrams per 100 milliliters of blood. As you'll learn in chapter 3, that's a level associated with heart attacks in our country.) Searching for an explanation other than blood-lipid levels, Drs. Bang and Dyerberg recalled the centuries-known but unexplained "bleeding tendency" of the Eskimos. Indeed, Eskimos are prone to frequent nosebleeds, their cuts take a long time to stop bleeding, and they tend to bruise easily. The doctors also knew that certain types of fatty acids can influence blood clotting. (Although clotting is important to stop bleeding when you have a wound, blood clots that can form in blood vessels leading to the heart and brain are a major cause of heart attacks and strokes.)

It then made sense to study differences in blood platelets—small, disk-shaped cells essential for blood clotting—between Eskimos and Danes. So it was back to Umanak in 1978 to once again draw some Eskimo blood samples. In fact, Drs. Bang and Dyerberg found that the reason for the bleeding tendency in the Eskimos was that their platelets had much less of a propensity to aggregate or clot together than did the platelets of Danes. And, since high levels of omega-3 fatty acids were found in the Eskimos' platelets, it was becoming obvious that diet was somehow responsible for the differences. The Danish physicians now had two highly plausible explanations for the low incidence of CVD in Eskimos—lower blood lipids and blood that was less likely to form clots. (Chapter 3 will further detail the relationship of fish oils to blood clots and lipids.)

Clues from the Japanese

The Japanese get away with it, too. They have a low incidence of heart disease despite the fact that a lot of people in Japan have high blood pressure—another major risk factor for CVD. But, quite the opposite of the Eskimo diet, traditional Japanese cuisine—with its mainstays of rice and vegetables—is extremely low in fat and high in carbohydrate. The commonality with the Eskimos is a love of fish, reflected by about a fivefold higher intake by Japanese than Americans.

You could argue that a low fat intake is solely responsible for the lower heart disease statistics in Japan. Fish, however, does seem to make a difference, as evidenced by a comparison between Japanese fishermen and farmers. Japanese who live in fishing villages eat about three times the level of fish oils of those living in farming villages. And the fishermen have a much lower incidence of heart disease and strokes. Lower still is the rate of heart disease among the Japanese who live in Okinawan fishing villages, consuming twice the level of fish oils of other Japanese fishermen. One study revealed that, compared to Americans, the Japanese have ten times as much EPA (one of the beneficial fish-oil fatty acids) in their blood and one-sixth the incidence of heart disease. Fish intake has also been correlated with a lower breast-cancer rate in Japan.

As with the Eskimos, fish oils have been associated with blood-clotting changes in the Japanese. Japanese fishing villagers who ate almost nine ounces of fish a day had much higher levels of omega-3 fatty acids in their diet and blood than farmers who consumed just three ounces of fish daily. And the fishermen's blood contained platelet cells that were less likely to clump together.

Now, the Eskimo dog team is giving way to the snowmobile; kimonos were long ago exchanged for blue jeans in Japan. Likewise, it is probable that the dietary habits of both populations will become increasingly westernized. Unfortunately, the evidence in hand indicates that when either the Japanese or the Eskimos adopt a more Western-style diet—typically, one that's about 40 percent fat with a fair amount contributed by saturated fats—the incidence of Western-style maladies, such as heart disease, escalates.

CHAPTER THREE

Zeroing In on
Cardiovascular Disease

DYERBERG AND BANG'S pioneer work linking the Eskimos' high fish intake with their low rate of heart disease marked only the beginning of a cascade of scientific studies that confirm and extend the early findings. Now, researchers all over the world are looking into the effects of fish and fish oil on hearts, blood, and blood vessels. But no study caught the public's eye like the recent Dutch study, mentioned in previous chapters, which made the headlines because it suggested that regularly eating just small amounts of fish can prevent heart attacks.

A LESSON FROM THE NETHERLANDS

Undoubtedly, the Dutch study attracted the media spotlight because of its revelation that just an ounce of fish a day—in contrast to the more than 14 daily ounces of marine fare eaten by traditional Eskimos —is associated with a marked decrease in deaths caused by heart disease. The discovery came about when Daan Kromhout, Ph.D., M.P.H., and his colleagues at the University of Leiden in the Netherlands studied the relationship between the amount of fish 852 men regularly ate and their number of deaths from heart disease over a 20-year period. None of the men had heart disease at the outset.

The researchers found that the 78 men who ate the *least* fish suffered the most deaths from heart disease. On the other hand, the *greater* the amount of fish regularly consumed, the lower the risk of dying from heart ailments. Men who ate an ounce or more of fish each day were about two and a half times less likely to die from heart disease than non-fish-eaters.

To see if there might be an alternative explanation for their findings, the investigators went several steps further to determine whether the fish-eaters had other habits that protected them from heart disease. Surprisingly, these men ate somewhat *more* total fat and cholesterol than men who ate no fish. And even after the scientists conducted special statistical tests to account for factors that would have placed the fish-eating men at smaller risk of heart problems—including lower blood pressure, lower blood cholesterol, and less cigarette smoking—they found that fish consumption *all by itself* correlated with a lower incidence of heart-related fatalities.

Also striking about the Dutch study was the finding that the intake of *lean* fish alone was associated with fewer heart-related deaths. Indeed, the fish-eaters in the study, on average, consumed only a third of their fish as oily varieties; the other two-thirds was lean and quite low in omega-3 fatty acids. This suggests either that just small amounts of omega-3s consumed for long periods of time are preventive or that there is something else in fish—in addition to its special oils—that protects against heart disease.

One question that's been raised about the Leiden study is whether the fish-eaters were more likely to die from causes other than heart disease compared to low fish consumers. Dr. Kromhout's research team is currently conducting a study to see if that is so. Some encouraging news in this regard has already been reported, however, in research involving nearly 2,000 middle-aged men who were followed for 25 years. Richard B. Shekelle, Ph.D., from the University of Texas School of Public Health and his coworkers found that men who ate the most fish not only had the lowest risk of dying from heart disease, but they were also less likely to die from other causes than non-fish-eaters.

THE MAKINGS OF HEART ATTACKS AND STROKES

No wonder the Dutch study raised eyebrows, when about a million and a half Americans have heart attacks each year, more than a third of which are fatal. But before going into the mechanisms that appear to give fish its cardiovascular advantage, a brief description of the process that causes most heart attacks, strokes, and what we've been calling CVD is in order. Called *atherosclerosis,* the disease process starts out as streaks of fatty tissue laid down in blood-vessel walls during childhood and adolescence. Slowly and chronically, fat and cholesterol accumulate at the sites of these streaks, along with a buildup of scar tissue, calcium, and white blood cells. Eventually, a raised fibrous plaque forms, narrowing blood vessels that serve as pipes, conducting the flow of blood to such vital organs as the heart and brain.

Contrary to common opinion, however, atherosclerosis does not appear to be the immediate cause of many heart attacks and strokes. Instead, the acute crisis probably stems from the formation of a blood clot consisting largely of clumped platelets, as well as red and white blood cells. This mound of cells—which is more likely to form in some people than others—can completely clog a blood vessel that's already narrowed by atherosclerosis. If the blocked vessel is one leading to the heart, blood flow to that vital organ is impaired; a heart attack is the result. Many strokes are caused by the same process, but the blockage is in atherosclerosis-narrowed blood vessels in or leading to the brain.

Sadly, by the time many people have physical symptoms of CVD, the ailment is far advanced. For instance, angina—chest pain that's often the first physical sign of narrowed coronary blood vessels—is commonly accompanied by a 50- to 75-percent blockage of one of the main arteries leading to the heart, according to Dr. Castelli. Of the participants in the Framingham Heart Study—a study to determine risk factors for CVD in thousands of Framingham, Massachusetts, residents and their families—every fifth man and every seventeenth woman has had a heart attack before age 60; 1 out of 15 men *and* women has suffered a stroke. Just about all of them feel "well" until the first day that an attack affects their hearts or brains.

RISK FACTORS FOR CARDIOVASCULAR DISEASE

Why does it have to get so bad before we begin to realize that our cardiovascular systems are failing? It really doesn't, because medical scientists have found that there are usually predisposing conditions—not necessarily symptoms you can feel—common to people with CVD that well precede overt heart attacks and strokes. Collectively known as *risk factors,* the well-established predisposing conditions are high blood pressure, cigarette smoking, elevated blood cholesterol, a family history of heart disease at an early age (specifically, a heart attack or sudden death before age 55 in a parent, brother, or sister), and diabetes mellitus. Indeed, medical scientists don't know exactly what causes atherosclerosis or clot formation, but they do know that—over and over again—most individuals who suffer heart attacks and strokes have a history of at least one of these danger signals. Generally speaking, the more risk factors you have, the greater your risk for CVD. In addition, men have a higher incidence of CVD than women. Other conditions thought to increase the risk of CVD include high blood triglycerides and a sedentary or stressful lifestyle. Severe obesity (30 percent or more overweight) also increases the odds of CVD, although it is not clear whether, in the absence of other factors, a less serious weight problem poses a risk all by itself. Nevertheless, overweight people often have elevated blood pressure, cholesterol, and triglycerides.

Doesn't it logically follow that the best way of preventing a heart attack or stroke is to do something about the risk factors you can change? That is, if you have high blood cholesterol or triglycerides, alter your diet to lower them (see "Fish and the Lipid Factors" on page 27); if you smoke cigarettes, kick the habit; get your weight down to a desirable level; for high blood pressure, follow your diet and—if you're on any—take medication to keep it down.

Despite the fact that such steps really can lower your risk of heart attacks and strokes, the emphasis in our society has been on *treating* CVD once someone already has it—not on preventing it in the first place. Witness the plethora of heart bypass operations, a handful of highly publicized mechanical-heart implants, and, now, new methods aimed at dissolving blood clots. But even if you elect or have no other recourse than a remedial one, you still have to take preventive steps to avoid winding up where you started. Heart bypass patients, for instance, were shown in one study to have major blockages of their bypasses ten years after surgery, particularly if their blood cholesterol and triglycerides remained high.

In a preventive vein, Dr. Castelli often refers to studies in which monkeys with CVD were placed on low-fat diets; in just a little over three years, 80 percent of their atherosclerosis was gone. "Why," he asks, "do you have to be a monkey to be put on the right therapy for this disease?" The fact is that you don't—most of the very tools are within your own grasp, one of them the decision to add more fish to your diet.

CLOSE-UP ON BLOOD LIPIDS

A fish-rich diet probably has the greatest direct impact on the lipid risk factors. (See the next section for the specific effects fish has on cholesterol and triglycerides.) Any step you can take to lower blood cholesterol can be significant when you consider how risky seemingly small elevations of this blood lipid can be. In the largest study ever on blood cholesterol and long-term death rates, the *Journal of the American Medical Association* recently revealed that 35- to 57-year-old men whose cholesterol was anywhere between 203 and 220 milligrams per deciliter (mg./dl.) of blood had a death rate from heart disease that was 73 percent higher than that of men with cholesterol readings below 182 mg./dl. Indeed, most people don't think of cholesterol levels in the low 200s as life-threatening, but these findings suggest a need for concern among the 50 percent of adult Americans who have cholesterol levels above the 200- to-230-mg./dl. range. (It goes without saying that people with higher cholesterol elevations should be doubly worried.)

Now for the good news—we currently have strong evidence that lowering elevated blood cholesterol does a lot of good: a huge study, funded by the National Heart, Lung, and Blood Institute (NHLBI), revealed that men who lowered their high blood-cholesterol levels by 13.5 percent had close to 25 percent fewer heart-disease-related deaths than did men who decreased their blood cholesterol by only 5 percent. Granted, the men who had the 13.5 percent drop in cholesterol were on both a diet and a drug to cut blood levels of the lipid. But their diets—at around 40 percent fat calories—could hardly be considered lean. We do know, however, that eating a low-fat, low-cholesterol diet can alone lower blood cholesterol substantially in many people.

The authors of the NHLBI study estimate that every 1 percent fall in blood cholesterol will bring about a 2 percent drop in the rate of heart attacks. Accordingly, a National Institutes of Health advisory panel concluded that, if the American public could be convinced to change its diet to bring about a 10-percent decrease in average blood cholesterol, 100,000 lives could be saved each year! This kind of a drop in cholesterol (or more) might well be accomplished by switching from our typical diet consisting of 40 percent fat calories to the recommended 30 percent. Doing just that brought about a 17-percent decrease in blood cholesterol in a group of men starting out with normal values (averaging 210 mg./dl.) who were studied by heart disease expert Scott M. Grundy, M.D., Ph.D., and his colleagues at the University of Texas Health Science Center.

How do you know if your blood cholesterol is too high? You go to your physician and ask for a simple blood test (from your arm or finger) to have it measured—a wise move for everyone by the age of 30 at the latest. (If it's normal, get it checked every 3 to 5 years after that.) But make sure you're given the numerical results, because medical labs often consider any reading in the 150- to-300-mg./dl. range to be "normal." You're better off going by the cutoff values for cholesterol that were established for people age 20 and older by a National Heart, Lung, and Blood Institute panel of experts (see table 1). The panel advises that blood-cholesterol readings above 200 mg./dl. be repeated; the average should be used as your cholesterol level. If you *are* found to have elevated blood cholesterol, the panel offers very specific guidelines for diet and, possibly, drug treatment. Consult your physician and a registered dietitian about how to proceed. (You can usually locate a registered dietitian by calling the dietary department of your local hospital.)

TABLE 1. National Heart, Lung, and Blood Institute
         Blood-Cholesterol Guidelines

Desirable blood cholesterol	Less than 200 mg./dl.
Borderline-high blood cholesterol	200-239 mg./dl.
High blood cholesterol	240 mg./dl. or more

One caveat about learning your cholesterol level: mild elevations cannot predict who is at risk for a heart attack. While many people with borderline-high blood cholesterol don't get heart attacks, half of Americans who do suffer attacks have blood cholesterol levels of less than 250. Here's where the value of a relatively new blood test comes in—measurement of HDL-cholesterol, the so-called "good" kind of cholesterol in the blood. You see, we now know that *total* cholesterol is made up of both unfavorable and beneficial types. The "bad" cholesterol is carried by low-density lipoproteins (LDLs) that tend to deposit the fatty substance in blood vessel walls, increasing the risk of heart attack and stroke. "Good" cholesterol, on the other hand, is transported by high-density lipoproteins (HDLs), considered to be the cholesterol scavengers of the body. HDLs are thought to remove cholesterol from blood vessels, leaving less behind to block blood flow to the heart and brain. The bottom line is: the lower your LDLs and the higher your HDLs, the lower your risk of CVD. (Exercise appears to be the most effective way to raise your HDLs; weight loss, cutting back on saturated fat and total fat, and eating more fiber from oats, fruit, and beans can help lower LDLs.)

So when you have your blood cholesterol checked, it's a good idea to ask for a reading on your HDLs, as well. That way, you'll know what percentage of your total cholesterol is the "good" type. (An HDL-cholesterol level below 35 mg./dl. is considered low, but it should be confirmed by a repeat test.) Medical laboratories often report the ratio of total cholesterol to HDL-cholesterol; you want a reading that's 4.5 or less. Someone whose total cholesterol measures a seemingly high 245 mg./dl., but whose HDLs are 65—giving a ratio of 3.8—doesn't have to worry so much about having a heart attack as someone with the same cholesterol reading but a low HDL score. Of course, you have to consider other risk factors, as well—you can't keep smoking, for instance, assuming that high HDLs will spare you from a heart attack.

You're no doubt anxious to get on with the story and learn more specifically what fish has to do with all this, but first a few general comments concerning triglycerides. As intimated earlier, blood triglyceride elevations have not been firmly connected with CVD. Nevertheless, people with CVD often have high triglycerides. Further, individuals with raised levels of these lipids commonly have other risk factors including high blood cholesterol and low HDL-cholesterol. In addition, they're often obese.

Not too long ago, a National Institutes of Health panel on triglycerides established a level of 250 mg./dl. of blood as the upper "normal" limit for adults. It certainly behooves anyone with triglycerides above this point—who also has other risk factors for CVD—to take steps to lower the lipid. That can be accomplished, in less severe cases, by losing weight, limiting alcoholic beverages, and avoiding fatty and cholesterol-rich foods. A fancy for fish may also come in handy, as you'll see momentarily.

FISH AND THE LIPID FACTORS

The remarkable effect that fish and fish oil can have on blood lipids was best demonstrated in a study published in the same issue of the *New England Journal of Medicine* as Dr. Kromhout's research from the Netherlands. Investigators from Oregon Health Sciences University —a foremost site of fish and fish-oil research in this country—found that a diet rich in marine oils had a "profound" effect on people with two different types of lipid abnormalities: blood-cholesterol and triglyceride levels "fell in every patient without exception."

The findings of the Oregon study, headed by Beverley Phillipson, M.D., are striking because a diet rich in salmon and fish-oil supplements had a far more positive effect on blood lipids than did the strict low-fat, low-cholesterol diet—in some cases amounting to just 5 percent fat calories, with almost no cholesterol—that patients with high blood lipids commonly have to follow. The fish-oil diet was much more liberal, with up to 30 percent fat calories and more than 300 milligrams of cholesterol.

To give you the specifics, when patients with a type of disorder that brings about an elevation of both lipids followed the high fish-oil diet, they saw their triglycerides drop from an average of 334 to a healthy 118 mg./dl.; cholesterol went from 324 to 236 mg./dl. In another group of patients with a relatively rare lipid abnormality that raises blood triglycerides to about 5 times the normal value, average triglyceride levels decreased from 1,353 to 281 mg./dl.—a drop of 79 percent! Similarly, cholesterol went from a heart-threatening 373 to a much more reassuring 207 mg./dl.

To see what would happen if vegetable oil was used in place of fish oil, some patients were subsequently asked to follow a diet supplemented with corn and safflower oil for a period of time. The vegetable oils had a much less positive effect on blood lipids than fish oil had. In fact, when fish oil was replaced with vegetable oil, the second group of patients experienced such an unhealthy return to high blood triglycerides that they had to be taken off the diet. Their cholesterol increased, too.

After learning of the research going on at Oregon Health Sciences University, Dr. Castelli also got some remarkable results when he had patients with extreme triglyceride elevations take fish-oil supplements. At a large conference on seafood and health, he talked about his dozens of patients with blood plasma that "looks like milk or cream instead of looking like Chardonnay or Chablis [the normal appearance]. . . . I tried every drug ever known to man and God on these people and nothing happened." With the fish-oil supplements, triglycerides in some of these patients went from a range of 1,500 to 2,000 down to 200 to 300 mg./dl. "And that's why we're giving you back all these fish . . . ," he added for the benefit of individuals who used to be forbidden oilier fish varieties.

Bear in mind that the Oregon study involved an experimental situation in which people with both cholesterol and triglyceride elevations ate salmon every day *and* took fish-oil supplements; their total omega-3 fatty acid intake was at least three times that of the Eskimos. Dr. Phillipson cautions against taking fish-oil supplements to lower your lipids because blood-clotting changes—changes that could conceivably lead to bleeding tendencies in some people—have been reported in people taking high doses. Likewise, I urge that fish-oil supplements be left in the hands of physicians who have experience with them and know how to monitor potential side effects. Again, it may seem somewhat unfair to fill your head with the wonders of consuming high levels of fish and its oils, only to turn around and tell you not to down tablespoons of fish oil or marine oil capsules. But you'll understand the reasons for not jumping on the supplement bandwagon later in chapter 5, "Why Not Pop a Pill?"

Nevertheless, the Oregon study still bears good tidings for some individuals who have cholesterol and triglyceride elevations, for it now appears that the very strict diets they traditionally have had to follow may be liberalized if they eat more fish. And oilier fish that used to be restricted because of their higher fat content now seem advisable.

Dr. Phillipson's study also suggests that formerly recommended vegetable oils may not be advantageous for all people who have lipid elevations. Likewise, people with different types of lipid abnormalities may respond differently to fish oils. Indeed, studies in which people with high blood cholesterol—but normal triglyceride levels—have been given fish oils have yielded inconsistent results. It's wise for anyone with high blood lipids to work closely with a physician and a registered dietitian to see how they respond to different levels and types of dietary fat. Remember, too, that even though a liberal intake of fish may allow you to eat more fat, the total level of fat in your diet should make up 30 percent or less of your calorie intake. Indeed, the evidence in hand suggests that you can't expect fish to wipe out a multitude of fatty indiscretions; you've got to make a fish-enriched diet part of a low-fat style of eating if lowering your lipids is an important goal.

What if you're a health-conscious person who doesn't have high blood cholesterol or triglycerides, but who wants assurance that your lipids stay at a heart-sparing level—will eating high amounts of fish and fish oil help you, too? Perhaps, according to another study conducted at Oregon Health Sciences University in which healthy adults consumed three different diets to see what the effects on blood lipids would be. One diet was rich in saturated fat; another contained large quantities of salmon fillets and salmon oil; and the third was rich in safflower and corn oils. The researchers concluded that, on a gram-for-gram basis, fish oil was more effective than the vegetable oils in lowering both cholesterol and triglycerides.

In general, however, studies of both healthy people and those with lipid elevations reveal that fish and fish oil have a greater impact on blood triglycerides than on cholesterol. That may be because part of the cholesterol-lowering ability is negated by the naturally high levels of cholesterol in some fish-oil supplements. Salmon oil, for example, contains about 140 milligrams of cholesterol per ounce (about half the daily recommended amount), compared to no cholesterol in vegetable oils.

As for the effect of fish oil on favorable HDL-cholesterol (the type of cholesterol you *want* to be high), the picture is unclear. Studies to date suggest that fish oil either has no impact or a slight elevating effect on HDL levels. Polyunsaturated vegetable oils, on the other hand, have been shown in some studies to lower HDL-cholesterol.

The question remains: Will simply upping your fish intake to a reasonable level favorably affect your blood cholesterol? The truth is that no one knows for sure. Renowned heart disease researcher Scott M. Grundy, M.D., Ph.D., from the University of Texas Health

Science Center at Dallas believes that eating a fish-rich diet may have more of an impact on blood cholesterol than does an increase in fish oil alone. Not only would substitution of fish for meat several times a week increase omega-3 fatty acid intake, but it could lower consumption of total fat and saturated fat—both foes of healthy blood-cholesterol levels. Further, eating more fish could help to decrease calorie intake, which would have "a cholesterol-lowering action in many people."

ANTICLOTTING FACTORS AND MORE

We now know that CVD involves a whole lot more than just cholesterol and triglycerides. Currently, there's a great deal of interest in blood-clot formation, which Oregon Health Sciences University's Scott Goodnight, Jr., M.D., refers to as the "coup de grace" because it leads to a stoppage of blood flow to the heart, causing a heart attack or to the brain, causing a stroke. There's strong evidence that fish oil plays a role in preventing or delaying these "final" events.

Recall Drs. Dyerberg and Bang's finding that Eskimos had platelet cells that were rich in omega-3 fatty acids and less likely to clump together. Since then, researchers who have fed people known amounts of fish oil in controlled studies have found similar effects on platelets. So far the studies suggest that fish oil prevents blood from forming undesirable clots in the following ways:

- *Prolongs bleeding time*—the length of time required for a tiny cut to stop bleeding under laboratory conditions. (The speed with which bleeding ceases is almost entirely dependent on the capacity of platelets to stick to an injured blood-vessel wall—something you don't want a high proclivity for if you've got CVD.)
- *Renders platelet cells less likely to aggregate or clump together.*
- *Lowers blood levels of certain chemicals* that are indicators of blood "stickiness."

Furthermore, people taking fish-oil supplements have been found to have less viscous blood, as well as red blood cells that are more pliable. Therefore, omega-3-enriched blood may be "thinner" than normal and capable of slipping through partially blocked blood vessels more easily, thereby improving blood flow to vital organs. In addition, there's evidence that fish oil can favorably alter the function of monocytes, which are a type of white blood cell involved in the early stages of atherosclerosis.

Fish oil may also have an impact on high blood pressure or hypertension—an ailment afflicting about one in four Americans that, if uncontrolled, markedly raises the chances of having a heart attack or stroke. Expressed as two numbers, blood pressure is the force exerted against the walls of blood vessels and chambers of the heart as blood is pumped through the circulatory system. If your blood pressure consistently reads higher than 140 over 90, the heart, kidneys, and blood vessels have to work under a strain. (The first number is called the systolic reading; the second is diastolic. An elevation of either is considered risky.)

Several studies suggest that diets supplemented with fish oil or oily fish have the ability to lower blood pressure in healthy people. But you may have to down two cans of mackerel daily to get that effect! Men with normal blood pressure who did just that experienced a significant drop in both diastolic and systolic readings. For men with mild hypertension, however, the same two cans of mackerel only lowered systolic blood pressure.

So far, the impact of fish oil on blood pressure is considered modest. Long-term studies are needed to determine the ultimate effect since, in the mackerel studies, the men only ate the fishy fare for two weeks. Raising your fish intake in order to maintain a healthy blood pressure certainly wouldn't hurt. But that should only be one part of the more important antihypertensive steps of keeping your weight down, taking blood-pressure medication when it's prescribed, and, in some cases, watching salt intake. (Some experts now believe that only half of the people with hypertension respond to a low-salt diet.)

BUT DOES IT DO ANY GOOD?

So much for lower lipids, less sticky platelets, "thinner" blood, altered monocytes, and maybe lower blood pressure; where is the proof that fish and its oils prevent atherosclerotic plaques from progressing or blood clots from forming? Is there any direct evidence that omega-3s prevent heart attacks and strokes? Some preliminary data from animal research indicate that marine oils can do the job. Several studies suggest that animals given fish oil had less severe heart attacks and strokes than animals not receiving the oil.

Recently, two provocative studies revealed that fish oil is capable of inhibiting atherosclerotic plaque formation in animals. At the University of Massachusetts Medical Center, Bonnie Weiner, M.D., and her colleagues fed a group of pigs—animals that can develop atherosclerosis and heart attacks, much the way humans do—a diet loaded with saturated fat. The pigs were given so much lard that their cholesterol soared from well below 150 to more than 560 mg./dl. of blood. On top of this fatty diet, some of the pigs were given a daily supplement of about 2 tablespoons of cod-liver oil. Even though the supplement had no effect on their high blood-cholesterol levels, the pigs on fish oil had significantly less blockage of their blood vessels than did unsupplemented pigs. While "minimal" atherosclerotic disease was evident in blood vessels leading to the hearts of pigs fed cod-liver oil, similar blood vessels of more than half the unsupplemented pigs were almost completely clogged.

Closer still to humans, rhesus monkeys fed a diet rich in highly saturated coconut oil had far more atherosclerosis than monkeys on diets in which part of the coconut oil was replaced with fish oil. Although animals fed fish oil experienced a marked lowering of blood cholesterol, it wasn't a great enough drop to alone account for the difference in plaque formation. The University of Chicago researchers conclude that fish oil somehow inhibited the development of athero-sclerotic plaques.

There have been very few studies published in which humans were used to demonstrate the specific benefits of fish and its oils. One of the few studies involved individuals with a history of angina who took daily fish-oil supplements for periods lasting up to two years. They reported much less chest pain and less need to use medication for angina. A reduction in chest pain was also noted in another study in which angina patients consumed cod-liver oil. As favorable as these findings sound, both studies need to be replicated because neither involved what scientists call a "control" group of patients who didn't take any fish oil. For the results of a study to be considered more reliable, patients receiving some form of intervention need to be compared with a similar group of patients who don't get the same treatment. In fact, a more recent study that was controlled did not confirm a benefit for angina patients who took fish-oil supplements.

Another problem with drawing conclusions about fish oil's advantages is that most of the research on prevention of heart disease has involved relatively large doses of omega-3s. At that, the majority of studies have gone on for just short periods of time. So, we're still left with the question, "What is the evidence that regular consumption of fish alone can prevent heart attacks and strokes in people?" Large population studies such as Dr. Kromhout's in the Netherlands certainly provide some evidence—but not proof—that fish eating has an advantage.

Research designed to answer more definitively the regular-fish-intake question would involve a tremendous amount of time, money, and effort. First, you'd need to engage a large number of participants for the results to be considered valid. Second, you'd have to find a group of people who would be willing to faithfully and regularly add an exact amount of fish to their diets—and do it for years. Then you'd have to check up on them quite often to make sure that they were really eating what they said they would eat. In addition, the people would need to keep good records of everything they ate so you, as a researcher, could make sure that there wasn't some change in their diets (other than eating more fish) that would explain the final results. You'd also have to closely follow the dietary habits of a similar group of people who didn't add more fish to their diets so you'd have a control group. Then you'd have to track the medical records of both groups of people—noting such factors as blood pressure and lipid levels, incidence of various diseases, weight changes, and causes of death—for many years to see if there were differences between the fish-eaters and non-fish-eaters.

The closest anyone has ever come to attempting to pull off this elaborate type of study was the investigation by Averly Nelson, M.D., mentioned in chapter 2.

A MAN AHEAD OF HIS TIME

During the 1950s Dr. Nelson—a Seattle heart specialist—first examined 206 heart-disease patients, most of whom were referred to him by other physicians because of high blood cholesterol and complications such as angina. Dr. Nelson was able to enlist 80 of the patients to follow a special diet that gradually increased weekly fish intake (at the expense of meat) to a level of three servings of oilier fish, plus two servings of leaner varieties. (Omega-3-rich salmon, tuna, herring, and trout were the mainstays of the fish fare.) In addition, his patients were allowed to eat low-fat dairy products, lots of fruits and vegetables, four or more servings of bread or cereal, a small amount of polyunsaturated vegetable oil or margarine, and moderate-sized portions of lean meat and poultry. (If this sounds like the *Eat Fish* Diet in chapter 13, you're not mistaken—Dr. Nelson *was* ahead of his time.)

Dr. Nelson got his patients to follow their diets by engaging them in an extensive educational program involving at least 20 to 30 hours of study and close work with a dietitian. To assess their understanding of their schooling Dr. Nelson quizzed his patients; to see if they complied with their diets, he periodically checked their blood-cholesterol levels. (As stern a master as he was, Dr. Nelson had a soft and realistic side, too—for he allowed his patients to go off their diets for one 24-hour period each week.) He followed the progress of all 206 patients over the course of 16 to 19 years.

The results of the study are quite remarkable: patients who followed the low-fat, fish-rich diet lived an average of 9 years before dying from atherosclerosis; nondieters survived just under 5 years. At the end of the study, 42 percent of 40- to 55-year-olds who had been on the diet, but only 15 percent of the nondiet group, were still alive. Even more striking, among 56- to 70-year-olds, 32 percent of those who followed the diet remained alive, but only 5 percent of nonfollowers survived.

Of course, no one knows for sure that the increase in fish alone was responsible for the differences in mortality. Admittedly, Dr. Nelson's study has a number of flaws from the researcher's vantage point—for example, we don't know whether people who went on the diet were also motivated to adopt other healthy habits, such as exercising more or losing weight. Or perhaps those who had the incentive to follow a diet were also more motivated to take their medication for controlling high blood pressure. Unfortunately, we'll probably never know the precise role that fish played because Dr. Nelson died shortly after his study was published in the journal *Geriatrics* in 1972; medical records on his patients were destroyed shortly thereafter. Nevertheless, his findings are so striking that, coupled with what we now know about fish and CVD, it's certainly possible that fish did in some way contribute to the differences in mortality.

You can make your own decision. But I believe that all of the studies on lipids and clotting, coupled with the finding of several different types of studies that fish-eaters have lower rates of heart disease, add up to plenty of good reasons for assuming that eating more fish can help ward off the nation's number-one killer.

HOW FISH OIL DOES ITS BUSINESS

Fish oil appears to accomplish its work largely by influencing the body's production of hormonelike substances called *prostaglandins* and *leukotrienes*. While some of these substances are necessary in the body —say, to help regulate blood pressure, reproduction, muscle contraction platelet aggregation, and inflammation—an imbalance occurs when people have diseases such as CVD, arthritis, and asthma. In an unbalanced state, prostaglandins and leukotrienes can have harmful effects on body tissues.

The body makes prostaglandins and leukotrienes from dietary fats, including vegetable oils, animal fats, and our friends the omega-3s in fish oil. The evidence in hand suggests that consumption of fish oils brings about a more favorable balance of these hormonelike substances in the body.

In the case of CVD, *thromboxane* and *prostacyclin* (two types of prostaglandins) play a major role. Thromboxane tends to make blood vessels constrict and induces blood platelets to stick, causing them to aggregate into blood clots. Quite the opposite, prostacyclin inhibits platelet aggregation and causes blood vessels to open up. A healthy cardiovascular system is thought to depend on a balance of thromboxane and prostacyclin.

Here's where fish oil comes into play. In comparison to other types of dietary fat, the omega-3 fatty acids—EPA in particular—is converted to a less active thromboxane. At the same time, EPA derived from fish oil produces significant amounts of antiaggregating prostacyclin. The end result: less-sticky platelets that have less tendency to form artery-blocking blood clots.

CHAPTER FOUR

The Fish Frontier

WHAT DO MALADIES as diverse-sounding as breast cancer, arthritis, asthma, diabetes, multiple sclerosis, systemic lupus erythematosus, psoriasis, and migraine headaches have in common? All are thought, in some way, to involve the immune system—the body's system of tissues and cells that helps ward off disease, fight infection, and cause inflammation with its subsequent pain, redness, or other discomforts to signal that something has gone awry in the body. Evidence is mounting that the immune system can be favorably influenced by the omega-3 fatty acids, as demonstrated in a widely reported study from Harvard University. Researchers found that, when healthy people took high doses of fish oil, certain white blood cells, cells which are involved in causing inflammation, lost two of their critical functions that lead to inflammatory reactions.

It makes sense that fish oil would be advantageous for the immune system since some of the body's white blood cells come from the same cells in our bone marrow as the platelets that have to do with heart disease. In addition, the immune system is influenced by the prostaglandins and leukotrienes that you now know are altered by fish-oil consumption. Indeed, most of the ailments mentioned in the previous paragraph are thought to involve prostaglandins or leukotrienes. Certain leukotrienes, for instance, likely play a role in causing the unpleasant symptoms of asthma.

It didn't take scientists long to surmise that, since fish oil can have an impact on prostaglandins, leukotrienes, *and* the immune system, the omega-3s might offer a route for treating—and possibly preventing—a host of ailments, opening up a whole new frontier of fish-oil research. You must realize, however, that far less is known about the connections among fish oil and the "frontier" ailments covered in this chapter than about the omega-3s and cardiovascular disease. While I

36

will continue to build the case for eating more fish, it is not with promises that a fish-rich diet will cure you or guarantee a life free of cancer, arthritis, and the like.

Instead, the idea is to give you a *perspective* on the building evidence that fish and its oils favorably alter the course of many diseases, at the same time knowing that it's far from clear how fish oil—or what amount—does its business when it comes to the "frontier" ailments. I hope that sharing the promising—albeit preliminary—findings about fish and such an array of ailments will leave you wondering how you can afford *not* to add more fish to your diet.

THE CANCER CONNECTION

Second only to CVD as a leading cause of death in our nation comes cancer. To be sure, most people now know that a fatty sustenance jeopardizes the well-being of their hearts. But did you know that the general consensus of experts is that as many as 35 percent of cancer deaths could be diet-related? Once again, the particular dietary culprit, as mentioned earlier, is fat. For some studies have shown an association between a high fat intake and "cancers of the breast, colon, rectum, prostate, and possibly pancreas, uterus, and ovaries," according to the National Cancer Institute (NCI).

In a recent monograph describing cancer-control objectives for the nation, the NCI spoke out loud and clear about the connection between diet and two particular forms of malignancy: breast and colon cancer. The agency estimates that, in a 10-year time span, it's possible that breast-cancer deaths—befalling more than 40,000 Americans a year—could be reduced by 25 percent if people were to cut their dietary fat from 40 to 30 percent of calorie intake. As for colon cancer, the NCI projects that—if we ate more fiber, at the same time cutting fat consumption—the death rate could be cut in half within a decade, saving 29,000 lives a year.

How, then, do you explain another Eskimo anomaly—that our Greenland neighbors, who traditionally enjoy a diet that's about 40 percent fat calories, are also practically free of both breast and colon cancer? By now, you can guess that the nature of their fatty fare— derived mainly from the sea—may well have something to do with the Eskimo advantage over us with these two forms of cancer.

How might fat that you eat predispose toward—or protect against —certain forms of cancer? Dietary fats can influence the endocrine system (which controls reproductive organs), immune-cell behavior, and prostaglandin synthesis—all of which have something to do with the development of breast cancer. And it's not just the amount of fat that seems to make a difference, for studies in animals suggest that the type of fat is important, too. Indeed, animal research suggests that high levels of polyunsaturated vegetable oils enhance the development and growth of some types of tumors. It seems that prostaglandins arising from vegetable-oil-derived fatty acids may be associated with an increase in an animal's tumor size.

Polyunsaturated fish oil, however, presents quite a different story, as shown most strikingly in studies on animals conducted by Rashida Karmali, Ph.D., from New Jersey's Rutgers University and the Sloan-Kettering Institute for Cancer Research in New York City. She found that high levels of omega-3 fatty acids inhibited the growth of breast and prostate cancer in rats, while corn oil led to an increase in tumor size. In a study by other researchers, the omega-3s blocked the development of chemically induced tumors in the breast, pancreas, and colon of rodents. Dr. Karmali suspects that one way omega-3 fatty acids impede tumor development is by blocking the formation of the types of prostaglandins that cause tumors to proliferate.

We still don't know how these animal studies involving unnaturally high doses of fish oil apply to people who regularly eat—or don't eat —fish. A clue may come from a Japanese study involving 100 prostate cancer patients and 100 cancer-free people. Prostate cancer occurred at the highest rate in those who never or only occasionally ate seafood. (Note, however, that there were other differences between prostate cancer patients and cancer-free people.)

Until we have more data, I'd say it's premature to start taking fish-oil supplements to ward off cancer. Very little research has been done with people to date, and we just don't know enough about the proper balance of fish oil and vegetable oil that might protect against cancer.

So where are you left if you're a woman who *knows* she's at increased risk for breast cancer—say, your mother, grandmother, or sister had it and you could lose a few pounds, to boot? Should you make an effort to change your diet? "Yes," says Dr. Karmali. She believes that someone who is really serious about lowering breast-cancer risk should lower fat intake so that it takes up only 20 percent of her calories. Not an easy change, since 20 percent of a 1,500-calorie diet would leave you with just 300 daily calories to spend on fat. Although some other researchers are less convinced about the relationship between dietary fat and breast cancer, cutting back on fat would certainly help anyone who's overweight to lose. Dr. Karmali also recommends eating more fish—not only will it up your omega-3 intake, but, as you know, a fish-rich diet can make it easier to cut back on fat and calories.

Just as with heart disease, you can't expect that eating more fish gives you carte blanche to eat whatever else you want and think that you'll be spared from cancer. In addition to cutting back on fat and keeping your weight down, the American Cancer Society urges a combination of other preventive dietary steps against cancer: eat more cruciferous vegetables (broccoli, cabbage, brussels sprouts, and cauliflower), consume plenty of high-fiber foods (whole grains, fruits, and vegetables), and increase foods rich in vitamins A (dark green and deep orange fruits and vegetables) and C (citrus fruits are the best sources). Although it's okay to eat them once in a while (I'll never give up my smoked oysters!), go easy on salt-cured, smoked, nitrite-cured foods—hot dogs, ham, bacon, and salt-cured fish, for instance —since cancers of the esophagus and stomach are quite common in countries where these foods are consumed in high amounts. Finally, some studies suggest that limiting consumption of alcoholic beverages may lower the risk of breast cancer in women.

ARTHRITIS

Long before it emerged as a possible remedy for heart disease, fish oil was used to treat arthritis. Maurice Stansby, veteran fish-oil researcher and scientific consultant to the National Marine Fisheries Service in Seattle, uncovered documents indicating that, in the late 1700s, personnel from a hospital in Manchester, England, routinely—and successfully—dosed arthritis patients with cod-liver-oil supplements to help their "squeaky joints." Mr. Stansby surmises that the fish-oil tradition was lost to history because it was so unpalatable—the only time patients would take their tonic was when it was forced upon them by attendants in the hospital. No wonder, when cod-liver oil of the day was extracted from rotten fish livers!

Interest in treating arthritis patients with fish oil was rekindled by the finding that manipulating fatty acids in the diets of arthritic animals was beneficial. A link with fish oil was also suspected because of evidence that leukotrienes and thromboxanes are involved in the kinds of inflammatory reactions causing the painful symptoms of arthritis. Accordingly, Harvard researchers decided to test out the effects of fish oil in people who have rheumatoid arthritis, a form of arthritis that can be severely disabling and affects seven million Americans. Richard Sperling, M.D., and his coworkers found a lowering of inflammatory biochemicals, along with a decrease in joint pain and tenderness, in rheumatoid arthritis patients who took fish-oil supplements. Although the results are considered preliminary since no control group was involved, Dr. Sperling thinks that fish oils have the potential to act as antiinflammatory drugs.

Support for Dr. Sperling's hunch comes from research conducted at

Albany Medical College in New York. Joel Kremer, M.D., found "modest" improvements in some symptoms of rheumatoid-arthritis patients who were on fish-oil capsules compared to a group of similar patients who did not take the supplements. The problem with this study is that the patients who took the capsules were also on a special diet, making it difficult to know whether fish oil or something about the diet was responsible for the differences. In a more recent study, Dr. Kremer placed people with rheumatoid arthritis on fish-oil supplements, but no special diet. Compared to a period of time in which they took a placebo (an inert supplement, often called a "sugar pill"), the fish-oil takers suffered significantly less joint tenderness and reported less fatigue. It's important to note that, although there appeared to be overall improvement in other symptoms of arthritis such as duration of morning stiffness and joint swelling, the effects of fish-oil supplements were not as definite.

Thus, fish oil cannot be viewed as any sort of a panacea for arthritis sufferers. Furthermore, the small amount of research that has been conducted in this area has involved large amounts of fish oil. Dr. Kremer's patients, for example, took ten to fifteen fish-oil capsules a day—surely a pharmaceutical dose. He issues words of caution when it comes to taking fish-oil supplements. But he does recommend that people who have arthritis eat more fish. At the very least a fish-rich diet can help keep weight down—an important move to minimize stress on weight-bearing arthritic joints.

ASTHMA

Anyone who struggles with asthma is all too familiar with the breathlessness, wheezing, and coughing brought on by an attack. Since these aversive symptoms appear to be caused largely by leukotrienes, the search is on for remedies that will antagonize leukotriene synthesis. Enter another potential use for fish oil—in one study, large doses brought about the formation of less aggravating leukotrienes in asthmatics. But Walter C. Pickett, Ph.D., senior research biochemist at Lederle Laboratories in New York, who was involved in this research, notes that it's not yet known whether the change in leukotrienes helps alleviate asthma symptoms.

In his book *Fish and Human Health*, Dr. Lands speculates that one reason why Eskimos have a low incidence of asthma may be that they have hefty amounts of omega-3 fatty acids in their diets continuously from birth. Possibly, marine oils have an impact in the early stages of asthma—before asthmatics are sensitized to substances that bring on asthma attacks. Dr. Pickett agrees that it's conceivable that eating fair amounts of fish starting early in life may influence the development of asthma later on.

DIABETES

Investigators are interested in the possibility that fish oil might somehow protect against diabetes—a chronic disease that appears to be related to an immune reaction which leaves the body deficient in insulin or incapable of using insulin correctly. (Insulin, a vital hormone produced by the pancreas, is needed to properly metabolize carbohydrate, protein, and fat.) Indeed, diabetes is rare among the Eskimos. The explanation may, in part, be genetic. But some speculate that their fish-rich diet provides a "natural" state of immunity that prevents the development of diabetes.

Once someone already has diabetes, fish oil may also be of benefit because people with this ailment are particularly prone to cardiovascular disease. People who have what is known as the Type II or "adult" form of diabetes suffer two to four times as many deaths and illnesses caused by heart attacks, strokes, and other vascular problems as do nondiabetics. No doubt, these cardiovascular misfortunes have to do with the fact that people with diabetes often have elevated triglycerides, low HDL-cholesterol levels, hypertension, and a tendency for platelets to aggregate.

Interestingly, one study suggests that Japanese diabetics—who have higher blood levels of EPA, one of the key omega-3 fatty acids —also have fewer cardiovascular problems than Westerners who have diabetes. In contrast, Japanese diabetics who live in Hawaii, where they tend to eat more Western-type foods, have a higher incidence of complications caused by atherosclerosis than do Japanese diabetics who stay in their homeland.

To determine if fish-oil supplements have the same heart-sparing benefits for diabetics as have been reported for nondiabetics, Margaret Albrink, M.D., and her colleagues at West Virginia University in Morgantown placed a small group of people with Type II diabetes on fish-oil supplements. At the end of a month, HDL-cholesterol (the good kind that we want to be high) took a marked jump and platelet aggregation was less. Although blood pressure was not lowered, triglycerides dropped from an average of 530 to 333 mg./dl.—not normal, but certainly an improvement. Before fish-oil supplements are recommended for diabetics, however, more research is needed because there is some evidence that high doses of omega-3 fatty acids impair blood sugar metabolism in people with the so-called adult form of diabetes.

Obviously, we have a long way to go before we know for sure how and in what ways fish and its oils help people who have diabetes. Nevertheless, Dr. Albrink encourages people who have diabetes to eat more fish. For even if you place aside the potential fish-oil benefits, fish itself is an excellent choice to help fill the common diabetic prescription for a low-fat diet that also helps with weight loss.

MULTIPLE SCLEROSIS

Decades ago, scientists reported that Norwegians living near the ocean —who also happened to eat large amounts of fish—had a much lower incidence of multiple sclerosis (MS) than did inlanders who were meat-eaters. Researchers have also found evidence that blood and blood cells of MS patients—who suffer from muscle weakness, lack of coordination, serious visual problems, and difficulty urinating—may have different unsaturated fatty acid content than that of healthy individuals.

Since fish-oil fatty acids are so unusual themselves, why not see if they affect the balance of fatty acids in MS patients and determine whether the change affects the course of the disease? That's exactly what investigators at the Royal Victoria Infirmary in England have been doing since 1981. Several hundred MS patients are involved in a study in which one group is taking fish-oil supplements and the other is not. The goal is to see if fish oil has an impact on overall disability and the number, duration, and severity of relapses. At this writing, the final results have not been published.

MIGRAINE HEADACHES

Serious migraine sufferers who receive no comfort from the host of traditional medicines used to treat their headaches may find welcome relief from fish-oil supplements, according to a study described by Robert Hitzemann, Ph.D., associate professor of psychiatry and behavioral science at the State University of New York at Stony Brook. Out of fifteen people who endured headaches much of the time and who were not helped by other medications, nine got significantly better when they took large doses of fish-oil supplements for six weeks. In general, headaches were less severe and some people suffered fewer attacks. In one dramatic case, a young graduate student who was so incapacitated by headaches that he rarely left bed in his darkened room was able to get up and go back to school when taking fish oil.

Unlike individuals who just occasionally get migraines, those who suffer severe and frequent migraines appear to have a deficiency of one of the omega-3 fatty acids—eicosapentaenoic acid (EPA)—in their blood. That's what led Dr. Hitzemann and his colleagues to test out fish oil in the first place. No one knows exactly why supplements of the omega-3s seem to work, but it may have something to do with a change in prostaglandins which help regulate platelet function and blood vessel dilation. And migraine pain is thought to be related to blood platelets and dilation of blood vessels in the head.

The remaining questions are whether fish oil continues to work on a long-term basis for migraine sufferers and whether there are side effects from regular use of fish-oil supplements. In addition, it's puzzling why six of the migraine sufferers did not get better (according to Dr. Hitzemann, a few got worse). He suspects the dose may not have been high enough for everyone.

Some of these questions may be answered in an upcoming study involving as many as one hundred patients who will be followed on fish-oil supplements for long periods of time. In the meantime, Dr. Hitzemann advises severe migraine victims, who have run the gamut of migraine drugs and found no relief, to consult with their physicians about the possibility of taking fish-oil supplements. He recommends the use of a detailed symptom diary to see if the fish oil really works.

LUPUS AND KIDNEY DISEASE

Results from animal studies forecast promising news for people afflicted with the relatively rare disorder known as systemic lupus erythematosus. Lupus is a chronic inflammatory disease that often leads to arthritis, skin rashes, sores, and weakness. Ultimately, lupus can damage blood vessels, cause severe neurologic problems, and result in fatal kidney damage.

Although we don't yet know what the effects on people with lupus will be, research in animals with an ailment similar to the human variety of lupus reveals that those on fish-oil supplements suffered significantly fewer deaths from kidney disease than animals on a diet high in saturated fat. In addition, a preliminary report on Japanese patients with another type of kidney disease suggests that those treated with fish oil had no advancement of disease after one year. Another group of kidney patients who were not taking fish oil became notably worse.

PSORIASIS

Psoriasis, a distressful and chronic skin condition characterized by redness and scaling, is known to involve irritating leukotrienes. Testing a theory that fish-oil consumption might lead the body to produce fewer inflammatory leukotrienes, researchers had thirteen psoriasis patients eat a special diet supplemented with fish oil. At the end of two months, eight patients experienced "mild to moderate" improvement. The psoriasis of the five other patients either stayed the same or became slightly worse.

The investigators—led by Vincent Ziboh, Ph.D., from the University of California-Davis—believe that fish oil may yield better results when used along with other remedies for psoriasis. (An interesting aside: two patients who also had moderately severe cases of a type of arthritis that can accompany psoriasis reported feeling much better.) Bear in mind that the diet the patients followed would be exceedingly difficult to replicate in everyday life. Just 5 percent of their dietary fat came from foods, while a whopping 25 percent came from liquid fish oil mixed in with orange juice.

More recently, however, researchers reported in the British medical journal *The Lancet* that the amount of fish oil in about 7 daily ounces of Atlantic mackerel had more promising effects for psoriasis sufferers. Twenty-eight psoriasis patients were given either fish-oil supplements or olive oil capsules. They were instructed to continue with their usual topical treatments for psoriasis and to follow their normal diets. At the end of eight weeks, people who took the fish oil supplements had significantly less itching, redness, and scaling. Olive oil brought about no change.

A PREVENTIVE HYPOTHESIS

Although people with any one of the "frontier" diseases can probably benefit from eating more fish, the truly dramatic results so far have been obtained in people consuming fish-oil supplements. Once again, we're talking about a therapeutic or druglike benefit. But what would happen if more of us decided to eat fish three to seven times a week— as opposed to the paltry American average of a little over once a week? Would we, like the Eskimos, experience fewer immune and inflammatory ailments? Of course, no one knows the answer. But fish-oil biochemist Dr. Lands speculates that, in the same way that the omega-3 fatty acids appear to interfere with the beginning stages of cardiovascular disease, the oils may also have a positive effect on early phases of immune and inflammatory diseases. He adds that, at this point, we can only speculate on the possible impact that a fish-rich diet can have "throughout one's entire childhood and adult life."

ARE FISH-OIL FATTY ACIDS ESSENTIAL?

Aside from the role that fish oils may play in preventing various diseases, there is reason to believe the omega-3s are essential nutrients for normal growth. An essential nutrient is one that the body cannot make at all or in adequate amounts, which, therefore, must be supplied by the diet in order to maintain health. Vitamins and minerals are examples of essential nutrients we have to obtain from foods.

At Oregon Health Sciences University in Portland, Martha Neuringer, Ph.D., and William Connor, M.D., found that rhesus monkeys—creatures with visual systems very similar to ours—who were deprived of omega-3 fatty acids during fetal life and as infants could not see as well and had abnormal retinas compared to monkeys fed adequate amounts of omega-3s. In addition, evidence from rat studies suggests that the omega-3s might be important for normal development of the brain and nervous system.

Note that if the omega-3 fatty acids are, indeed, found to be essential in our diets, just tiny amounts are probably all we require. Drs. Neuringer and Connor speculate that we probably need about 1 percent of our total calories as omega-3 fatty acids—amounting to 20 calories' worth for someone who needs 2,000 calories a day. (The preventive level of omega-3s, however, may turn out to be much higher than that.)

Since the eyes and nervous systems of humans develop largely before birth, Drs. Neuringer and Connor believe that it's especially important for pregnant women to consume adequate amounts of omega-3 fatty acids. They advise prospective mothers to eat two weekly meals of relatively oily fish. For breast-feeding mothers, too, they advocate fish eating since the fatty-acid composition of mothers' milk reflects what they eat.

CHAPTER FIVE

Why Not Pop a Pill?

LET ME START TO make my case by giving you an assignment. Flip back to the beginning of the "frontier" diseases in chapter 4. Starting with cancer, quickly skim through each ailment, but plug in the word "aspirin" any time you see the words "fish oil" or "omega-3 fatty acids." Now, if aspirin had in fact been tested with each of the "frontier" diseases and the same discoveries had been made as with fish oil, would you then be ready to commence a daily course of high —or even low—doses of aspirin? Would you be willing to take a drug—and that's how these therapeutic uses of fish oil should be viewed, as drug uses—on the basis of a handful of preliminary tests?

Remember that it often takes many years of use before all potential adverse effects of drugs are revealed. Referring to the unknowns of taking fish-oil supplements in a recent presentation, Steven Plakas, Ph.D., and Anthony Guarino, Ph.D., chief of the Food and Drug Administration's Fishery Research Branch, state, "History tells us that with virtually all clinical trials with new agents, the early results are predominantly good. It is only after more widespread use of a substance that the less desirable effects are manifested." This scenario can be applied to aspirin, which once was viewed by many as an innocuous over-the-counter drug. But we now know that aspirin causes gastrointestinal bleeding in some individuals. And aspirin has been linked with the rare, but sometimes fatal illness Reye's syndrome in children.

Certainly, just as with fish oil, there are ailments that daily doses of aspirin can benefit. The pain of rheumatoid arthritis, for instance, can be alleviated by regular aspirin intake. And aspirin made the headlines because of the recent study showing that the risk of heart attacks was cut markedly in men who took an aspirin every other day. But that doesn't mean we should all go out and start taking aspirin supplements.

The same holds for fish-oil supplements—available as capsules, liquid concentrates, or fish-liver oils. Because of easy accessibility of marine oils—now sold in health-food stores, pharmacies, and even some supermarkets—the temptation for people to "doctor" themselves is great. One concern about self-therapy is that people who catch wind of fish-oil benefits—either from ads for fish oil or popular media reports—and who decide to treat themselves for an ailment may do so in lieu of proper medical attention. Some fish-oil companies do advise people to check with a physician before taking their products. But the reality is that many individuals do not consult their doctors before using over-the-counter remedies. Besides, how is your everyday physician to know the proper way to prescribe fish-oil supplements when even top researchers in the field are uncertain?

HOW MUCH SHOULD YOU TAKE?

For someone considering taking fish-oil supplements, it's important to be aware that—whether the goal is treating a disease already in existence or preventing some ailment from occurring down the road —it's not yet clear what amounts of omega-3 fatty acids are beneficial. It's likely that effective therapeutic and preventive levels of omega-3s vary from person to person and depend on whether someone is healthy or suffering from an illness. The action of omega-3 fatty acids also depends on your total fat intake and the kinds of fats you're eating. In fact, many of the studies on CVD and the "frontier" diseases involved carefully controlled diets, as well as taking fish-oil supplements. Not only would it be difficult to follow a strict diet on your own, but there is no way yet of knowing the ideal amount of dietary fat you should be consuming along with your fish-oil capsules.

Not only that, but you never know what you're getting with commercial fish-oil supplements since they vary greatly in their levels and proportions of omega-3 fatty acids. Case in point: of two different fish-oil products from the same company, one offers a daily dose of 750 milligrams of omega-3s while another provides 1,077–2,154 milligrams of the fatty acids per day, depending upon whether you take one or two capsules with each meal. (For comparison's sake, a three-and-a-half-ounce portion of pink salmon contains about 1,000 milligrams of the omega-3s.) Moreover, the January 1988 issue of the *Tufts University Diet & Nutrition Letter* reports that many major brands of fish-oil supplements have far lower levels of omega-3 fatty acids than are listed on their labels. In part, that's because vitamin E, which is added to the supplements to prevent the breakdown of the fatty acids, is not added in adequate amounts.

POTENTIAL SIDE EFFECTS

If you were to take the number of capsules or tablespoons recommended on most fish-oil-supplement bottles—which ranges from one dose a day to two with each meal—you probably wouldn't experience any ill effects, but you also wouldn't come close to the levels researchers have found to be advantageous for treating various ailments. Indeed, a number of studies involved taking anywhere from ten to eighteen fish-oil capsules a day. Not only should you ask yourself how long you could down so many pills on a daily basis, but you also need to realize that doses high enough to provide some benefit may be toxic in other ways.

The potential adverse effect that seems to most concern experts in the field is the bleeding tendency mentioned previously. As you know, omega-3 fatty acids can alter platelet function, and that could mean a delay in the time it takes blood to clot if you should receive a wound. It appears that the longer you take fish oil and the higher the amount, the greater the interference with clotting. One problem is that, even without taking fish-oil supplements, there is individual variation in the amount of time it takes for wounds to stop bleeding, making it difficult to specify a potentially harmful level of omega-3s that applies to everybody. It's conceivable that an amount of fish oil that has no effect on one person may lead to a bleeding tendency in someone else. People who regularly take doses high enough to interfere with blood clotting could run into serious hemorrhaging if they have to undergo surgery or are involved in an accident.

The University of Massachusetts Medical School's Marc Fisher, M.D., believes that the greatest risk of excessive bleeding—even for those who stick with label recommendations for daily amounts of fish oils—are posed for those who have a bleeding tendency already. People fitting this description include alcoholics and hemophiliacs, as well as individuals who bruise very easily. Also in jeopardy are people who regularly take other medications that can interfere with blood clotting—such as aspirin and anticoagulants ("blood thinners"). They may experience a "double dose" effect if they also take fish-oil supplements. One person involved in a University of Massachusetts study— who was on both fish-oil supplements and aspirin—experienced considerable bleeding as a result of a fall while shoveling snow. The effect of regularly taking the two remedies together may well have been worse than if either one had been taken alone.

A MATTER OF TIME

Not only have doses been high in studies suggesting a favorable impact of fish oil on various diseases, but, as I already mentioned, the research has involved taking fish-oil supplements for short periods of time—just a matter of weeks or a few months in most cases. Since the evidence in hand indicates that you'd have to keep taking fish oil to continue to receive the benefits, much more research must be conducted to know the long-term efficacy and safety of taking concentrates of the omega-3s. Only time will tell if those who take fish-oil supplements really do continue to get better, become worse, or develop serious side effects.

Some researchers fear that long-term use of high doses of fish-oil supplements will increase the body's need for vitamin E—a vitamin you may need more of when your polyunsaturated-fat intake is high. Although some commercial fish-oil products have vitamin E added as a preservative, the amounts of the vitamin are typically quite small. Besides, vitamin E tends to decompose as it protects the oil from spoiling. Fortunately, signs of vitamin E deficiency have not been reported in Greenland Eskimos or in studies involving people who took large amounts of fish oil. Nevertheless, no one knows what might ensue if large doses of fish oil were consumed for long periods of time.

GETTING MORE THAN YOU BARGAINED FOR

Some fish-oil supplements can add a hefty dose of cholesterol to your daily intake—without even letting you know it on the label. One popular brand provides more than 150 milligrams of cholesterol per ounce, as does cod-liver oil. That's half of your day's maximum allotment from about two tablespoons of oil. Fortunately, some cholesterol-free fish-oil supplements are making their way onto the commercial market. Unless the label indicates that a supplement is cholesterol-free, the manufacturer should be consulted to determine cholesterol values.

You also may be getting potentially toxic levels of certain vitamins if you get your omega-3s from fish-*liver* oils. Just one teaspoonful of cod-liver oil, for example, nets you a whole day's recommended amount for vitamins A and D, two fat-soluble vitamins that can be harmful if taken in high amounts for long periods of time. (Vitamin D excess can cause blood vessels to calcify, plus harm the kidneys, lungs, and bones; vitamin A toxicity can result in damage to the liver, skin, bones, and red blood cells.) To attain the levels of omega-3 fatty acids used in some of the "frontier" disease studies, you might have to consume 3, 5, or even 20 teaspoons of cod-liver oil. All it would take to exceed the advisable upper limits for vitamin D are 2 to 3 daily teaspoons, while 5 or 6 teaspoons of the fishy stuff could net you unsafe levels of vitamin A. Since fish-oil *capsules* are produced from fish bodies—not from their livers, where vitamins A and D are stored —they don't contain high levels of the vitamins.

Fish-oil supplements can also add to your calorie and fat intake. Recommended amounts on product labels may only provide you with an extra 50 to 70 daily calories. But if you were to approach the levels used in research studies (without cutting back on sources of fat in your diet), hundreds of extra calories—most of them from fat—would be added to your daily regime. All it takes to add an extra ten pounds to your frame in a year's time is an extra 100 calories per day above what your body needs to maintain its current weight.

Some people have also expressed concern about the possible presence of contaminants, such as mercury and polychlorinated biphenyls (PCBs), in fish-oil supplements. It's a legitimate issue since chemical contaminants are likely to concentrate in fish body fat and livers. Nevertheless, a recent study on a number of commercial fish-oil supplements conducted by the FDA's Fishery Research Branch revealed that only about one in twenty had significant levels of PCBs.

Reputable companies remove contaminants and heavy metals in processing fish oil, checking to make certain that no harmful substances remain in the finished product. But Drs. Plakas and Guarino of the FDA point out that the extent to which cleanup procedures are used by fish-oil companies is uncertain—such precautions "may not be employed by low-budget operations." If you have questions about any particular fish-oil product, don't hesitate to pick up the phone and call the manufacturer. (For more on contaminants in fish, see chapter 7.)

CONFRONTING THE REAL ISSUE

Okay, you get the message—large doses of fish oil can be risky. But what's the harm in popping a few pills or downing a teaspoon or two of liquid fish oil to up your daily omega-3 intake? It probably won't hurt most people, but you have to ask yourself if you're skirting the fact that you'll have to change your diet and lifestyle, too, if you want to do all you can to ward off many of the ailments connected with the omega-3s. Indeed, you cannot count on fish-oil supplements to spare you from CVD and the like in lieu of changing your diet and altering risk factors. As indicated earlier, many of the studies showing beneficial effects of fish-oil supplements employed them in conjunction with a fat-controlled diet. Even the literature that accompanies some fish-oil products cautions users to incorporate the marine oils into a low-fat diet that includes more fish, plus tells them to quit smoking, exercise more, and control their weight.

The problem with popping a pill or potion is that it tends to give you a false sense of security; it's tempting to think that you don't have to make any changes in the rest of your life. As respected biomedical researcher Edwin L. Bierman, M.D., from the University of Washington School of Medicine puts it, taking fish-oil supplements avoids "biting the bullet" with the American diet, which is too high in saturated fat and cholesterol. In other words, just taking a fishy pill isn't enough!

Now, I'm not saying that I don't foresee a day when omega-3 fatty acids will be used to treat—and maybe prevent—certain diseases. The data we have so far look too promising to be that skeptical. Even now some experts are ready to advise that people who have severe migraine headaches or blood triglyceride levels in the thousands—people who have found no relief from other accepted remedies for their conditions—take fish-oil supplements under the guidance of a physician. Other health professionals, however, urge that more research should be conducted before fish-oil supplements are routinely used as drugs for treating diseases.

There may also come a time when people who don't or can't eat fish will be advised to take a daily low-dose omega-3-fatty-acid supplement—much the way many women now take iron or calcium supplements because they don't get enough from the foods they eat. But, as is likely to be the case with the omega-3s, the ideal way to get these two minerals is from foods which contain a natural balance of nutrients. (Chapter 6 elaborates on the many nutritional advantages that fish has over fish-oil supplements.)

DO THE OMEGA-3S HAVE IT ALL?

Although the omega-3 fatty acids undoubtedly have potent abilities, don't lose sight of the fact that there might be something in marine creatures other than, or in addition to, these fatty acids that spares regular fish-eaters from diseases such as CVD. Recall the much lower incidence of CVD in the men in the Dutch study who consumed just one or two fish meals a week—only a third of their fish came from oilier types. Moreover, the researchers found that higher intakes of lean fish alone were associated with a lower risk of CVD.

No one knows exactly what it is about fish that provides the protective edge—for high fish consumption was not associated with lower blood-cholesterol levels in the Dutch men. Moreover, even the highest fish consumers did not eat the amount of fish found to be associated with favorable platelet changes in other studies.

One thought that the Dutch investigators put forth is that levels of a trace mineral, called selenium, provided by fish may protect against CVD. Their theory is based on a study from Finland revealing that people with low blood-selenium levels had a higher risk of cardiovascular deaths. The bottom line is that it's entirely possible that a combination of fish components protects against certain diseases.

SPEND IT ON FISH

Fish-oil supplements don't come cheap—maximum doses recommended on labels of some of the more popular products can run you anywhere from $195 to more than $500 a year. Just think what you'd have to spend in order to arrive at the levels of omega-3 fatty acids found to be effective in research studies!

Needless to say, I'd much rather see you spend your money on fish. That way, you'll be getting more omega-3s and whatever else there might be in fish that seems to keep people healthy. And you'll automatically be on your way to the low-fat, lower-calorie diet we all should be eating. At that, you won't be running the risk of potential side effects of fish-oil supplements, since there simply is no evidence that eating reasonable amounts of fish several times a week—or even once a day—will harm you. Quite the opposite: all indications are that eating more fish will do you a world of good.

CHAPTER SIX

Facts and Fallacies about the Nutritional Goodness of Fish

OILY FISH ARE FATTENING. Seafood is too salty. Oysters heighten your libido. Shellfish are taboo on low-cholesterol diets. Such are popular notions kicking around about our piscine friends. Take the fish "fact or fallacy" quiz in this chapter to find out how much you really know about the nutritional merits of fish. (Also, watch for "Seafood Nutri-facts," a new labeling program that provides nutrition information for more than sixty species of fish at fresh and frozen seafood cases.)

HOW FISH STACKS UP NEXT TO OTHER PROTEIN FOODS

Although I can't hide my bias that fish is the best protein food around, I'm not about to berate meat and poultry. Meat, for one, has cleaned up its act when it comes to fat (for example, leaner cattle are being bred, and butchers are trimming off more fat), and skinless poultry has long been considered a low-fat food. My goal is simply to show you how fish compares with meat and poultry.

Fact or fallacy? The protein in meat and poultry is superior to that in fish.

Fallacy. All three provide high-quality protein containing the essential amino acids which the body needs in order to make its own proteins. (Amino acids are the building blocks that compose proteins; the essential amino acids are the ones the body can't synthesize itself and, therefore, must obtain from foods.) A three-and-a-half-ounce cooked serving of meat, poultry, or fish provides well over a third of the daily recommended amount of protein for a man or woman.

An advantage of many types of fish over meats is that you don't have to consume as many calories to meet your protein needs. As you can see from the comparison of lean types of protein foods in table 2, you need to eat more than double the calories from lean ground beef to get 15 grams of protein—the US RDA—than you would from low-fat fish such as cod. (See sidebar for an explanation of the US RDAs.)

Fact or fallacy? The protein in fish is easier to digest than the protein in meat.

Fact. When was the last time you needed a knife to cut fish? You probably never put a knife to cooked fish because, compared to meat, it has less tough connective tissue and shorter muscle fibers—both factors that render it more digestible than meat. Moreover, the connective tissue that *is* present in fish is usually softened in cooking, while some tough tissue usually remains in cooked meat. Although the difference in toughness between a good cut of meat and a soft portion of fish is not of great significance for most healthy people, it does make boneless fish an ideal protein choice for small children and the elderly, who may have trouble chewing or with digestion.

Fact or fallacy? On an ounce-for-ounce basis, meat is much higher in cholesterol than fish.

Fallacy. Many people are surprised to learn that, although meat is somewhat higher in cholesterol than fish, the difference isn't that great. A 3½-ounce serving of the lean portion of cooked beef, pork, or lamb runs from about 80 to 95 milligrams of cholesterol. Chicken (with skin or without) is in the same range.

Granted, a 3½-ounce portion of cooked fish—averaging about 65

TABLE 2. Calorie Counts per 15 Grams of Protein in Various Foods

Food	Calories per 15 grams of protein
Cod, baked or broiled	70
Chicken breast, roasted, no skin	80
Beef, top round, broiled	90
Lamb, leg, shank portion, roasted (lean part only)	95
Pork (fresh), leg, shank portion, roasted (lean part only)	115
Beef (lean—21 percent fat), ground, broiled	164

Sources: Based on data from the U.S. Department of Agriculture, Human Nutrition Information Service Handbooks 8–5, 8–10, 8–13, and 8–15; *Food and Nutrition News,* March/April 1987; National Livestock and Meat Board.

The RDAs and US RDAs

Anyone who reads the sides of cereal boxes or takes vitamin supplements has come across the US RDAs on labels. They are a kind of condensed version of the more extensive Recommended Dietary Allowances or RDAs, which are the levels of most major nutrients —including protein and many vitamins and minerals—considered by experts to meet the daily needs of nearly all healthy people. Since nutritional needs vary according to age and sex, there are separate RDAs for seventeen different age and sex groups—from infants to older adults to pregnant and lactating women.

For the purpose of comparing the nutritional value of products to the RDAs on food labels, the government has devised the US RDAs, which more or less combine the RDAs into single values for various nutrients. The US RDAs serve as general guidelines for children ages four and up as well as adults. For the most part, the US RDAs represent the highest RDA values for any age group. For example, the highest RDA for iron is 18 milligrams—for premenopausal women and teenagers. Therefore, the US RDA that you see foods compared to on nutrition labels is also 18 milligrams.

You'll see that, throughout this chapter, I often mention what percentage of the US RDA for a particular nutrient a 3½-ounce serving of fish provides. That's because nutritionists commonly report nutritional values for 100-gram portions of foods that are about 3½ ounces. Although 3½ ounces is certainly not a large portion of fish, meat, or poultry, most nutritionists consider that amount to be adequate.

---

milligrams of cholesterol—is lower than meat and poultry. But cholesterol values for all of these protein foods are well below the recommended daily 300-milligram limit.

Fact or fallacy? The leanest cuts of meat contain far more fat than the leanest types of fish.

Fact. The problem with meat isn't so much its cholesterol content as it is the fat level. Even lean cuts of meat, such as broiled top round of beef, contain about 6 grams of fat per 3½-ounce cooked serving. But the many types of very low-fat fish—including cod, flounder, pollock, and most shellfish—contain no more than 2 grams of fat for the same-size portion.

Take a look at table 3 (page 56) to compare fat and calorie content of specific types of fish with other types of protein foods. As you can see, you could feast on 3½-ounce portions *each* of cod, sole, crabmeat, and shrimp before you'd arrive at the total fat level in a single 3½-ounce serving of beef top round or lean leg of lamb. And less fat means you get to eat a larger portion for the calories. Consider, for instance, that 100 calories' worth of steamed shrimp nets you a 3½-ounce portion; if you spent the same 100 calories on a lean, broiled hamburger, you'd wind up with a serving not much more than a third that size.

Fact or fallacy? Since higher-fat fish, such as sockeye salmon, provide more fat than sirloin steak, then the steak is a more healthful choice.

Fallacy. The *type* of fat in the two protein sources is quite different: 41 percent of the fat in broiled sirloin steak is saturated, while just 17 percent of salmon's fat is of the less healthful saturated type. Even lean top round steak has 35 percent saturated fat.

TABLE 3. Approximate Calorie and Fat Content of 3½-Ounce Portions of Cooked Protein Foods (lean, edible portion only)

Food	Calories	Fat (grams)	% calories from fat
Cod [a]	105	less than 1	8
Flatfish (flounder, sole) [a]	117	1.5	12
Swordfish [a]	155	5	29
Salmon, sockeye [a]	216	11	46
Crab, blue [b]	102	2	18
Shrimp [b]	99	1	9
Chicken breast, roasted (no skin)	165	3.5	19
Chicken breast, roasted (with skin)	197	8	37
Beef, top round, broiled	191	6	28
Sirloin steak, broiled	208	8.5	37
Ground beef, lean (21% fat), broiled	272	18.5	61
Lamb, leg, shank portion, roasted	180	6.5	33
Pork (fresh), leg, shank portion, roasted	215	10.5	44

Sources: U.S. Department of Agriculture, Human Nutrition Information Service Handbooks 8–5, 8–10, 8–13, and 8–15; *Food and Nutrition News,* March/April 1987; National Livestock and Meat Board.
[a] Cooked without added fat by a dry-heat method, such as baking, broiling, or microwaving.
[b] Cooked by a moist-heat method, such as boiling, poaching, or steaming.

Percent Fat and Percent Calories From Fat

At this point, it's important to make some distinctions about terminology used to describe fat content of foods. When nutritionists talk about "percent fat" in a food, they're referring to fat as a proportion of the food's total weight—usually in the raw state. For example, since bluefin tuna is about 5 percent fat by weight, then a pound of the raw fish contains .05 × 16 ounces or eight-tenths of an ounce of fat.

"Percent calories from fat," on the other hand, tells you what proportion of a food's total calories are contributed by fat. You can determine the percentage for yourself if you know the number of calories and grams of fat in a given portion of food. Consider a 3½-ounce portion of bluefin tuna that provides 144 calories and 5 grams of fat. Knowing that fat has 9 calories in each gram, you multiply 5 grams times 9 to arrive at 45 calories, which is the number of calories contributed by fat. Then divide 45 by 144 (the total number of calories in the piece of fish) and you'll wind up with 31 percent fat calories.

The difference, in large part, is explained by salmon's omega-3 fatty acid content—cooked, it provides more than 1,200 milligrams of EPA and DHA, while beef has none of these beneficial fatty acids to speak of. Neither do chicken, pork, or lamb provide appreciable levels of the two omega-3s. For comparison's sake, the fat in cooked chicken breast is 28 percent saturated, pork is about 35 percent saturated, and the fat in many cuts of lamb is about 50 percent saturated.

Fact or fallacy? Because of its saturated-fat content, meat should be excluded from a diet designed to prevent heart disease.

Fallacy. Reasonable amounts of lean meat—that is, non-greasy, fat-trimmed cuts with little white marbling through the flesh—have every right to be part of a well-balanced, low-fat diet. As suggested earlier, the past several decades have brought about efforts on the part of breeders to substantially lower body-fat content of cattle, pigs, and sheep. In addition, meats are good sources of protein, iron, zinc, and B vitamins.

The problem is that many Americans go well beyond the American Heart Association's recommendation to eat *no more* than 6 ounces *total* of lean beef, pork, lamb, and veal (as well as skinless poultry and fish) each day. And when they go for meat, they opt for the fattier, marbled cuts. Since meats tend to provide more total fat than fish—and a larger proportion of it is saturated—the higher your meat intake, the more likely you are to exceed the recommendation to consume a diet containing 30 percent fat calories, with less than 10 percent coming from saturated sources.

THE NITTY-GRITTY ABOUT FISH FATS

Assuming the fish-health story has you hooked, you're probably eager to know which fish are the most healthful. On the other hand, you've been told to keep your total fat intake low, which would imply that the leanest fish are your best bets. Yet you've also heard about the merits of the oils in fish—a suggestion that maybe you ought to go with the fattier species. My advice for accomplishing both goals is to pick your weekly choices from a mix of very low-, low-, and medium-fat fish, as well as oily types.

Table 4 groups fish according to these classifications. The information comes from the most recent U.S. Department of Agriculture data on the nutritional composition of fish. Note that until this point, I've been comparing nutritional data for *cooked* protein foods. Unfortunately, however, there just isn't much information available on cooked fish. Therefore, in table 4, I've elected to compare 3½-ounce portions of *raw fish*—for any one type of raw fish, you can figure that a 3½-ounce cooked portion would have roughly 20 percent more calories, fat, cholesterol, and omega-3 fatty acids. (Because of moisture loss the nutrients become more concentrated.)

Fact or fallacy? The fattier the fish, the higher its calorie content.

Fact. Since fat is the most "fattening" of all nutrients—at 9 calories per gram versus 4 calories per gram for carbohydrate and protein—fish such as mackerel, with about 14 grams of fat in each 3½-ounce portion, is bound to have more calories than a very low-fat fish like cod, with less than 1 gram of fat for the same amount. Considering, however, that Atlantic mackerel—containing just 205 calories—has more calories than any other type of fresh fish listed in table 4, I wouldn't deem any unprocessed finfish or shellfish a high-calorie protein food. What really jacks up the caloric value of fish is the butter, margarine, oil, cream, cheese, and the like added in cooking.

Fact or fallacy? When it comes to fat content, one salmon steak is the same as any other.

Fallacy. Any one piece of fish is likely to have different fat and omega-3 fatty acid composition than the same-size piece from a different fish of the same species. In addition, there are marked variations

TABLE 4. Calorie, Fat, Cholesterol, and Omega-3 Fatty Acid Content of 3½-Ounce Portions of Raw Fish (edible portion only)

FINFISH

Very Low-Fat Finfish—2 percent or less fat by weight

Fish	Calories	Fat (grams)	Cholesterol (milligrams)	Omega-3s[a] (milligrams)
Cod, Atlantic	82	0.7	43	184
Cod, Pacific	82	0.6	37	215
Cusk	87	0.7	41	—
Dolphinfish (mahimahi)	85	0.7	73	108
Flatfish (flounder, sole)	91	1.2	48	199
Grouper, mixed species[b]	92	1	37	247
Haddock	87	0.7	57	185
Hake—*see* Whiting				
Monkfish	76	1.5	25	—
Ocean perch, Atlantic	94	1.6	42	291
Perch, mixed species[b]	91	0.9	90	253
Pike, northern	88	0.7	39	107
Pollock, Alaska (walleye)	81	0.8	71	372
Pollock, Atlantic	92	1	71	421
Pout, ocean	79	0.9	52	—
Rockfish, Pacific, mixed species[b]	94	1.6	35	345
Sea bass, mixed species[b]	97	2	41	595
Snapper, mixed species[b]	100	1.3	37	311
Tuna, skipjack	103	1	47	256
Tuna, yellowfin	108	1	45	218
Whiting, mixed species (includes hake)[b]	90	1.3	67	224

[a] Omega-3 fatty acid values include EPA (eicosapentaenoic acid) and DHA (docosahexaenoic acid) only.
[b] Analyses of more than one species of this generic name are included because the species are similar in nutritional content and/or there are not enough data available to include a separate listing for individual species.

TABLE 4. Calorie, Fat, Cholesterol, and Omega-3 Fatty Acid Content of 3½-Ounce Portions of Raw Fish (edible portion only), *continued*

FINFISH

Low-Fat Finfish—2.1 to 5 percent fat

Fish	Calories	Fat (grams)	Cholesterol (milligrams)	Omega-3s[a] (milligrams)
Bass, freshwater, mixed species[b]	114	3.7	68	595
Bass, striped	97	2.3	80	754
Bluefish	124	4.2	59	771
Catfish, channel	116	4.3	58	373
Croaker, Atlantic	104	3.2	61	220
Halibut, Atlantic and Pacific	110	2.3	32	363
Mullet, striped	117	3.8	49	325
Porgy (scup)	105	2.7	—	——
Salmon, chum	120	3.8	74	627
Salmon, pink	116	3.5	52	1,005
Sea trout, mixed species[b]	104	3.6	83	372
Shark, mixed species[b]	130	4.5	51	843
Smelt, rainbow	97	2.4	70	693
Swordfish	121	4	39	639
Tilefish	96	2.3	—	430
Trout, rainbow	118	3.4	57	568
Tuna, bluefin	144	4.9	38	1,173
Turbot, European	95	3	—	——
Weakfish—*see* Sea trout				
Wolffish	96	2.4	46	623

[a] Omega-3 fatty acid values include EPA (eicosapentaenoic acid) and DHA (docosahexaenoic acid) only.
[b] Analyses of more than one species of this generic name are included because the species are similar in nutritional content and/or there are not enough data available to include a separate listing for individual species.

FINFISH

Medium-Fat Finfish—5.1 to 10 percent fat

Fish	Calories	Fat (grams)	Cholesterol (milligrams)	Omega-3s[a] (milligrams)
Butterfish	146	8	65	——
Carp	127	5.6	66	352
Herring, Atlantic	158	9	60	1,571
Mackerel, Pacific and jack, mixed species[b]	157	7.9	47	1,441
Mackerel, Spanish	139	6.3	76	1,341
Orange roughy	126[c]	7[c]	20	——
Pompano, Florida	164	9.5	50	568
Roe, finfish, mixed species[b]	140	6.4	374	2,346
Salmon, Atlantic	142	6.3	55	1,436
Salmon, coho (silver salmon)	146	6	39	814
Salmon, sockeye (red salmon)	168	8.6	62	1,172
Whitefish, mixed species[b]	134	5.9	60	1,258

Oily Finfish—10.1 percent fat or more

Fish	Calories	Fat (grams)	Cholesterol (milligrams)	Omega-3s[a] (milligrams)
Eel, mixed species[b]	184	11.7	126	147
Herring, Pacific	195	13.9	77	1,658
Mackerel, Atlantic	205	13.9	70	2,299
Sablefish	195	15.3	49	1,395
Salmon, chinook (king)	180	10.4	66	1,355
Shad	197	13.8	——	——
Turbot, Greenland	186	13.8	46	919

[a] Omega-3 fatty acid values include EPA (eicosapentaenoic acid) and DHA (docosahexaenoic acid) only.
[b] Analyses of more than one species of this generic name are included because the species are similar in nutritional content and/or there are not enough data available to include a separate listing for individual species.
[c] Actual values may be considerably lower because more than 90 percent of the fat is a waxy substance that may not be metabolized. Dr. Joyce Nettleton's *Seafood Nutrition* reports that orange roughy has 65 calories and 0.3 grams of fat per 3½-ounce portion.

TABLE 4. Calorie, Fat, Cholesterol, and Omega-3 Fatty Acid Content of 3½-Ounce Portions of Raw Fish (edible portion only), *continued*

SHELLFISH

Crustaceans

Fish	Calories	Fat (grams)	Cholesterol (milligrams)	Omega-3s[a] (milligrams)
Crab, Alaska king	84	0.6	42	—
Crab, blue	87	1.1	78	320
Crab, Dungeness	86	1	59	307
Crab, snow (queen)	90	1.2	55	372
Crawfish, mixed species[b]	89	1.1	139	173
Lobster, American (northern)	90	0.9	95	—
Lobster, spiny, mixed species[b]	112	1.5	70	373
Shrimp, mixed species[b]	106	1.7	152	480

Mollusks

Fish	Calories	Fat (grams)	Cholesterol (milligrams)	Omega-3s[a] (milligrams)
Clams, mixed species[b]	74	1	34	142
Mussels (blue)	86	2.2	28	441
Octopus	82	1	48	157
Oysters, Eastern	69	2.5	55	439
Oysters, Pacific	81	2.3	—	688
Scallops, mixed species[b]	88	0.8	33	198
Squid, mixed species[b]	92	1.4	233	488

[a] Omega-3 fatty acid values include EPA (eicosapentaenoic acid) and DHA (docosahexaenoic acid) only.
[b] Analyses of more than one species of this generic name are included because the species are similar in nutritional content and/or there are not enough data available to include a separate listing for individual species.

PROCESSED FISH

Fish	Calories	Fat (grams)	Cholesterol (milligrams)	Omega-3s[a] (milligrams)
Anchovies, canned in olive oil (drained)	210	9.7	—	2,055
Caviar, black and red	252	17.9	588	—
Crab, imitation Alaska king	102	1.3	20	—
Gefilte fish, commercial with small amount broth (sweet recipe)	84	1.7	30	120
Herring, Atlantic, pickled	262	18	13	1,389
Mackerel, jack, canned (drained)	156	6.3	79	—
Salmon, pink, canned (solids with liquid and bones)	139	6.1	—	1,651
Salmon, sockeye, canned (drained, with bones)	153	7.3	44	1,156
Sardines, Atlantic, canned in soybean oil (drained, with bones)	208	11.5	142	982
Sardines, Pacific, canned in tomato sauce (drained, with bones)	178	12	61	1,604
Scallops, imitation	99	0.4	22	—
Shrimp, imitation	101	1.5	36	—
Tuna, light, canned in soybean oil (drained)	198	8.2	18	128
Tuna, light, canned in water (drained)	131	0.5	—	111
Tuna, white (albacore), canned in soybean oil (drained)	186	8.1	31	—
Tuna (albacore), white, canned in water (drained)	136	2.5	42	706

Source: U.S. Department of Agriculture, Human Nutrition Information Service Handbook 8–15.
Notes: Missing numbers indicate lack of reliable data or uncertain presence. All values are approximate and vary from one fish to the next and/or according to brand.
[a] Omega-3 fatty acid values include EPA (eicosapentaenoic acid) and DHA (docosahexaenoic acid) only.

among different species of fish that are in the same family. The reasons are numerous and depend on the following:

- *Age and size.* Older fish tend to be larger and have had a chance to accumulate more fat than younger, smaller fish.
- *Season of the year.* The fat content of mackerel, for example, may be double in the autumn of what it is after December.
- *Salt content of the water.* In general, saltwater fish tend to have higher omega-3 fatty acid levels than freshwater fish.
- *Temperature of the water.* Fish that live in colder waters tend to contain more omega-3s.
- *Diet of the fish.* The more omega-3 fatty acids fish regularly eat, the more omega-3s their bodies contain. Those raised on fish farms are commonly fed diets rich in vegetable oil's omega-6 fatty acids and, therefore, have been reported to contain significantly lower levels of omega-3 fatty acids than their wild counterparts.
- *Spawning status.* Salmon, for instance, are fattiest just before their spawning run; while traveling, they use up their fat stores.
- *Distance traveled before spawning.* As a case in point, observe the vast differences in fat content among the various species of salmon listed in table 4. Chinook salmon tend to have large fat stores because they travel great distances. Pink salmon, on the other hand, have much lower fat levels because they travel just several hundred yards to spawn.

What all of this means is that the pink salmon you serve tonight may have somewhat different fat and omega-3 fatty acid content than the pink or chinook salmon you serve a month from now. It may also contain different fat levels than those listed in table 4. Another implication of fat variability is that a fish, such as butterfish, may at one time be classified as "medium-fat," yet at other times it may be "oily."

Although the values in table 4 represent the best available scientific data, in many cases the figures on nutritional composition of fish are based on limited data—for instance, analysis of just a small number of fish caught at one location at one time. Therefore, I recommend that you use the tables only to get a rough idea of how one type of fish compares to another.

Fact or fallacy? The fattier the fish, the higher its omega-3 fatty acid content.

Fact—at least generally speaking. In table 4, you'll see that as you move from the very low-fat fish through the oily ones, the omega-3 values tend to increase markedly. There are, however, some notable exceptions. For instance, even though the U.S. Department of Agriculture (USDA) data indicate that pink salmon is low-fat, it has levels of omega-3 fatty acids that are more like those of medium-fat and oily fish. Quite the opposite, fatty eel has a low omega-3 level.

Observe, too, that even though total fat levels in canned water-packed light and white (albacore) tuna are not far apart, the white variety is much higher in omega-3s. Also note that popular shellfish —almost all of which are very low-fat—tend to have more omega-3 fatty acids than well-liked, very low-fat finfish such as cod, sole, and haddock.

Fact or fallacy? Since oil-packed tuna and sardines are obviously oilier than their counterparts canned in water or tomato sauce, it's safe to assume that they're higher in the omega-3 fatty acids, EPA and DHA.

Fallacy. Unless the ingredient listed specifically includes sardine oil, fish canned in oil is usually packed in vegetable oils that add omega-6 fatty acids as well as calories to the products. Moreover, there is evidence that vegetable oils actually leach considerable amounts of omega-3 fatty acids from the fish into the oil, which is usually discarded.

Sometimes fish is packed in soybean oil, which does contain an omega-3 fatty acid called linolenic acid. Linolenic acid is also provided by some vegetables as well as by a new cooking oil derived from rapeseed, called canola oil. But linolenic acid has a different chemical structure than EPA and DHA—it's not known how its biological activity compares with fish oil's omega-3s. Some preliminary evidence suggests that linolenic acid may play a role in lowering blood pressure. But, in general, there's little scientific information on its biological effects. At present, the consensus seems to be that omega-3 fatty acids from vegetable oils are not as physiologically active as those in fish oils. Incidentally, if soybean oil is even partially hydrogenated—as it often is in margarines—its omega-3 fatty acid level can be cut by more than half.

Because they're much lower in fat and calories, I advise using water-packed tuna and sardines canned in tomato or mustard sauces over oil-packed varieties. (Although they have quite high levels of omega-3 fatty acids, Atlantic sardines packed in oil also provide close to half the daily recommended limit for cholesterol.) If you use the oil-packed types, drain them well. Canned salmon and mackerel usually come canned without added oil. I do recommend you remove as much skin as possible because it has a layer of fat under it and because it can impart a strong fishy taste.

TABLE 5. The Effect of Breading and Frying on Fat and Calorie Levels of 3½-Ounce Portions of Fish

Fish	Calories	Fat (grams)	Saturated fat (grams)
Pollock, Alaska, baked, plain	113	1.1	0.2
Pollock, Alaska, fish portions and sticks* (frozen and reheated)	272	12.2	3.1
Shrimp, boiled	99	1.1	0.3
Shrimp, breaded and fried*	242	12.3	2.1
Clams, steamed	148	2	0.2
Clams, breaded and fried*	202	11.2	2.7

Source: U.S. Department of Agriculture, Human Nutrition Information Service Handbook 8–15.
* Cooked in hydrogenated vegetable oil (not palm or coconut)

Fact or fallacy? Smoking, canning, freezing, and frying do not destroy the omega-3 fatty acids in fish.

Fact. Smoke it, can it, freeze it, or fry it—but you won't significantly affect the omega-3s in fish. When it comes to imitation shellfish, however, made from a minced-fish (usually Alaska pollock) paste called surimi, processing is likely to have a negative impact. The USDA provides no information on omega-3 fatty acids in the imitation crustaceans, but the modest natural amounts of omega-3s in Alaska pollock are largely "washed out" when surimi is made. (For more on surimi-based products, see page 152.)

Although frying doesn't seem to have a major effect on omega-3 fatty acid levels in fish, it can substantially raise total fat levels—and the increase is not in the omega-3s, EPA and DHA. Table 5 shows you that fish fried in hydrogenated vegetable oil (like shortening) absorbs as much as a 12-fold increase in total fat and significant elevations of saturated fat and calories. Although the saturated-fat levels of these fried seafoods are still well below those of lean beef, their total fat levels are much higher.

THE FISHY CHOLESTEROL SAGA

I regret all the years that I—along with most other dietitians—denied shellfish to my patients on low-cholesterol diets. I can only plead that we just didn't know then what we now know about the cholesterol content of fish.

Fact or fallacy? Most shellfish are now considered to be good for the heart.

Fact. The old restrictions on shellfish for the cholesterol-conscious have been greatly eased, for it is now known that most are low in cholesterol. Shellfish got their reputation as blood-cholesterol-raisers because of outdated scientific methods that detected cholesterollike substances (called noncholesterol sterols) as well as real cholesterol (also a sterol) in shellfish. Thus, the readings on cholesterol in many shellfish were falsely high. A small portion of oysters, for example, was once thought to contain more than 300 milligrams of cholesterol. But newer scientific methods that eliminate the noncholesterol sterols reveal a cholesterol value for oysters of around 55 milligrams.

It turns out that cholesterol composes only 30 to 40 percent of the total sterols in mollusks—that is, clams, mussels, oysters, and scallops—hence the low cholesterol readings that you see for most mollusks in table 4. (You can't miss the one exception—high-cholesterol squid, the only mollusk that comes close to eggs in cholesterol content.)

Unlike plant-eating mollusks (the so-called vegetarians of the sea), crustaceans tend to have higher cholesterol levels because most feed on small animals. And practically all of the sterols in a crustacean are from cholesterol. Nevertheless, a 3½-ounce serving of even those crustaceans highest in cholesterol—namely, American lobster, shrimp, and crawfish—provides just one-third to one-half the daily recommended 300-milligram limit for cholesterol.

Still, the American Heart Association's advice to the general public is to limit intake of shrimp and lobster to no more than a single serving of either of the two fish per week. My personal feeling is that, unless you're on a very strict low-cholesterol diet, the higher cholesterol content of shrimp and lobster is not of great concern because of their very low-fat and low-calorie nature. Besides, not many of us can afford to eat shrimp or lobster much more than once a week.

Some experts also feel that the cholesterol that *is* present in shellfish may be—at least in part—offset by the omega-3 fatty acid content, which represents a substantial proportion of the fat in crustaceans and mollusks.

Fact or fallacy? Certain components of shellfish may interfere with the body's absorption of cholesterol, thus offsetting its potentially harmful effects.

Fact. The medical journal *Metabolism* reported in 1987 the results of a study in which Marian Childs, Ph.D., and her colleagues at the University of Washington Department of Medicine found that men on a strict low-fat diet that was rich in clams and oysters absorbed 25 percent less cholesterol than they did while eating crab- or chicken-rich diets which were just as low in fat. The drop in cholesterol absorption was thought to be related to noncholesterol sterols, which oysters and clams have in high amounts, but crabs and chickens do not.

Like many studies, this one was somewhat contrived since the men were provided all of their carefully-calculated meals by a research center. Dr. Childs's group conducted another study in which healthy men substituted oysters, clams, or crabmeat for the animal-protein foods—such as meat, eggs, milk, and cheese—in their normal diets. For each set of three weeks' testing, the men substituted each type of shellfish for animal-protein foods. But they were allowed to prepare their own foods and, for the most part, eat whatever else they wanted in addition to the shellfish.

Compared to the animal-protein diet that the men had been following before the study began, all three shellfish diets brought about a significant drop in LDL-cholesterol. It's interesting that even the crabmeat diet was associated with a drop in this detrimental type of cholesterol since it contains very few noncholesterol sterols. Although noncholesterol sterols may have interfered with cholesterol absorption when the men ate oysters and clams, the researchers believe that an additional reason the shellfish diets had their cholesterol-lowering effects was because they were lower in total fat and higher in omega-3 fatty acids than the meat, eggs, milk, and cheese diet.

It's intriguing, too, that huge quantities of higher-cholesterol shellfish don't seem to have much of an impact on blood-cholesterol levels. When Dr. William Connor and his colleague Dr. Don Lin fed an almost 1-pound mixture of crab, lobster, and shrimp to healthy men each day for three weeks (what torture!), their cholesterol only climbed to 192 from an average of 184 mg./dl. when they were on a low-cholesterol diet. The elevation was "considerably lower" than blood-cholesterol increases found in other studies in which people were fed similar amounts of cholesterol from egg yolks.

Although it remains to be seen what effects different shellfish have on people who already have high blood cholesterol, Drs. Connor and Lin see no reason why all types of shellfish can't be eaten on low-cholesterol diets, as long as portions are in the 3- to 4-ounce range.

Fact or fallacy? Because they're higher in fat content, oilier finfish are much higher in cholesterol than lean types.

Fallacy. According to seafood researcher Maurice Stansby, with the National Marine Fisheries Service, there is no relationship between oil content and cholesterol levels in fish. Notice, for example, that sablefish—the highest-fat fish included in table 4—contain just 49 milligrams of cholesterol. Very low-fat dolphinfish, on the other hand, provide 73 milligrams. With a few exceptions (such as eel at more than 100 milligrams), cholesterol levels in higher-fat fish are similar to those in lower-fat types. All in all, it's hard to come by a finfish that provides more than 75 milligrams of cholesterol per 3½-ounce raw serving.

Fact or fallacy? Cholesterol values for a given type of finfish or shellfish are quite stable and vary little from one fish to the next.

Fallacy. As is the case with fat content of fish, cholesterol levels are subject to the whims of nature and vary from one fish of the same family or species to the next. Take the case of squid, which has been reported to contain anywhere from 80 to 400 milligrams of cholesterol per 3½-ounce portion. Different shrimp species also vary greatly in cholesterol content. Some experts advise that when you see a cholesterol value for any one type of fish, you figure a range of plus or minus 20 percent. Once again, use table 4 only for approximate comparisons.

Fact or fallacy? Fish roe, caviar, and lobster tomalley are gourmet foods that are good for you.

Fallacy. If you glance again at table 4, you'll see that fish roe and caviar are the only seafoods that top the egg for cholesterol content at 374 and 588 milligrams respectively. Lobster tomalley (the liver), that some people view as a delicacy, has also been reported to be high in cholesterol.

ON VITAMINS AND MINERALS IN FISH

Just think of what you'll be missing if you get your omega-3s from a bottle—that is, pills or oils—instead of from the real thing. Marine fish are the richest natural food source of iodine, a mineral needed for proper thyroid function. And they're among the few foods that provide respectable amounts of fluoride, important for protection against cavities and maybe osteoporosis. Fish are also a reliable source of selenium, which may play a role in preventing heart disease and possibly cancer. Quiz yourself to see what else you'll miss out on if you take fish-oil supplements instead of eating fish.

Fact or fallacy? No other natural food has as much zinc as oysters.

Fact. The truth of this statement may perpetuate the myth that oysters are an aphrodisiac. Indeed, zinc is necessary for sexual development, but there's no evidence that the mollusks will increase your sexual desire. Eastern oysters provide about 90 milligrams of zinc—that's 6 times the US RDA—in each 3½-ounce raw or canned serving. Raw Pacific oysters also top the US RDA at around 17 milligrams. Other good zinc sources in the seafood world are crab and lobster.

Fact or fallacy? Like meat and poultry, fish is low in calcium.

Fact and fallacy. In general, fish is not considered a good calcium source since most types provide less than 50 milligrams (5 percent of the US RDA) per 3½-ounce raw portion. The three exceptions are salmon, mackerel, and sardines—but only when they're canned *with bones.* A 3½-ounce serving of canned pink or sockeye salmon provides more than 200 milligrams of calcium—20 percent of the US RDA. The same amount of canned jack mackerel or Pacific sardines packed in tomato sauce contains around 240 milligrams, while Atlantic sardines packed in oil give you over 350 milligrams—that's more than a cup of milk has to offer. So leave the skeletons in canned fish—if they bother you, the bones are usually so soft that you can crush them with your fingers or a fork before adding the fish to a recipe.

Fact or fallacy? When it comes to iron content, fish doesn't begin to compare with meat.

Fact and fallacy—it all depends on the type of fish. A 3½-ounce raw portion of popular white-fleshed fish, such as cod, sole, or haddock, provides a milligram or less of iron—a mere drop in the bucket compared to the US RDA of 18 milligrams. But few people realize that certain shellfish surpass lean red meat with its 2 milligrams of iron per 3½-ounce raw portion. The same amount of blue mussel meat provides double that amount, while clams contain a whopping 14 milligrams of iron. Pacific and Eastern oysters will net you 5 to almost 7 milligrams per serving. Other good fish sources of iron are crawfish, shrimp, canned sardines, and light, water-packed tuna—all in the 2- to 3-milligram range. (Like the iron in meat and poultry, the form of iron in fish is more readily used by the body than iron from plants.)

Fact or fallacy? In general, fish has little to offer in the way of vitamins.

Fallacy. Overall, fish is considered a respectable source of B vitamins—similar to most land animals. Dark-fleshed fish such as mackerel and salmon are apt to be higher in B vitamins than lighter fish. Raw-fish lovers should be aware that certain fish, including shellfish, carp, mackerel, and fresh sardines, contain an enzyme that can make the B-vitamin thiamine unavailable to the body. (Cooking inactivates the enzyme.)

Generally speaking, fish flesh is not a good source of fat-soluble vitamins, such as A and D. But some oilier fish like herring and mackerel are among the few natural food sources of vitamin D. And canned sardines provide fair amounts of vitamin A. According to Dr. Nettleton, high-fat fish do provide some vitamin E, but the data on vitamin E content of fish are scanty.

THE TRUTH ABOUT SODIUM

Is finfish a high-sodium or low-sodium food? What about shellfish? Does processing have a marked impact on sodium levels in fish? See if you know the answers.

Fact or fallacy? Because marine fish spend their lives in salt water, they're naturally high in sodium.

Fallacy. Fish have physiological mechanisms to prevent their bodies from becoming as salty as the sea around them. (The chemical name for salt is sodium chloride; about 40 percent of sodium chloride is sodium.) Unprocessed finfish are considered low in sodium since their maximum level is around 100 milligrams per 3½-ounce raw portion. That's only 5 percent of the daily 2,000-milligram allotment for sodium allowed many people on low-sodium diets. Most shellfish tend to have somewhat more sodium—in the 100- to 300-milligram range, with a few even higher. King crab, for instance has 836 milligrams of sodium per 3½-ounce serving. For the most part, however, fish becomes a high-sodium food only when large amounts of salt are added in processing, in cooking, or at the table. (Although there is no RDA for sodium, the group of scientists that decides on the RDAs specifies 1,100 to 3,300 milligrams as a "safe and adequate" range for sodium for most healthy adults.)

Fact or fallacy? Canned fish are high in sodium.

Fact and fallacy. Table 6 shows you the impact processing has on sodium levels of various types of fish. If you compare USDA data for canned clams and crabmeat with their steamed counterparts, you'll see that sodium values are affected little, if any, by canning. Sodium values do, however, vary from one canned product to the next and can be considerably higher. If the sodium level is not listed on the label, you can try checking with the manufacturer. Canned tuna and salmon are much higher in sodium than the unprocessed fish. To get around the higher sodium levels in these canned products, you can buy reduced-sodium or no-added-salt versions. But you can save yourself the expense of special low-sodium foods if you simply place canned fish in a strainer and rinse it with cool water. A study published in the *Journal of the American Dietetic Association* showed that rinsing water-packed tuna for one minute washed out nearly 80 percent of the sodium, bringing the level close to that of low-sodium canned tuna.

(Notice the high sodium levels of processed fish at the bottom of table 6, as well as the impact of smoking, pickling, and making imitation shellfish. Unfortunately, rinsing or soaking these foods to remove sodium would make an inedible mess out of them.)

TABLE 6. Sodium Content of 3½-Ounce Portions of Selected Fish

Fish	Sodium (milligrams)
Clams, steamed	112
Clams, canned (drained)	112
Crab, blue, steamed	279
Crab, blue, canned (drained)	333
Crab, imitation	841
Tuna, fresh bluefin, baked[a]	50
Tuna, light, canned in water (drained)	356
Tuna, light, canned in oil (drained)	354
Salmon, sockeye, baked	66
Salmon, sockeye, canned (drained)	538
Salmon, lox	2,000
Haddock, raw	68
Haddock, smoked	763
Anchovies, canned in oil (drained)	3,668
Caviar, black and red	1,500
Gefilte fish, commercial, with small amount of broth (sweet recipe)	524
Herring, pickled	870
Sardines, Atlantic, canned in oil (drained)	505
Sardines, Pacific, canned in tomato sauce (drained)	414

Source: U.S. Department of Agriculture, Human Nutrition Information Service Handbook 8–15.
[a] Cooked fresh bluefin tuna is used for comparison because the USDA provides no data for cooked fresh yellowfin or skipjack tuna that are the types of tuna usually used in canned, light-meat products.

Fact or fallacy? Fresh fish purchased in a fish market or grocery store may contain *added* sodium that's not naturally present in the fish.

Fact. Between the time they're caught and the time they're filleted, whole fish may be held in refrigerated sea water, rinsed in a brine (salty) solution, or chilled in an icy brine mixture. Saltwater solutions help preserve fish because the presence of salt prevents water from freezing at 32° F. Fish can, therefore, be stored at low temperatures —which are ideal for maintaining freshness—without freezing. Since fish are dead at this point, however, they no longer have their natural regulatory mechanisms that prevent their bodies from taking up sodium, and they absorb the mineral from their salty holding solutions.

Consumers who have to watch their sodium intake are really in a bind because the extent of these practices and their exact impact on sodium levels are not known. (One study published in the journal *Food Technology* revealed that the natural levels of sodium in fish stored in refrigerated sea water increased 5 to 10 times.) Moreover, there's really no good way to tell if fresh fish has added sodium because it usually lacks nutrition labels and ingredient listings. (Some experts say that you can spot heavily brined fish because of its unusual shininess and tacky feeling.)

Dr. Roy Martin, the National Fisheries Institute's (a fish industry group) vice president for science and technology, was able to offer some useful guidelines about fish holding processes that add sodium. In the first place, refrigerated seawater storage is not commonly used for fish caught on the East Coast. The practice is far more prevalent on the West Coast, where it may be used for fish such as pollock, cod, and rockfish. If you rinse suspect fish, it will help lower sodium content. But don't soak it or you'll ruin the texture.

Dr. Martin maintains that brine freezing is used primarily in the shrimp industry, but may also be employed for some less commonly eaten fish such as croaker and spot (both members of the drum family). Warm-water fish are more likely to be brine-frozen than are cold-water species. If you're concerned about sodium in shrimp, Dr. Martin recommends boiling it with seasonings other than salt.

Some sodium is lost when fish is cooked, but the extent depends on the method you choose. A study sponsored by the U.S. Fish and Wildlife Service suggests that boiling and steaming are more effective than broiling and baking for lowering sodium levels in fish. If you're concerned about your sodium intake, you may want to stick with moist-heat cooking methods. I'd also advise that you be assertive and ask your fish dealer if he knows or can find out whether your favorite types of fish have been stored in salt solutions.

Another preservation method, used primarily for frozen fish, is dipping in sodium-containing preservatives such as sodium tripolyphosphate. These additives are used to prevent moisture loss upon thawing and must be listed on ingredient listings for frozen fish. Dr. Martin points out that since fish fillets are quickly dipped in the sodium-containing additives, there would only be a 5 to 7 percent increase over the natural sodium levels in fish. Rinsing will not have much of an impact on fillets treated with these additives.

All in all, sodium levels of fish do not pose a health threat for most people. The next chapter addresses some more serious concerns about eating fish.

CHAPTER SEVEN

The Truth about Pollutants, Pesticides, and Poisons in Fish

AMERICANS WANT SAFE, wholesome food—food that's untouched by carcinogens, contaminants, and chemicals. But we also want unlimited quantities of food, choices galore, low prices, and top-quality items—from red and spotless tomatoes to blemish-free apples. In the nonfood realm, we pride ourselves on weedless lawns; depend on disposable cups, plates, and plastic containers; and feel entitled to boundless energy resources. It all adds up to a lot of "wants" for which we pay a price—namely, unwanted chemicals in our environment.

Some of the pesticides and herbicides that give us perfect produce and show-off lawns, as well as the chemicals composing industrial products that contribute to our comfortable lives, can wind up in the food served at our tables. And fish is no exception, since many unwanted chemicals ultimately leach their way into the rivers, lakes, and oceans that fish inhabit. Indeed, reports that the nation's fish supply is tainted with industrial chemicals and heavy metals have some people running scared from a food that clearly has so many benefits.

Just how valid are fears of fish contaminants? Is fish any more risky than other foods? If there are some concerns about eating fish, how can you minimize the potential risks? Admittedly, definitive answers to these questions don't exist. But this chapter will help you gain a perspective on the safety of our fish supply, both from chemical and microbiological standpoints. You'll see how I came to reach the conclusion that the benefits of eating fish 3 to 7 times a week far outweigh any conceivable risks.

BASICS ABOUT ENVIRONMENTAL CONTAMINANTS

There are two types of environmental contaminants that can enter our fish supply: *organic chemicals,* including agricultural pesticides and industrial chemicals like polychlorinated biphenyls (PCBs) and *metals,* such as mercury. As with most other foods, it's virtually impossible to assure a pristine fish supply—one that's totally free of undesirable chemicals. Therefore, the Food and Drug Administration (FDA) has set "action" levels for a number of contaminants that, based on scientific studies, it deems safe enough to be allowed in fish. These allowable levels are usually specified as so many parts of contaminant—2 or less in most cases—per million parts of fish. (The University of Wisconsin Sea Grant Institute equates 1 part per million to a single cup of milk out of 16 milk truckloads!)

The actual monitoring of contaminant levels in fish and the waters they inhabit is largely carried out by the states—through their environmental protection, fish and wildlife, and public health agencies. If levels of a contaminant are found to be higher than the FDA's acceptable limit for a particular species, commercial and/or recreational fishing of that species may be forbidden. In 1986, for example, commercial and recreational fishing of striped bass were banned in both New York and Rhode Island, in part because PCB levels were considered too high.

Sometimes advisories warn that fishermen and their families eat no more than one fish meal per week of species found to be contaminated in certain bodies of water. Because some undesirable chemicals can be transferred to unborn children or through breast milk, an additional warning is commonly added that pregnant and breast-feeding women completely avoid species of fish found to have high contaminant levels. Likewise, it may be advised that infants and small children abstain from suspect fish because youngsters' bodies are still growing, and their small size may make them more susceptible than adults to a pollutant's effects.

Many environmental contaminants are stored in internal organs and fatty tissues of fish. Therefore, compared to leaner types, fattier fish have a greater propensity for storing fat-soluble chemicals. Size may be more important—larger fish of a species have lived longer and therefore have had more time to accumulate pollutants. And large predator-type fish that eat smaller contaminated fish tend to build up unwanted chemicals. Bottom feeders, such as carp and catfish, are also susceptible to chemical accumulation because contaminants often settle in sediment in bodies of water where the fish feed. Furthermore, fish like bluefish and striped bass that tend to migrate up and down the coast, spending a fair amount of time in shallow coastal areas, are prone to contamination. (Both fish are also predators.)

Don't panic and think that you should stop eating all fish that fit any of the above criteria. The available evidence suggests that fish contamination problems are usually limited to *recreationally caught* fish from polluted freshwater ponds, lakes, and streams or from sheltered ocean bays and harbors near industrial sources of pollution. On the other hand, most *commercially caught* fish is taken offshore or deep at sea where the waters are much cleaner.

THE PISCINE PCB STORY

No other organic chemicals in fish have received the press coverage given to PCBs, a group of industrial substances used as coolants and lubricants in electrical equipment from 1929 until the late 1970s. PCBs were also used to make plastics, carbonless copy paper, adhesives, paints, and varnishes.

Because PCBs have been linked to ailments such as cancer in animals—and, likewise, may be hazardous to people—the government banned the manufacture of the chemicals in the late seventies. Nevertheless, PCBs will be with us for decades because hundreds of millions of pounds are estimated to still be in use in items made before the ban. Moreover, the PCBs that were once dumped into rivers, lakes, and open landfills are long-lasting because the chemicals break down very slowly over time.

PCBs have also found their way into ocean harbors near large cities. Here, as well as in polluted lakes and streams, fish can accumulate PCBs in their fat and internal organs. Since PCBs are fat-soluble, oilier and older fish dwelling in contaminated waters tend to build up the highest levels. Lake Michigan lake trout, for example, can live as long as 10 years and so tend to accumulate more PCBs than chinook salmon that only live in the lake for 3 to 4 years. Similarly, people who regularly eat contaminated fish tend to build up PCBs in their fat tissue.

The FDA's current limit for PCB levels in the edible part of fish is 2 parts per million (ppm). (Note that fish is not alone—the FDA also has limits for PCB amounts in dairy products, poultry, and eggs.) When authorities find PCB levels to be above the allowance for certain species of fish, advisories are issued to commercial and recreational fishermen. Sometimes, only larger fish of a given species are found to have unacceptable contaminant levels.

If you purchase your fish in commercial channels, you really don't need to worry because most PCB-contaminated fish are caught by recreational fishermen in polluted lakes, streams, or harbors. Some areas with a long history of PCB contamination and subsequent restrictions on catching certain fish are the Great Lakes, the Hudson River in New York, and Boston and New Bedford Harbors in Massachusetts.

Fortunately, several studies suggest that adults who have a history of eating PCB-contaminated fish do not have increased rates of illness. Other studies, however, indicate that the risks may be greater for unborn babies and nursing infants whose mothers have been exposed to PCBs. In fact, one of the more worrisome stories that I covered as executive editor of the *Tufts University Diet & Nutrition Letter* concerned more than 240 mothers who, despite warnings to the contrary, had a 16-year history of eating Lake Michigan salmon and lake trout several times a month. Compared to a group of women who ate no Lake Michigan fish, mothers who consumed the contaminated fish gave birth to babies who were 7 to 9 ounces lighter (their size was still normal) and born 6 to 12 days earlier. Moreover, the babies of fish-eating mothers tended to exhibit abnormal reflexes, general weakness, and slower responses to stimuli. It is expected that these differences will be outgrown, but the long-term effects remain to be studied.

The moral of the story is that people need to heed public health advisories about eating recreationally caught fish. In particular, young women who intend to have children, as well as pregnant or nursing mothers, should avoid eating any fish found to exceed allowable federal levels for contaminants. The same advice is warranted when feeding young children.

Although the data on PCB levels in saltwater fish are more sketchy than for freshwater species, I feel reassured about the available information on PCB levels. According to John Wessel—the FDA's director of the contaminants policy staff—the agency routinely samples saltwater fish and rarely finds any with greater than the allowable 2 parts per million.

In addition, a comprehensive study on bluefish recently released by the government suggests that "the levels of PCBs in bluefish in commercial distribution do not present a health concern for the general consuming public." The National Oceanic and Atmospheric Administration (NOAA) study analyzed 1,200 bluefish samples from the Atlantic coast from North Carolina to Massachusetts. In all cases, fish smaller than 20 inches in length were within the 2 ppm acceptable limit for PCBs.

Some larger fish, however, from each location tested did exceed 2 ppm. Thus, the NOAA report concluded that bluefish may pose a health threat for recreational fishermen—who take in as many as

80 to 90 percent of bluefish caught—and their families who eat PCB-contaminated fish "day after day, year after year." The concern is much less for the majority of us who eat commercially caught fish, since bluefish tend to be eaten as part of a wide variety of seafoods.

Because bluefish are among the saltwater fish most susceptible to contamination, Robert Kifer, Ph.D., director of the National Marine Fisheries Service Utilization Research Laboratory in Charleston, South Carolina, maintains that, if bluefish don't pose a problem, then the remainder of saltwater finfish are likely to be safe to eat. As affirmation, a comprehensive review of available data on chemical contaminants studied in New England seafoods over the past 20 years revealed that PCB levels tend to be low in offshore species of finfish which comprise most commercial sources. The report—headed by Judith McDowell Capuzzo, Ph.D., a zoologist at the world-renowned Woods Hole Oceanographic Institution on Cape Cod—found that even just outside of highly polluted New Bedford Harbor, nonmigratory fish do not show high PCB levels. Finfish and shellfish taken from coastal areas near urban centers, however, tend to have unacceptable amounts of contaminants. Fortunately, most heavily polluted areas are not commercial fishing grounds and our main commercial fish spend their time at sea, rather than in harbors.

Be aware, however, that Dr. Capuzzo's report warns that there are serious contamination problems in urban harbor locations along the New England coastline. Even though contamination is not currently affecting offshore fish, commercial resources may be in jeopardy if pollution of inshore areas continues.

A FEW WORDS ABOUT OTHER FISH CONTAMINANTS

I've devoted a lot of space to PCBs because they've been studied more extensively than most other fish contaminants. That doesn't mean that other organic chemicals (such as pesticides) are of no concern in the fish we eat. In fact, insecticides such as DDT, mirex, and kepone have been found in lakes and rivers, and in coastal areas where they can accumulate in certain freshwater and saltwater fish. (The FDA has action levels for all three pesticides.) But Dr. Capuzzo believes that PCBs serve as relatively good indicators of the extent of other organic contaminants in marine environments. Indeed, the NOAA study on PCBs in bluefish also examined the levels of 10 pesticides in bluefish and found that all were within the FDA's acceptable limits.

Dr. Capuzzo's report suggests that, in cases where the use of a chemical contaminant has been controlled, such as DDT, levels in fish clearly decline with time. And many pesticides used in the past have

80 to 90 percent of bluefish caught—and their families who eat PCB-contaminated fish "day after day, year after year." The concern is much less for the majority of us who eat commercially caught fish, since bluefish tend to be eaten as part of a wide variety of seafoods.

Because bluefish are among the saltwater fish most susceptible to contamination, Robert Kifer, Ph.D., director of the National Marine Fisheries Service Utilization Research Laboratory in Charleston, South Carolina, maintains that, if bluefish don't pose a problem, then the remainder of saltwater finfish are likely to be safe to eat. As affirmation, a comprehensive review of available data on chemical contaminants studied in New England seafoods over the past 20 years revealed that PCB levels tend to be low in offshore species of finfish which comprise most commercial sources. The report—headed by Judith McDowell Capuzzo, Ph.D., a zoologist at the world-renowned Woods Hole Oceanographic Institution on Cape Cod—found that even just outside of highly polluted New Bedford Harbor, nonmigratory fish do not show high PCB levels. Finfish and shellfish taken from coastal areas near urban centers, however, tend to have unacceptable amounts of contaminants. Fortunately, most heavily polluted areas are not commercial fishing grounds and our main commercial fish spend their time at sea, rather than in harbors.

Be aware, however, that Dr. Capuzzo's report warns that there are serious contamination problems in urban harbor locations along the New England coastline. Even though contamination is not currently affecting offshore fish, commercial resources may be in jeopardy if pollution of inshore areas continues.

A FEW WORDS ABOUT OTHER FISH CONTAMINANTS

I've devoted a lot of space to PCBs because they've been studied more extensively than most other fish contaminants. That doesn't mean that other organic chemicals (such as pesticides) are of no concern in the fish we eat. In fact, insecticides such as DDT, mirex, and kepone have been found in lakes and rivers, and in coastal areas where they can accumulate in certain freshwater and saltwater fish. (The FDA has action levels for all three pesticides.) But Dr. Capuzzo believes that PCBs serve as relatively good indicators of the extent of other organic contaminants in marine environments. Indeed, the NOAA study on PCBs in bluefish also examined the levels of 10 pesticides in bluefish and found that all were within the FDA's acceptable limits.

Dr. Capuzzo's report suggests that, in cases where the use of a chemical contaminant has been controlled, such as DDT, levels in fish clearly decline with time. And many pesticides used in the past have been replaced with less persistent and less risky types. Nevertheless, the Woods Hole report suggests that, because little information is available on the distribution of currently used pesticides that might affect fish resources, monitoring of newer chemicals should be put in place. In addition, the report stresses that there are no action levels or routine testing programs for oil-derived contaminants, such as petroleum hydrocarbons—some of which are carcinogenic. Since little data are available concerning organic chemicals in shellfish, Dr. Capuzzo also believes that they should be more closely monitored.

Potentially harmful heavy metals, such as mercury and cadmium, can occur naturally in bodies of water or result from pollution. Mercury has, by far, received the most attention. Unlike fat-soluble PCBs, mercury is believed to combine with proteins in fish. The metal is most likely to accumulate to levels that surpass the FDA's acceptable limits in large fish—namely, swordfish and shark, and, to a lesser extent, tuna and halibut—that live a long time and/or eat smaller fish.

In very high doses, mercury can adversely affect the central nervous system. Yet the effects of long-term consumption of low levels are not known. (According to Susan Faria's *The Northeast Seafood Book,* published by the Massachusetts Division of Marine Fisheries, there has never been a recorded case of mercury poisoning from swordfish in this country.)

Because swordfish is the most likely commercial species to be mercury-contaminated, the FDA keeps a close watch on swordfish shipments. When mercury levels exceed the FDA's limit, regulatory action is taken. At this writing, for instance, there's a detention placed on all imported swordfish because samples from some foreign countries were found to have mercury levels that exceed the FDA's safe limit. Once suppliers prove that their swordfish complies, it can be sold. The FDA also monitors domestic swordfish for mercury levels and takes steps to prevent its marketing when amounts are too high.

According to John Wessel of the FDA's contaminants policy staff, the agency rarely finds fish other than swordfish that exceed the 1-part-per-million limit. For the most part, the tuna that are sampled comply. Note that other metals, such as lead and cadmium, can occur in fish. But little research has been done in this area.

When it comes to shellfish, the National Shellfish Sanitation Program (see page 164) tracks metals in oysters, clams, and mussels. These bivalves are more likely to accumulate metals than crustaceans and most finfish. Although an up-to-date report that the FDA completed on shellfish (primarily clams and oysters) was not yet finalized at this writing, Wessel is reassuring that the data indicate that levels of metals, such as mercury, cadmium, and lead, do not pose a health threat. In the aftermath of the Chernobyl accident, you may also wonder about radioactive contamination of fish. According to Wessel, the FDA's sampling of imported fish, primarily from Scandinavian countries, uncovered no increase in radioactive substances. In this nation, the agency periodically monitors fish near suspect sources of nuclear material, but has found no evidence of contamination.

THE LOWDOWN ON FISH CONTAMINANTS— ARE WE REALLY PROTECTED AND HOW CAN YOU PLAY IT SAFE?

When you consider the many species of fish available to us, along with the various bodies of water in which fish are caught, you may wonder how federal and state governments can adequately monitor contaminants in fresh- or saltwater fish. The truth is that, given limited resources and funding, they probably can't. Lee Weddig, president of the National Fisheries Institute (which, as you'll recall, represents the interests of the fish industry), agrees that monitoring of fish for contaminants in this country is "rather sparse" and should be stepped up. By the same token, he maintains that the evidence we do have indicates that most fish do not pose a public health risk. He points out that when contaminants *are* picked up in fish, levels are usually within the FDA's acceptable allowances. Overall, fish are far more beneficial than harmful.

In case you're still leery, I suggest you place your concerns about fish contaminants in context with the status of unwanted chemicals in other foods. As I was writing this very chapter, for instance, the National Academy of Sciences issued a report on laws regulating pesticide residues in fresh and processed foods, including fruits and vegetables as well as meat, milk, and poultry products. It concluded that the government lacks adequate data on the carcinogenicity of many pesticides and that the current laws governing pesticide residues in foods do "not provide the best protection of public health."

Consider also the safety of drugs given to cattle, pigs, and chickens that can show up as residues in foods. A 1986 House of Representatives investigation accused the FDA's Center for Veterinary Medicine of allowing the sale of tens of thousands of animal drugs never shown to be safe or effective; approximately 4,000 of them are potentially harmful to people and animals. At the time, Tufts School of Veterinary Medicine's Dean Franklin M. Loew, D.V.M., was quoted in the *Tufts University Diet & Nutrition Letter* as saying that the cursory spot-checking for drug residues in meat, milk, and eggs is not reliable enough to assure human safety.

My goal is not to make you paranoid about everything you eat. For the most part, Americans enjoy a safe, wholesome food supply. The point is that there are some small risks with many things that we eat. Remember, too, that if we want to continue to enjoy our plentiful supply of near-perfect, relatively inexpensive foods, some trade-offs are bound to be made.

With any unwanted chemical, you also have to keep in mind the frequency and level of exposure. There are many food substances that we tolerate—or even require—in small doses which are harmful if taken in excess. Vitamins A and D are perfect examples. (See page 49.)

On the other hand, that doesn't mean we shouldn't make every effort to minimize risks when we can. Some of the steps that you can take to be certain your potential exposure to fish contaminants is minimal are as follows:

- *Be choosy about where your fish comes from.* The safest bets are fish purchased from reputable commercial dealers. Go very easy on rec- reationally caught fish from rivers, lakes, and sheltered coastal areas that are near sources of industrial pollution.
- *Heed advisories that tell you to limit consumption of certain recreationally caught species.* Before going fishing, check with state environmental, fish and wildlife, or public health organizations to see if any warn- ings have been issued.
- *Vary your fish intake.* Pick your 3 to 7 weekly fish meals from a mix of high-, medium-, and low-fat fish. Don't go overboard with any one kind, particularly if it has a history of on-and-off contamina- tion. For example, make swordfish and bluefish occasional rather than everyday items.
- *Avoid eating the viscera, skin, and fatty sections of fish*—contaminants tend to concentrate here.
- *When eating fish that you're suspicious of, take preparation precautions that may lessen intake of fat-soluble contaminants.* Specifically, you should remove the fatty sections from fish flesh. Start by skinning the fish, cutting away a shallow layer of flesh under the skin. Then cut away the strip of fat that runs along the lateral lines on each side of the fish. Also cut away the ½- to ¾-inch flap of flesh that runs along the fish's belly. (When you cut a fish open lengthwise, two such flaps result.) Likewise, remove the fatty portion along the top of the fish's back, as well as any dark-colored sections of flesh.

To allow some of the fat to drip off while cooking, grill, bake, or broil fish on a rack. Don't use pan drippings to baste fish. If you poach or steam suspect fish, be sure to discard the cooking liquid.

When you add it all up, there doesn't seem to be any reason to fear eating fish 3 to 7 times a week, provided you follow the guidelines outlined above. In fact, experts who study fish contaminants don't let their knowledge stop them from frequently eating fish—Stuart Wilk, Ph.D., who headed the PCB-bluefish study, eats fish 3 to 4 times a week; and Woods Hole's Dr. Capuzzo eats fish just about every day!

ALLERGIES AND ADDITIVES

In my work as a nutrition counselor, patients often complained of an "allergy" to seafood. In reality, however, true food allergies appear to affect less than one percent of the population. At that, fish is not among the most common offenders, which include cow's milk, egg whites, peanuts, wheat, and soybeans. Although fish allergies are rare, they're more common in populations that eat or process a lot of fish. Reactions, such as asthma attacks, have even been reported as the result of simply breathing in steam from cooking fish.

Keep in mind that a far more common response to eating allergenic foods is an upset stomach—also a sign of food poisoning. Therefore, it's important not to give up fish based on a one-time reaction. If you suspect you're allergic to fish, get verification from a physician certified by the American Board of Allergy and Immunology so you don't have to sacrifice unnecessarily.

If you really are allergic, it's possible that it will turn out that you react to just one species of fish. Whatever the allergy, you'll then have to carefully read labels of processed foods, such as surimi-based products and frozen dinners, and ask about ingredients in restaurants so you can avoid the offenders. Be aware that allergenic substances in fish are not destroyed by cooking.

A family of additives commonly used as preservatives in fresh, frozen, canned, or dried shrimp can cause allergic-type reactions— some of them severe—in a small percentage of people who have asthma. Known as sulfites, the additives are used on some shrimp that's available to prevent the development of black spots that occur as the shellfish ages. Sulfites may also be used as preservatives for frozen lobster, dried cod, and processed scallops. (The specific names of the sulfiting additives are sulfur dioxide, sodium sulfite, sodium and potassium bisulfite, and sodium and potassium metabisulfite.)

If detectable levels of sulfites are present in packaged foods, the additives must be included in the ingredient listings. But when eating in a restaurant or buying bulk products—such as shrimp from the seafood case—there is no way for people who know they're sulfite-sensitive to tell whether fish has been treated unless they ask to see the box that the fish came in. (The additives must be listed on the bulk-package label.) It's a tough situation for sensitive people, but so far none of the 17 reported deaths that have implicated sulfites have been linked with fish products. (The FDA recently banned the use of sulfites in fresh fruits and vegetables, and it plans to regulate the use of sulfites in other foods shortly.)

Concerning other additives, I've already discussed the fact that phosphates such as sodium tripolyphosphate and sodium pyrophosphate can somewhat increase sodium content of fish products (see page 74). Likewise, monosodium glutamate (often used in surimi-based products) can add to your sodium intake.

Dilute chlorine washes are commonly used to help remove bacteria from fresh fish. According to Dr. Joyce Nettleton in *Seafood Nutrition,* tiny amounts of chlorine may be detectable in the final product. But chlorine is a natural body constituent, present primarily in the form of chloride. And most people consume plenty of chloride in the form of common table salt without any apparent ill effects.

There are also several other additives commonly used to preserve processed fish, but I see no need to be concerned about them—it's more important to have wholesome, unspoiled fish. As seafood expert Sue Faria says in *The Northeast Seafood Book,* "Although some consumers are against additives, nobody wants fish which is not fresh."

It's possible that the use of certain additives might be lessened if a petition to allow irradiation of fish is approved. Low doses of gamma rays would be used to kill or inactivate bacteria and parasites, as well as prolong shelf life of fish products. If irradiation of fish does come to pass, I have no qualms that the process is safe, based on extensive research I did for the *Tufts University Diet & Nutrition Letter.*

SEAFOOD "POISONINGS"

Certain fish and shellfish—as they come from their natural habitats—can pass a number of different types of "poisonings" to people. Although avid fish-eaters should be aware of the illnesses that may be contracted by eating fish, they shouldn't fret unduly because most cases are unusual and/or can be prevented by a few simple precautions.

Paralytic shellfish poisoning

Cast aside the old wives' tale that shellfish should only be eaten during the months with an *r* in them. Contrary to popular opinion, the adage is not a guide for preventing paralytic shellfish poisoning (PSP) caused by what's commonly known as "red tide." The illness results when people consume mussels, oysters, clams, or scallops harvested in areas where toxic microorganisms known as dinoflagellates are thriving. The organisms proliferate at certain times of the year and are most common in Maine, Massachusetts, Oregon, California, Alaska, and Washington.

Another myth is that the organisms responsible for PSP always create a red tide—on the contrary, water color is definitely not a reliable indicator of PSP risk. In actuality, the dinoflagellates can color the water green, yellow, or black, as well as reddish-brown. Besides, according to seafood technology specialist Robert J. Price, Ph.D., at the University of California-Davis, most red tides are harmless.

PSP can result when filter-feeding clams, mussels, oysters, and scallops—all bivalves that obtain food and oxygen by pumping and straining large volumes of water through their internal filtering systems—live among the toxin-producing dinoflagellates. All four mollusks can accumulate the microorganisms, but mussels tend to accrue them the fastest. You can't count on cooking to destroy the toxins because they're heat-stable.

Lobsters, crabs, shrimp, and finfish do not accumulate the PSP-causing organisms and are almost always safe to eat during red-tide outbreaks, as is the muscle meat of scallops. (I say "almost always" because, in one incident, PSP-toxin was found in internal organs of mackerel from off the coast of New England. But there was no evidence of toxin in the mackerels' flesh.) While affected bivalves eventually purge themselves of the dinoflagellates when they subside, Dr. Price points out that the viscera of scallops (popular in Europe) should never be eaten because they can remain toxic year-round.

Although the toxins don't harm the bivalves themselves, they impair nerve conduction in people. The symptoms usually come on within 30 minutes after eating affected shellfish and can include tingling and numbness of the mouth, lips, face, neck, and extremities. Nausea, vomiting, diarrhea, and abdominal cramps are also likely. In severe cases, muscle weakness, paralysis, and serious breathing difficulties can occur. The poisoning usually lasts from a few hours to several days, and some deaths have been reported. If you ever suspect you have PSP, contact your local poison control center and seek immediate medical attention. (The same advice applies to any of the fish "poisonings.")

In this country, PSP tends to occur when people collect their own shellfish; PSP outbreaks are uncommon in commercially harvested mollusks. One of the functions of state agencies involved in the National Shellfish Sanitation Program is to monitor shellfish beds for PSP potential and to place restrictions when necessary. But whether or not warning notices are posted in your favorite gathering spot, it's wise to call local public-health authorities before harvesting your own shellfish.

Ciguatera poisoning

Most commonly reported in association with fish caught near Florida and Hawaii in this country, ciguatera poisoning also occurs in vacationers in the Caribbean, Pacific islands, and West Indies. The illness is usually caused by eating large fish that feed in tropical reefs. It's thought that they acquire the ciguatera poison when they consume small fish that have been feeding on toxin-producing microorganisms. The more commonly implicated fish, according to Cornell University's Robert Gravani, Ph.D., are grouper, barracuda, red snapper, and sea basses. Note that, within the same species, one fish may bear the toxin while another is "clean." In other words, barracuda from one reef may be safe from ciguatera, yet barracuda from another reef may be poisonous.

Some studies have reported that the toxin tends to concentrate in the fish's viscera, brain, and eyes, while the flesh is contaminated to a lesser extent. Ciguatera toxin is not destroyed in cooking.

The symptoms of ciguatera poisoning usually occur within six hours of eating affected fish and may include tingling of the mouth, intense itching, abdominal pain, nausea, vomiting, diarrhea, aching, and blurred vision. Sometimes victims have a reversal of temperature sensations—they experience hot as cold and vice versa. In rare, severe cases, paralysis, convulsions, and even death can occur. Peculiarly, a group of people who all eat the same fish can be affected very differently—some may have a serious reaction, others mild, while the rest never get sick. The symptoms may only last for a short time, but they sometimes hang on for many months.

In certain areas where ciguatera poisoning is common, public health officials have adopted measures to minimize the hazard. In Hawaii, for instance, some fish aren't marketed because they're risky. But there's concern that the call for exotic fish in larger U.S. cities will trigger more reports of ciguatera poisoning on the mainland.

Indeed, two recent cases were reported in people who had eaten Floridian barracuda in Vermont restaurants.

To minimize the risk of ciguatera poisoning, don't eat the liver, intestines, eyes, brains, roe, or sex organs of tropical fish. When traveling, avoid eating unusually large reef fish and species that have a history of carrying ciguatera toxin in the region. Public health officials should be able to guide you.

Pufferfish poisoning

Pufferfish—also called globefish, swellfish, blowfish, balloonfish, porcupinefish, ocean sunfish, filefish, and triggerfish—carry a nerve toxin that can be deadly. Nevertheless, puffers are a delicacy in Japan, where they're known as *fugu* and are prepared by licensed chefs who are specially trained in removing the poisonous viscera, gonads, roe, and skin without contaminating the white meat. The symptoms of pufferfish poisoning may be as mild as tingling of the mouth and sweating. But vomiting, severe muscle weakness, paralysis, and even respiratory arrest can occur. Deaths usually result when fishermen don't clean their catch properly.

Puffers vary in toxicity, with more poisonous species coming from tropical regions and off the coasts of Japan and China. At the present time, the FDA prohibits pufferfish *imports*. On the domestic scene, pufferfish grow in Atlantic, Pacific, and Gulf of Mexico waters. According to Douglas Park, Ph.D., an FDA specialist in seafood toxins, the agency has not fully determined the potential toxicity of domestic species. Reports suggest that puffers caught off the north to mid-Atlantic coast—often sold as sea squab—are not toxic if the fish are cleaned correctly; fish from warmer waters are more likely to be harmful. Even though pufferfish are available commercially in this country —and reports of pufferfish poisoning are rare—Dr. Park advises consumers to be aware that *all* puffers carry the potential to cause illness.

Scromboid poisoning

If you stick with a reliable seafood seller, scromboid poisoning is extremely unlikely because the illness results from eating improperly refrigerated fish. It usually occurs in tuna, mackerel, bonito, and swordfish, but scromboid poisoning has also been linked with Pacific amberjack and mahimahi. When such freshly caught fish are left in the warm sun for too long, bacteria in their flesh can convert an amino acid to histamine, the main substance thought to be responsible for the symptoms of scromboid poisoning. One outbreak implicated fish stored at room temperature for just 3 to 4 hours. The fish may have a sharp or peppery taste, but then again, there may be no signs of decomposition.

Experienced anywhere from several minutes to an hour after contaminated fish are eaten, the symptoms can include skin rashes and edema, gastrointestinal problems, headache, palpitations, tingling, flushing, and itching. Most people suffer from just a few of these problems, which usually last for 4 to 12 hours. But some scromboid-related deaths have been reported.

According to a recent article in the journal *Emergency Medicine,* scromboid poisoning is sometimes mistaken for an allergic reaction. Therefore, it's important to note the taste and species before ruling out a type of fish for life. Since histamine is not broken down in cooking, it's essential that fishermen prevent its formation by promptly refrigerating their catches.

Old-fashioned, "man-made" food poisoning

Rest assured that all of the previously described maladies are rarities in everyday American life. You're much more likely to be plagued by food poisoning caused by human error—that is, from external sources of bacteria (as opposed to organisms that appear in fish as they're harvested—read about raw-fish risks, starting on page 89), such as salmonella, in fish that's been improperly handled or stored by people.

Be they transferred by unclean hands, sneezes, utensils, cutting boards, containers, rodents, or insects, bacteria that cause food poisoning commonly get into foods from fecal contamination, dirt, or secretions from throat and nasal passages. Fish can also pick up bacteria when it comes into contact with more likely food carriers such as poultry.

The most common symptoms of food poisoning resemble intestinal flu—nausea, diarrhea, cramping, vomiting, and fever. Your best safeguards against these unpleasantnesses are cleanliness, thorough cooking, and proper storage of protein foods. Specifically, be sure your hands and anything else that comes into contact with fish are clean. Unless you wash them with hot water and soap first, don't use utensils, cutting boards (use plastic, not wood because it can't be cleaned adequately), or containers that contacted raw seafood (or meat or poultry) for cooked fish—otherwise, you can recontaminate the cooked item. Cook all fish thoroughly, and refrigerate it as soon as possible after cooking—the longer it sits at room temperature, the more chance any bacteria present have to thrive. When thawing frozen foods, do it in the refrigerator or the microwave oven rather than on the counter.

THE RISKS OF RAW SEAFOOD

Remember the song about sweet Molly Malone, the fishmonger who cried, "Cockles and mussels, alive, alive oh"? It's speculated that she met her fate "of a fever" by eating her own contaminated shellfish wares. Although that's an old story, the relatively new passion for eating raw or lightly cooked shellfish and finfish is spurring concern that a number of illnesses are on the rise because of harmful organisms —organisms that, for the most part, are killed with adequate cooking —picked up by fish in their natural environments.

Raw clams, oysters, and mussels

Because these filter-feeders pump large volumes of water in seeking out food and oxygen for survival, they also pick up and concentrate disease-causing bacteria and viruses if they happen to be bedded in polluted waters. In fact, the level of harmful bacteria in mollusks can be as much as 20 times higher than that in their surrounding waters. Although most of these organisms don't bother the shellfish them-selves, people who eat raw or undercooked mollusks can contract gastrointestinal illnesses, hepatitis A, typhoid, and cholera.

Since the National Shellfish Sanitation Program was created in 1925, once-common typhoid fever and cholera from shellfish are now rare. (For more on the NSSP, see page 164.) But we're currently plagued with some newly identified bacteria and viruses that can cause illnesses ranging from upset stomach to death, primarily in people who eat raw mollusks.

The sanitary quality of shellfish-growing areas is determined largely by measuring levels of certain fecal bacteria that serve as indicators that waters are sewage-contaminated and may harbor harmful bacteria and viruses that mollusks can pick up. In badly contaminated areas, harvesting is prohibited. But mildly contaminated shellfish may be harvested, provided they're "purified" under permit in controlled con-ditions. In the *depuration* process, the contaminated bivalves are trans-ferred to tanks of purified seawater where they purge themselves of pathogenic organisms within several days.

Although buying or harvesting mollusks from approved waters is a good way to hedge your bets against contracting illness, studies now suggest that it's no guarantee. For, according to *Emergency Medicine,* outbreaks of sickness have been reported when mollusks were supposedly taken from legally sanctioned waters. It's thought that the test showing absence of fecal bacteria in shellfish growing areas may not apply to *viral* contamination. In addition, current shellfish depuration methods are probably not adequate to rid mollusks of viruses.

Viruses. Shellfish can be exposed to more than 100 viruses from sewage, but only two are known to pose a major problem as far as human illness is concerned—namely Norwalk virus and hepatitis A virus. Relatively new to the risk scene for raw and undercooked mollusks, Norwalk virus causes short-lived gastroenteritis with the symptoms of nausea, vomiting, diarrhea, and abdominal cramps. The virus was not thought to be a major problem in shellfish until a *New England Journal of Medicine* report linked the virus to a 1982 epidemic of gastroenteritis that affected more than 1,000 New Yorkers who had eaten clams or oysters. Although most afflictions were associated with consuming raw clams or oysters, 1 out of every 4 victims had eaten only *steamed* clams. The standard minute or so of steaming required to open clams just doesn't seem to be adequate for killing viruses.

The fact that the clams and oysters involved in the epidemic came from the waters of Rhode Island and Massachusetts—and possibly New York, North Carolina, and Prince Edward Island—suggests that the problem of mollusk contamination may, at times, be widespread. Nevertheless, according to FDA microbiologist Scott Rippey, Ph.D., cases of shellfish-related gastroenteritis have decreased appreciably since the early 1980's.

In an editorial that accompanied the *New England Journal* report, Herbert L. DuPont, M.D.—an expert on infectious diseases at the University of Texas Health Science Center—advises that clams be steamed for four to six minutes (after the water returns to a boil) for the internal temperature to become hot enough to inactivate viruses. That should render the mollusks safe, without turning them to rubber.

As far as less-common hepatitis A virus is concerned, 10 of the people involved in the New York epidemic became infected after eating raw or steamed clams. Hepatitis A infection usually starts out with malaise, a loss of appetite, nausea, vomiting, and fever. After 3 to 10 days, jaundice can set in and urine may darken. Some cases are so mild, they're mistaken for the flu. But others become serious enough that liver damage and, possibly, death can occur. Again, Dr. DuPont points out that thorough cooking—that is, steaming for four to six minutes—should be adequate for destroying hepatitis A.

Bacteria. Mollusks can pick up any number of bacteria in their natural surroundings, but only certain ones are harmful or pathogenic. The mere presence of a few bacteria isn't likely to make you sick, however. It's when bacteria multiply that food becomes contaminated. According to Marleen Wekell, Ph.D.—the director of the FDA's Seafood Products Research Center in Seattle—bacterial contamination of shellfish in the U.S. is usually the result of human mishandling. It's leaving mollusks in the sun or failure to refrigerate them adequately at home that allow pathogenic bacteria to multiply to the point where food poisoning becomes a real possibility.

One type of mollusk-transmitted bacterium that's raised the concern of public health officials is *Vibrio vulnificus,* an organism that usually causes mild infection. But it can bring on blood poisoning and death in people with chronic ailments such as liver or kidney disease, blood-cell disorders, alcoholism, AIDS, or other diseases that impair the immune system. Since several studies have linked the illness with eating raw oysters, people with any of the high-risk disorders should abstain from eating raw mollusks.

All bacteria can be killed with adequate cooking. But a light steaming or poaching can't be counted upon to do the trick.

Is raw worth the risk? It is true that most reports of mollusk-related illness can be traced to raw or inadequately cooked seafood and/or to illegally-harvested shellfish from polluted waters. But the FDA still maintains that most oysters, clams, and mussels being harvested are clean and safe to eat—that is, if they're from approved growing areas —and advice to cook all shellfish is unwarranted for most healthy people. The FDA does recommend, however, that all shellfish be cooked for people who have cancer, diabetes, liver disease, chronic gastrointestinal illness, or any condition resulting in impaired immunity. To play it safe, I'd add pregnant women, small children, and the elderly to the list. (New information suggests that raw oysters from the Gulf of Mexico are particularly risky from April through October.)

The problem is that there's no way for consumers to tell if mollusks are contaminated—a clam or oyster that looks, smells, and tastes okay is not necessarily free of bacteria and viruses. On the other hand, Dr. DuPont points out that the rarity of serious mollusk-associated outbreaks of severe illness—coupled with the fact that millions of people get away with eating raw shellfish without suffering dire consequences —make it "difficult to take too strong a stand against retailers and the practice of consuming raw shellfish. In fact, poultry-associated salmonellosis and campylobacteriosis have more public health importance."

Indeed, a 1987 National Academy of Sciences report criticizes the USDA's poultry inspection program for inadequately protecting consumers from food poisoning caused by such organisms as campylobacter and salmonella. The report indicates that half of the estimated two million yearly cases of campylobacter infection—which typically causes gastroenteritis—are thought to be poultry-related. Likewise, many of the two million yearly salmonella cases are linked with eating poultry. (Of course, if you handle poultry properly and cook it well, these organisms are killed.)

If you do choose to eat raw or lightly cooked mollusks, here are some tips to minimize the risk of illness:

- *Buy only from reputable seafood sellers,* not from the back of a truck or a roadside stand. When in doubt, ask to see certification tags. (Certification is explained on page 165.)
- *Check with public health authorities* to make sure the waters are safe before harvesting your own shellfish.
- *Promptly refrigerate shellfish,* holding them between 32° and 40° F.
- *Abstain from eating raw seafood when traveling in developing areas* of the world, such as Latin America and Africa.
- *Avoid shellfish from a questionable source.* If you decide to take the risk, at least be sure to thoroughly cook mollusks from areas in which shellfish-related outbreaks of illness have recently been reported.

If you're a healthy person who just can't relinquish your passion for raw mollusks, be forewarned that—even after taking all the precautions listed above—you still run the risk of gastroenteritis, which can put you out of commission for 1 to 4 days. What's worse, you may contract longer-lasting hepatitis A and be ill for 1 to 3 weeks.

People who develop bacterial or viral gastroenteritis after eating clams, oysters, or mussels usually get better on their own within several days. But if diarrhea and vomiting persist or are severe, a physician should be contacted. In addition, afflicted people should notify their local health department and/or FDA regional office (listed in the government section of the phone book's white pages) so the source of contamination can be tracked down.

On sushi, sashimi, ceviche . . .

A decade ago, most Americans would have squirmed just thinking about eating uncooked finfish. Now, some sophisticated palates can't get enough of the raw fish that goes into making sushi, sashimi, and ceviche. But many gourmands are unsophisticated in their knowledge of the risks involved in eating the raw fare. Although fish processors examine fish for parasites and remove them, occasionally some slip through. Even if the fish is marinated or slightly cooked, partakers can contract parasites that sometimes inhabit raw fish flesh. Fish tapeworms and roundworms are the two groups of parasites that currently have the attention of experts in the field, who are concerned that increased reports of parasitic infections in the U.S. may be related to the current passion for raw fish. *The risks discussed below, however, pertain to raw or undercooked fish. If fish is properly frozen or cooked, the risks are of no concern.* The risks of parasites exist in many other types of food, e.g., pork, which is why we eat it well-done.

Tapeworm infection. Both fresh- and saltwater fish—including pike, salmon, and perch—can transmit tapeworms that go unnoticed in many infected people until the unsightly worms are passed in their stools. In some victims, tapeworms grow to be many feet long and can cause nausea, diarrhea, cramps, fatigue, weight loss, and vitamin B$_{12}$ deficiency.

In 1980 a particularly bad outbreak of tapeworm infection was reported in Pacific Coast states, where the number of cases jumped nearly four times in one year. According to a report in the *FDA Consumer,* public health officials at the Centers for Disease Control became aware of the outbreak because so many physicians requested a tapeworm-killing drug that only the CDC supplied at the time. The majority of the 59 cases were linked to eating salmon—a popular sushi ingredient—or rockfish. (It so happens that salmon were heavily infected with tapeworm larvae in 1980.)

Although most victims said they ate the fish raw, a small number had it smoked, pickled, or cooked. The incidence of fish tapeworm infection today is not known since the antitapeworm drug that clued in officials in the 1980 outbreak is now available by prescription.

To protect yourself against tapeworm infection, fish should be thoroughly cooked or frozen for 72 hours at -4° F. Marinated fish used to make ceviche or gravlox can still harbor viable tapeworms if it is not frozen properly beforehand. Smoked fish should be safe if it's cooked as it is smoked; cold-smoking methods won't kill tapeworms. Joe Regenstein, Ph.D., from Cornell University's Department of Food Science, points out that commercially prepared lox from this country and Canada is safe to eat because it's brined *and* smoked and is usually made from frozen fish. It's wise to stick with lox purchased from a reputable delicatessen or supermarket. Be very cautious, however, if you're ever presented with home-smoked lox. Note that lox and other smoked fish should be kept in the refrigerator.

Roundworms—Anisakis. Of the two parasites you're most likely to contract from eating raw fish in this country, tapeworm is the lesser evil. For tapeworm infection can be cured with drugs, and its symptoms are usually less serious than those of *Anisakis* infection, called anisakiasis. No medications are currently available to treat anisakiasis, and the consequences may be grave enough to warrant surgery.

Mackerel, squid, herring, salmon, tuna, cod, and pollock are among fish that carry the larvae of anisakids. The larvae usually concentrate in internal organs, but are occasionally present in the flesh. Fish acquire the roundworm when parasite-infested feces of marine mammals—such as seals, whales, and dolphins—are dropped into the water and eaten by small crustaceans that, in turn, are eaten by other fish. It's thought that West Coast fish are more infected with the parasites than East or Gulf Coast species because of the larger marine mammal population in the Pacific.

Several surveys reported in the late 1970s suggested that the presence of *Anisakis* larvae, as well as some other parasites, was widespread in fish commonly sold in U.S. markets. According to FDA parasitologist Thomas Deardorff, Ph.D., more recent surveys give no reason to believe that the figures on roundworm occurrence in fish have declined.

If you happen to eat *Anisakis*-infected raw fish you may be lucky enough to experience no symptoms and simply excrete the parasite. But if you're among the unlucky, the roundworm can bore into the lining of the stomach and intestines and attach, causing excruciating pain and sometimes nausea and vomiting. Anisakid worms may be coughed or vomited up. On the other hand, they may have to be removed by a physician with forceps and the aid of a viewing instrument inserted into the stomach.

If the parasites attach to the intestinal wall, the only options are surgical removal or just treating the symptoms until the parasites die in a few days. Anisakiasis victims may also wind up in surgery because the symptoms mimic those of other ailments, including ulcers and stomach cancer.

As with the health threats of raw mollusks, it's important to get raw-finfish risks in perspective. According to Dr. Deardorff, only about 50 cases of anisakiasis were reported in the U.S. from the late 1950s to mid-1987. Many people eat raw fish without becoming sick. A concern, however, is that most cases occurred in the 1980s, which may reflect the raw-fish fad of recent years. Moreover, experts believe many more cases of anisakiasis go unreported.

Adequate cooking is a surefire way to get rid of anisakids. The 10-minute rule—that is, baking fish at 450° F for 10 minutes per inch of fish thickness—appears to be adequate to kill the roundworms. Anisakids will also likely meet their demise if you can get your freezer as low as -4° F and freeze fish for 4 to 5 days. In fact, the FDA has recommended that all fish products—with the exception of oysters, clams, and mussels—destined for consumption in the raw be thoroughly frozen before being sold in restaurants. Irradiation is also being tested as a means for eradicating parasites.

If you choose not to kick the raw-fish habit . . . Be aware of the risks—Dr. Deardorff maintains that many raw-fish lovers are unaware of the possibility of illness. Should you make your own sushi, sashimi, or ceviche, freeze the fish for 4 to 5 days at -4° F beforehand. Dr. Deardorff cautions against eating cod, Pacific rockfish, or salmon raw or undercooked because they've been linked to the majority of cases of fish parasitic infections in this country.

Don't count on marinating to spare you, since tapeworms can survive the process, and anisakids can live as long as 51 days in a vinegar solution. As with raw shellfish, I'd recommend that anyone with a chronic disease, as well as pregnant women, young children, and very old people, lay off raw finfish.

PART II

Selecting, Storing, and Cooking Fish

CHAPTER EIGHT

A Fish Glossary

MOST OF US ARE familiar with cod, haddock, salmon, sole, flounder, and swordfish. Yet, if you only count finfish, there are some 20,000 known species—with well over 100 kinds available for eating in this country. As mentioned earlier, one of the best parts of adding more fish to your life is the variety. But few of us are taking advantage of the plethora of fish that are out there.

The goal of this chapter is to expand your fish repertoire and familiarize you with what I call the "new" fish—fish that are relatively new to the commercial scene, although many have been enjoyed for centuries by people in other cultures. Some you may have come across but were hesitant to try because you didn't know what to do with them. Others are teeming in the oceans, just waiting for you to create the demand that will thrust them into commercial markets. In addition this chapter will provide nutritional and general information on the "old" fish—the more familiar fish varieties.

GETTING OUT OF THE FAMILIAR-FISH RUT
(OR TRY IT, YOU'LL LIKE IT)

"How do you know you don't like it if you've never tried it?" These familiar words, issued from parent to wary child faced with trying a new food, I now pose to you regarding the "new" fish. For if you're like the majority of Americans, you're stuck in the cod-flounder-haddock tradition, a tradition that has fostered dwindling supplies and soaring prices for all three fish. Faced with these frustrations, you probably don't eat fish very often and turn to more accessible poultry and beef.

If you don't want to foot the bill for your old fish favorites *and* you're really serious about adding more fish to your life, the best advice is to open up to trying new and different kinds of fish. Just the other day, I stood behind another customer at the supermarket seafood counter who was complaining about the $5.98-per-pound price of cod, at the same time asking, "What's this pollock at $1.98 a pound?" A savvy "new" fish consumer, he had the right idea and agreed to try pollock instead of cod—that is, after reassurances from the clerk that pollock's darker color would lighten up when cooked.

PLENTY OF FISH IN THE SEA

What if we all decided to follow the *Eat Fish* recommendation to have fish 3 to 7 times a week, but only stuck with the familiar few fish? Given the fact that supplies are already down, it's quite obvious that we'd soon have *no* fish to eat at all. But there are so many other fish possibilities going to waste—fish-trawling operations from Massachusetts alone throw back 20 to 30 percent of what they catch from along the continental shelf. It all adds up to an estimated 50 to 75 million pounds of rejected fish each year. One explanation for the discards is small size, but another major reason is lack of a market, relegating the throw-backs to such status as "trash fish," "underutilized species," and "lowly species."

Some seafood companies and restaurateurs, however, are catching on fast to consumer interest in many "new" fish that were once considered "trash" because they weren't popular. We're beginning to see aggressive marketing of such nontraditional fare as catfish, cusk, hake, pollock, squid, and skate. Such novel fish are often much less expensive than familiar species, but some "new" fish—orange roughy, crawfish, monkfish, and red drum, for instance—are in such demand that they're commanding record prices. Once considered underutilized and highly available, some of the "new" fish are now hard to come by. Still, there are many others—for instance, mackerel, skate, and ocean pout—that are plentiful and waiting for your demand. Indeed, over the next several years, the supply of so-called "underutilized species" is expected to climb more than 100 percent.

OVERCOMING AESTHETIC OBSTACLES

Many restaurants are setting the pace for exposing the public to the "new" fish—witness skate-wing entrees going for as much as $25 in some posh establishments. Why is it that people are willing to try the "new" fish when dining out, but not at home?

One encouragement for trying unique fish in restaurants is that you don't have to see the raw materials that go into making your meal. To be sure, an obstacle in the way of willingness to try some of the "new" fish is their appearance. (I must agree that uncleaned skate, squid, and monkfish are among the homeliest creatures I've encountered.) But what if you'd never seen a shrimp or lobster before? One look at their beady eyes, sharp claws, and insectlike bodies and you'd likely be dissuaded from taking your first bite!

You're also more likely to try "new" fish in a restaurant because the dirty work is done for you—the skate wings have been skinned and filleted; the squid has been gutted and "de-inked." But if you're willing to pay for it, many fish dealers will perform the cleaning services. If not, you're likely to find that, after your first attempts, the effort to clean many fish is not greater than that involved in skinning and deboning chicken. Besides, just think of all the effort you're willing to go through to get a couple of ounces of meat from that difficult lobster!

The preceding discussion may lead you to believe that most "new" fish are messy and difficult to prepare. Quite the contrary, the majority are commercially available as fillets and they're just as easy to cook as your old favorites.

IF YOU WANT IT, ASK FOR IT

If you've never seen skate wings, ocean pout, hake, mullet, or any number of the "new" fish at the seafood counter, it may well be because you're not asking for them. After all, why should a store stock fish that there's no demand for and is a risky bet for profit-making? Once you let your seafood dealer know what "new" fish you want, however, he may see that there's something in it for himself and will readily supply you with your new favorites. When I gave the owner of my local seafood market a list of "new" fish that I wanted to try, within the course of one week he got me skate wings, squid, and "yellow eel." Another week, a different dealer provided me with tautog, tilefish, and monkfish.

The next step is to educate your seafood dealer—mine didn't know how to fillet a skate wing. I told him how (it's simple—see page 148), then offered my recipe for Tarragon Skate Wings Sautéed in Bread Crumbs and Lemon Butter. That way, I figured he'd be more likely to try skate himself and stock it in the future. Nor did my seafood seller know that the "yellow eel" he'd sold me was really ocean pout —no relation to eels. Certainly ocean pout fillets—which can be nicely stuffed and rolled—are more marketable than eel meat.

None of this means that you have to completely relinquish cod, flounder, and haddock. I'm merely suggesting that you become receptive to trying "new" fish. If more people would, ocean stocks of traditional fish favorites would have a chance to replenish themselves, and market prices might go down.

A PROBLEM OF NOMENCLATURE

How do you know that the fish you're buying is what the sign says it is—particularly if it's been skinned and filleted? The fact is you don't, because most fish are named according to a somewhat arbitrary, unofficial system.

Although there are complex-sounding biological names for species of fish, they're of little value when consumers go to the fish market. After all, would you know that *Homarus americanus* refers to the American lobster? Federally regulated common names do exist for some fish, but states don't necessarily abide by them within their own borders.

Basically, names of fish depend on where you live and who you're buying from. Although fish sold in interstate commerce are supposed to be identified by "common or usual names," you may run into a situation where seafood retailers have applied "dress-up" names to make certain fish seem more appealing. Pollock, for instance, may be sold as Boston bluefish, squid as calamari, and dolphinfish as more exotic-sounding mahimahi. And even though it's illegal, names of more desirable seafoods are sometimes applied to those of lesser value. A case in point is that of calico scallops, at times sold as similar-looking, but more highly-prized bay scallops.

Individual states can have their own rules for naming certain fish— for instance, Pacific Ocean perch sold in certain West Coast states may be sold as snapper within state borders. But these fish are unrelated to the red snapper caught in Florida's waters. You may also find that what's named flounder in one community is sold as sole in the next. And the confusing "scrod" name is actually a size designation that can apply to any number of small white-fleshed fish, including haddock, cod, and pollock.

To muddle matters further, the same name may be used for more than one species. "Whitefish," for instance, may refer to any fish with white meat, or it may apply to a specific freshwater member of the trout family (see page 161). Also confusing, some fish are not even in the same family they're named for—white sea bass, for instance, are not bass at all but are actually members of the croaker and drum family. Fortunately, the National Marine Fisheries Service, along with the FDA, are in the process of standardizing market names of fish so that only one name will apply to fish sold in interstate commerce.

A FEW WORDS ABOUT THE GLOSSARY

Because of the naming mayhem, most entries in the fish glossary begin with "also known as"—a list of common aliases that particular fish may go by. Next you'll come to "market forms" to let you know how the fish is usually purchased. (See pages 168–69 for definitions of terms such as *drawn* and *dressed*.) "Points of interest" addresses intriguing facts about each type of fish. "Eating quality" describes the color, taste, and texture of each fish after it's cooked. "Preparation" gives you cleaning tips, cooking methods, and recipe ideas. "Trade-offs" lists some of the other fish for which you can substitute the "new" fish in recipes. Trade-offs are not listed for the "old" fish.

I must tell you that "eating quality" and "trade-offs" are somewhat subjective because, to date, there has never been a coordinated scientific effort to define the culinary qualities of various types of fish. Thus, two fish cookbooks may describe the same fish somewhat differently. Furthermore, the color, taste, and texture of a specific fish species can vary depending on the time of year, freshness, the age of the fish, and its diet.

Concerning "trade-offs," the suggestions are by no means exhaustive because little is known about how well fish work in place of one another in recipes. The National Marine Fisheries Service is in the process of scientifically examining many types of fish under varying cooking conditions. They're developing "edibility profiles" that will give consumers a better sense of what unfamiliar fish taste like. The profiles will also let consumers know what fish can be used interchangeably in recipes. It's expected that several more years will pass before the project is completed.*

In the meantime, I urge you to experiment because many different types of fish may work well in the same recipe. Don't, however, expect all recipes to taste exactly the same with "trade-off" fish because there *are* flavor and texture differences. Moreover, a particular "new" fish may work well in place of a more familiar fish in one recipe, but not in another. (Be sure to adjust cooking times according to fish thickness.)

---

* I pooled my information about the "new" fish from a variety of professional seafood handbooks and fish cookbooks. I also consulted the following individuals: Robert Learson, director of the Northeast Fisheries Center Laboratory of the National Marine Fisheries Service in Gloucester, MA; Beth Hubbard, sales and marketing consultant for the M. F. Foley Company in New Bedford, MA; Ralph Boragine, executive director of the Rhode Island Seafood Council; Linda Odierno, coordinator of Fisheries and Aquaculture Development, the New Jersey Department of Agriculture, David Steuiber, Ph.D., at the University of Wisconsin Department of Food Science; and Joyce Taylor, seafood education specialist with North Carolina State University Seafood Laboratory.

When you get to the descriptions of "nutritional value" for each fish, you'll see that I've primarily focused on fat,** calorie, and cholesterol content. I say little about protein levels because all but a few fish provide 15 grams or more—plenty of high-quality protein for a meal. (For more details on the nutritional content of various fish, see chapter 6.)

I used nutritional data for 3½-ounce portions of *raw* fish (only the edible part) because there is little information available on the content of cooked "new" fish. Calorie, fat, and cholesterol values change little when that 3½-ounce raw portion is cooked. (Note, however, that a 3½-ounce *cooked* portion of any one type of fish *is* higher in calories, fat, and cholesterol than a 3½-ounce *raw* serving of that same fish—see page 58.)

The fish glossary is by no means all-inclusive—you may come across others in your locale. I attempted to cover those with greatest availability and to include some "new" fish from various parts of the country.

Anchovy

Market forms: In the U.S. anchovies are usually sold in processed form, the most familiar being canned fillets (sold flat or rolled), salted and packed in oil.

Points of interest: It's hard to think of those lifeless-looking canned squiggles as the silvery, big-eyed fish that they are when they're alive! Although there are more than 15 species of anchovies in our nation's waters, the small fish are more often used as bait than as food. The natural flesh of anchovies is white—not the characteristic reddish color resulting from months of salt-curing. Saltwater fish.

Eating quality: Once you've eaten a processed anchovy, you never forget its strong, salty taste. Because a little goes a long way, anchovies are typically used to enhance the taste of other foods—say, pizza, antipasto, or Caesar salad.

Nutritional value: With nearly 10 grams of fat per 3½-ounce serving, anchovies canned in olive oil are high in fat compared to other fish, even if they're drained. (The same-size portion of fresh anchovies has about half that amount of fat.) More than 3,500 milligrams of sodium

** I used the same fat classifications (by weight) that I used in chapter 6: *very low-fat*—2 percent or less fat; *low-fat*—2.1 to 5 percent fat; *medium-fat*—5.1 to 10 percent fat; *oily*—10.1 percent fat or more.

are also present in the canned version! (This can vary from one product to the next.) On the positive side, for just a little over 200 calories, you get high amounts of omega-3 fatty acids, as well as lots of calcium and iron, from a serving of European canned anchovies. (The USDA provides no data on cholesterol.)

Bass, black sea

Also known as: sea bass, blackfish. It's not uncommon to see black sea bass confused with striped bass (see the next entry) or tautog (*also* known as blackfish).

Market forms: drawn, dressed, fillets.

Points of interest: Along with groupers, black sea bass are true members of the sea bass family, unlike many other so-called basses. (White sea bass, for instance, actually belongs in the croaker and drum family.) Saltwater fish.

Eating quality: The firm, white flesh of black sea bass is considered mild and delicate in flavor.

Preparation: A delight for the uninitiated seafood cook, black sea bass "can be cooked by any method and is one of few fish that's difficult to ruin by lack of culinary skill . . . ," according to A. J. McClane's *Encyclopedia of Fish Cookery.* Popular in Chinese cooking, black sea bass can be steamed with a seasoning of chopped scallion, crushed garlic, grated ginger, soy sauce, and sesame oil. It also works in chowders.

Nutritional value: Black sea bass is *very low-fat* with just 97 calories per serving.

Bass, striped

Also known as: striper, rockfish (in the middle Atlantic states). (Striped bass is a member of a different biological family than black sea bass)

Market forms: drawn, dressed, fillets, steaks. (To protect against substitutions, it's recommended that fillets be purchased with their striped skin on.)

Points of interest: Now a veritable rarity on the commercial market, striped bass was once a "premier fish of the Atlantic coast," according to *The Seafood Handbook,* published by *Seafood Business.* Landings have steadily declined because of a combination of overfishing, pollution, and a natural cyclical decline in numbers. In addition, some states have closed commercial striped-bass fisheries as a conservation measure and because of high PCB levels (see page 77). Like salmon, striped bass are anadromous—that is, they normally live in salt water but travel to freshwater rivers to reproduce.

Eating quality: The prized white meat of striped bass is known for an excellent, distinct flavor and firm texture. Under the skin is a darker-fleshed section that's oilier and more strong-tasting.

Preparation: Striped bass can be cooked just about any way you please —bake, broil, poach, stuff, sauté, fry, or stew.

Nutritional value: Striped bass is *low-fat* with just 97 calories and 80 milligrams of cholesterol in a 3½-ounce portion. (Incidentally, fresh-water bass is *low-fat* and provides 114 calories and 68 milligrams of cholesterol.)

Bluefish

Also known as: tailor, skipjack (not to be confused with skipjack tuna), blue snapper. (As mentioned earlier, don't mistake so-called "Boston bluefish," which is pollock, for true bluefish.)

Market forms: usually sold as fillets or head-on and gutted; also available in steaks and smoked.

Points of interest: The tough guys of the sea, bluefish go for just about any bait and put up a whale of a fight. As such, they attract far more sport fishermen than commercial. Bluefish have gluttonous appetites which they satisfy primarily by feeding on smaller schooling fish. As migratory creatures, they move inshore, then out to sea, as well as north and south, depending on the season of the year. Its predatory and migratory behaviors play into the bluefish's propensity for concentrating contaminants, such as PCBs, as you saw in chapter 7. Saltwater fish.

Eating quality: Despite the foregoing forbidding description, bluefish has a well-deserved popularity on the East Coast. The moist meat has a distinct, full flavor. And its dark color lightens up upon cooking.

Preparation: For a milder taste, cut out the darker, stronger-tasting midline meat in an uncooked fillet by making two shallow, angled cuts along either side of the line. Be careful not to cut all the way through the fillet if you want to leave it intact. Because bluefish tends to spoil rather quickly, it should be cooked soon after it's caught or purchased. Until then, chill it in the back lower part of your refrigerator. Bluefish is best baked, broiled, or grilled; it can also be stuffed. To bring out the best in bluefish and lighten the flesh somewhat, complement it with the tartness of lemon juice, tomatoes and tomato juice, vinegar, orange juice and grated orange rind, or wine. Cold, leftover bluefish is tasty served on a bed of lettuce with low-calorie salad dressing or mayonnaise.

Nutritional value: Popular opinion has it that bluefish is very oily, but it's actually *low-fat.* A serving has 124 calories and 59 milligrams of cholesterol.

Butterfish

Also known as: dollarfish, Pacific pompano, pomfret, shiner, skipjack.

Market forms: drawn, dressed, smoked, whole.

Points of interest: Largely an East Coast phenomenon, butterfish are caught in the Atlantic Ocean from Nova Scotia to the Gulf of Mexico. There's also a West Coast member of the butterfish family known as Pacific pompano, as well as some European cousins called pomfret. Don't mistake butterfish for sablefish (see page 140) which is occasionally marketed as butterfish and sold as fillets. Butterfish are much smaller than sablefish. Saltwater fish.

Eating quality: You can probably guess from the name that butterfish are rich in oil—they're said to melt in your mouth. Don't be put off by the dark color of butterfish because it lightens up when cooked. And the soft, fine texture firms upon cooking. The flavor of butterfish is rated as delicate and excellent.

Preparation: Because they're so small, butterfish are usually prepared whole. They're said to be best if cooked by splitting, then broiling or baking with the skin on. Their superfine scales can simply be rubbed off. You can also fry, grill, or sauté butterfish. Try cooking *en papillote* with vegetables or in a cucumber-yogurt sauce (see page 198).

Trade-offs: Although less oily and lighter-tasting than mackerel, butterfish can be used in most mackerel recipes.

Nutritional value: A *medium-fat* fish, butterfish provides just under 150 calories and only 65 milligrams of cholesterol per serving.

Carp

Market forms: dressed, fillets, whole.

Points of interest: Carp is widely distributed in freshwater habitats across the U.S. But it's most popular in Chinese and Central European cuisines. Although it's not big on the commercial scene, carp is often used to make gefilte fish.

Eating quality: The quality of carp meat depends on the season and the quality of the water in which it's caught. Generally speaking, winter carp caught in clear, flowing streams offer the best eating. Carp contains some tough and unappealing dark-colored flesh that's best cut away before cooking. The lighter sections can be incorporated in many recipes. Somewhat coarse and meatlike, carp can contain annoying bones. Its flavor has been described as distinctive and rich.

Preparation: If you have to perform the skinning honors for carp, first bring a large kettle of water to a boil. Submerge the whole fish or fillets, and after the water returns to a boil, time it for about 25 seconds. The skin can then be readily rubbed off while the carp is still hot. Before it's used in a recipe, carp is often tenderized for an hour in a dry, salty mixture that's then rinsed off. If you follow this course, don't add extra salt in cooking. Stuff and bake, broil, fry, grill, poach, steam, or use in soups, stews, and sweet-and-sour sauces. Try carp fillets baked with stewed tomatoes and sliced onions.

Nutritional value: Carp is *medium-fat* but provides only 127 calories per serving. It has 66 milligrams of cholesterol.

Catfish

Also known as: many confusing, regional names. There are 28 species in North America, but the 3 most popular are channel, white, and blue catfish.

Market forms: fresh and frozen fillets and steaks, dressed. (Most sales are of boneless fillets.)

Points of interest: Aquaculture (fish farming) now provides most commercially sold catfish in this country. From Florida through Kansas, many farmers transformed their fields to catfish ponds years ago. Among America's most popular fish, catfish are eaten most often in Southern and Central states. But catfish are rapidly gaining a following in other parts of the nation. In fact, many areas now boast catfish as the leading fish product in volume sales. Freshwater fish.

Eating quality: The taste of catfish—which eat just about any living or dead thing—depends largely upon their diet, a factor that's controlled in aquacultured fish. A delight for those who are annoyed by bones, catfish have a quite simple skeletal structure that makes for boneless eating. The white meat offers a fine, firm texture and somewhat sweet taste.

Preparation: The low-fat virtues of catfish are most commonly done away with by deep-fat frying. But other cooking methods are becoming more popular. Catfish can be prepared any way you please—from placing them in aspic to stewing. They can also be "blackened" (see page 197) and are good basted with a sauce and grilled. Try microwaving fillets with vegetables (see page 271) or "slim-frying" them in a cornmeal coating (page 251).

Trade-offs: Catfish work well in many recipes for flatfish. You can also substitute catfish for cod, pollock, ocean perch, rockfish, or whiting in many recipes.

Nutritional value: Catfish is *low-fat* and provides 116 calories along with 58 milligrams of cholesterol per serving.

Clams

According to *Seafood Business,* we down more clams in America than anywhere else in the world. There are so many different types of clams that it's easiest to address them individually.

Soft-shell clams. Also known as steamers, squirt clams, long neck clams, and belly clams, they are sold primarily for steaming and frying. *Au naturel,* they have thin, white shells and dark siphons (often called "necks") that retract when touched. Unlike other types of clams, the soft-shell variety can't close tightly. Before eating, the piece of skin covering the tip of the neck should be removed.

Hard-shell clams. Also called quahogs (pronounced "ko-hogs"), bay quahogs, and hard clams, these have thicker, roundish shells that *do* close tightly when touched. Their uses vary according to size. The smallest hard-shell clams, called littlenecks, are the most expensive; they're usually served raw or steamed. Cherrystones are larger, but also may be served on the half shell or steamed. More often, however, cherrystones are used in chowders, casseroles, and appetizers (such as "clams casino"). Larger still are chowders—rather tough creatures best used in recipes calling for chopped or minced clams. (Note that there's a deep-sea clam, called the ocean quahog, mahogany quahog, or black clam. It, too, is used for minced-clam products, as well as clam strips for frying.)

Surf clams. These have whitish shells that are larger and more oval-shaped than quahogs. (They're the washed-ashore shells that I used to collect as a kid on Atlantic Coast beaches.) Surf clams are processed for minced-clam products or strips for fried clams.

All of the above are more East Coast phenomena, which take up most of the commercial clam market. But the Pacific Coast sports some clams of its own: Manila clams (sometimes marketed as littleneck clams), butter clams, and horse clams (similar to East Coast steamers). At a weight of as high as five pounds comes the geoduck (pronounced "gooey duck"). It's the largest North American clam, found only in the Pacific Northwest.

Preparation: For tips on purchasing clams, see pages 164 and 171. Storage guidelines are on page 174, and cleaning suggestions are on page 183. Turn to page 200 for steaming directions. (A discussion of shellfish safety concerns begins on page 89.)

Nutritional value: Very low-fat, a 3½-ounce portion of raw clams (the USDA provides data for "mixed species") comes close to fulfilling the hard-to-meet RDA for iron for premenopausal women. A serving offers only 74 calories and 34 milligrams of cholesterol.

Cod

Also known as: codfish; fillets from smaller cod are often sold as scrod.

Market forms: Atlantic cod can be purchased drawn, dressed, smoked, dried, or salted. But you're probably most familiar with Atlantic cod as fresh or frozen fillets. Steaks can also be had, as can tongues and cheeks of larger cod. Pacific cod (sometimes called "true cod") is closely related to the Atlantic variety. Fresh Pacific cod comes in fillet form, dressed, and whole. Frozen, you may see fillets, as well as fish portions and sticks.

Points of interest: Cod is the most demanded species for fish sandwiches served in fast-food restaurants. A cod statue in the Massachusetts State House marks cod's favored place in New England history.

Eating quality: Atlantic and Pacific cod can be used interchangeably. Most people are familiar with cod's large, firm, white flakes and mild flavor.

Preparation: Cod is so versatile that you can cook it any way you please —from poaching to broiling, microwaving to stewing. Its subtle flavor can be dressed up (with a spicy sauce) or down (with lemon and a dab of butter or margarine). If you adjust cooking time according to thickness, cod can be used in recipes calling for haddock, halibut, cusk, hake, pollock, flounder, or sole.

Nutritional value: Very low-fat fish, both Atlantic and Pacific cod provide 82 calories per serving. At 43 milligrams, Atlantic cod provides 6 more milligrams of cholesterol than Pacific cod.

Crab

Like clams, crabs come from nature in many styles.

Blue crab. The most common type of crab on the commercial market in this country, these small creatures—measuring 5 to 7 inches across the shell—are captured in Atlantic waters from Maine to Florida, as well as in the Gulf of Mexico. You can buy blue crabs live or fresh-cooked. Lump, flake, and claw meat is also available in frozen form. In addition, you can purchase pasteurized crabmeat which, compared to fresh crabmeat, keeps much longer in the refrigerator. Steaming is considered the best cooking method for fresh blue crabs (see page 200) and will turn the shells red. (Most domestically packed canned crabmeat is from blue crabs.)

Soft-shell crab. For soft-shell crab lovers, it may come as a surprise to learn that their passion is none other than blue crab sans the hard shell. It turns out that blue crabs periodically shed their shells and can be eaten whole before their new shells harden. Soft-shell crab is available fresh and frozen. Once the apron or flap underneath the crab's body is taken off—and the "face," intestines, and gills are removed—the remainder of the soft-shell blue crab is eaten, shell and all. Woe to the health-conscious; the delicacy is typically pan-fried in butter.

King crab. These giants—which are more closely related to hermit crabs than to true crabs—can easily have legs running three feet long. Although there are other species, the Alaska red king crab is most commonly sold in the U.S. Be it leg, claw, or body meat, the bulk of king crab is sold frozen in this country. If the meat was precooked, as it commonly is, any additional cooking should be minimal.

Dungeness crab. This is most popular on the West Coast, where it is captured from California to Alaska. Not only can you buy live Dungeness crabs, but meat from various parts of the body is sold fresh-cooked and frozen. Unlike the white body meat, you'll find that claw meat has a reddish or pinkish hue. Dungeness crab lends itself to boiling, steaming, frying, and baking. If the struggle to remove meat from whole crabs seems barely worth the effort, you'll appreciate the Dungeness variety because it's comparatively easy to remove the flesh from the crustacean's thick legs and shoulders.

Snow crab. It's also known as tanner crab and queen crab. Canadian fishermen capture it in the North Atlantic, as do fishermen in the North Pacific. Still large, snow crabs run about half the size of king crabs. Snow crabmeat is usually marketed in the cooked, frozen form, but it's also available canned. You can substitute snow crab for king crab—some people think the snow type tastes even better.

Jonah and rock crabs. Both Dungeness crab relatives are sold in the Northeast, where they may not be distinguished from one another at point of purchase. Since both are small, the yield is limited—say a dozen rock crabs to one pound of meat. Thus, both Jonah and rock crabs remain underutilized. It will be interesting to see if a newly developing market for *soft-shell* rock crabs takes off. Compared to other types of crab, rock and Jonah produce light meat with a brownish cast.

The list of types of crab goes on. You may come across red crab, which is similar to snow crab and is marketed primarily as frozen, cooked and picked meat. Floridians are likely familiar with stone crabs caught in their waters—only the large claws are eaten.

For crab purchasing guidelines, turn to pages 164 and 171. Storage tips are on page 174. Steaming directions are on page 200.

When it comes to canned crabmeat, most is imported from countries such as Thailand, Malaysia, and Japan. If the label of canned crabmeat products simply specifies "crab" on the ingredient listing, there's no telling what type of crab it came from.

Nutritional information: The USDA provides nutritional data for blue, king, Dungeness, and snow crab. All 4 are *very low-fat,* providing 84 to 90 calories per serving. Cholesterol ranges from 42 milligrams for king crab to 78 milligrams for blue crab. Crabmeat is a good source of zinc. Sodium levels of king and snow crab are on the high side, at 836 and 539 milligrams respectively.

Crawfish

Also known as: Crayfish, crawdads, écrevisse (in gourmet circles).

Market forms: live, fresh and frozen whole, tail meat—cooked or raw, fresh or frozen.

Points of interest: If you're like me, the thought of crawfish brings back childhood memories of discovering small lobsterlike creatures under rocks in your local creek. But today, these freshwater crustaceans— once known as "poor man's food"—are considered gourmet treats, going for a late-1986 wholesale price of nearly $3.00 a pound for peeled tail meat. The demand for crawfish has largely been spurred by their popularity in Cajun cooking. Most crawfish in this country come from fish farms, which are spreading from Louisiana to Texas, California, and a number of other states. Hopefully, the price will come down as more crawfish are produced.

Eating quality: Crawfish taste similar to lobster. Most of the meat is in the tail with small amounts in the claws.

Preparation: Like lobsters and crabs, crawfish should be cooked live because the meat of dead, raw crawfish spoils quickly. Live crawfish should be washed well and placed in ice-cold water, which will temporarily stun them and make them easier to handle. Soak for 5 to 8 minutes, stirring occasionally to help get rid of dirt. Afterward, scoop out and drain the crawfish. Then bring a large kettle of water to a boil. (For a savory broth, add lemon juice, garlic, and chopped onions to the water.) Drop crawfish, 2 or 3 at a time, into the boiling water. When they're all in, cover tightly, bring the water to a boil again, and cook for about 10 minutes. Stir once or twice to move them around well. Drain thoroughly. It's easiest to remove the meat while the crawfish are still warm.

To eat as is, crack open the claws (you may need the aid of a sharp knife) and suck out the meat and tasty juices. Twist and pull off the tail. If you hold the tail with both hands and twist at the middle of the shell, it should open up. (You can also remove the tail meat by cutting the shell along the side lines where the top and bottom join.) Then remove the vein, as you would with shrimp. Be patient, for it takes about 7 pounds of whole crawfish to get a pound of meat! If you like, dunk the fruits of your labor in lemon juice or cocktail sauce (see page 237). You can also substitute crawfish for shrimp or lobster in salads, soups, appetizers, jambalaya, and creamed dishes. A tasty way to serve raw, cleaned, and shelled crawfish is broiled in a little olive oil with lemon juice, paprika, chopped parsley, and minced garlic. It's also good stir-fried with vegetables.

Trade-offs: Use crawfish meat just as you would lobster or shrimp.

Nutritional value: Crawfish is *very low-fat* and offers just 89 calories per serving. At 139 milligrams, its cholesterol level is fairly high.

Cusk

Also known as: Smaller cusk may be marketed as scrod. Cusk fillets are sometimes sold as whitefish fillets.

Market forms: fresh and frozen skinless fillets, salted.

Points of interest: Members of the cod family, cusk tend to be less expensive. Saltwater fish.

Eating quality: Although its white flesh is firmer than that of other cod family members, cusk tastes similar to cod with its mild flavor. Cusk holds well on a warming tray because of its firm texture.

Preparation: If it's not skinned (it usually is), it's worth it to pay for the service since cusk skin is slimy and difficult to remove. Cusk fillets have a single strip of bones that should be removed. (See "Mackerel" for directions.) It runs down the center for about two-thirds of the length. The M. F. Foley Company's Beth Hubbard suggests cutting cusk "on the bias" (in medallions) for the most pleasing texture.

Cusk is best if baked or broiled and served with seasonings and sauces to dress up its mild taste. It works well in soups and stews or cooked in parchment with vegetables. Cusk can also be poached, steamed, grilled, or sautéed. For barbecuing, you can cut cusk into chunks, marinate them, and skewer with vegetables. Try cooked cusk leftovers in a Waldorf salad or quiche.

Trade-offs: Although it tends to be somewhat chewy and dense, cusk can be used in just about any recipe calling for white-fleshed fish. Specifically, you can substitute cusk for cod, haddock, hake, pollock, grouper, wolffish, and pout.

Nutritional value: Very low-fat, cusk provides just 87 calories and 41 milligrams of cholesterol per serving.

Drum/croaker

Also known as: The names of drums are many and confusing since there are so many family members. For instance, there are black drums, red drums, and banded drums. Then there are white sea bass, which actually belong in the drum and croaker family. Drums are named for their specialized "drumming" muscle that makes a loud sound audible on land. Some make a loud, croaking sound—thus, the croaker name. Atlantic croakers are the most common of the croaker species. Other names drum-family members can go by are crocus, golden croaker, grodin, corvina, and hardhead.

Red drums (sometimes referred to as channel bass) caught in the Gulf and Southern Atlantic waters are often called redfish, made popular in the Cajun-cooked "blackened redfish." These so-called redfish should not be mistaken for ocean perch, which are also commonly called redfish.

Weakfish are also drums, but their eating quality is so different that they're handled in a separate category (see page 160). Be aware, too, that a freshwater drum called the sheepshead exists. But its coarse, lean, white meat is considered mediocre.

Market forms: dressed, fillets, whole, flaked and breaded.

Points of interest: Until recently, drums were relatively scarce because of overfishing and climate changes. But they're making a comeback in fish markets along the Atlantic Coast. Drums are also caught in the Gulf of Mexico and on the West Coast.

Eating quality: Because of the number of species, the taste and texture of drums varies. Generally speaking, drums are firm in texture with a light to moderate flavor. The flesh is white in color. Croaker has a more distinctive taste than that of other drums.

Preparation: Drums are not recommended for raw dishes, such as ceviche or sashimi, because they may harbor harmful parasites. When cooked properly, the parasites are killed. Drums work well in stews, soups, and light sauces. They're also good pan-fried, and whole fish can be grilled. Try serving with a low-fat lemon sauce or stir-frying strips with broccoli and mushrooms. You can also bake, broil, poach, and steam drums.

Trade-offs: Larger drums can be used in almost any seafood recipe. Try them in place of cod, haddock, snapper, and whiting. Croaker can substitute for monkfish, swordfish, weakfish, or spot in certain recipes.

Nutritional value: Atlantic croakers are *low fat,* providing 104 calories and 61 milligrams of cholesterol per serving. Red and black drums tend to be *very low-fat* and have less than 100 calories in 3½ ounces.

Eel

Market forms: dressed (skinned and unskinned), fillets, live, smoked, steaks. May be fresh or frozen.

Points of interest: For many, the mere mention of eel conjures up an image of squirming snakes. But these true fish—with tiny scales and gills—are a delicacy in Europe and the Far East. In this country, eel is most available at Christmastime because of its popularity in certain ethnic dishes. At other times of the year, it can be hard to find eel outside of large metropolitan areas. American eel can actually be caught in fresh or salt waters of the Atlantic and Gulf coasts, for they spend most of their lives in fresh water or brackish coastal streams and estuaries, returning to the sea to spawn.

Eating quality: Eel meat is considered rich and very firm, and at the same time smooth, delicate, and sweet-tasting. Its grayish color turns white upon cooking. About the only bone you have to deal with in eel is the long backbone, which can be easily removed.

Preparation: Eels have a tough skin that should be removed before cooking. When buying whole eels, you can figure on about a half-pound per person. Because eel meat is so firm, it may need to be cooked longer than many other fish. Eel can be baked, broiled, fried, grilled, poached, or stewed. Try skinless eel chunks dredged in seasoned flour and sautéed in a small amount of oil with chopped shallots, parsley, and garlic. To firm the flesh before using it in a recipe, it's sometimes recommended that you first parboil eel for a few minutes in water with salt and vinegar or lemon juice.

Trade-offs: Although its flesh is whiter, eel can be used in some mackerel recipes. Cooked eel meat can be used in place of white, flaky fish in cold seafood salads. Eel also works well in many meat recipes.

Nutritional value: One of the highest fat fish, eel is *oily.* Yet, according to USDA data, eel provides a low level of omega-3 fatty acids and is fairly high in cholesterol (126 milligrams). Despite its fat level, a serving of eel nets you just 184 calories.

Flounder and sole

Believe it or not, there are more than 200 species of flounder and sole in U.S. waters. But no true sole is available on a commercial scale here. Indeed, a number of flounders are marketed as "sole" because it sounds more posh. Flounder and sole are actually from two different biological families. Although both are considered flatfish, flounders tend to be roundish, while sole are more oval and thick-bodied. (About the only time you come across real sole in this country is when Dover sole is imported from Europe.)

As for flounder, the chief Atlantic types are as follows.

Winter flounder. These are called "blackbacks" when they weigh 3½ pounds or less; those weighing more are sold as "lemon sole." Lemon-sole fillets are among the thickest and meatiest—they're also quite flaky. Blackbacks yield both white and gray fillets, depending on the side of the fish they come from.

Gray sole. Also called "witch flounder," it is one of the most popular and more expensive types on the East Coast. Despite its name, the flesh is very white.

Yellowtail flounder. These provide delicate, thin fillets.

Dab. Also sold as American or Canadian plaice, its white flesh is not as moist as that of some other types of flounder. Like lemon sole, dab gives you thick, firm fillets.

Summer flounder. This fish may also go by "fluke." Because it's a large fish, you may come across quarter-cut fillets or even steaks.

Summer-flounder flesh tends to be a bit less moist and coarser-textured than that of some of its cousins.

Pacific Ocean flounders include the following.

Dover sole. The most common West Coast flounder, this large thick-bodied fish produces fine-textured fillets. It's not related to the European Dover sole mentioned earlier.

Petrale sole. The number-one West Coast choice when it comes to taste and delicate texture, sometimes it's called "brill sole."

Rex sole. This is a type of flounder that's often cooked whole because it produces smaller, thinner fillets.

English sole. These are also on the small side. To confuse matters, English sole may also go by "lemon sole."

Arrowtooth flounder. Usually sold frozen, it's less valuable because the meat breaks up quite easily.

European species of sole are also available in this country—particularly in the winter when prices for domestic flounder soar. You may come across European plaice, and European turbot (different from the Greenland turbot discussed on page 160), as well as true Dover sole.

Market forms: You almost always encounter flounder—be it fresh or frozen—in fillet form. But sometimes it's available whole and dressed. Fillets may be marketed with the skin on, particularly if they're from the preferred white sides of the fish.

Points of interest: Flounders have a curious appearance—they're not only flat and saucerlike, but both eyes are on the same side of the fish. As the fish swims horizontally through the water, its white eyeless side faces the ocean floor, while its darker mottled side faces upward.

Eating quality: It's hard to find someone who dislikes the mild, delicate flavor and snow-white meat of boneless flounder and sole fillets. If you're put off by the darker color of some fillets (which come from the darker-skinned side of certain species, such as blackbacks), you can rest assured that the meat whitens upon cooking. You'll also likely save money with grayish fillets since they tend to be less expensive.

Preparation: Simple cooking methods, such as sautéing or lightly pan-frying, best suit flounder and sole. You can also steam, poach, bake, microwave, oven-fry, and broil fillets, as well as cook them *en papillote*. Because fillets tend to be on the thin side, you need to be careful not to overcook them. This can be an advantage for people on the run— as the West Coast Fisheries Development Foundation puts it, Pacific sole is "the natural fast food." Because they produce long, narrow fillets, gray sole and Pacific Dover sole lend themselves especially well to rolling with a stuffing. Just about any type of fillet can be stuffed sandwich-style or lightly sauced. (For tips on filleting flatfish, see page 183). You can use flounder and sole fillets in any recipe calling for white-fleshed fish, adjusting cooking time according to thickness.

Nutritional value: The USDA lumps the various types of flounder and sole together as "flatfish." *Very low-fat,* they provide 91 calories and 48 milligrams of cholesterol per serving.

Grouper

Market forms: Most grouper is sold whole, but we're seeing more fresh fillets on the market. It's also sold dressed and as steaks. You can find grouper in fresh or frozen form.

Points of interest: The many different species of grouper are members of the sea bass family. Examples are black, Nassau, red, and yellowfin groupers, as well as the jewfish and gag.

Eating quality: Groupers have a fine, firm texture. Their meat is white and mild-flavored. With fillets, you don't have to cope with any small bones.

Preparation: Be sure to remove the skin of groupers because it's tough and strong-tasting. Grouper works especially well in chowders because of its firm texture. But it tends to dry out in broiling. An easy recipe is to coat grouper chunks with a small amount of oil or melted margarine. Add chunks to a microwaveable dish and top with a mixture of bread crumbs and herbs. Cover and microwave at full power until done; serve with lemon wedges. Grouper can also be fried, grilled, poached, sautéed, steamed, and stewed.

Trade-offs: Grouper works well in almost any recipe calling for light, delicate fish. Try it in place of cod, haddock, porgy, snapper, or halibut.

Nutritional value: Grouper is *very low-fat* with 92 calories and only 37 milligrams of cholesterol per serving.

Haddock

Also known as: scrod when fillets come from 1½- to 2-pound haddock; snapper when they're taken from fish weighing less than a pound and a half.

Market forms: Although you can buy haddock drawn and dressed, it's most commonly sold in fillet form, either fresh or frozen. While frozen fillets may be sold skinless, fresh haddock usually comes skin-on so buyers can distinguish it from other white-fleshed fish, such as cod. Smoked haddock fillets are called "finnan haddie."

Points of interest: Haddock lovers can tell if they're buying the real thing—which usually commands the highest price of all cod-family members—by a black line that runs down the side of a skin-on fillet. In addition, the skin will have a blotch, known as the "Devil's thumbprint" or "St. Peter's mark," up where the "shoulder" of the fish would be. Haddock's price can be attributed to its great popularity in the Northeast, as well as to its less plentiful numbers in recent years. Haddock is found only in the North Atlantic Ocean.

Eating quality: If you like cod and flounder, then you're bound to like the mild taste of haddock. It's considered one of the most delicately flavored fish with its flaky, white flesh. Haddock is thought of as less firm than cod.

Preparation: Just as with cod, you can do almost anything with haddock—bake, broil, microwave, cook *en papillote,* poach, or use it in chowders and stews. Since you're probably paying premium prices for haddock, I'd suggest you don't hide its flavor with anything more than a light sauce. Haddock can be used interchangeably in recipes calling for cod, flounder, sole, halibut, cusk, and hake. Finnan haddie should be refrigerated and kept no more than 4 or 5 days.

Nutritional value: Another *very low-fat* fish, haddock offers only 87 calories and 57 milligrams of cholesterol in a single serving. Note that smoking haddock can boost the sodium value of fresh haddock from 68 to more than 700 milligrams.

Hake

Also known as: There are many different types of hake, including white and red hake from the Atlantic, Atlantic whiting (which is really silver hake), and Pacific whiting (or Pacific hake).

Market forms: What's commonly sold as fresh hake fillets is usually white hake. Both types of whiting are often sold headed and gutted, but Pacific whiting is also available in fillet form. (Atlantic whiting are generally small, weighing about a pound each.) Frozen whiting is usually imported.

Points of interest: Hake are related to cod but are often less expensive. Fillets may be sold as scrod or whitefish. Whiting has a reputation as one of the least expensive fish going. Saltwater fish.

Eating quality: Hake flesh is softer and more flavorful than that of other cod family members. Some types of hake flesh are an off-white color that turns white when cooked. Atlantic whiting has a mild, delicate flavor that's sometimes described as sweet.

Preparation: Because of its soft texture, some guidelines suggest slightly undercooking hake—8 rather than 10 minutes per inch of thickness. The crumbliness also means that you should keep your preparation methods for the hake family simple—recommendations include baking, sautéing, or using in fish cakes. But hake can also be broiled, grilled, poached, fried, or steamed.

Hake fillets work in many recipes calling for lean, white fish fillets —tomato-onion sauces are great accompaniments. Headed and gutted whiting can be grilled in a wire rack over hot coals after marinating in any combination of soy sauce, olive oil, lemon juice, brown sugar, grated ginger, chopped onions, garlic, and sherry. Whiting is also tasty baked in dry white wine with garlic and parsley. Hake is not recommended for chowders and stews because it will totally fall apart in cooking. The crumbliness, however, may be an asset for small children. Hake cannot be frozen for as long as some other types of lean, white fish.

Trade-offs: A most versatile fish, hake works best as a substitute for cod, haddock, and pollock. It can also be used in place of flounder, sole, and red snapper. Whiting works as a milder alternative in some rainbow trout recipes; if you ever come across whiting fillets, use them as you would flatfish such as flounder.

Nutritional value: Hake is *very low-fat* with about 90 calories plus 67 milligrams of cholesterol per serving.

Halibut

Market forms: fresh or frozen steaks, chunks, fillets (usually cut into smaller pieces known as "fletches").

Points of interest: The biggest flatfish in the oceans, the larger female halibut averages 100 to 200 pounds. Although halibut comes from both the East and West coasts, Pacific halibut makes up the major U.S. supply.

Eating quality: Halibut's delicious white meat is firm and mild-tasting but a bit more flavorful than flounder. The meat is a little on the sweet side. Halibut steaks have a large center bone that can easily be lifted out after cooking.

Preparation: Another versatile fish, halibut can be cooked almost any way. It's especially good marinated and broiled, as well as poached and served with a light hot or cold sauce (See Oven-Poached Halibut with Florentine Sauce on page 310). You can substitute halibut for flounder and sole in many recipes if you adjust cooking time for thickness. Use Pacific and Atlantic halibut interchangeably.

Nutritional value: Halibut falls into the *low-fat* category with its 110 calories and 32 milligrams of cholesterol.

Herring/sardines

Also known as: Sea herring. Shad are the largest herring-family members. Small, young herring are commonly sold as sardines. (McClane's *Encyclopedia of Fish Cookery* points out that the name "sardine" doesn't refer to any one type of fish; instead, it's a collective term applied to certain small herring family members that have soft bones.)

Market forms: Fresh herring is available in the drawn and dressed form, but it's hard to come by. You're likely familiar with the more common processed forms of herring—smoked and salted (as in kippered herring), pickled, or in a sour-cream sauce. Shad comes drawn, dressed, and as fillets. The smallest sardine-type herring are canned in dressed form, while the larger ones are packed as small steaks. Sardines are canned in oil, tomato or other sauces, and mustard; some are also smoked.

Points of interest: When you look at the omega-3 fatty acid levels of herring (see page 61), it should come as no surprise that their diets are largely made up of plankton. Saltwater fish.

Eating quality: The dark, full-flavored meat of fresh herring has a fine, soft texture that firms when it's pickled and smoked. Beware that large herring have many small, hairlike bones. Shad, for instance, has a reputation as a bony fish despite its good tasting, sweet, and delicate meat. Shad meat is lightish in color and soft in texture. Sardines have a soft, fine texture.

Preparation: Herring can be broiled or sautéed. One idea is to fillet herring, roll it in oatmeal, and broil it. Herring also works in milk-based chowders. An English dish layers herring in a baked "pie" with sliced potatoes and apples. The oily nature of shad makes it ideal for broiling.

Processed herring products are used as appetizers, as well as in salads and dips. To get rid of fat and calories, drain and blot sardines packed in oil. One main-dish serving idea for sardines is to gently fold them into a curried low-fat cream sauce (see page 296). You can also cut sardines into chunks and serve them as part of a salad made with chopped apples, celery, green grapes, and a low-fat salad dressing.

Nutritional value: Of the fish in the *medium-fat* category, Atlantic herring is on the high side for fat, while Pacific herring is high enough to make it into the *oily* fish group. Both are loaded with omega-3 fatty acids and have less than 80 milligrams of cholesterol per 3½-ounce serving. Calorie values are 158 for Atlantic and 195 for a serving of Pacific herring. Kippered and pickled Atlantic herring have more calories than the fresh version; both forms of processing boost sodium levels of natural raw herring from 90 to more than 850 milligrams. Shad is also an *oily* fish that has 197 calories per 3½ ounces.

Sardines are an excellent source of calcium because they're processed with their soft bones. When canned in oil and drained, they have a little more than 200 calories per 3½-ounce serving. Atlantic sardines have 142 milligrams of cholesterol, but USDA data indicate that Pacific sardines have less than half that amount. Sardines tend to be salty and can have upwards of 400 milligrams of sodium per serving.

(Nutrient values of sardines and other processed herring products can vary greatly from one product to the next.)

Lobster, American

Also known as: Northern lobster.

Market forms: The vast majority of American lobsters are sold live. But you can also buy freshly cooked whole lobsters, as well as fresh and frozen lobster meat.

Points of interest: Caught from Maine to New Jersey, American lobsters are slow growers, taking as long as 5 to 8 years to attain a weight of 1 pound.

Eating quality: Need I tell you that lobster meat is out of this world, with its sweet, distinctive taste and firm texture? Contrary to popular opinion, large lobsters are not necessarily tougher than their small counterparts. (It's overcooking that makes them tough.) Live lobsters can come with either a hard or soft shell, depending on whether a hard shell has had a chance to re-form after molting. Since the soft-shell variety tends to have less meat that's more watery, its price is generally lower. People who relish the green tomalley (the liver) or "coral" (the roe of females) in lobsters may be disappointed to learn that they're loaded with cholesterol.

Preparation: When trying to decide how much live lobster to buy for a crowd, you can figure that about a third of its weight is edible. (Purchasing guidelines are on pages 164 and 171). Boiling is considered the easiest way to cook live lobsters. Simply fill a large pot with enough water to cover the lobsters you intend to cook. Bring the water to a full boil, then drop the live critters in, head first. When the water returns to a boil, start timing, figuring 10 to 12 minutes for a 1-pound lobster and adding 2 to 3 minutes more for each additional pound. Cooking will turn the dark shells to their familiar bright red.

Incidentally, the reason why lobsters and crabs are cooked while still alive is that their uniquely textured flesh tends to harbor bacteria which proliferate once the crustaceans die. The only time it's safe to cook dead lobsters or crabs is when they're killed right before cooking.

Lobsters can also be steamed (see page 200), baked, broiled, or grilled. Before baking, broiling, or grilling, however, a whole lobster should be killed and split. A humane way to instantly do the deed is to place the lobster on its stomach on a hard surface. Then quickly insert the point of a sharp knife in the spot where the tail and body join. (The dead lobster may still move, but that's only its reflexes— not writhing in pain.) To split an uncooked lobster, Ruth Spear, in her book *Cooking Fish and Shellfish,* advises placing the body on its back and slitting the undershell right down the middle. Next, a heavy knife will allow you to split the lobster, starting at the head, from one end to the other. You may need a mallet or hammer to add force to the knife as it cuts through the hard shell on the lobster's back. Then take out and discard the small internal sac near the eyes, as well as the milky sac behind the eyes. The milky sac is the stomach, which should come out with the attached intestinal vein that runs down the tail section near the back shell. (Storage recommendations for lobster are on pages 175 and 176).

Nutritional value: American lobster is *very low-fat* and provides 90 calories, as well as 95 milligrams of cholesterol per serving. (See chapter 6, page 66, for a discussion of cholesterol in shellfish.) American lobster is quite a good source of zinc.

Lobster, spiny

Also known as: rock lobster. (Spiny lobster is sometimes called crawfish or crayfish but they are not one and the same.)

Market forms: Since the meat is all in the tail, spiny lobster is usually sold as cooked and uncooked tails, which may be frozen. In season, you may also encounter spiny lobster live.

Points of interest: These clawless creatures are grouped as either warm- or cold-water, depending on where they're caught. We receive cold- water lobster tails—which are considered firmer and better-tasting— from Australia, South Africa, and New Zealand. Our domestic supply is warm-water and comes mainly from Florida.

Eating quality: In *The Encyclopedia of Fish Cookery*, A. J. McClane says of spiny lobster, "Compared to the American lobster, its texture is coarser but of good flavor and tender when freshly prepared."

Preparation: Spiny-lobster tails can be boiled, deep-fried, broiled, or steamed. Baking is not advised because it toughens the meat. How- ever you cook it, spiny lobster should be cooked for a short time to assure tenderness. Since frozen or partially frozen tails tend to be tough if cooked as is, it's wise to thaw them completely in the refrigerator beforehand.

Nutritional value: Spiny lobster is also *very low-fat* and provides 112 calories per serving. With its 70 milligrams of cholesterol, spiny lobster is an excellent source of zinc.

Mackerel

Market forms: drawn, dressed, fillets (usually with skin), smoked, whole, canned.

Points of interest: Truly an underutilized fish species, mackerel is a member of the tuna family. The Massachusetts Division of Marine Fisheries estimates that only about 73 million of the greater than 2 billion pounds of mackerel off the Northeast Coast were caught in 1985. Indeed, many people are unfamiliar with mackerel—in a taste test sponsored by the Massachusetts Seafood Marketing Program, more than half of 500 participants had never tasted the fish. Eighty-five percent of them, however, liked the sample they were given.

Eating quality: In general, mackerel flesh can be described as oily and firm. The flesh tends to be darker than that of most fish. Mackerel flavor is considered to be full and pronounced, but can be sweet and light when the fish is fresh. Spanish mackerel is considered to be about the best for eating because of its lighter-colored, leaner flesh and milder flavor. Atlantic and Pacific mackerel are very similar and have darker flesh. King mackerel (sometimes mistakenly called kingfish, which is a lean, white, mild-flavored fish) also has dark flesh and a somewhat stronger taste.

Preparation: The oily nature of mackerel keeps it moist and tender, suiting the fish for broiling and grilling. A good soaking in a lime marinade will help firm and whiten the flesh, plus cut the oily flavor. Mackerel is often prepared as fillets, but may be cooked whole or—if the fish is large—in steaks. (I usually see drawn or dressed mackerel on the market, but ask my fish dealer to fillet it for me.) To remove bones from raw mackerel fillets, lie them skin side down. Feel for the center strip of bones (called pin bones) and cut with a sharp knife along each side. Firmly grasp one end of the strip and gently pull it out. Allow one large or two small fillets per person.

Since there's little worse than old mackerel, it's best eaten the day of purchase. It just doesn't keep well because of its rich oil reserves. Very fresh mackerel can be held for a day or two, but keep it in the coldest part of your refrigerator—away from the door. If you're dealing with whole mackerel, be sure to wash the cavity out well before cooking because it can be quite bloody.

Mackerel is complemented by acidic, tart marinades and sauces. Tomatoes, dry wine, and lemon work well with mackerel. You can also try it in soups and stews, steam it for salads, pan-fry, or bake. Mackerel is delicious in a yogurt sauce (see Mackerel with Creamy Cucumber-Dill Sauce on page 294) or a garlic sauce (see Mackerel in Creamy Garlic Sauce on page 281).

Trade-offs: bluefish, butterfish, herring, freshwater trout, and shad. Mackerel also works in some salmon and whitefish recipes. Cooked or canned mackerel can be used just like canned tuna and canned salmon.

Nutritional value: As you already know, mackerel is a higher-fat fish that's rich in the omega-3s. But it's not high in cholesterol, with less than 80 milligrams in a portion. At around 14 grams of fat per serving, Atlantic mackerel provides about double the level of total fat found in Pacific and Spanish mackerel. A portion of Atlantic mackerel has 205 calories—48 calories more than Pacific; 66 more than Spanish. Atlantic mackerel also has the highest omega-3 fatty-acid levels.

Mahimahi

Also known as: dolphinfish, dorado.

Market forms: most often skin-on fillets, but occasionally dressed.

Points of interest: No, dolphinfish are not our mammalian friends, the dolphins or porpoises. It's more appealing to call dolphinfish mahimahi—true finfish usually caught near Florida or Hawaii. Once a fancy of sportfishermen only, mahimahi is gaining an important footing in the commercial market. Watch for more frozen mahimahi from Ecuador, Japan, and Taiwan. Saltwater fish.

Eating quality: Mahimahi is delicious, with a flavor that's mild, delicate, and unique. The meat is a little like swordfish—light and firm —but mahimahi has a moist, large flake when cooked. Along the middle of its sides, mahimahi has dark meat that you may choose to remove.

Preparation: From broiling to poaching, you can cook mahimahi practically any way you want. If you keep the skin on during cooking, it helps to hold the flesh together. Mahimahi is great in a sweet-and-sour sauce or served as an appetizer—just cut in squares, marinate with lime juice, a little oil, and garlic, then broil. Thin steaks make great sandwiches. Try marinated mahimahi in Minty-Lime Grilled Mahimahi on page 275.

Trade-offs: halibut, fresh tuna, swordfish, shark, tilefish, black and red sea bass.

Nutritional value: Mahimahi is *very low-fat* and provides 85 calories per serving; it has 73 milligrams of cholesterol.

Monkfish

Also known as: allmouth, anglerfish, baudroie, bellyfish, frogfish, goosefish, lotte, monktail, sea devil.

Market forms: fillets, whole tails.

Points of interest: How did such an ugly fish attract so many names? Truly one of the most hideous finfish in the sea, monkfish were discarded as "trash fish" until about a decade ago. Now lotte, as the French call it, is sold in sophisticated restaurants and even made an appearance on Julia Child's TV show. Fortunately, monkfish is sold sans its ugly head—tail meat is the delicacy. Saltwater fish.

Eating quality: Sometimes called "poor man's lobster," monkfish really does resemble the expensive crustacean in both taste and texture. The white flesh of cooked monkfish has an unusually firm and meaty texture. The taste is mild, slightly sweet, and delicate. Tail-end fillets have no bones.

Preparation: If you're dealing with a whole tail, filleting is a simple task. Simply skin, then cut along the tail bone on either side and remove the two fillets. You'll find that each fillet has a tough grayish membrane on one side that's best pulled off before cooking.

You'll have your greatest successes with monkfish if you bake, broil, poach, or sautée it. Try lightly breaded and baked medallions (see Breaded Monkfish Medallions on page 276). The mild flavor of monkfish is enriched by light sauces and marinades. Its firm texture lends itself to skewering for kebabs or thin slicing (freeze for an hour first) for Chinese cuisine. Monkfish adds body to soups and stews, such as bouillabaisse. Try Saucy Monkfish and Scallops on page 286. If mixed with lobster or shrimp, monkfish will assume their taste. The lobster in lobster salad can be stretched by adding an equal amount of monkfish that's been cut in ¾-inch cubes and poached. Be forewarned that monkfish tends to shrink more than most other fish when it's cooked, especially if thick pieces are used.

Trade-offs: Monkfish works well in any dish that calls for scallops or firm, white fish. You can also substitute it in some recipes calling for lobster.

Nutritional value: Monkfish is *very low-fat* with just 76 calories and a mere 25 milligrams of cholesterol per serving.

Mullet

Also known as: Lisa. There are many species of mullet, including black, silver, and striped mullet. The last two are the most important commercial species in the U.S.

Market forms: drawn, dressed, fillets, whole.

Points of interest: Three-quarters of the nation's mullet comes from Florida. Mullet is recognized as one of Florida's most valuable finfish. Saltwater fish.

Eating quality: About a third of the meat you get in mullet fillets is dark and strong-flavored. But the remaining white meat is described as mild, sweet, and nutlike. Mullet flesh is firm but tender when cooked.

Preparation: Mullet can be baked, broiled, grilled, sautéed, smoked, or stuffed. Try it broiled, brushed with a sauce made of small amounts of olive oil and vinegar, lemon juice, crushed garlic, and Italian seasonings. You can also bake it whole with a stuffing of shrimp, bread cubes, onions, and celery. Mullet is not a good candidate for freezing, particularly if the dark meat is left intact.

Trade-offs: According to my sources, mullet really stands alone; it's difficult to compare it to other types of fish.

Nutritional value: Striped mullet is *low-fat* and provides 117 calories and 49 milligrams of cholesterol per serving.

Mussels

Also known as: blue mussels, moules.

Market forms: live, shucked, cooked meats, smoked, pickled. Live mussels are sold by the quart or the pound—you get anywhere between a dozen large and 15 to 20 smaller mussels per pound. A quart contains 1½ to 2 pounds.

Points of interest: Until recently, these bluish-black shelled mollusks were not popular in the U.S. As the demand is increasing, we'll likely see more farm-raised mussels, which tend to be plumper and of more uniform size than their naturally grown counterparts. Cultivated mussels are also unlikely to have the pearls that can form in large wild mussels. If you harvest your own, first check with local public health authorities to be certain that the intended waters are not polluted or plagued with red tide, for mussels are more severely affected by red tide than are other bivalves. (See page 85 for more on red tide.) If you happen to find one of the tiny crabs that sometimes live inside mussel shells, it's okay to go ahead and eat both the crab and the mussel.

Eating quality: Because they don't bury themselves in sand the way clams do, mussels tend to be much less gritty. Cooked mussels sport an orange, cream, or tan color and offer a delicate, slightly sweet taste. When cooked properly, they're very tender.

Preparation: If you're using them as appetizers, figure on 10 to 12 mussels per person; for entrées, allow 18 to 24 for each diner. Cultivated mussels are cleaned and ready to use. But if you're starting from scratch with uncleaned live mussels, start by running them under cold water, pulling out the tough, brown fibers with your fingers (aided by a dull knife blade) or pliers. (Known as the beard, these fibers are used by the mussel to fasten itself onto hard surfaces; it's recommended that you don't de-beard mussels until right before you're ready to serve them.) To remove debris stuck on the shell, scrub with a stiff brush or plastic pot scrubber. Throw out any mussels that feel unusually heavy because they're probably filled with sand or mud that you'll never adequately remove.

It's important to make sure that all the mussels are alive by holding each one between your thumb and forefinger and gently trying to slide the top shell across the bottom one. Since shells of live mussels resist moving, discard any that slide easily. Live mussels will also close up if they're gaping—test them by tapping on the counter. Finally, soak the live mussels in a large pan of cold water for an hour or so. To avoid scooping up the sand that settles on the bottom, lift the mussels out of the water when you're ready for cooking. (Because soaking can dilute flavor, some experts say not to do it. Mussels that are commercially available shouldn't need to be soaked.)

To cook, use a pan that's large enough that you can add the mussels in a shallow, uncrowded layer. Don't immerse them in water—you only need a cup or so of liquid to steam mussels. Try adding a bit of wine, chopped vegetables, and some herbs for flavor. Cover the pot and steam—usually 6 to 7 minutes is adequate cooking time for the amount of mussels you'd serve to 4 people. Shake the pan a couple of times during cooking. Be sure not to overcook or you'll wind up with shrunken, tough meat. Since cooked mussels should open up, discard any that remain shut after heating.

You can eat the entire meat as it is or dip it in lemon juice, cocktail sauce, or (if you must) butter or margarine. The broth can be saved for soups, but drain it carefully to leave behind any sand. Mussels are especially good in Italian sauces and served with pasta (see Steamed Mussels Marinara on page 236). They can also be added to cold salads. You can freeze raw or cooked mussels, but use them soon because the texture will deteriorate.

Trade-offs: Use mussels as you would clams; you may even find that they are more versatile. Mussels also often work in place of oysters.

Nutritional value: Mussels are *low-fat* and have only 86 calories and 28 milligrams of cholesterol per serving. At 12 grams, protein content is a bit lower than that of other seafoods. But that slight disadvantage is far outweighed by the high amount of iron in mussels—about 4 milligrams in a single serving.

Ocean perch and Pacific rockfish

Also known as: A confusing kettle of nomenclature, Atlantic Ocean perch (also called redfish and rosefish), Pacific Ocean perch, and West Coast rockfish are all members of the same fish family. Ocean perch may also be called sea or saltwater perch, although they're not kin to freshwater perch such as yellow perch. To muddle matters further, Pacific Ocean perch can be called snapper in California, Oregon, and Washington. They're not related, however, to the red snapper caught off the coast of Florida.

Market forms: drawn, dressed, fillets (fresh and frozen), whole. Atlantic perch are usually sold skin-on as are most other reddish-skinned rockfish. Otherwise, fillets are commonly sold skinless. Frozen fillets come from Iceland and Canada, as well as the U.S.

Points of interest: Ocean perch—from both the Atlantic and Pacific—have made it big in the Midwest; they're the number-one retail seafood in many areas.

Eating quality: Ocean perch and rockfish fillets taste similar to one another. The flesh can be white or pinkish, depending upon whether the fish were bled at sea. When cooked, colored meat tends to turn white. Ocean perch and rockfish cook up firm and tender with a fine flakiness. Their taste is mild and delicate, but more flavorful than popular white-fleshed fish such as flounder and cod.

Preparation: Ocean perch and rockfish fillets are best broiled, fried, poached, sautéed, and steamed. Allow about two fillets per person. The skin is very tough and should be removed before cooking. If not, serve fillets skin-side down so people can scrape away the flesh, leaving the skin behind. Ocean perch and rockfish go hand in hand with almost any kind of sauce. Try whole fish in a sweet-and-sour sauce. Fillets are tasty baked with tomato sauce, garlic, onions, green pepper, and oregano; top with low-fat cheese and bread crumbs.

Trade-offs: You can use ocean perch and rockfish fillets as you would flounder—with the added advantage that they're less likely than flounder to fall apart when cooked. In many recipes, you can also substitute ocean perch and rockfish for freshwater catfish, grouper, porgy, orange roughy, and tilapia.

Nutritional value: Pacific rockfish and ocean perch are *very low-fat* and provide under 100 calories per serving. They offer less than 45 milligrams of cholesterol.

Orange roughy

Also known as: deep sea perch, Australian sole.

Market forms: skinless fillets—flown in from New Zealand to major U.S. cities. Virtually all orange roughy is or has been frozen. If it's sold as "fresh," it just means that the fish wasn't refrozen after filleting and skinning.

Points of interest: Unknown as a fish species just a decade ago, orange roughy made the U.S. commercial scene in 1982 and took off within a year. The demand soared—and led to rising prices—because of a well-coordinated marketing program and orange roughy's versatility. Watch for other foreign imports such as leatherjacket (with flesh similar to orange roughy's), painted sweet lips (a stand-in for red drum), scarlet red snapper (a substitute for Gulf of Mexico red snapper), and cod-like hoki. Saltwater fish.

Eating quality: The pearl-white fillets hold up extremely well under a variety of cooking methods. Orange roughy's meat tastes delightfully light and mild—somewhat like sole—but tends to be slightly on the sweet side. The flesh is firm but tender.

Preparation: You name it and you can do it with orange roughy—from baking to stewing. For those who never have any success cooking fish, these fillets are considered indestructible. For a quick supper try marinating orange roughy in teriyaki sauce (see page 313) and tossing it on the grill. Or you can simply sautée fillets coated with a little flour, salt, and pepper in a small amount of margarine. Orange roughy is also good with an orange sauce (see page 314) or lightly sautéed in a small amount of margarine, white wine, mushrooms, and herbs. (Once thawed, orange roughy should not be refrozen.)

Trade-offs: sole, flounder, cod, haddock, halibut, Greenland turbot, ocean perch, rockfish, tilapia.

Nutritional value: The available USDA data suggest that orange roughy is *medium-fat* and around 125 calories per serving. But the actual fat and calorie values may be much lower because most of the fat is a waxy substance that may not be metabolized. Therefore, orange roughy is probably *very low-fat* and likely offers less than 100 calories per serving. Cholesterol content is very low at 20 milligrams.

Oysters, Eastern

Also known as: Atlantic oyster, American oyster.

Market forms: live, fresh-shucked, frozen shucked, canned, smoked.

Points of interest: The U.S. surpasses all other countries in its production of oysters. The Eastern oyster, which is found from Cape Cod to the Gulf, takes up about 85 percent of the nation's oyster harvest.

Oyster numbers have been on the decline because of shoreline development, disease, natural predators, and pollution. (The West Coast supplies the Pacific oyster, as well as the small Olympia oyster. In addition, farmed oysters are available.)

Eating quality: The way an oyster looks and tastes depends on what it eats and where it's caught. The flavor depends on the type of algae oysters eat—some oysters taste a bit coppery, while others are more salty. Regardless, oysters are described as "tender and succulent." Coloring is usually cream, tan, or gray. But don't hesitate to eat variations that are greenish, reddish, pinkish, or brown. Names of oysters on restaurant menus often reveal their origin—say, Chesapeake Bay oysters or Blue Point oysters (from Long Island). It's true that oysters are less tasty in the summer because they spawn then. But contrary to popular rumor, it's safe to eat them during summer months lacking the letter *r* in their names (that is, unless a health advisory has been issued).

Preparation: I must confess that I'm among those who relish raw oysters —the risks of this fancy are spelled out on page 89. They're also great deep-fried. On a more healthful note, however, oysters can be poached, baked, sautéed, broiled, steamed, stewed, escalloped, and used in stuffings. One rule of thumb in cooking oysters is never to boil them—it rubberizes the meat. Unfortunately, the cooking guidelines for best eating, which advise heating at a low to moderate temperature just until the thin edges of the oyster begin to show signs of ruffling, may not be adequate to inactivate harmful organisms (see page 185). Purchasing guidelines are on pages 164 and 171; storage suggestions are on page 176; and cleaning instructions are on page 183. There are a number of ways to open oysters, but the easiest (and safest) is on page 184.

Nutritional value: Both Eastern and Pacific oysters are *low-fat* mollusks. While the USDA has no data on cholesterol in Pacific oysters, Eastern have just 55 milligrams. Both are excellent sources of iron and outstanding for their zinc contributions.

Perch

Also known as: lake perch or yellow perch. But the name "perch" is loosely applied to a number of unrelated freshwater and saltwater fish species. True perch are members of the *Perca* family; most are freshwater creatures with our yellow perch among them.

Market forms: Most yellow perch is available in fillet form. You may also find it whole and dressed.

Points of interest: Yellow perch are small, generally running less than a pound in weight. They comprise one of the most important Great Lakes commercial species of fish and command some of the highest prices of lake fish. Great numbers of yellow perch are also caught recreationally.

Eating quality: Yellow perch has solid, firm white flesh.

Preparation: Because of its small size, most yellow perch is pan-fried. But it can be cooked by just about any cooking method. Fillets are quite easy to obtain from whole fish and can be used in most recipes calling for firm, white-fleshed fish fillets.

Nutritional value: Freshwater perch, in general, are *very low-fat* with only 91 calories and a somewhat high 90 milligrams of cholesterol.

Pike

Market forms: fillets and steaks, fresh and frozen. Also available drawn and dressed.

Points of interest: Pike is primarily a game fish, but some is imported for commercial sale from Canada. Of the five North American pike species, only the northern pike and muskellunge (the largest pike) are of culinary importance. Incidentally, what's known as walleye or yellow pike is really a member of the freshwater-perch family.

Eating quality: All the books say that pike is underrated as a food fish in this country. Although it does tend to be on the bony side, pike meat is sweet and white with a firm flake. When choosing a cooking method, you should take into account the fact that pike tends to be somewhat dry.

Preparation: Most people pan-fry pike, but McClane stresses that baking and poaching are the best cooking methods. Pike can also be steamed, broiled, and grilled. Moist stuffings counteract pike's rather dry nature. Since the length of pike can present a problem, it's fine to cut the fish into individual serving sizes (center cuts can be stuffed and cooked) or—with larger fish—cut it into steaks. When handling a freshly caught pike, scaling is much easier if you deal with the dense, slimy coating on the skin by pouring boiling water over the fish. This will coagulate the slime and loosen the scales.

Nutritional value: Per serving, *very low-fat* northern pike provides 88 calories and 39 milligrams of cholesterol.

Pollock (Atlantic)

Also known as: Boston bluefish, a confusing name chosen to attractively market pollock. But pollock is not related to true bluefish—a darker, oilier fish. Small pollock can be marketed as scrod in the U.S.

Market forms: drawn, dressed, fillets (skinless), smoked, steaks, whole; some fillets and steaks are frozen.

Points of interest: As popular haddock and cod supplies dwindle, Atlantic pollock, which is similar in taste and texture, is gaining an important footing in the commercial market. Available year-round, the cost of pollock is generally much lower than that of its counterparts.

Eating quality: The meaty flesh of pollock has a thin layer of dark, maroon-tinted meat on one side. If the dark side has turned brown, dark tan, or gray, it's a sign that the fillet is not fresh. The remainder of a pollock fillet is off-white or creamy tan, but it whitens with cooking. Pollock is more flavorful than cod and haddock. The Pacific Coast sports its own type of pollock, known as Alaska pollock; it's an entirely different species. Softer in texture than the Atlantic variety, the snow-white meat of Alaska pollock is a prime ingredient for fish sticks.

Preparation: Cook pollock any way you want. The meaty texture lends itself well to soups and stews. If you like, you can remove the somewhat stronger-tasting darker flesh that appears just under the skin. Try pollock baked with a covering of bread crumbs (see page 252) or in a creamy casserole with broccoli (see page 278).

Trade-offs: Use pollock as you would cod, haddock, or hake. It works well in any recipe calling for lean, white fish. Because of its meaty texture, you can even try substituting it in some meat and poultry recipes (see Fillet of Pollock Parmigiana on page 282).

Nutritional value: The *very low-fat* nature of pollock is reflected in its low calorie content—92 in a serving. Pollock has 71 milligrams of cholesterol.

Pompano

Also known as: Florida pompano (note that Florida pompano is a different fish than the member of the butterfish family known as Pacific or California pompano).

Market forms: dressed, drawn, fillets, whole.

Points of interest: Florida supplies most commercially caught pompano. Saltwater fish.

Eating quality: With its reputation as one of the more expensive fish going, pompano is prized as one of the tastiest. Its white meat is firm but delicate.

Preparation: You can cook pompano almost any way, but broiling, grilling, baking, sautéing, and cooking *en papillote* are most highly recommended.

Nutritional value: Despite the fact that it's comparatively low in omega-3 fatty acids, Florida pompano is one of the fattier fish in the *medium-fat* fish category. It contains 50 milligrams of cholesterol.

Porgy

Also known as: scup, paugie, fair maid.

Market forms: drawn, dressed, occasionally fillets, whole.

Points of interest: Porgies have a following on the East Coast, where they are often used as panfish. Mediterranean ethnic groups tend to favor porgies. Although the names scup and porgy tend to be used interchangeably, scup is just one of the many types of porgy. Saltwater fish.

Eating quality: Porgy offers firm, coarsely-grained flesh. The light-colored meat tastes rather mild and delicate but has its own distinctive, slightly sweet flavor—not unlike that of freshwater trout. Beware—porgies are known for having many small, sharp bones.

Preparation: If you have a choice, select larger porgies because they make it easier to separate the flesh from the bones. Scaling the fish can be a chore since scales tend to adhere tightly—the job is easier if the fish is wet. Simple cooking methods are recommended, such as pan-frying, grilling, and poaching. Or try steaming porgy Chinese-style. To pan-fry, just dip the fish in milk, then flour with seasonings. Brown in a small amount of margarine, lemon juice, and parsley. You can also stuff dressed scup with sautéed onions, tomatoes, zucchini, and green peppers. Cover and bake in a little white wine. To tell if the meat is done, slide a fork down the length of the backbone—if ready, the flesh will lift away from the bone.

Trade-offs: butterfish, rockfish, ocean perch.

Nutritional value: Porgy is *low-fat* and provides 105 calories in a serving.

Pout

Also known as: ocean pout, yellow pout, muttonfish. Pout's long, narrow body has also earned it the names eelpout, yellow eel, and conger eel, although it's not an eel at all.

Market forms: fillets.

Points of interest: Pout is caught in both the Atlantic and Pacific oceans. It's most plentiful in New England from September through May. But you've probably never seen pout in the fish market or grocery store because you and other consumers are not asking for it. In fact, you're missing out, as shown in one taste test in which pout was favored over well-liked flounder! If you do find it, you'll likely discover that pout is much cheaper than flatfish, cod, and haddock. Once popular, pout lost its favor because of a tendency to harbor parasites. Fortunately, processors now remove these harmless—albeit unpalatable—parasites. Truly underutilized, pout largely remains an unknown to most people.

Eating quality: Pout's white meat bears few bones. Its fillets are long and thin, cook up firm, and have a sweet, mild taste.

Preparation: Some say pout fillets are best poached. Their shape lends itself to rolling and stuffing. Pout can also be fried, stir-fried, or used in soups. Since its texture is so firm, a tasty way to serve pout fillets is to lightly bread them and sauté as cutlets. (Try pout fillets in place of skate wings in the recipe on page 257). Note that broiling tends to dry out pout. According to Ralph Boragine of the Rhode Island Seafood Council, pounding pout fillets with the flat side of a knife will make them less likely to curl when cooked, as well as more tender and flaky.

Trade-offs: A multipurpose fish, pout can be used in most recipes calling for lean, white fish. Specifically, use pout in place of flatfish, cod, pollock, ocean perch, cusk, and wolffish.

Nutritional value: Pout is another *very low-fat* fish; a serving provides a mere 79 calories and 52 milligrams of cholesterol.

Red snapper

Market forms: unskinned fillets, drawn, dressed, head-on gutted.

Points of interest: Red snapper is the best-known, most popular, and most economically valuable of the 15 snapper species found in U.S. waters. As mentioned previously, don't confuse it with Pacific Ocean perch, which is sometimes marketed as snapper. When sold in a different state than caught, only true red snapper may be legally sold as such. Despite its high demand, the supply of red snapper is not large because it's fairly difficult to catch. In fact, most red snapper is sold to restaurants. Not surprisingly, red snapper prices run on the high side. You may come across the following red snapper relatives on the commercial market: yellowtail, silk, mutton, vermillion, mangrove, and lane. Saltwater fish.

Eating quality: From the culinary vantage point, red snapper has a reputation as a premier fish. Its light meat is firm and mild with a flavor all its own. In general, other members of the snapper family have slightly darker meat that's less expensive than red snapper.

Preparation: Red snapper can be cooked just about any way, but because of its bright-red skin, it presents itself especially well when the whole fish is stuffed and baked. You can also poach red snapper or cook it *en papillote.* Fish cookbooks remind their readers to ask for the head, bones, and skin of red snapper to make a tasty stock. Red snapper lasts quite a long time if refrigerated properly.

Nutritional information: The USDA provides values for 3½ ounces of "mixed species" of snapper as follows: 100 calories and 37 milligrams of cholesterol. Snapper is *very low-fat.*

Sablefish

Also known as: Alaska cod, black cod. Sablefish is sometimes sold as butterfish.

Market forms: Sablefish is commonly marketed as smoked fillets and chunks, but fresh steaks and fillets are becoming more available.

Points of interest: Caught in the Pacific Ocean—from Alaska down to California—sablefish is not related to its sometimes namesakes, cod and butterfish. According to the trade journal *Seafood Business,* market demand for sablefish has yet to catch up with the amount of sablefish available.

Eating quality: The white, oily flesh of sablefish has a rich, distinctive —yet delicate—flavor. Cooked meat has an unusually velvety texture that's also flaky and tender. The moist flesh does not dry out easily.

Preparation: The oiliness of sablefish begs for marinating, then broiling or grilling. A simple marinade of lemon juice, grated lemon peel, salt, and small amounts of brown sugar and oil will do. You can also bake, poach, steam, or stew it. Try microwaved sablefish, topped with oregano, lemon juice, chopped scallions, minced garlic, salt, pepper, and tomato slices. (The fat content of sablefish makes for short refrigerator life—one to two days at best for fresh and one month for frozen.)

Trade-offs: Sablefish is considered in a class of its own, but you can try it in recipes calling for other oily fish.

Nutritional value: Sablefish is *oily* and an excellent source of omega-3s. It provides 195 calories, but only 49 milligrams of cholesterol per serving.

Salmon

Market forms: steaks, fillets, whole, chunks, smoked, canned. High-quality frozen salmon is available year-round and often commands a lower price than fresh. If you buy previously frozen salmon, don't refreeze it.

Points of interest: Salmon are anadromous, which means that they live in salt water, returning to the freshwater streams and rivers where they were born to reproduce. There are 6 major salmon species marketed in this country; one from the Atlantic, the others from the Pacific Coast. Differences are as follows.

Atlantic salmon. It's difficult to come by wild Atlantic salmon; most Atlantic salmon available in the U.S. is farm-raised and imported. It may be marketed according to its source—Norwegian or Icelandic salmon, for instance. (Some Atlantic salmon is also farm-raised in Maine and Canada.) The rich-tasting flesh of Atlantic salmon is pink to red or orange when raw; it tends to turn pink when cooked. Although its texture is still considered firm, Atlantic salmon flesh tends to be somewhat softer than that of some other species.

Chinook salmon. A market competitor of Atlantic salmon, chinook or king salmon is considered the finest and most expensive of the Pacific salmons. You may see it marketed according to where it was caught, a determinant of quality. Like Atlantic salmon, chinook is relatively soft. Its oily meat is red in color.

Coho salmon. The medium-red flesh of coho salmon—also called silver salmon (not to be confused with silverbrites or chums below)—is a bit lighter in color than that of chinook salmon. Coho is also less oily and firmer. When cooked, it tends to turn orange or pink.

Sockeye salmon. You often see it as red salmon and, sometimes, as blueback salmon. It's prized for its deep-red flesh. Canned sockeye salmon commands a premium price.

Chum salmon. Also called silverbrites and semibrites, chum salmon tend to have meat that's on the orange side and is lighter in both color and taste than other Pacific types. It tends to turn pink to gray upon cooking. Most chum salmon is frozen, but some is canned.

Pink salmon. Outnumbering other Pacific species, pink salmon or "humpies" are also the smallest. Their flesh is softer and pinker compared to other types of salmon. West Coast markets sometimes carry it fresh, but most pink salmon is canned.

Preparation: Keep salmon icy cold and use it promptly because of its relatively high oil content. Uncanned, smoked salmon should also be refrigerated. Salmon steaks and fillets are meant for broiling or grilling. Salmon also lends itself to poaching, sautéing, steaming, and baking. Lemony or lime-based marinades complement its unique flavor. Even though it's not a terribly bony fish, be sure to check fresh salmon carefully for bones—any that are present are usually firmly embedded. You can pull them out with needle-nose pliers or fingernails. Cold, cooked salmon and canned salmon make healthful hamburger substitutes in patties (see Salmon Burgers on page 256), as well as work nicely in cold salads and mousses.

Nutritional value: Even though we tend to think of salmon as fatty fish, only chinook salmon falls into the *oily* category; not surprisingly, it's also the highest in calories of the salmons at 180 per serving. Atlantic, coho, and sockeye are all *medium-fat* fish which average around 150 calories per portion. In the *low-fat* group come chum and pink salmon—they're also lowest in calories at 120 and 116, respectively. All 6 types of salmon are good omega-3 sources, but at more than 1,000 milligrams each, Atlantic, chinook, sockeye, and pink have significantly more than chum and coho. None of the salmon types has more than 75 milligrams of cholesterol (see page 60 for more detail).

Even though sodium levels of canned and smoked products vary considerably from one brand to the next, you can bet that both processes markedly boost the naturally low sodium levels in fresh salmon. The USDA lists canned pink salmon at 554 milligrams of sodium per 3½-ounce serving; smoked chinook salmon has 784 milligrams. Canned salmon is an excellent source of calcium, however, when it's processed (and eaten) bones and all. Incidentally, lox is a salt-cured, lightly smoked salmon that's soaked in fresh water to remove some of the salt. Nevertheless, lox can still be very salty—the USDA places lox at 2,000 milligrams of sodium per portion. (But sodium levels in different lox products can vary.) Gravlox—which is raw salmon marinated in salt, sugar, and seasonings—would also be quite high in sodium.

Scallops

Market forms: shucked muscle meats. Most scallops are sold fresh, but frozen are also available. Three major types of scallops are available on the U.S. market.

Sea scallops. These are the largest type, which can grow as large as 2 inches in diameter. The majority are from the Atlantic Coast, but a small number come from the Pacific.

Bay scallops. Also known as Cape Cod scallops, they run from ½ to ¾ inch in diameter. Most are found from Cape Cod to Long Island.

Calico scallops. The smallest type, these meats are about ½ inch across. They're mainly taken from the Florida coast. Some people consider calicos to be less tasty and tougher than bay scallops—calico scallops are definitely less expensive.

Points of interest: When you eat a scallop, you're actually downing the oversized muscle that opens and shuts the mollusk's two shells. Unlike us, Europeans eat the entire scallop meat.

Eating quality: Most people are familiar with the sweet taste and firm texture of this mollusk that often pleases the most ardent fish hater. Scallops are usually milky white in color, but are fine to eat if they're tannish, light pink, orangeish, or blue-tinged.

Preparation: Scallops can be broiled, baked, stir-fried, escalloped, poached, oven-fried, pan-fried, and sautéed. (It's a good idea to dry scallops well before pan-frying or sautéing.) Sea scallops are ideal for marinating and grilling. And scallops, in general, are wonderful in light cream sauces, tomato-based dishes, and in cold salads. ("Ceviche" or marinated raw scallops are quite popular, but I'm not keen on raw seafood, as you saw in chapter 7.)

Whatever cooking method you choose, make it quick—for overheating yields a dry, chewy scallop. This is especially important for calico scallops, which are commonly steamed open for shucking. The result is that you buy a partially cooked scallop with a whitish, sharp outer edge. (This allows you to distinguish them from bay scallops.) You can use the different types of scallops interchangeably in recipes if you adjust cooking time according to the size. Sea scallops often have to be cut when used in recipes calling for smaller scallops. Frozen scallops should be thawed in the refrigerator and can then be used just like fresh ones. (Purchasing guidelines for scallops are on pages 164 and 171. Storage suggestions are on page 176).

Nutritional value: Scallops are *very low-fat;* they provide just 88 calories and 33 milligrams of cholesterol per serving.

Sea trout—see "weakfish."

Shark

Also known as: A number of different kinds of shark are caught as food fish in the U.S. See below for the specifics on blacktip, blue, and mako shark, as well as dogfish.

Market forms: steaks, occasionally fillets.

Points of interest: Shark meat calls to mind a dinner party thrown by a food scientist friend of mine back in the mid-seventies. Guests were shocked to learn that the gourmet fish they were eating was none other than the stereotypical man-eater. Now recovered from an image problem, shark is no longer disguised as "grayfish," "whitefish," or "catch of the day" on restaurant menus. Mako shark in particular has established a name for itself and is preferred by some to swordfish. One distinction that sharks have from other kinds of fish is an unusually high blood level of urea, which gives off a strong ammonia odor if the fish aren't bled and/or iced immediately after they're caught. Saltwater fish.

Eating quality: A real plus is the lack of bones in shark meat—the result of a nonbony skeleton made up of cartilage. The taste, color, and texture of different kinds of shark meat vary—some are similar to swordfish; others have white, mild-tasting meat. (See individual descriptions below.)

Preparation: Although a lingering essence of ammonia is not harmful, I wouldn't buy shark that has a strong smell. If just a hint of ammonia odor remains, however, you can neutralize it by soaking the raw fish in a weak acidic solution for at least 4 hours in the refrigerator. Use ½ teaspoon lemon juice or 1 tablespoon vinegar for each pound of fish plus enough cold water to cover it. A soaking in milk or buttermilk for a half-hour or so before cooking will also do the trick. Shark tends not to keep well, so use it as soon after purchase as possible.

Dogfish. The British—with their fancy for dogfish in fish and chips —receive much of our catch of this small shark. The little sold here may be marketed as "grayfish" or just plain "shark"—in steak or fillet form. Since the white meat of dogfish is firm, smooth, and mild-flavored, cook it as you would any lean fish such as cod.

Blue shark. More available on the Pacific Coast, this shark offers snow-white meat of a mild flavor. Described as similar to halibut, blue-shark meat can be baked, broiled, fried, poached, or sautéed. If you purchase it frozen, thaw blue shark in the refrigerator before cooking to allow some of its watery juices to escape. Then blot well before cooking.

Blacktip shark. Blacktips also have very white flesh. Because it's somewhat dry, be careful not to overcook it. A good bet is to stir-fry blacktip-shark meat.

Mako shark. The most popular member of the shark family from the culinary standpoint, mako shark is a close competitor of swordfish in color, taste, and firm, dense texture. But mako shark is usually less expensive than swordfish. Better still, mako tends to be moister and less fishy-tasting than swordfish. (Sometimes a smaller fish, mackerel shark, is marketed as mako; the two taste just about the same.) Mako shark can be baked, broiled, grilled (try it marinated, chunked, and skewered), steamed, and stir-fried.

Trade-offs: In many recipes, you can use mako shark in place of swordfish, bluefish, mackerel, mullet, shad, or tuna. Swap mako shark for swordfish in Sweet'n' Sour Swordfish on page 293 or use it in Broiled Basil Swordfish on page 253.

Nutritional value: In general, shark is *low-fat* and offers approximately 130 calories in a 3½-ounce raw portion; cholesterol levels are around 50 milligrams.

Shrimp

Types/market forms: Of the more than 300 species of shrimp worldwide, *The Seafood Handbook* by *Seafood Business* mentions three important commercial groups. The largest is warm-water or tropical shrimp, which includes the white, brown, and rock shrimp caught in our own waters. Another group is cold-water shrimp from New England, Alaska, the West Coast, Norway, and Canada. Finally, there are numerous types of freshwater prawns which are largely caught in Asian countries. Incidentally, McClane points out that, although the term "prawns" properly refers to freshwater shrimp species, and "shrimps" to all marine types, the terms are not always used properly on the commercial market.

As mentioned in chapter 9, most shrimp marketed in this country is frozen or has been previously frozen. What you buy as fresh, raw shrimp has commonly been sold to retailers in frozen block form. They thaw it and should display it as "previously frozen" so buyers know not to refreeze the shrimp. (Occasionally, you'll come across locally caught shrimp that's never been frozen, but it's quite rare.)

Raw, frozen shrimp is typically sold headless and in the shell—regardless of species or color, this form of shrimp is called "green." You can also buy shrimp peeled, peeled and deveined, cooked and peeled, flash-frozen (in the frozen-food case), and canned. The cost of shrimp is usually determined by size, ranging from extracolossal to tiny; the larger the shrimp, the more expensive.

Points of interest: Speaking of money, shrimp is our most valuable seafood resource. In addition to domestically caught wild shrimp, we have access to aquacultured shrimp and imported shrimp, sources which are expanding. In fact, more than half of our available shrimp is imported from places such as Mexico, Ecuador, Central America, and India. Thailand produces the majority of imported canned shrimp. Most shrimp is preserved with sulfites, a concern for certain asthmatics (see page 83).

Eating quality: I hardly need to describe the taste and texture of shrimp to the American public. There are differences, however, that you may not be aware of in the different types of shrimp on the commercial market. So-called brown shrimp, for example, has a somewhat stronger taste than white shrimp. Rock shrimp is known for firmness and flavor that's somewhat lobsterlike. Cold-water shrimp is considered to have a slightly sweet taste compared to other types; it's usually smaller than warm-water shrimp. Cold-water shrimp doesn't have to be deveined before eating.

Preparation: Guidelines for steaming shrimp are on page 201, but you can also bake (with stuffing), broil, fry, boil, sauté, or stir-fry shrimp. As with most shellfish, cooking time—which depends on the size of shrimp and whether it's thawed or frozen—should be as short as possible to assure a tender result. The idea is to cook shrimp until the meat changes from translucent to an opaque white—just until the meat loses its glossy appearance and curls up. To stop the cooking process, immediately rinse shrimp in cool water. When using the type of peeled, deveined shrimp that you buy from the frozen-food case, there's no need to thaw before cooking. (The package should have directions.) Since shrimp runs on the expensive side, stretch it by adding it to soups, casseroles, salads, and dips. You may want to slightly undercook shrimp that will undergo additional cooking in a casserole or a sauce. In fact, you're probably better off not precooking shrimp intended for a slow-cooking sauce—simply add raw shrimp at the end of the cooking time and heat just until done.

Although larger shrimp lose a smaller percentage of their body weight when cooked, a general rule of thumb is that every two pounds of raw, headless shrimp will yield about a pound of cooked, peeled, and deveined shrimp. Some people feel that shrimp is more tasty if cooked in the shell; it's also easier to peel cooked shrimp. (For guidelines on cleaning shrimp, turn to page 184. Purchasing tips are on pages 164 and 171.) Since canned shrimp is already cooked and peeled, just cook long enough to heat them through in recipes. (I like to rinse and drain canned shrimp before using.)

Raw, unfrozen shrimp can be stored in a covered container in a very cold refrigerator (see page 175) for 3 to 4 days; cooked shrimp should be refrigerated and eaten within 5 days.

Nutritional information: The USDA lumps the various types of shrimp together as "mixed species." As such, shrimp is *very low-fat;* per 3½-ounce portion, it provides 106 calories and 152 milligrams of cholesterol. (See page 66 for a discussion of cholesterol variability in fish.)

Skate

Also known as: ray, raja, rayfish. (Skates and rays are not really the same, but the names tend to be used interchangeably commercially. The two are similar-tasting. Actually, there are a number of species of both skates and rays.)

Market forms: wings—whole, trimmed and skinned, or filleted.

Points of interest: I was as hesitant as the next person to try this odd-looking, kite-shaped fish. In fact—based solely on the fish's homely appearance—skate was the one fish that my family refused to try when I researched this book. It's their loss—for I found skate-wing fillets to be among the best seafoods I've eaten. You probably won't find skate in your fish market unless you ask for it because it's a fish that's often tossed back or sold as bait. Yet in Europe, skate wings are prized.

Like sharks, skates have cartilage (running crosswise through the center of each wing) rather than a bony skeleton. The center body portion of skate is cut out and discarded by fishermen at sea—only the wings are landed. It's often said that "imitation scallops" are punched out of skate wings and sold to unsuspecting consumers. In reality, however, the practice is not common. Besides, you can identify scallops by their vertical striations, while punched skate would have horizontal lines. Saltwater fish.

Eating quality: Simply put, the meat is delicious. Once the wings are skinned, it's a pleasant surprise to find that they resemble pearly angel's wings. Skate's white-colored flesh is mild and delicate in flavor —much like that of scallops. Similar to crabmeat in texture, cooked skate wings have long fibers or strands of meat and no bones. Freshly caught skate is about the only fish that gets better with age—the taste and texture improve when it's kept for several days in the refrigerator.

Preparation: Since each skate wing yields two thin fillets, one small wing or half of a large wing is plenty for each person. If your stomach is at all weak, try asking your fish dealer to fillet it for you—or at least to skin it. If you decide to tackle the job yourself, the edibility of both skinned and skinless wings is said to be enhanced by soaking them before cooking in a solution consisting of 2 tablespoons white vinegar per quart of water. Refrigerate in the solution for 2 to 3 hours. Very fresh skate wings with skin intact can form a slimy coating that can be wiped off or scraped with a knife.

Although you can skin them raw, the easiest way to skin and fillet whole skate wings is to start by poaching them. For extra flavor, you can add wine, onions, parsley, carrots, and celery to the cooking water. Lower the wings into the hot liquid (you'll need one large pan for each wing that you cook). Make sure that the liquid covers the fish. Bring the broth to a boil, then lower it to a simmer, cover, and poach for about 5 minutes. At this point, the skin should start to bubble up. Remove the wings from the water and run cold water over them until they're cool enough for handling. Then simply peel the skin off both sides using your fingers and a small paring knife. Gently scrape off any gelatin-like material under the skin. Note that the fish is only partially cooked at this point. From here, you can place the entire skinless wing back in the hot poaching liquid, cover, and resume simmering for another 10 to 15 minutes or until it's done. The cartilage in large cooked wings is tender enough to cut through if you want to divide a large wing for two people. Serve with a light sauce, allowing diners to eat by pulling a fork down the rows of cartilage. Some chefs feel that skate is best this way, but you can cook fillets just about any way you like—bake, broil, sauté, or as chunks in chowders and stews.

If you want to use skinless fillets in a recipe, don't poach them for the second time. (This method also works for skinless raw wings.) Remove fillets from the cartilage by turning a sharp knife flat and (with the blade pointing away from you) slicing off the meat on one side of the cartilage. Start at the thick side of the wing and slowly work off the meat. Use the cartilage as a guide, staying as close to it as you can. Try to keep the fillet in one or two large pieces. It does tend to separate into strands toward the tip of the wing. Repeat on the other side of the same wing.

When preparing fillets, bear in mind that they tend to be thin and fast-cooking—faster still if you partially precooked them as described above. Skate is also good steamed with a fresh vegetable topping or wrapped in foil and grilled with a barbecue sauce. (See Tarragon Skate Wings Sautéed in Bread Crumbs and Lemon Butter on page 257.)

Trade-offs: Skate fillets really lend themselves to just about any seafood recipe. I could see them working well in flounder and sole recipes or shredded, in place of crabmeat. Skate fillets can also substitute for cod or haddock. Skate meat can be cut into small pieces and used in scallop recipes.

Nutritional value: The USDA offers no data, but other sources suggest that skate is *very low-fat* and has about 90 calories per 3½ ounces.

Smelt

Also known as: Rainbow smelt, which are the most widely sold type of smelt in this country. They're caught in the Great Lakes, as well as in numerous New England harbors. Other types of smelt exist, such as the eulachon or candlefish, a West Coast smelt that may be sold as "Columbia River smelt."

Market forms: Since they're small, running 6 to 8 inches in length, smelt typically come whole, drawn, or dressed. It takes 10 to 12 smelt to make a pound. Smelt are available fresh, and a number of supermarkets carry them frozen.

Points of interest: Smelt are related to salmon and can adapt to both fresh and salt water. Sea smelt are anadromous. A popular recreational fish, smelt is also caught commercially.

Eating quality: Smelt are known to have a distinctive, sweet taste and a smell that some describe as "cucumberlike," others as "violetlike." The meat is white with a rich, at the same time delicate and mild, flavor. Smelt bones are soft enough that you can eat them—from head to tail—particularly if small fish are crisp-fried. The bones of larger cooked smelt can be lifted out in one piece.

Preparation: Most smelt lovers prefer the whole fish pan-fried in a light batter or broiled. But you can also bake, steam, or grill them. To save on calories with pan-fried smelt, simply dip them in seasoned flour and sauté in a nonstick frying pan with a small amount of oil or margarine. You can substitute the various types of smelt for one another in recipes. Be sure to eat fresh smelt within a day or two because they spoil quite quickly. You can also freeze smelt—*Seafood Soundings* newsletter recommends placing smelt head-down in an airtight container. Then fill it to the top with water and freeze. That way, frozen smelt should keep for six months—they need only be thawed enough to separate them before cooking.

Nutritional value: Rainbow smelt are *low-fat* and offer 97 calories plus 70 milligrams of cholesterol per serving.

Squid

Also known as: calamari, inkfish.

Market forms: cleaned tubes and rings, whole, smoked, dried. You may also come across squid steaks—cut from a whole piece of a large squid. Frozen squid is usually whole—sometimes it's better than fresh because it freezes so well.

Points of interest: Another unpalatable-looking seafood, this octopus relative is one of the most underutilized of marine creatures. It may help if you think of squid as "calamari"—its Italian and gourmet name. Realize, too, that squid is fancied in Europe and Japan and is growing in popularity in restaurants here.

The part of the squid that you eat is the mantle—a long, cone-shaped tube that's closed at one end. The mantle houses a thin, transparent, plasticlike shell (called a pen or quill) along with internal organs and an ink sac that the squid uses to emit a cloud of ink to shroud its escape from predators. The pen, organs, and ink sac should be removed in cleaning squid. Squid also have ten appendages—usually referred to as tentacles in cookbooks—sticking out from their heads, as well as wing-like fins. Both tentacles and fins can be eaten. And they are economical—I recently purchased a 3-pound frozen box for just $2.59.

Eating quality: Fresh squid have cream-colored skin with reddish-brown spots. As they begin to age, the skin takes on a pinkish hue. In the hands of inexperienced preparers, cooked squid has received an unfair reputation for being tough. While the white meat is firm, it can be very tender if prepared correctly. Its flavor and texture are usually described as being most similar to clams. Squid flesh has a mild, almost bland taste that tends to assume the flavor of its co-ingredients in a recipe.

Preparation: Figure on one to three squid per person, depending on the size of the squid, the appetites involved, and the recipe in question. You'll wind up with about 4 ounces of meat for each half-pound of whole squid that you purchase. If whole squid makes you squirm, seafood dealers will often clean it for you. But you can save yourself some money by performing the following cleaning procedure:

1. If the squid is frozen, thaw it in the refrigerator. Place a single squid fin-side down and cut off the tentacles just before the eyes. If you want to save the tentacle section (to chop and use in a sauce or stuffing), you need to remove the hard beak that squid use for feeding. Near the spot where you made the cut, feel for a hard, round sac. Press, pop it out, and discard.

2. Reaching inside the mantle, feel for the clear, plastic-like pen. Firmly grip the pen and head and pull them out along with the internal organs and ink sac. Don't hesitate to probe around or turn the mantle inside out to make sure all the innards are removed. Slice off the fins, which can be chopped and saved for a stuffing. (Some people also save the ink sac and use its contents to add flavor, color, and thickness to sauces.)

3. On the outside of the mantle, you'll find a skin or membrane that can be peeled off and discarded. Rinse and drain the mantle, which is now ready for stuffing, cutting open as a fillet, slicing cross-wise into rings, or chopping.

Squid is great stuffed with a low-fat ricotta cheese and spinach filling (see page 284) or bread crumb stuffing. Squid slices and pieces work well in Italian sauces (see Squid Rings Marinara on page 283), stir-fry dishes, soups, and stews. Steamed or poached squid rings are great marinated and served in cold salads. Simply combine the cooked rings with lemon juice, vinegar, a pinch of sugar, a small amount of olive oil, chopped onion and celery, and pimientos.

Squid is peculiar when it comes to being cooked. If you want tender meat, heat it for either a very short time—say a minute or two if stir-frying, sautéing, or frying—or long and slow by simmering or slow steaming. For their book *Seafood as We Like It*, authors Anthony Spinazzola and Jean-Jacques Paimblanc experimented with cooking squid varying amounts of time and found that rings poached in simmering water are the most tender after 1½ to 2 minutes. When stuffed or stewed, the optimal time for the squid varies from 5 or 6 up to 10 or 12 minutes—not long enough to cook a stuffing thoroughly. To adequately heat the stuffing, you'd wind up with tough squid. Fortunately, they found that when stuffed squid is allowed to cook for 50 to 60 minutes, it begins to soften again.

Trade-offs: Squid rings and chopped squid work well in many clam recipes.

Nutritional value: Squid is *very low-fat* and low in calories at 92 per serving. Cholesterol is high, however—233 milligrams.

Surimi products

You probably know them by names like "Seaflakes," "King Krab," "Sea Stix," or simply "imitation" seafoods. But these are actually names for varying products made from a processed fish material called surimi. I've treated surimi products in a class by themselves because —although they're sold as fresh or frozen seafoods—they're technically "seafood-analogue products" that are quite different from the real thing.

Also known as: Sea Bites, Copy Crab, Krab Stix, Sea Legs, and other brand names that individual manufacturers deem descriptive of their processed fish products made from surimi. "Kamaboko" is more of a generic term that's sometimes used to name surimi-based products.

Market forms: The most popular surimi product in this country is imitation crabmeat—in chunks, flakes, and leg-shaped pieces. You can also buy simulated lobster, scallops, and shrimp made from surimi. Surimi products are available frozen, unfrozen, and breaded. Today, seafood salads that you buy in most supermarket delicatessen sections and in many restaurants are made with surimi products.

Points of interest: Surimi is not the finished food that you eat—rather, it's a paste used to make surimi products. The paste is typically made from Alaska pollock and, less frequently, from fish such as croaker.

The process of making surimi is often carried out right on board ship where the pollock is deboned by machine, then subjected to several rinsing processes to remove blood, fat, and fishy odors. From here, the minced fish that results is strained and mixed with other ingredients—typically sugar, sorbitol (a sugar alcohol that's commonly used to sweeten "sugar-free" gum), and/or phosphate-containing additives—that improve freezer storage and keep the fish protein from toughening. At this point, you have tasteless, uncooked surimi paste which is usually frozen in blocks that will later be structured into the substitute seafoods you can eat.

The making of the final surimi products entails thawing the surimi paste, chopping it, and blending it with other substances to give it shellfishlike taste and texture. The added ingredients you might find listed on the label include a bit of real shellfish meat (the amount added by different manufacturers is quite variable), shellfish flavor extract or artificial flavoring, salt, water, starch, egg white, and monosodium glutamate. In molded products, such as imitation shrimp, fat may be added in the form of vegetable oil, lard, or cream.

The next step is taking the surimi paste with its added ingredients and processing by heat in order to make chunk, flake, or fibrous products having texture like that of shellfish. A touch of natural or artificial red coloring is commonly added to the surface of the newly formed products so they look like real crab, shrimp, or lobster meat. The end result is a cooked seafood-analogue product that's ready to eat.

In the past, most surimi products sold in the U.S. were made in Japan. But a number of U.S. processors currently manufacture products from surimi. In addition, researchers in this country are experimenting with using other fish possibilities for making surimi—namely freshwater catfish, hake, menhaden, and whiting. And some fast-food chains are even working on developing surimi-based hot dogs, salami, caviar, and "chicken" patties.

A real advantage of surimi-based products is their price—at this writing, seafood flakes and sticks are selling in fish markets for anywhere from several dollars to just under $6.00 a pound. Compared to frozen snow crab at $9.00 a pound and king crab (if you can find it)—in the shell, no less—for $10.95, the imitation products can't be beat—that is, if you like their taste. But just because surimi foods can save you money doesn't mean that they're not generating a huge income for manufacturers. According to *Seafood Business,* in 1985 we ate some 88 million pounds of the stuff—up 85 million pounds from 1980! The forecast for 1988 was that about 120 million pounds would be consumed.

For several years, the labeling of surimi products has been a hot issue because manufacturers are required to label them as "imitation" whenever the shellfish substitutes are represented as natural products. Although many manufacturers don't think it's fair, "imitation" is required because surimi products are considered to be less nutritious than the foods they resemble.

Exceptions to this rule are surimi products not marketed as specific seafoods (say, as a seafood stuffing for pasta)—they don't have to declare "imitation," but their labels must clearly state their composition. All packaged surimi products must list their ingredients in decreasing order of predominance—a handy thing for allergic people who need to identify products with real shellfish in them.

Eating quality: If it's good, it's really good; if it's not, it's so-so. Indeed, the taste and texture of surimi products are highly variable depending upon the individual product. Some people see little difference from the real thing, while others find surimi products to be rubbery and "fake-tasting." Coming from somewhere in the middle, I find that the high-quality flakes I can purchase at my favorite fish store work well in cold salads, casseroles, and omelettes. But I've found other products to be much tougher and too sweet-tasting (because of the additives). I must admit that in a restaurant, I won't order any type of seafood salad unless it's made from the real thing.

Preparation and trade-offs: You can eat these seafood analogues as they are or mix them into casseroles, sauces, salads, and stuffings—just as you would with genuine shellfish. Because surimi products are so variable in quality, I'd suggest experimenting with different brands to find one you like. Remember that surimi foods are already cooked and require less cooking time when added to hot dishes than raw shellfish. In recipes, you might try mixing imitation with real shellfish to get the taste and texture you want.

Nutritional value: Like quality, the nutritional value of imitation seafoods varies from product to product. As a nutritionist, I'd have to agree with the government that surimi products are inferior to shellfish—but not so inferior that most people shouldn't eat them periodically. The biggest drawback, particularly for those on sodium-restricted diets, is the high sodium level—often well over 600 milligrams for a small serving. Surimi products are also lower in protein than shellfish. Cooked blue crab, for instance, provides about 20 grams of protein for a 3½-ounce serving compared with 8 to 15 grams for typical surimi products. But few Americans lack adequate protein in their diets, and other foods that you'd have in a meal—say, a glass of milk—could easily make up the protein difference.

Another shortcoming of surimi is that substantial amounts of water-soluble nutrients, including niacin and potassium, are lost in processing. As for our friends the omega-3 fatty acids, the relatively low levels that Alaska pollock has to begin with are diminished to almost nothing in making surimi. Thus, your imititation shellfish provides very small amounts of omega-3s compared to the more than 300 milligrams you get from a small serving of crabmeat.

The good news is that, when stacked up against many other protein foods, surimi products tend to be very low in calories, fat, and cholesterol—sometimes lower than real shellfish on all three counts (although we've already decided that shellfish don't really pose a cholesterol threat). When fat is added to imitation molded shellfish, however, it may be from a saturated source such as lard, but a gram or two isn't all that substantial.

Swordfish

Market forms: Swordfish usually comes as boneless fresh or frozen steaks; sometimes swordfish chunks are sold. Previously frozen swordfish is commonly sold in fresh-seafood cases and should not be refrozen by the purchaser.

Points of interest: So much simpler than other commercial fish, there's only one species of swordfish. It's found in the Pacific, as well as the Atlantic. Periodic concerns about mercury in swordfish (see page 80) have not deterred consumers from this favorite fish. Of late, fresh swordfish is available year-round because of increasing imports.

Eating quality: The color of raw swordfish meat depends on the fish's diet; it may be pink (sometimes marketed as "salmon sword" in New England), tan, off-white, or even orangeish. Most steaks have a dark maroon-colored section. You can spot older swordfish meat when it turns grayish and the dark meat becomes brown. The dense, firm texture of swordfish appeals to meat lovers. When it comes to taste and texture, mako shark is the only fish that's similar to swordfish.

Preparation: Swordfish is best if broiled, grilled, or baked. When using dry-heat cooking methods, stick with steaks that are at least three-quarters of an inch thick since swordfish tends to dry out. It's also wise to cover swordfish with a light topping or sauce (see Broiled Basil Swordfish on page 253) or to marinate it. Frequent basting helps to keep swordfish moist. Swordfish can also be poached, steamed, and sautéed.

Nutritional value: Swordfish falls into the *low-fat* category with its 121 calories and 39 milligrams of cholesterol per serving.

Tilapia

Also known as: Tilapia has been sold as "St. Peter's fish," the name it is given in Israel, but what is known world-wide as St. Peter's fish is actually a fish called "John Dory" in the U.S.

Market forms: fillets.

Points of interest: Tilapia is rapidly becoming an important farm-raised food fish. It's primarily grown in Israel and imported here, but is making its way onto American fish farms. Freshwater fish.

Eating quality: Tilapia's finely flaked meat is firm, white, lean, and moist. It has a sweet, nutlike taste. Tilapia's taste and texture are considered excellent.

Preparation: Tilapia can be baked, broiled, sautéed, or steamed.

Trade-offs: flounder, sole, ocean perch, rockfish, orange roughy.

Nutritional value: The USDA offers no data on tilapia, but other government sources suggest it is *low-fat* and offers about 100 calories per 3½ ounces.

Tilefish

Also known as: Eastern sea bass, golden bass, golden snapper, tile bass.

Market forms: drawn, dressed, fillets, steaks, whole.

Points of interest: Primarily caught in the Atlantic, tilefish is growing in favor and availability. (There is a Pacific tilefish—sometimes called ocean whitefish—but it's of limited availability and variable in quality; it sometimes has a bitter taste.)

Eating quality: Described as "exceptional at table," tilefish resembles a cross between lobster and scallops in taste and texture, although when I recently tasted it for the first time I found it somewhat sweeter than both. Its white flesh is firm and dense, yet moist and flaky. Whole fish yield thick steaks and fillets that can be cut into medallions (see page 182).

Preparation: Tilefish can be baked, broiled, grilled, or poached. It's excellent in chowders and stews. Try it cold in a cabbage slaw or fruit salad. It also works well in a highly seasoned tomato sauce or a sweet and fruity sauce (see Tilefish Medallions in Sherried Orange Sauce on page 314).

Trade-offs: You can use tilefish in any recipe calling for cod or haddock, but be prepared for a more distinctive flavor. Tilefish can also be swapped for pollock, grouper, sea bass, mahimahi, flatfish, red snapper, and rockfish in some recipes.

Nutritional value: Tilefish is *low-fat* and provides 96 calories per serving.

Trout

Market forms: Lake trout is available dressed, as fillets, and smoked. Rainbow trout—available fresh and frozen—come to us dressed, dressed and boned, butterflied, and smoked. Live trout is sometimes available in tanks.

Points of interest: Numerous trout species live in fresh U.S. waters. Lake trout are the largest trout in North America and are caught in large, cool freshwater lakes. Rainbow trout account for most commercially sold trout. They're widely raised by hatcheries for markets and restaurants. Steelheads are an esteemed anadromous subspecies of rainbow trout caught in the Pacific Northwest.

Eating quality: Color, texture, and flavor of trout meat varies greatly depending on the species, size, and where it's caught. The flesh of lake trout, for instance, can vary from white to red. Full-flavored and firm in texture, lake trout is on the oily side compared to other trout. Larger lake trout tend to have a higher proportion of body fat than smaller ones. Farm-raised rainbow trout have whitish flesh, but the meat of their wild counterparts can range from pale orange to deep red; when cooked, rainbow-trout meat is white to pale pink. Rainbows also have firm flesh, as do steelheads. Steelheads are considered a delicacy with their pink, flavorful flesh. Trout, in general, have a simple skeleton that can be lifted out of a cooked fish quite easily.

Preparation: For the most part, different types of trout can be used interchangeably, but their use depends on size. Small, 6- to 9-inch dressed fish are usually pan-fried; larger trout can be cooked by most other methods. Specifically, lake trout are good cut into steaks and broiled. Large lake trout can be used in place of similar-size salmon. Try them baked (and stuffed), poached, steamed, sautéed, or grilled. Likewise, all of these cooking methods apply to rainbow trout and steelheads.

Note that just-landed trout has a tendency to curl if it's cooked within 6 to 8 hours after catching. To prevent problems, Ruth Spear advises lightly coating fresh trout with seasoned flour and refrigerating it overnight.

Nutritional value: Rainbow trout is *low-fat* and offers 118 calories per serving. Its cholesterol level is 57 milligrams. (The USDA does not provide specific information on lake trout or steelheads, but Dr. Nettleton reports that lake trout are *medium-fat,* low in cholesterol, and have 162 calories per serving.)

Tuna (fresh)

Market forms: chunked, drawn, dressed; but usually marketed as boneless steaks.

Points of interest: After you try fresh tuna, you may have a hard time going back to what most Americans know as tuna—the canned variety. Although we eat almost a third of all tuna caught in the world, less than 5 percent of that is in the form of fresh and frozen tuna. Nevertheless, the demand for fresh steaks is growing and restaurants are sporting more grilled tuna on their menus. Tuna's newfound popularity can also be attributed to the current popularity of sashimi. The price of fresh tuna fluctuates according to its availability and quality, but it can be a good buy when stocks are up. Saltwater fish.

Eating quality: Don't expect fresh tuna to taste anything like its canned counterpart. Fresh tuna is most like swordfish and shark, but it has its own unique—and delicious—flavor. Its very firm texture is compact and fine-grained—a most appealing quality for meat lovers. In fact, some say cooked, fresh tuna meat is similar to veal. With the exception of albacore tuna, which turns white upon cooking, most types of tuna are reddish-brown when raw and turn brownish or light tan after cooking. In general, the lighter the color of tuna, the milder its flavor.

Preparation: Tuna doesn't stay fresh long, so use it as soon as possible after purchase. Some advise removing any strips of dark meat present as they might be bitter-tasting. You can leach some of the blood out of dark tuna, thereby lightening its color, if you soak it in a saltwater bath before cooking. But I'd advise trying it without brining to avoid increasing the sodium content. Besides, tuna is good just as it is. You can bake, braise, broil, and stew tuna. Try poaching it and serving it cold with a light dill or cucumber-yogurt sauce. Or marinate tuna in a teriyaki sauce and toss it onto the grill for a quick supper. Another easy idea is a light sauté in lemon juice, a little olive oil, and Italian herbs.

As is the case with shark, tuna taste and color depend upon the type. Following are some of the tunas you may encounter in the seafood market.

Albacore. This tuna has light red to pinkish meat that turns whitish upon cooking. (In the U.S., only albacore tuna can be labeled as "white meat tuna" when it's canned.)

Bluefin. With dark red or brown raw flesh (small fish are lighter), bluefin is prized in Japan, where choice cuts can go for more than $2 per pound. Bluefin tuna tends to have a stronger flavor than many other types. You can find it on the East Coast in the summertime.

Bigeye. Not too familiar in the U.S., its meat is lighter in color than that of the bluefin.

Skipjack. It has stronger-tasting meat than the albacore. Although similar to yellowfin tuna, skipjack meat may be darker and stronger.

Yellowfin. Falling somewhere between albacore and bluefin in color, its dark red meat becomes grayish-white when cooked. (Yellowfin and skipjack are major canning choices for "light meat tuna.")

Trade-offs: shark, swordfish, mahimahi. You can use the different types of tuna interchangeably with one another, but you may like the darker type more if you first marinate it in lemon or lime juice and a small amount of oil. Cooked fresh tuna can be used just like canned tuna. You'll find that fresh tuna works well in some chicken and meat recipes.

Nutritional value: Skipjack and yellowfin tuna are *very low-fat* with less than 110 calories in a serving. Bluefin tuna is *low-fat* and offers 144 calories per portion. Cholesterol levels for all three kinds of tuna are less than 50 milligrams. (The USDA does not provide data for other types of raw tuna.)

Turbot, Greenland

Also known as: Greenland halibut, although a federal regulation now prohibits marketing turbot as such.

Market forms: Most Greenland turbot is available as frozen fillets.

Points of interest: Actually, what we know as Greenland turbot is not *the* true European turbot (see the "Flounder" entry). Greenland turbot *is* a flatfish, however, inhabiting the northern part of both the Atlantic and Pacific oceans. Primarily sold in cafeterias, modest restaurants, and supermarkets, Greenland turbot sold in this country is imported.

Eating quality: Despite its fat content, Greenland turbot is often used as a less expensive alternative to sole and flounder. It's not unknown for even-cheaper arrowtooth flounder to be substituted for Greenland turbot. You can tell the difference because turbot is a much firmer fish when cooked; arrowtooth flounder tends to fall apart. Turbot has a mild flavor and dense, white meat.

Preparation: Greenland turbot can be baked, broiled, poached, steamed, fried, or sautéed.

Nutritional value: Compared to other flatfish, Greenland turbot is much higher in fat, falling into the *oily* fish category. It provides 186 calories and 46 milligrams of cholesterol per portion.

Weakfish

Also known as: grey sea trout.

Market forms: dressed, fillets, whole.

Points of interest: Weakfish—so named because fishing hooks easily tear from their fragile mouth tissue—are considered the most important commercial species of sea trout. Although members of the drum family, weakfish have their own distinctive taste and texture. Their availability—now considered "reasonable"—waxes and wanes greatly. In the 1950s weakfish were almost nonexistent.

Eating quality: Weakfish have high-quality, sweet, and very delicate meat. The white-colored flesh is fine and unusually soft and fragile.

Preparation: Sometimes weakfish is frozen to firm and improve its texture. If you plan to freeze it, check first with your fish dealer to see if it came to him frozen—you really shouldn't freeze it a second time. Weakfish lends itself to baking, broiling, pan-frying, and stuffing whole. Because of its tendency to break apart easily, be especially careful when you turn it. Weakfish works well in croquettes and mousses. Try it amandine or baked with herbs such as tarragon.

Trade-offs: Although the flavor is stronger, weakfish fillets can be used like flatfish fillets. Weakfish can also substitute for baked or broiled cod, haddock, pollock, and hake. Some recipes calling for croaker, sea bass, and striped bass will work with weakfish.

Nutritional value: Weakfish is *low-fat* and provides 104 calories plus 83 milligrams of cholesterol per serving.

Whitefish

Market forms: dressed, fillets, steaks—all in fresh or frozen form. Also available smoked.

Points of interest: True whitefish—as opposed to the catch of the day often described as "whitefish"—is a member of the trout family. Whitefish from the Great Lakes constitute a large commercial freshwater fishery. Offered by white-tablecloth restaurants in that part of the country, whitefish is considered a delicacy.

Eating quality: Whitefish offers pure-white meat that is moist and somewhat sweet. The taste has been described as "cucumberlike" or "melony." (The flavor can vary, however, depending on where it's caught.) With fillets, you should be prepared for some small, fine filamentlike bones.

Preparation: Higher in fat content than most white-fleshed fish, whitefish lends itself well to baking, broiling, and grilling. It's also tasty poached and served cold. Whole whitefish is a good bet for stuffing.

Trade-offs: Whitefish fillets can be used in just about any broiled-fish recipe (say, for salmon or scrod), as long as you leave the skin on. It also works well in recipes for baked fish, but expect a different taste than you're used to. (Because the flavor is unique, I can't recommend any specific "trade-offs.")

Nutritional value: Although fat content varies according to the lake in which it is caught, whitefish is generally *medium-fat* and provides fewer than 150 calories per serving. The omega-3 fatty acid content is very high—particularly for freshwater fish. The cholesterol level is 60 milligrams.

Wolffish

Also known as: ocean catfish, loup de mer (French).

Market forms: usually fillets (frozen fillets may be imported), sometimes steaks.

Points of interest: Although often called ocean catfish, wolffish are not related to catfish, and the taste and texture are different. Nevertheless, restaurants have been known to pass off wolffish as freshwater catfish.

Eating quality: Wolffish have strong jaws with teeth capable of grinding hard-shelled mollusks. This diet results in a unique firm and fine white flesh that's flaky when cooked. The flesh is considered similar to haddock. To me, wolffish and cusk taste similar.

Preparation: Bake, broil, poach, or steam. Try it broiled, then top with sliced parslied potatoes. You can also add small wolffish pieces to clam chowder (page 240).

Trade-offs: cod, haddock, cusk, pollock, pout, or any white-fleshed fish.

Nutritional value: Wolffish is *low-fat* and offers just under 100 calories per serving; it has 46 milligrams of cholesterol.

CHAPTER NINE

Stocking the Best Fish
the Right Way

NOW THAT YOU KNOW why fish is so good for you, you need to know how to purchase good fish and keep it at top quality once you get it home. If you're one of the many who suffer under the misconception that a fishy smell just goes with the territory when you serve seafood at home, this chapter will change your notions and your ways with fresh and frozen fish.

WHO'S IN CHARGE OF FISH QUALITY CONTROL?

You are the one who is primarily responsible for purchasing and preparing quality fish because—unlike meat and poultry products, which are inspected through mandatory government programs—fish and shellfish are not required to be inspected by any government agency before reaching your table. Nevertheless, some well-established voluntary programs are in place for the fish industry.

The major quality-control program—the National Seafood Inspection Program—comes out of the U.S. Department of Commerce and is conducted by the National Marine Fisheries Service. The inspection service is available on a voluntary basis to fish processors, packers, and brokers who are willing to foot the bill for services, estimated to cost about one cent per pound of inspected product. Participating companies—usually large processors and packers of seafood—and their wares are inspected by licensed Department of Commerce inspectors who examine fish for wholesomeness and quality.

For you, the consumer, there are two signs that fish has been inspected. One is the "Packed Under Federal Inspection" (PUFI) mark (see page 164) that signifies a product is safe, wholesome, properly labeled, and has "reasonably good flavor and odor" as it leaves participating processing plants. The other seal bestowed by the inspection program is the "U.S. Grade A" insignia (below) applied to products meeting certain *quality* critiera, as well as PUFI standards. The Grade A seal goes one step further than the PUFI emblem, assuring that a fish product is of top quality, uniform size, and almost free of blemishes. Grade A criteria exist for more than 20 fish products including frozen fish fillets, fish sticks, frozen shrimp, and fresh fillets of certain species. But many fish products have no established Grade A criteria and, therefore, aren't eligible for the emblem.

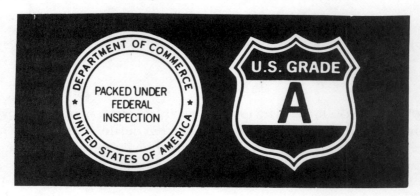

Although it's a favorable sign if you come across Grade A and PUFI symbols when you're shopping for fish, don't knock yourself out trying to purchase only inspected items. For in 1986 only an estimated 11.6 percent of all fish consumed in the U.S. was inspected by the Department of Commerce program—at that, less than 4 percent received the Grade A stamp of approval and most inspected products were in the frozen category. Now, that doesn't mean noninspected fish is of inferior quality—bear in mind that manufacturers have to pay to be part of the inspection program, and many obviously choose not to participate.

There have been efforts to establish a mandatory fish-inspection program in this country. Currently, the National Oceanic and Atmospheric Administration of the Department of Commerce is charged with developing such a program should it ever be mandated.

Another important voluntary quality-control effort is the National Shellfish Sanitation Program, administered by the Food and Drug Administration. It monitors the safety of clams, oysters, and mussels sold in interstate commerce by nearly 30 states (most of them coastal), as well as a small number of foreign countries. The shellfish control agency in each participating state is responsible for evaluating the quality of the waters in which these bivalves are harvested. When waters are unsafe, they're prohibited to harvesters. State officials certify shellfish dealers participating in the program as having only harvested or purchased these particular shellfish from safe areas. In addition, certified dealers have to maintain sanitation standards in their processing plants.

To find out if clams, mussels, or oysters that you purchase have come from certified dealers, you can check the label of prepackaged items to see if there is a certification sticker. If you buy unpackaged mollusks, your seafood seller should be able to tell you if they came from certified dealers because certification tags come on the bulk packages in which the shellfish arrive.

Be aware that even inspected fish and certified shellfish are occasionally mishandled once they leave the processor. The bottom line is that it's up to *you* to buy your finfish and shellfish from reputable dealers —either respected local seafood stores or major supermarkets. The odds of purchasing unsafe or poor-quality seafood soar when you deal with roadside hucksters. (For more on fish safety, see chapter 7.) The other way you can protect yourself is to troubleshoot by applying "Safe and Sound Seafood Signals" (see page 169).

THE FIVE FOES OF FISH QUALITY
(OR HOW FISH GOES BAD)

If you had to catch your chickens by chasing wild birds through the forest or kill cattle feeding on your backyard weeds, how do you think your poultry and meat would taste? Certainly not the same as the flesh from animals raised and slaughtered under today's controlled conditions. But think of the way we get most fish—they're hunted in the wild under a variety of uncontrolled circumstances. Indeed, before a fish is even hooked or netted, its quality is determined by its age, diet, spawning status, size (smaller fish tend to spoil faster than large), species, and the quality of its watery environment. Furthermore, some fishing methods are more likely to land quality fish than others.

Unless you're an avid fisherman, you can't directly control any of the aforementioned factors that determine the goodness of fish, but you *can* detect and influence the "five foes of fish quality" once it's out of the water, namely *bacterial growth, enzyme activity, too-high temperatures, oxidation,* and *dehydration.* Just like people, healthy fish have *bacteria* on their skin and in their intestinal tracts, as well as in gills. While the flesh of a living fish is essentially bacteria-free, once it dies, the bacteria from the skin and innards can multiply and invade the flesh (particularly if a fish is carelessly cleaned). Herein lies the major source of that fishy smell that deters so many prospective fish lovers.

Fish flesh deteriorates more rapidly than beef and poultry because it harbors bacteria that can withstand fairly low temperatures—that is, they can grow in the refrigerator. Moreover, compared to other protein foods, fish flesh is made of smaller molecules that bacteria can readily devour and use to proliferate. As the bacteria go to work, they rampantly release *enzymes,* which are proteins that help living fish metabolize nutrients and build muscle proteins. In a dead fish the enzymes are out of control and more or less self-digest its flesh.

The higher the *temperature* at which fish is held, the faster the bacteria grow and multiply and the speedier the enzymes work—for every 10° F jump above the freezing point, the rate of fish spoilage doubles. Therefore, you can exert the greatest influence over fish spoilage by holding it at 32° F or less (fish doesn't start to freeze until about 27° F). If your refrigerator runs at the common reading of 40° F, you're setting the stage for rapid fish deterioration.

The two final fish foes—*oxidation* and *dehydration*—are most likely to occur in frozen fish. (With unfrozen fish, bacterial spoilage generally precedes oxidation and the resultant odor would likely deter you from eating it.) Oxidation takes place when oxygen in the air reacts with the polyunsaturated fats in fish, yielding a rancid product with off-color, odor, and poor taste. Meat from land animals is much less likely to turn rancid because of its relatively low proportion of polyunsaturated fatty acids. On the other hand, because of their healthful polyunsaturates, fattier fish become rancid much more quickly than leaner varieties.

Dehydration—resulting from water loss in fish flesh and yielding tough, dried-out eating quality—happens most often in frost-free freezers that "suck" the moisture from improperly wrapped foods. The major deterrents to both oxidation and dehydration are low temperatures, proper wrapping, and avoiding keeping fish too long.

Bear in mind that you can't reverse any of the five foes of fish quality —restoring a spoiled fish is about as easy as resurrecting a dead one— but you can retard their development.

FINDING THE RIGHT PLACE TO BUY FISH

Some people actually think that fish isn't fresh unless it smells fishy. Quite the contrary; to put it crudely, fresh fish doesn't stink! If it does, it's on its way out. In fact, as mentioned earlier, that fishy odor is—understandably—a major reason why many people don't eat more fish.

If the fish you purchase is consistently smelly, then you're probably shopping at the wrong store. The right place to buy fish is one that greets you with no terribly offensive odor as you approach it. Look around the shop or seafood counter—are they clean and neat? I once entered a seafood store that looked reasonably sanitary on the customer side of the counter. But accompanying my youngster to the shop's restroom revealed a filthy behind-the-counter scene. (Needless to say, I did not return.)

Get to know the employees and/or owner where you shop for fish. I like to shop where personnel are knowledgeable about their fish wares —where does their supply come from? How long have they had it? Was it previously frozen? What can I do with it? These are just some of the questions that your fish seller should be able to answer.

The right fish store will keep fish in a special seafood case, on lots of ice. But the fish fillets and steaks should not directly touch the ice, which will leach away moisture and flavor, not to mention foster odor buildup. Instead, fish steaks should be displayed in a single layer— fillets can be stacked two deep—on a thin metal tray or, at the very least, on a paper or plastic-film barrier to the ice. If on a tray, look for puddles of fish juice—a promoter of spoilage and a sign that the fish has been sitting around too long.

Shelled shellfish meat and peeled raw or cooked shrimp are not supposed to be directly on ice either. And live shellfish have no business being buried in ice. On the other hand, whole or dressed fish (see page 168 for the difference) can be right on "the rocks" as long as the head end faces downward to foster good drainage of bacteria from the gut cavity. Under no circumstances should price tags be stuck into fish or shellfish flesh because the perforation promotes spoilage. Instead, tags should be wedged in ice or lemons placed close to the fish.

It's wise to stay away from cooked seafoods stored right next to raw products. That's because raw fish are more likely to harbor bacteria that can contaminate cooked foods. When buying prepackaged raw fish, always check the "sell by" date. A fair amount of juice inside the package is a sign of poor quality. Ideally, packaged fish should come in single layers—not rolled up or folded over. Know, too, that many supermarket self-service display counters, such as the meat counter, are not ideal for maintaining fish quality because they're too warm. Any fish that you buy should feel cold—not just cool—to the touch.

The ultimate quality-control check when buying fish is your nose. Don't hesitate to ask if you can smell the fish that you're about to buy. Like red meat and poultry, even top-quality fish has a scent of its own. But the smell should not be strong, ammonia-like, sour, or what most of us call just plain "fishy." Rather, the terms used to describe the smell of good fish are "ocean-fresh"—like a fresh sea breeze—sweet, mild, slightly "seaweedy," even "cucumberlike." In-dividual species—especially the oilier ones—sometimes have their own unique scents, but the smell should not be objectionable. You need to give prepackaged fish a second chance because it's more likely to have a fishy smell when you first open it. Don't pass judgment until you rinse it off, pat it dry, and then give it a whiff.

Since fish spoils quickly, buy it at the end of your shopping trip. It bruises easily, too, which will speed spoilage. So see that fish is packed at the top of your shopping bag—preferably in with frozen foods. Unless it's a frigid winter day and you drive without the heater on, go directly home so you can promptly refrigerate your catch. If you have to run errands in between, either bring along a cooler or ask that your fish be packed in a plastic bag, then in some ice.

If, after all of these precautions, your purchase still smells fishy, take it back to the store. Most fish sellers or supermarket managers want to know if you're not satisfied. If they won't accept your return or their fish is consistently fishy, I'd advise that you find a new seafood seller.

MARKET FORMS OF FINFISH

Most people in this country prefer to buy their fish as fillets and steaks. But real connoisseurs prefer fish closer to the natural state because they're easier to assess for freshness. Before learning some of the market terminology for fish, recognize that finfish are often categorized into two general groups—*roundfish* and *flatfish*. Most finfish are roundfish with streamlined, more cylindrical bodies that taper at each end; their eyes are on either side of their heads. Flatfish, on the other hand, include sole, flounder, halibut, and turbot with their platter-shaped bodies that are dark on one side and white on the other; both eyes are on the dark side.

Following are the major forms in which you can purchase roundfish and flatfish in the market.

Whole fish come to you *au naturel,* just as they're caught—head, gills, guts, and all. You don't often see finfish sold whole because their entrails encourage quick deterioration. Before using whole fish, you've got to gut them (the sooner the better) and usually scale them. About 45 percent of a whole fish is edible—the rest is waste. (If you ever buy live finfish, seafood expert Joyce Nettleton, D. Sc., R.D., advises having the dealer kill them for you since fish struggling out of water becomes less sweet and they toughen.)

Drawn fish are gutted for you—but may still need to be scaled. If you cook a drawn fish as is and let your diners pick away at the bones, about half of the fish can be eaten. But if it's skinned, filleted, and boned, each pound of drawn fish will yield only about a third of a pound of meat.

Dressed fish come to you with guts, head, scales, tails, and often fins removed. You can cook dressed fish as is. The term *pan-dressed* is sometimes applied to small fish that still have heads and tails. (Note that a recipe calling for "whole" fish usually requires whole, dressed fish.) You can figure that dressed fish are about two-thirds edible.

Fillets are cuts from the fleshy sides of fish—the muscular part that runs along the backbone and ribs is cut off from front to back. Sometimes fillets have skin that you can either leave on in cooking, ask to have removed, or cut off yourself (see page 183). Although many fillets are practically boneless, you can't assume that they are. Whether or not a fillet has bones depends on the fish species and how it's filleted. If it's important to you to have boneless fish, tell your dealer —but be prepared to pay a bit more. (I always check carefully for bones when feeding fish to children. See page 183 for suggestions about removing bones yourself.) Fillets have very little waste and are ready for cooking.

Steaks are slices cut crosswise (as opposed to lengthwise fillets) straight down through the fish's body. Steaks run about an inch thick and typically come skin-on and bone-in. If a fish has a very large circumference, you may be buying just a piece of one of its steaks. Steaks from large roundfish such as tuna and swordfish are usually boneless and have almost no waste. When cooking, leave the skin on to help hold the flesh together. Bone-in steaks are close to 85-percent edible. Sometimes 4- to 6-inch-thick cross sections of large, dressed fish are available as fish "chunks" or "roasts."

SAFE AND SOUND SEAFOOD SIGNALS

In addition to using your nose, put your other senses to work to determine whether market forms of fish are at their best. The guidelines below apply to most fresh- and saltwater fish, but realize that freshwater fish tend to have more natural surface slime. And, quite obviously, not all the comments for whole, drawn, and dressed fish apply to each form—headless fish, for example, don't have eyes!

HOW MUCH FISH TO BUY

Since there's so little waste with fish fillets and steaks, you can tell fairly well by eyeing them if you have enough to feed your brood. But, when it comes to dressed and drawn fish or unshucked shellfish, it's much more difficult to know how much to buy. Following is a chart that gives ranges for amounts of various forms of fish to buy per person. Whether you go with the lower or upper end of the scale depends on the appetites and ages of your diners, as well as other ingredients in a recipe. In general, I'd go with the higher figure if

TABLE 7. Safe and Sound Seafood Signals

	Top-quality signals	*Poor-quality signals*

FILLETS AND STEAKS

Color	Glistening, bright, almost translucent	Creamy or milky, discolored, blood spots
Flesh	Firm, elastic—springs back when depressed	Spongy, soft, doesn't spring back
	Tight—doesn't separate into segments	Separated into segments[a]
	Cleanly cut edges	Ragged, curled edges
	Moist but not slimy	Dry or slimy

WHOLE, DRAWN, AND DRESSED FINFISH

Body cavity	Clean, no blood or viscera	Traces of blood and viscera
Eyes[b]	Clear, bulging, bright, black pupils	Dull, cloudy, sunken, bloody
Flesh	Firm, elastic (springs back when depressed)	Spongy, soft
	Tightly adhered to bones	Loose from bones
Gills	Red or pinkish red	Gray, brown, or greenish
	Clear, thin mucus	Thick, sticky, yellow mucus
Skin	Shiny, bright metallic colors	Dull, faded colors and markings
	Moist with transparent outer slime	Dry or with thick milky or yellowish slime
	Scales (if present) tightly adhered to skin	Many missing scales

LIVE CLAMS, MUSSELS, AND OYSTERS

Shells tightly closed: —if open, they shut when tapped on a hard surface —can't pry apart by hand	Shells: —won't shut when tapped —can pry apart by hand
Shells intact, moist	Cracked, chipped, dry shells
Necks of soft-shell clams twitch when touched	Necks don't move

SHUCKED CLAMS, MUSSELS, AND OYSTERS

Plump meats, covered with their own juice

Shriveled, dark, dry meats, too little or excessive juice

Clear juice, free of shells and sand

Opaque juice, shells and sand present

LIVE LOBSTERS AND CRABS

Lively—legs move when tickled

Little or no movement

Hard shells (unless soft-shelled variety)

Soft shells

Feel heavy for size (there is more meat)

Light for size

When picked up, lobsters turn tails under

Tails hang limp

COOKED LOBSTERS AND CRABS

If in shell, the shell is bright red and hard

Discolored, soft shells

Lobster tails curled under and snap back when pulled out

Tails don't curl or snap

Picked meat:
—lobster: snow-white with red tints
—crab: white with red or brown tints
—no shell fragments, cartilage

Off-color, dried-out meat
Off-color, dried-out meat
Shell and cartilage fragments in picked meat

RAW SHRIMP[c]

Translucent shells with grayish green, pinkish tan, or light pink tint

Blackened edges or spots on shells

Moist

Dry

Firm flesh

Soft flesh

---

[a] This doesn't apply to species with very little connective tissue, such as Atlantic bluefish.

[b] Eyes are not the best quality indicators for a number of reasons. They may be cloudy from ice contact. Or they may be sunken because the fish was brought up from ocean depths under severe pressure. Furthermore, the rules don't necessarily apply to small-eyed fish, such as salmon.

[c] Most raw shrimp sold in the U.S. has been frozen and is sold as is or thawed. The same criteria apply to cooked shrimp as to raw, but look for pink or red-tinted shells.

TABLE 8. Amount to Buy per Person

Finfish fillets	¼ to ⅓ pound
Finfish steaks:	
bone-in	½ pound
boneless	⅓ pound
Whole finfish	¾ to 1 pound
Drawn finfish	¾ pound
Dressed finfish	½ pound
Live hard-shell clams, oysters	6 to 8
Live soft-shell clams (steamers)	12 to 18
Shucked clams, oysters	⅓ to ½ pint
Live lobsters, crabs	1 to 1½ pounds
Cooked lobster, crab, or shrimp meat	¼ to ⅓ pound
Scallops	¼ to ⅓ pound
Whole shrimp	1 pound
Unpeeled shrimp, headless	⅓ to ½ pound
Peeled shrimp, headless	¼ to ⅓ pound

(For amount to buy for mussels, skate, and squid, see chapter 8.)

you're serving a plain version of the fish—say, broiled or poached without a sauce. But if you'll be doctoring up the fish a fair amount, you can probably get away with less.

COUNTING YOUR PENNIES

If you're wondering which market form is most economical, it's not an easy, on-the-spot job to determine. It really depends on the edible portion (or yield) of fish meat—without waste, such as the skin or shells, head, tail, and bones.

If you keep in mind that each pound of drawn fish will net you about a third of a pound of fillets, you can figure out if it's cheaper to fillet a drawn fish yourself or to buy precut fillets. Let's say a type of drawn fish is going for $1.99 a pound—if only a third is going to be used, you can multiply the cost times three to see that the actual cost per pound of fillets is close to $6. Now if that same fish is available at $3.99 a pound in fillet form, it's obvious which is the better buy. If, on the other hand, drawn fish is cooked as is, people who know how to eat around the bones can consume approximately half the fish, making the price of fillets and drawn fish about the same.

When contemplating fish prices, you have to consider the taste of those you're serving, as well as your time. If you're feeding small children who can't—or adults who won't—eat cooked, drawn fish, then you're wasting money to serve it that way. As for time, even people who are on a fairly tight budget may not want to bother doing their own filleting.

While we're on the subject of budgets, you may be under the impression that fish is the most expensive protein food around. To see if that really is the case, I did an informal before-and-after survey in which I compared the costs of certain types of fish, chicken, and beef —as purchased—with the weight and costs per serving of the edible portion after cooking (skin, bones, and obvious fat removed). Was I ever surprised to find that a 3½-ounce ready-to-eat serving of fairly high-priced fresh tuna (at $4.98 a pound) ended up costing $1.33, compared to $2.03 for the same-size portion of "economy pack" T-bone steak going for $3.94 a pound! Look at it this way: if, for a family of four, you swapped fresh tuna for steak once a week, you could save $145 a year!

Certainly, the cost of chicken parts and ground beef is less than that of fish such as fresh tuna. But the cost discrepancy is not what label prices imply by the time you account for the discarded skin and bones from the chicken or the fat lost in cooking hamburger. For example, at the time of my survey, fresh tuna was about three times as expensive as unsplit chicken breast, going by label prices. But when I accounted only for the part you actually eat, a serving of tuna costs just one-and-a-half times as much as the chicken. Besides, nobody's telling you that you have to eat fish costing nearly five dollars a pound to get the benefits; you can alternate more expensive types with cheaper options.

Your best bet for saving money when you buy fish is to watch supermarket fliers so you can plan meals around what's on special for any given week. In general, you can expect fish prices to be higher when the weather is bad or very cold. Some experts advise planning meals or shopping for fish with a recipe or two—not a particular type of fish—in mind. See what's cheapest at the store, then be willing to experiment with lower-priced fish that you've never had before. (See chapter 8 for ideas about what fish can be used interchangeably.) For instance, the original recipe I developed for Pout Fillets with Spinach and Wheat Germ Stuffing called for expensive flounder fillets. When I saw pout fillets at $1.99 a pound, I decided to give them a try and wound up with an improved recipe.

To work in a healthful number of fish meals each week, the game plan that works well for me is to roughly map out a week's worth of dinners, keeping in mind what I already have on hand and several fish recipes I'd like to try. Then, the night I go to the grocery store, I buy enough reasonably priced fresh fish for one meal for the same or the next night, since I find it doesn't keep too long. Since my seafood specialty store—which has the freshest fish—is farther from home, I go there on a different evening and stock up on enough fish for another dinner or two. (If the fish is fresh and stored properly, you don't have to feel compelled to serve seafood two nights in a row.) Sometimes I call ahead to see what's available—and economical—that week. Then for a fourth fish meal, I might make something with inexpensive canned tuna or salmon, frozen fish fillets, or imitation crabmeat.

To stretch higher-priced fish, such as shrimp and scallops, you can serve them in casseroles or sauces made with low-fat milk. Be sure to save leftovers for lunch—they can be heated in a microwave oven, which many workplaces now have. Leftover plain fish can be used in seafood salads and soups. You can even use fish heads or lobster bodies to make a fish broth or to flavor soups.

STORING FISH TO KEEP IT FRESH

Over and over again, seafood handbooks and cookbooks say you should use fresh fish within a day or two of purchase. That certainly makes it difficult to eat fish 3 to 7 times a week, particularly if you live a distance from your seafood seller. But, according to Susan Faria, seafood specialist and author of *The Northeast Seafood Book,* the 2-day rule simply doesn't hold if you buy top-quality fish and store it properly. Indeed, fresh, well-kept fish that's been gutted will stay in Grade A shape for 8 to 9 days after it's caught and remain edible for about 2 weeks. In fact, some research suggests that, compared to just-caught fish, fish 3 to 9 days off the hook tastes even better! Oilier fish, such as mackerel, however, have a maximum hook-(or net-)to-skillet life of about a week.

The big ifs that determine how long you'll actually be able to keep bought fish are quality and age at time of purchase, the market form and species of fish (leaner fish keep the longest), and how you store it at home. "Finding the Right Place to Buy Fish" on page 166 gives you guidelines for finding the store that's most likely to supply you with fresh, well-kept fish. In all likelihood, my local seafood-store owner, who makes frequent trips to the coast of Rhode Island, can supply me with better-quality fish than my favorite supermarket, stocked by a more distant New Jersey processor. True, I can often get good fish at the supermarket, but when I buy it there, I find that I have to have sharper eyes and nose and must use the fish more quickly. There's no question that some supermarkets are better than others at stocking fresh seafood.

As far as market form is concerned, drawn fish that have only the viscera and gills removed last the longest because minimal flesh surface is exposed to the air. But most of us tend to stick with fillets and steaks whose freshness is at the mercy of our fish dealers and our hands once we get them home.

If you're really serious about upping your fish intake and would like to keep it on hand for more than a day or two, I'd suggest investing in a refrigerator-freezer thermometer—you can get one for several dollars at a discount department store. That way, you can see if your fridge is set at 31° or 32° F, the recommended temperatures for holding fish. When I first checked mine, I found that it was set at the 40° F temperature so typical of home refrigerators. But the thermometer enabled me to make the right adjustments to get it just below 32 degrees. It's wise to check yours because a recent survey, published in the *Journal of the American Dietetic Association,* revealed that one out of five participating households had refrigerators operating at 50 degrees or higher—temperatures at which harmful bacteria can conceivably grow. (Be aware that at this low temperature other foods in your refrigerator may freeze.)

One way to hold fish fillets, steaks, and shellfish meat at a temperature of 32 degrees—particularly if you don't want to set your fridge quite that low—is to contain them in a waterproof bag and bury them in ice. According to Sue Faria, high-quality lean fish, such as cod and flounder, purchased at retail stores, can keep as long as 3 to 4 days at 32° F, while oilier varieties will keep a maximum of 2 to 3 days. Gutted and gilled fish can be placed right on crushed ice. Just pack the belly cavity with ice and place the fish belly side down in a container. Top with ice and refrigerate. Whenever you keep fish in ice, be sure to change the ice as it melts—and keep a large plate under it or your fridge may wind up with hard-to-get-rid-of fish odors.

The ice is not as important if your refrigerator is set below 33° F or you plan to use the fish right away. But however you hold it, keep fish in the coldest part of your refrigerator—usually in the meat compartment or on the bottom shelf. Always place it toward the back, away from the opening and shutting door that lets warm air in. It's okay to store well-wrapped, prepackaged fish as you purchase it, but place a plate underneath in case it drips.

Below are guidelines—largely from Sue Faria—for storing shellfish in the refrigerator. Storage times assume that you're keeping top-quality fish at 32° F.

Live shellfish. Shellfish should be kept alive until you're ready to use them. Store in the refrigerator in a leakproof, open container or else they won't have enough oxygen to survive. Although you want to keep them moist, submerging live shellfish in fresh water will do them in. Instead, cover with a damp, clean cloth, moist paper towels, or lettuce leaves. Hard-shell clams and oysters should survive for 7 to 10 days in the refrigerator, while mussels and soft-shell clams last 4 to 5 days. Lobsters and crabs will keep about 2 or 3 days. Make sure all shellfish are alive before using (see pages 124 and 130)—throw out the dead ones. It's okay to cook lobsters and crabs if you know they died in the last hour. By breaking off a crab claw or lobster tail you can probably tell if the meat is still okay—it should have "the aroma of the ocean."

Shucked clams, mussels, and oysters. To keep meats from drying and darkening, store in a covered, leakproof container and smother them with their own liquid. If you don't have enough liquid to cover them, you can stretch it with a homemade brine made of 1 teaspoon salt to 1 cup of water. The shucked meats should keep for 7 to 10 days.

Cooked lobster and crab. If you want to keep them whole, wrap tightly and store no more than 2 to 3 days. You can separate lobster tails and claws, wrap each piece tightly, and keep for about 3 or 4 days. Any cooked, shelled shellfish can be refrigerated for 3 to 4 days if you wrap it well.

Smoked fish and shellfish. Contrary to the popular notion that smoked foods last indefinitely, the smoking performed on fish in this country does little more than enhance its flavor. Therefore, smoked seafoods should be held (in the refrigerator) for no more than about a week.

Canned fish and shellfish. For ideal storage, keep in a cool, dry place no longer than a year. Once open, transfer to a plastic container, cover, and refrigerate for up to 5 days.

BUYING THE BEST FROZEN FISH

If the thought of frozen fish conjures up images of tough, dried-out "block" fillets or breaded fish sticks and fillets, then you're behind the times. The frozen fish industry has new quality standards and technology that allow for "flash-freezing" of fish, often within hours after they're caught. Then the frozen products are kept at very low temperatures capable of maintaining fish quality for months. Nowadays, you often hear it said that good frozen seafood is a far better bet than fresh fare of questionable quality.

Freezing affords consumers year-round variety and reasonable prices for fish—not to mention the convenience of being able to eat it when you're ready to. Stocking a regular supply of frozen fish is a great way to supplement the fresh fish you buy so you have no trouble getting in your weekly quota of 3 to 7 fish meals. In fact, many retailers now expand their supply by selling previously frozen, thawed fish along with the fresh. Although thawed fish should be marked as such at the seafood counter, it may not be—you can always ask so you can be sure not to refreeze it.

Freezing will markedly slow down or halt bacterial and enzyme spoilage, but dehydration can still occur in frozen fish, leaving you with meat that's tough, dried out, and woody when cooked. Signs of dehydration—typically called freezer burn—are whitish, dull, cottony patches and papery, dry-looking edges. Oxygen, too, can still get to the oils in frozen fish, causing rancidity which can result in orange coloring and offensive odors.

If you want quality frozen fish, be on the lookout for untorn, tightly wrapped packages with little space left around the fish. A buildup of ice crystals or water stains on packaging are possible signs of thawing and refreezing, a real deterrent to good eating quality. If fish is stacked high in freezer cases—above the load line or frost mark—it's probably not cold enough. Never buy fish that doesn't feel solidly frozen. It's wise to check the expiration date if there is one—select the package that gives you the most time leeway. If you have reason to suspect that a supermarket freezes some of its own fish, it's doubtful they have the facilities to do the job properly. Once again, don't hesitate to ask questions.

As suggested for fresh fish, it's wise to save frozen-fish purchases until the end of your shopping trip because just a half-hour at room temperature can initiate the thawing process. When you get the fish home, freeze it immediately, placing it away from the door. But realize that home freezers are not ideal for storing frozen fish for long periods—they're simply not cold enough. Ideally, your freezer should be set at 0° F or less. Chest freezers are best for holding fish; upright frost-free freezers are the worst because they can leach water from your catch. If your freezer is set at 10° F or higher, you really shouldn't keep frozen fish more than a week if you want the best eating quality. (See below for more on storage times for frozen fish.)

FREEZING YOUR OWN FISH

At the outset, you have to accept the fact that you can't freeze fish as well as commercial processors. Home appliances are not capable of freezing as fast or holding fish as cold as commercial freezing equipment. Slow freezing fosters the formation of large ice crystals which expand and burst fish muscle cells, damaging the texture. Commercial processors, however, use a number of different methods that render fish solidly frozen within 1 to 2½ hours (at home, it can take many hours). Fast freezing results in smaller ice crystals and much less damage to fish tissue. Some seafood experts say not to bother freezing fish yourself, especially if you don't have a chest freezer—advice that I feel is a bit extreme and impractical for the serious and regular fish-eater.

Whatever you do, don't take the time to freeze fish of suspect freshness. And never try to salvage old fish by freezing because it will probably deteriorate even more when frozen.

There are steps you can take to do the best job possible with home fish freezing. Start with fish that you know is fresh and of the highest quality. If it isn't already "undressed" or cut into steaks and fillets, make sure that it's scaled, gutted, degilled, and rinsed clean of blood and viscera before freezing. Fish that weigh 2 pounds or less after cleaning should be frozen whole; larger fish can be cut into steaks and fillets. When fish has light and dark sections, it's best to remove and discard the darker parts, which are higher in oil and more prone to oxidation.

The main goals in home fish freezing are to keep air out and moisture in. Proper packaging will help you accomplish both. Start with the right plastic wrap—made from polyvinylidene chloride, polyester, or polyvinyl chloride, according to Sue Faria. Polyethylene, commonly used in plastic wraps and bags, is not recommended because it allows passage of some water vapor and air.

Certain plastic-bag and -wrap packages do state what the plastic is made of, but many do not. Some companies, however, list toll-free phone numbers on their labels, so call and find out what goes into their products. You can use heavy wraps specially made for freezing, but you may get confused since I found one product made of nonrecommended polyethylene that boasted it was "ideal for freezing." Because they puncture easily and don't form tight seals, wax paper, aluminum foil, and freezer paper are not advised for wrapping, but the last two may be used as an outer wrap over the plastic layer.

Fresh prepackaged fish should be removed from its original container and rewrapped before freezing. When you wrap any fresh fish for freezing, you want to form a tight skin around it, pressing out air. For drawn and dressed fish, press the wrap into the belly cavity. Seal any edges with tape, cover with another layer of wrapping, and date the package. For easy separation, package steaks and fillets individually or layer them with waxed paper in between. It's best to freeze no more than one pound of fish per package.

Since you should freeze fish as fast as possible, it's ideal if you can set your freezer at its lowest temperature about 2 hours before you add the fish. In general, freeze no more than 3 pounds of fish per cubic foot of freezer space in a day's time. Try to place fish packets directly against freezer walls and floors where it's coldest. Because temperature fluctuations hasten dehydration, keep the fish toward the back or bottom of the freezer—away from the door. For the best eating quality, keep the temperature below 0° F. In general, lean fish that are less than 2 percent fat can be frozen for 4 to 6 months; fattier fish keep for about 2 or 3 months.

If you anticipate holding fish in your freezer for a while—say, two months or more—you can preserve the quality longer by coating already-frozen fish with an icy glaze. After you've solidly frozen the fresh fish as quickly as possible (you can do it by placing fillets or steaks in a single layer on a cookie sheet and covering with a layer of foil or waxed paper), take each piece and quickly dip it in ice-cold water. A glaze will automatically form. After each fish piece has been dipped, place the batch back in the freezer, uncovered, for another 10 to 20 minutes. Repeat this dipping and freezing process 5 or 6 times until a thick ice coating is formed. Then wrap, label, and freeze.

You can also make a protective dipping solution of 4 teaspoons ascorbic acid (the chemical name for vitamin C that's sold as Fruit Fresh in supermarkets) to 1 gallon of water. Hold the fish in the solution for 30 seconds, then wrap and freeze. Rinse in cold water before cooking.

To freeze shucked clams, oysters, and mussels, place in small freezer containers, cover with their own strained juices (if necessary, supplement with the homemade brine described on page 176), cover, and freeze. Be sure to leave about a half-inch space between the liquid and the lid to allow for expansion of the liquid. Figure on keeping the shellfish no more than 4 months. Fresh scallops can also be frozen for up to 4 months if you tightly pack them in covered freezer containers or double plastic bags meant for freezing (press out air). Generally speaking, properly wrapped *cooked* seafoods can be frozen for about 3 months.

Fish aficionados are sort of like coffee fanatics who insist on grinding their own beans—if you get hooked on fresh fish, you may decide that the only way to go is to cut your own fillets and steaks from dressed or drawn fish. Not only is it easier to identify quality fish in these forms, but they keep better than precut fillets and steaks.

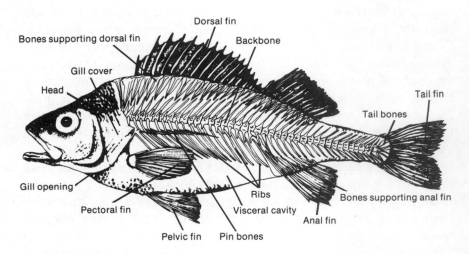

Round fish structure

For starters, you'll need a decent fillet knife—one with a blade about 6 inches long that's relatively thin and narrow with some, but not too much, flexibility. Then go to work with the following procedures, which you may or may not have to do, depending on the fish's destiny. If, for instance, you only plan on cutting skinless fillets, you don't have to scale or defin the fish. All fish-cleaning procedures require a sharp knife. Note also that you don't have to proceed in this order and that there are other ways to perform the various cleaning duties.

Drawing and dressing whole finfish

Since most retail fish dealers don't sell fish whole, you're more likely to need the following skills if you catch your own. (Recall, however, that about 20 percent of the fish eaten in this country is estimated to be caught recreationally.) Do the honors as soon as possible because intact internal fish organs are responsible for quick fish deterioration and possible bacterial contamination.

Before you even start cutting, you have to cope with fish slime, which harbors bacteria and makes fish difficult to handle. As Kenn and Pat Oberrecht, authors of *Keeping the Catch,* put it, "If fish had handles, they would be a lot easier to grip." To keep fish slime to a minimum, rinse whole and cut fish well, and frequently wash off your hands and any utensils that contact the fish. To cope with the slimiest fish, which include flatfishes, tautog, northern pike, and skate, you can scrape off the slime with the back of a knife blade and/or soak them in a "desliming" solution made of 1 part vinegar to 3 parts cold water. Rubbing the skin with salt helps to make handling easier, too. (In either case, rinse the fish before cooking.)

Scaling can be done using a fish scaler, a knife blade, or a teaspoon. Scales can make a big mess, so you may want to do the honors on a newspaper or underwater. First rinse, but don't dry, the fish. Holding the fish by the tail and starting at the tail end, simply scrape against the scales and toward the head in short, firm strokes. Go all the way up to the head, under the belly, and then to the other side. Be sure to clean up right away as dried-on scales are difficult to remove from the counter.

Remove the gills, which can impart an unpleasant taste if you plan to cook the fish head-on. Lift the gill covers and cut near the "chin" and at the base of the skull to remove the accordion-shaped gills.

Gut the fish by making an incision with the point of a sharp knife along the fish's belly—from the anus all the way up to the fish's "chin" or gills. Be careful to cut through only the meat, not the internal organs. (In roundfish, the entrails are at the bottom of the widest part of the fish; in flatfish, they're located in the front quarter of the body, just beneath the gills.) Next, just pull out the organs by hand. You may need to run a knife along either side of the kidneys— that dark red line of tissue on either side of the backbone. You can scrape out any kidney material left behind with a spoon or an old, clean toothbrush. Submerge under cold, running water and rinse all traces of blood from the stomach cavity.

Behead the fish by slicing right through it, just behind the gill covers. You may need to use a heavy knife to get through the backbone of larger fish.

Remove the fins by either of two methods. You can simply cut them off with a sharp knife or scissors, which leaves behind their root bones. But to get rid of the bones, Sue Faria advises making a V-shaped cut down into the flesh at the base of each fin—including the large dorsal fin on top—with the root bones in the middle of the cut. Then with your hands or pliers, grab hold of each fin at the end nearest the tail and pull toward the head. Fins should come out, root bones and all. (If you plan to cook drawn or dressed fish, the flesh may hold together better if you leave on the dorsal and anal fins.)

Cut off the tail at its base if you don't like its looks. Rinse the remainder of the fish's body thoroughly.

Steaking fish

Steaking is meant for firmer-textured fish that weigh 5 pounds or more. To avoid dried-out cooked steaks, you want to slice cross sections of no less than ¾ inch. If not done already, gut the fish and remove its scales, fins, and head. Lay the cleaned fish on its side and, starting at the head end, start making ¾- to 1-inch slices. Your cuts should go straight down through the backbone and continue until the fish starts to taper. Then, if you like, you can stop the steaking and turn the tail end into two fillets. If you have an electric knife, you'll find that it works well for producing uniform steaks and getting through the backbone.

Filleting

You don't have to gut fish before filleting if you do the job immediately after a fish is caught. The head and tail need not be removed, and scales can be left on if you intend to skin the fillet. To avoid cutting yourself when filleting, always place the knifeless hand that does the steadying behind the blade. There are many ways to fillet a roundfish, but the experienced authors of *Keeping the Catch* say the easiest method—and one that works for most species—is to lay the fish on its side with the backbone facing you. With a sharp knife, make a cut behind the head (behind the pectoral fin) down to—but not through—the backbone. (Continue the cut down to the belly.) When you feel the knife hit the backbone, turn the blade flat, facing it toward the tail. Angle it slightly into the backbone, and with long, smooth slicing strokes, run the knife along the backbone until you reach the tail, at which point you can angle the blade upward and cut off the fillet. (You may need to saw a bit when you hit rib and pin bones—see below.) Trim any ragged edges off your fillet, then turn the fish over and repeat the whole process on the other side.

Whether or not you wind up with a bony fillet depends on your skill, the skeletal structure of the species, and how the fish responds to cooking (some fish bones are edible after cooking). There are wide variations—some fish have free bones peppered throughout the belly; others have only a spine. You may be able to feel bones in your raw fillet by running your hand across the flesh. To remove the "belly" bones running through the thicker end of a fillet, cut them away by sliding a knife under the bone tips and slicing underneath until they're free. In addition, you may choose to remove the pin bones present in many fish. If they run in a strip, you can cut along each side and simply lift it out. Any individual remaining bones can be removed with your fingers, tweezers, needle-nose pliers, or a knife. (It's a good idea to keep a kitchen pair of tweezers so they're handy whenever you find bones in fish.)

Large flatfish, such as flounder, can be cut into 4 fillets—2 from each side. Place the side with the eyes facing upward and make a cut down the backbone (which runs down the center of the side of the fish facing upward)—all along it from the gill cover to the tail. Then make a cut through the fleshy section behind the head. Starting at this cut, slide a flexible knife blade between the backbone and flesh, lifting away the fillet as you go. (Avoid the root bones of the fins.) Fillet the other half of this same side, then turn the fish over and remove the two fillets on the other side.

Skinning a fillet

With the fillet placed skin side down, hold the tip of the tail or tail-end down with your fingers or a fork held by your noncutting hand. Close to the tip and using a sharp knife, make a cut down—but not through—the skin. Then, holding the knife horizontally with the blade away from the noncutting hand, slip it between the flesh and the skin and slide it down the length of the fillet, using a light back-and-forth sawing motion to separate the skin from the flesh. Keep the knife as flat against the skin as you can and push the knife in one direction while you pull the skin the other way.

HOW TO CLEAN SHELLFISH

Clams, mussels, and oysters

If you buy them at a fish market, these mollusks may only need to have their shells scrubbed or simply rinsed. Ask your seafood dealer how you should handle them. If you do your own digging, you'll need to purge clams of the grit they accumulate as they bury themselves in the sand. Actually, clams will expel the sand for you if you simply cover them with clear sea water or with a solution consisting of ⅓ cup salt to 1 gallon of cool tap water. Allow to sit for half an hour, drain, and repeat the process several times. (If you object to the dark appearance of clam guts, it's said that you can add some cornmeal to the water—the clams will eat it, replacing their stomach contents with what some people see as more pleasing-colored contents.) After soaking, scrub the shells with a stiff brush or a plastic pot cleaner.

Oysters and mussels don't accumulate much sand. For oysters, just rinse and scrub the shells under cool running tap water. (See page 130 for details on cleaning mussels.)

If you want to use raw, shucked mollusks in a recipe, the easiest way to get them to open up is to steam them just until the shells give way enough to insert a knife tip. Watch closely if you want the meat to be uncooked. If you're wondering why I'm not offering guidelines for shucking shellfish so you can eat them raw, it's because I can't—in good conscience—advise you to eat them that way. (See "The Risks of Raw Seafood" on page 89.) Besides, shucking raw mullusks with a knife can be dangerous—my father has stitch marks on one of his hands to prove it!

Cleaning shrimp

Start by pulling the heads off if they're still on. You can peel and devein shrimp before or after cooking. If you peel cooked shrimp, the shell is easiest to remove within 20 minutes of cooking. Starting at the head end, take hold of one side of the legs with their attached shell and "unwrap" the shell from the body. You can also pull the legs off, then remove the shell. The tail can be pulled off or left on for decoration or as a handle for eating.

The "vein" is actually the shrimp's intestinal tract, which is harmless if the meat is cooked. Most people choose to remove it for aesthetic reasons. In larger shrimp, it's really a good idea to take out the vein because it can be quite sandy and gritty. To devein, take a sharp knife and make a shallow cut from the head to the tail along the back of each shrimp. With your fingers, a knife, or a toothpick, lift out the exposed vein and rinse.

Now that your fish has been properly chosen, stored, and cleaned, you're ready to cook it. The next chapter tells you how to "cook it right."

CHAPTER TEN

Cook It Right

NEXT TO SMELLY FISH, the worst fish is overcooked fish. Be it baked, broiled, or fried, fish that's been subjected to heat for too long a time becomes dry and tough. Fish simply can't take the heat the way red meat and poultry can because it has so little connective tissue, tissue that would require relatively long cooking to soften it for eating. Therefore, to keep fish juicy and tender after you cook it, the basic guidelines are *high temperature, short time,* and *watch it.*

WHEN IS IT DONE?

Most experts currently go by what's known as the Canadian cooking rule, which holds that unfrozen finfish—whether whole, steaks, or fillets—should be cooked for about 10 minutes per inch of thickness, measured at the thickest part of the fish. For baking, the oven should be preheated to 450° F. (Some references say 400° F.) The 10-minute rule also applies to most other cooking methods (the specifics start on page 188) and should be scaled up or down according to the thickness of the fish. Thin, half-inch fillets, for instance, need only be cooked for 5 minutes, while thick one-and-a-half-inch steaks require about 15 minutes of heat exposure. If the edges of a fillet are thinner than the rest of the piece of fish, simply fold them under to make the fillet of uniform thickness.

For frozen fish, up the cooking time to 20 minutes per inch. And add 5 minutes to the calculated cooking time for each inch of thickness if you cook fresh or frozen fish in a sauce. Extra time may also be needed if your fish is stuffed or cooked with vegetables.

The Canadian rule is only approximate—you still need to watch fish closely as it cooks, and you should test it for doneness before the calculated time is up. In general, firm, dense fish like swordfish and tuna cook more slowly than delicate, flaky types of the same thickness. And because they're naturally "greased," oily types of fish can withstand a bit longer cooking than leaner varieties. For the record, the moistest, most flavorful forms of fish are those cooked with skin and bones intact. Leaving heads and tails on also helps to prevent the loss of tasty fish juices.

You know it's done when the watery, translucent appearance of raw fish flesh assumes an opaque cast. The color of most types of finfish also becomes snowy white or lightens after cooking. The texture will change, too—most raw fish isn't flaky and the flesh sticks to any bones that are present, at least if the fish is fresh. But cooked fish flakes and readily separates from the bones. Test for doneness by inserting a sharp knife tip or a fork in the thickest part of the fish (behind the head in whole fish) and gently pulling back on the flesh. Properly cooked fish should split along its natural separations. The color and texture changes happen very quickly, so keep a close eye on your catch as it cooks and take it away from the heat the instant that the center registers "done." Try to have the rest of a meal ready to go so you can serve fish the moment it's cooked through.

There's no question that the art of fish cookery takes some practice. But you need to be adventuresome and try new cooking methods if you want to add more fish to your diet yet never tire of it. Just think, if you have access to 20 different kinds of fish in a year's time and you apply each of the 10 or so cooking methods discussed in this chapter, you have the potential for creating 200 different—and easy—fish dishes!

THE CATCH-22 OF FISH COOKERY

Many culinary experts now balk at the traditional cook-till-it-flakes guideline for finfish because they believe that fish tastes better when it's slightly underdone. Accordingly, the going recommendation on the part of a number of seafood chefs is to cook fish only to the "medium-rare" point that occurs just as flakes are beginning to form. Basically, medium-rare fish is like medium-rare steak—it's hot on the outside and warm on the inside. The problem is that this new advice for succulent fish eating is not without risks from a food-safety standpoint. When you eat any type of meat, poultry, fish, or shellfish that's not thoroughly cooked, there's always the possibility of contracting certain types of food poisoning.

It's well documented that fish can transmit some harmful parasites —tapeworms, flukes, and roundworms—to people who eat it *raw*. (See "On sushi, sashimi, ceviche . . ." on page 92.) But I can't tell you exactly what the risks of eating fish medium-rare are since even the experts don't agree. Robert Learson, director of the National Marine Fisheries Service Laboratory in Gloucester, Massachusetts, is not worried about eating finfish medium-rare because most fish parasites are not harmful to humans—any that are would likely be killed if fish were cooked medium-rare. On the other hand, Joseph Licciardello, Ph.D.—a research food technologist who works with Learson—believes that you should eat all fish well cooked to play it safe. He admits that most harmful agents that might be present in fish appear on the surface and are inactivated by brief cooking. There are, however, potentially harmful—albeit uncommon—organisms that can still survive in the interior of undercooked fish. Indeed, Dr. Roy Martin, with the National Fisheries Institute in Washington, D.C., stresses that the presence of these internal organisms is not an everyday occurrence, and doesn't think medium-rare fish presents a health concern.

Of course, the risk may depend on how you define medium-rare—for some people it may mean barely warmed. A report of fish tapeworm infection in the *Southern Medical Journal* revealed that one couple found out the hard way that a "very light" cooking of salmon is not adequate.

To put things in perspective, the risks of eating medium-rare finfish are probably no greater than those of eating medium-rare beef. Obviously, many beef lovers are willing to take a small risk every day, usually without suffering any ill consequences. Thomas Deardorff, Ph.D., an expert on fish parasites at the FDA's Fishery Research Branch, reassures that "the vast majority of fish available in this country is safe." Nevertheless, he maintains that the safest bet for assuring the death of finfish parasites is to cook fish until the thickest part is opaque, flakes easily, and is *hot* to the touch. (That doesn't mean you have to cook it to death.) Some of the finfish that Dr. Deardorff cautions against eating medium-rare are cod, Pacific rockfish, and salmon because they've been linked to the majority of parasitic infections reported in North Americans. Shellfish, too, should be thoroughly cooked to kill any harmful organisms that might be present. (For more on risks of eating raw and underdone fish and shellfish, see chapter 7.)

As mentioned earlier, freezing at very low temperatures will also kill fish parasites. Dr. Deardorff's preliminary findings suggest that freezing at $-4°$ F for 4 to 5 days will do the trick. You need a freezer thermometer (see page 175) to determine if your freezer is cold enough. As for commercially frozen fish, viable parasites are highly unlikely because of the even lower temperatures to which it's subjected. Pickling, marinating, and cold smoking, however, do not do away with all harmful organisms.

THE MANY METHODS OF FISH COOKERY

The remainder of this chapter is devoted to simple fish-cooking techniques that allow you to enjoy the light, natural taste of fish—without a lot of added calories and fat. With moist-heat cooking methods like poaching, steaming, microwaving, and cooking *en papillote,* you don't have to add a single bit of butter, margarine, or oil. But dry-heat methods—including broiling, baking, and grilling—often require a small amount of fat or a light sauce to keep the fish moist. You can usually get away with using much less fat than the amount called for in typical recipes. (See chapter 11, "Working from Your Own Recipes.")

It's important to try to match the type of fish you have in hand with a suitable cooking method. Moist-heat methods, for instance, complement leaner fish that dry out easily. Because of their built-in lubrication, oilier species are great broiled or grilled but don't work so well with some moist-heat methods.

To thaw or not to thaw?

When working with frozen fish, you have to decide whether to thaw it before cooking. Many fish connoisseurs now agree with Raquel Boehmer, editor of *Seafood Soundings* newsletter, that "across the board, frozen finfish is best cooked without being defrosted." It's true that you don't need to thaw fish for most techniques as long as cooking time is increased. That way, fewer juices are lost, thereby preserving more flavor and nutrients than in thawed fish. For some recipes—say, for rolled or stuffed fish—you have to thaw. And certain sauce recipes work best if fish is thawed. But many times you need only partially defrost frozen fish. (Specific guidelines for handling frozen fish are given under each cooking method.)

Never thaw fish at room temperature because the outer parts will defrost and can start to spoil before the center is ready. The ideal way to thaw fish is in your refrigerator overnight, which should be adequate for one-pound portions of fillets and steaks; whole fish may take longer. Be sure to place it on a plate to catch any drippings. Incidentally, it's safe to refreeze fish that's been thawed in the refrigerator, but the quality of the fish will greatly suffer.

If you need to speed things up, tightly wrapped fish can be placed under cold, running water or immersed in very cold water—allow about 30 minutes per pound of fish. Don't use warm or hot water which will thaw outer surfaces too fast and may start the fish cooking.

Fish can also be thawed in a microwave oven. The National Fisheries Institute says that it requires about 6 to 8 minutes at 30 percent power to defrost a pound of fish. Fillets and steaks should be placed in a covered dish that's vented at one corner. Rotate the dish at the halfway point and continue microwaving in 30- to 60-second intervals, then resting, until the fish is defrosted. Or you may choose to follow the instructions given in your owner's manual. Mine suggests a combination of microwave thawing at a low power, then standing in cold water. Times vary with the amount of fish and their market form. However you thaw frozen fish, keep it refrigerated until ready to use—preferably within two days.

Baking

A versatile cooking method, baking works for just about any kind of fish and any market form. Because it is a dry-heat method of cookery, baking is best applied to whole fish, thick steaks and fillets, and oily fish. You can certainly bake thinner and leaner varieties, but you may need to add a small amount of fat, bread-crumb topping, light sauce, or liquid to prevent drying out. To humidify your oven while baking fish, you can plant a pan or two of water on a lower rack.

First, allow about 20 minutes for the oven to preheat to 400° to 450° F. While that's warming, lightly grease a shallow baking dish with margarine or oil, or coat with a nonstick vegetable spray. One tablespoon of diet margarine adds just 50 calories to a recipe. Another trick to prevent sticking is to place lemon slices under the fish. Delicate fish that tends to crumble can be placed into the baking dish on a greased sheet of foil with edges extended over the sides for lifting out at the end of baking time.

The topping on baked fish can simply be lemon juice and herbs for thicker and oilier pieces. If your fish needs a bit of fat, a tablespoon of melted margarine, butter, or oil will do for four people and can be stretched by mixing with several tablespoons of lemon or lime juice. Bread crumbs and crushed crackers or flake-type cereals can be used as tasty toppings that help seal in moisture.

You don't usually need to cover baking fish, but some recipes say to cover the dish loosely with greased foil, a good moisture-saving idea for leaner types. (This would make for soggy crumb-topped fish, however.) You can also bake fish (covered or open) in a small amount of liquid—a broth, seasoned water, or milk. I enjoy lean fish fillets baked in a bit of milk and topped with crushed cracker crumbs and a very light drizzling of margarine.

As for time, apply the 10-minute rule of thumb for each inch of thickness or until the fish is done. Add 5 minutes per inch if you bake fish in a sauce.

Another way to bake fish of any market form is to wrap it in foil (securing at the top to hold in the juices), place it on a cookie sheet or baking dish, and cook at 400° to 450° F for 10 minutes per inch. For larger and thicker portions, you may need to add an extra 5 minutes per inch of thickness for the heat to penetrate the foil. Foil-baked fish actually steam-cooks—because of moisture retention, you don't have to add any fat. For added flavor liberally top it with lemon or lime juice, seasonings, a bit of white wine, and/or fresh, thinly sliced vegetables.

Frozen fish can be baked as is unless you're rolling or stuffing it. For one-pound frozen blocks of fish, which run about an inch thick, Raquel Boehmer recommends removing from the freezer for 20 minutes before baking. Then cut into several portions with a heavy knife and bake in a preheated 450° F oven for about 20 minutes. Use frozen steaks and fillets as they are in recipes, baking about 20 minutes per inch of thickness and adding about 5 minutes per inch if baked in a sauce or in foil.

Basic baked fish recipes: Cod Fillets with Lemon-Herb Butter, page 261, and Simple Cod Fillets with Buttery Crumb Topping, page 263.

Broiling

Oily fish were made for broiling—they require no fat or sauce and are delicious basted with a simple lemon or lime and herb mixture. Any type of fish fillet or steak can be broiled, but cuts of at least ¾-inch thickness are best suited for the intense, dry heat. Thinner pieces and lean types of fish need some type of coating or periodic basting while broiling. Try a light coating of reduced-calorie mayonnaise or plain yogurt mixed with herbs. Lemon juice, wine, herbs, and a small amount of olive oil or melted margarine make a nice basting mix. You can also marinate fish before broiling and baste with the marinade.

For thinner fish, place the oven rack so the top of the fish will be about 4 inches from the broiler element. Thicker pieces need about 6 inches of space so the outside doesn't char before the inside is done.

Allow about 10 minutes for the broiler to preheat. While that's going, place your fish in a single layer on a broiler pan or rack over a baking sheet. Grease the rack using oil, margarine, nonstick spray, or diet margarine. If the skin is still on fillets, place them skin side down. (For easy cleanup, I usually cover the pan underneath with foil.) You can add a small amount of water to the lower pan for moistening, but don't let it touch the fish. Then place your fish under the broiler, leaving the door slightly ajar. Apply the 10-minute rule for timing, but keep a close eye on the fish.

Baste lean and thin-sliced fish before and several times during cooking. If pieces are less than one inch thick, you don't have to turn them. Fish of an inch or greater thickness should be turned once, about halfway through the calculated cooking time. If you want to top-brown fish cooked by another method, slightly undercook it, then place under the preheated broiler for a minute or two. Watch closely.

Small drawn and dressed fish can also be broiled. To facilitate heat penetration, make a few shallow slashes through the skin before cooking. Larger drawn and dressed fish can also be broiled if they're split and placed flat on the greased broiler rack.

Frozen fish can be broiled without thawing if you move the oven rack at least a notch lower than you'd use for unfrozen fish. Use the same coatings (to avoid overbrowning, you may want to add them toward the end of cooking) or basting mixes and broil for about 10 minutes per inch of thickness on each side.

Basic broiled fish recipe: Broiled Basil Swordfish, page 253.

Grilling

Grilling is not just for steak, burgers, and hot dogs anymore. Fish cooked over the coals is a treat you can't afford to miss because the smoky flavor complements the natural taste of fish. Almost any variety or market form can be grilled if you do it right, but thick, firm steaks and fillets—from bluefish or tuna, for example—are ideal. As with broiling, the types of fish best suited for grilling are oilier: mackerel, trout, butterfish, sablefish, and salmon. They require little or no basting, while drier fish like halibut and swordfish need to be marinated or basted first. Oily or firm thick cuts can be placed directly on a well-greased grill.

Fish that isn't firm should be placed in a hinged wire rack or cooked on the grill covered with heavy-duty foil—poke small holes in the foil to allow the smoky taste to come through; this is also a good method for scallops. Thinner outer portions of fillets should be tucked under for uniform thickness.

Well-oiled, firm-textured drawn and dressed fish can be placed directly on the grill. If the flesh is not particularly firm, you're better off placing drawn and dressed fish in a special fish-shaped wire basket before grilling. Two- to 3-pounders cook more evenly if you make diagonal slashes through the skin in the thicker areas of the fish.

Be sure to oil anything that touches the fish—wire baskets, foil, skewers, and the grill itself. The more you can leave on the fish—heads, tails, and skin—the moister the finished product will be. Fillets with skin should be cooked skin side down. Grilled fish of any sort is always juicier if you baste it with marinade or barbecue sauce while cooking.

If using a gas or electric grill, make sure that it's preheated before adding the fish. When using charcoal, start the fire 30 to 40 minutes ahead of time. Coals are ready when they have an ashy white coating. Spread them into a single layer. Since fish tends to stick to an unclean grill, make sure it's been washed first. Dry, then grease the grill well and preheat it over the hot coals. Large drawn and dressed fish and thick steaks need about 6 inches between themselves and the coals, while smaller pieces of fish require only 4 inches. You can place slices of orange or lemon under the fish to help prevent sticking to the grill. It's best if the fish has just come out of the refrigerator because the coldness will slow down the fast rate of cooking. Keep a squirt bottle of water handy to quell any flames that might char your fish.

Perhaps more so than with any other method, you have to keep your eye on grilling fish because the intense heat is variable and unpredictable—being at the mercy of air currents and humidity. The 10-minute rule only roughly applies, so stay close by grilling fish, checking for doneness before the time is up.

In their book *Fish on the Grill,* Barbara Grunes and Phyllis Magida recommend that fillets be turned only if thick and firm. For steaks and fillets that are an inch or more thick, apply the 10-minute rule, turning at the halfway point. Small, whole fish take 6 to 9 minutes per side, while large, whole fish require 11 to 20 minutes on each side. Cooking times may be longer if fish is very thick or stuffed. I'd advise having your stuffing nice and hot before filling a dressed or drawn fish destined for grilling.

Authors Grunes and Magida offer an indirect method of grilling that can be used if a slower rate of cooking is desired and/or you don't feel like watching the fish closely. When the hot charcoal is whitish, divide it into two small banks on each side of the grill. Lay the fish on the grate over the spot between the two piles of charcoal, and cook for about 15 to 18 minutes per inch of thickness. To catch drippings, a metal pan can be placed in the very bottom of the grill between the two piles of charcoal.

Live clams, oysters, mussels, crabs, and lobsters can be roasted directly on the grill. Furthermore, any type of fish or shellfish can be wrapped in foil and placed over the coals, but you really wind up with a steamed product. Sea scallops and shrimp make nice kebab items, as do chunks of firm fillets or steaks. You can also weave thinner fillet strips on skewers. Since you only need to cook kebabs for 9 to 15 minutes total, you may want to parboil harder vegetable additions like peppers and onions. Turn kebabs about every 3 minutes until all sides are done.

It's sometimes recommended that frozen fish be thawed before grilling. But if you can distance the fish from the coals or cook it indirectly, you can grill fish in the frozen state.

Basic grilled fish recipe: Sesame-Soy Halibut Steaks, page 262.

Marinating

Marinades give fish flavor and spare them from drying out, particularly when you're broiling or grilling. For heavier-tasting fish, try blends of soy sauce, vinegar, brown sugar, and fruit juice. A mixture of white wine, lemon or lime juice, and herbs complements light, leaner varieties. If the fish is dry and lean, add a touch of oil to your blend.

Acids in marinades containing lemon or lime juice, vinegar, or wine also tenderize fish. So don't let more delicate types sit too long in such marinades or you may wind up with a mushy texture. Usually an hour or so is adequate for marinating fish. Use a glass, enamel, or plastic container—not metal, which may dissolve in acid—to hold marinating fish. And be sure to refrigerate the fish, turning several times, as it bathes.

Basic marinated fish recipe: Scallop-Shrimp Kebabs, page 312.

Microwave cooking

Some seafood experts reject microwave cooking so completely that it's not even listed as a method in a number of fish cookbooks. But many people I know swear by it when they want a moist, tender piece of fish that doesn't entail a lot of fuss or have added calories from fat. A common problem with microwave cooking of fish is timing—here's a case where the 10-minute rule just doesn't apply. You really need to experiment with how long you cook fish, following the guidelines in your oven's manual. Indeed, cooking time varies with the power of the oven, the thickness and density of the fish, other recipe ingredients, and the amount you're cooking. In general, however, you can figure that microwave cooking times are ¼ to ⅓ of those used for conventional recipes. And you can usually use ¼ less liquid when you convert regular recipes for the microwave oven.

Basic fish cookery in a microwave entails placing the fish in a flat, shallow microwaveable baking dish. You can lightly grease the dish if you like. Thicker parts of fish should be positioned toward the outside of the dish. Cover with waxed paper or plastic wrap with a few holes poked in it or a corner pulled back for venting.

Fillets are usually cooked at high power—a very rough guide is 3 minutes per pound of boneless fillets. Add a minute or so to the cooking time for fish cooked in a sauce or with vegetables. Whole fish can be cooked in a covered, shallow dish or wrapped individually in plastic or waxed paper and placed on a plate with tails aimed toward a corner of the oven. Thick cuts of fish often cook more evenly at medium to medium-high settings and recipes calling for eggs, cheese, milk, and mayonnaise may require less intense heat so they don't curdle.

If you don't have a moving carousel in your oven, turn the dish 180 degrees about halfway through the cooking time. Microwave-cooked fish should be removed from the oven when the outer portions are opaque, but the center is still slightly translucent. It will finish cooking (covered) during the standing time.

Frozen fish should be thawed before cooking in a microwave oven. Follow the directions in your owner's manual.

Following are some of the things you can do with fish in the microwave oven. (Apply the general principles discussed above for placement of fish, rotating, and standing. Your owner's manual may offer more specific guidelines for each method.)

- *Steaming.* Just place a damp paper towel over fish arranged in a baking dish and cook for the allotted time.
- *Poaching.* Prepare a poaching liquid of your choice (see page 199) and bring it to a boil in the microwave oven. Cover the fish with the hot liquid, cover and vent, then microwave at full power.
- *Breaded fillets.* If you have a special microwave browning skillet, it's possible to wind up with a crispy breaded product. Without the skillet, however, crumb toppings and coatings will be moist.
- *Sauce recipes.* If you're using a sauce recipe designed for conventional cooking, you may find that it turns out runny because of the fish juices released in microwaving. You can rectify the situation by removing the cooked fish from the sauce, setting it aside on a warm platter, and covering it. Then mix together a tablespoon of cornstarch with a tablespoon of cold water for each cup of sauce that

you wish to thicken. Blend the cornstarch and water into the sauce and microwave at full power, whisking several times, until the sauce thickens and bubbles. Now it's ready to pour over the fish.

• *Reheating fish leftovers.* Since leftover fish is easily overcooked, it's important not to heat it too long in the microwave oven. Casseroles and sauce dishes work the best for reheating.

Basic microwaved fish recipe: Simple Sole Amandine, page 271.

Oven-frying

If your fancy is fried fish—yet you want to go the healthful route— oven-frying (sometimes called the Spencer method) is for you. With a small amount of fat, some bread crumbs, and a very hot oven, you can simulate the taste and texture of fried fish. When serving a crowd, oven-frying is also an ideal way to cook a large batch of fish at once. Although the method is best-suited to fillets, any market form or type of fish—oily or lean—can be used. But your pieces of fish should be less than an inch and a half thick. You can also oven-fry shrimp and scallops.

Oven-frying is not really frying at all, but entails baking fish in an oven that's been preheated to a temperature of 500° to 550° F. The oven rack should be placed in the upper third of the oven. While the oven is warming, dip each fish piece in some sort of liquid that will bind the crumbs. Your binder can be any of the following: milk, beaten eggs mixed with some milk, low-calorie salad dressing, but-termilk, yogurt, or reduced-calorie mayonnaise thinned with milk. Sometimes the fish is lightly coated with flour before dipping it in the binder.

After thoroughly coating fish pieces with the binder, let them drip a bit, then coat each one with crumbs. It's easiest if you spread a layer of crumbs on a flat plate and press each side of the fish into them. Bread crumbs are only one option—you can substitute cornmeal, crushed crackers, wheat germ, oatmeal, or crushed flake-type cereal. Add some seasonings, such as onion or garlic powder, parsley, dry mustard, Parmesan cheese, or salt and pepper.

After the fish is coated, place it in a single layer on a well-greased cookie sheet or flat baking dish; drizzle with a light trickling of melted margarine, butter, or oil (a tablespoon or two is all you need for four servings); and bake in the preheated oven. Watch closely, for the 10-minute rule may be too generous with cooking time. Don't cover, turn, or baste the fish while it's baking.

Beware of the intense heat released when you open the oven door.

You'll find that the high temperature and crumbs lock in fish juices while yielding a crispy golden crust. Oven-fried fish served with lemon wedges or low-calorie tartar sauce (on page 237) can't be beat!

Frozen fish should be at least partially thawed before oven-frying.

Basic oven-fried fish recipe: Easy Oven-Fried Cusk Fillets, page 264.

Pan-frying

Yet another way for fried-fish lovers to enjoy crispy fish without all the grease, pan-frying lends itself best to thin cuts of fish—no more than ½ inch thick. You can also pan-fry small drawn or dressed fish such as butterfish, whiting, and trout. The procedure is similar to oven-frying, but it's done on top of the stove.

Select a heavy skillet large enough to accommodate the fish without crowding pieces. A nonstick pan enables you to get away with using less fat. You can also use an electric frying pan. The burner should be set at medium to medium-high or an electric pan at 350° to 375° F. Add a tiny amount of oil—a light coating that covers the bottom of the pan is all you need. Heat until the oil is hot, but not smoky. I've also successfully pan-fried in diet margarine (in a nonstick pan) or in a small amount of butter stretched with lemon juice—heat until the mixture sizzles (see basic recipe below).

To prepare the fish for frying, follow the steps listed for oven-frying —dip in a moist binder, then coat with crumbs. You can also coat moist fish with a light dusting of flour and herbs. Add the coated fillets to the hot pan in a single layer, uncovered. Apply the 10-minute rule, cooking half of the time on one side—until it's golden brown. Then gently turn, taking care to lift the crispy coating. Cook the rest of the time on the other side, then drain on paper towels if the fish seems greasy. Very thin fillets need only be breaded and coated on one side—serve with the browned side facing up.

You can also lightly pan-fry fish without precoating with crumbs or flour. Over a burner set at medium to medium-high, heat margarine, butter, or oil until quite hot. You can also use the lemon juice—butter (or margarine) mixture described above with herbs such as parsley and chives. Dry white wine works nicely in place of the lemon juice, too. Then apply the 10-minute rule, turning once while cooking.

Frozen fish, some say, should be thawed or partially thawed before pan-frying—unless it's sliced very thin. But a comprehensive article on fish cookery that appeared in *Sunset* magazine recommends the following. Allow a 1-pound package of frozen fish to stand at room temperature for about 15 minutes or until it can be cut into serving-size pieces; individually frozen fillets and steaks just need to be rinsed in cold water and patted dry. Coat portions for pan-frying and heat the fat as described above. For fish less than ½ inch thick, fry for 5 to 6 minutes total over medium-high heat. Increase the total time by a minute or two for ½- to ¾-inch portions and cook for half the time on each side. For 1-inch-thick pieces, drop the heat to medium-low and cook for 20 to 25 minutes. In all of these cases, check to make sure the fish is done before serving it.

Relatively new to the pan-fried fish scene, Cajun "blackened" fish has gained a restaurant following but can easily be prepared right in your own kitchen—and with less fat. Blackened fish is simply fish coated with a hot, spicy herb mix that's cooked in a very hot cast-iron skillet. Among the fish you can use for blackening—in fillet or steak form—are red drum, pompano, tilefish, swordfish, fresh tuna, cusk, shark, halibut, mackerel, and bluefish. Cuts of fish should be no more than an inch thick.

The basic seasoning mix, brought to fame by Louisiana's chef Paul Prudhomme, consists of:

1 tablespoon sweet paprika	¾ teaspoon white pepper
2½ teaspoons salt	¾ teaspoon black pepper
1 teaspoon onion powder	½ teaspoon dried thyme
1 teaspoon garlic powder	leaves
1 teaspoon ground red pepper (preferably cayenne)	½ teaspoon dried oregano leaves

The recipe makes enough seasoning mix for 4 pounds of fish, so scale it down if you're not sure you'll like it. I also think you can easily cut the salt back to 1½ teaspoons. After you coat your fish pieces evenly with the seasoning mix, the cooking method suggested by the Massachusetts Division of Marine Fisheries involves preheating a large cast-iron skillet over high heat until it's very hot. (It could take as long as 10 minutes to heat the pan.) When you add just a small amount of corn or peanut oil to coat the bottom of the pan, it should smoke. (When blackening fish, be prepared for a lot of smoke. If you disconnect your smoke alarm, make sure you put the batteries back in later.) Add the fish and cook (uncovered) on both sides, allowing 2½ minutes per side for 1-inch-thick fish pieces. Less time is required for thinner fish. If the fish looks charred, it's supposed to. It should also be done on the inside.

Basic pan-fried fish recipe: Tarragon Skate Wings Sautéed in Bread Crumbs and Lemon Butter, page 257.

Fish *en papillote*

Although it sounds fancy and laborious, cooking *en papillote* is merely baking fish in sealed parchment-paper pockets. The method is most often used for thin fillets and steaks, but is also apropos for small drawn or dressed fish and most shellfish. Not only does the paper pocket lock in natural juices, but it makes serving and cleanup simple.

For each portion of fish, cut a square of parchment paper (which you can buy at gourmet shops) that, in length and width, is 3 to 4 inches more than double the size of the piece of fish. Fold the paper in half and, beginning at the fold, cut out a large half heart or semicircle. Because they are what you'll be cooking in, the half heart or semicircle need to be several inches larger than the fish. Open your artwork into a heart or circle and place the fish on one side of the fold. Top with vegetables, such as sliced onions or scallions, red or green pepper slices, zucchini and carrot strips, and mushrooms. You can add some seasoning along with a bit of wine, lemon juice, lime juice, and/or a small amount of butter, margarine, or oil. Then fold over the fishless side of parchment paper so that the edges of both halves of the paper meet. Starting at one end of the package, crimp the edges tightly closed by folding over (just a small amount) twice every 1½ to 2 inches. To help seal the edges, you can brush them with beaten egg before folding. Repeat the procedure for each piece of fish to be served.

Although I don't find it to be necessary, some recipes advise greasing the outside of each closed pocket. When assembled, place them on a cookie sheet and bake in a preheated 400° to 425° F oven, applying the 10-minute rule. But add a couple of extra minutes to the calculated time because it takes a short while for the heat to penetrate the paper. You essentially wind up with a steamed product in a puffed-up, browned package. If you like, carefully cut an X in the top of the paper to allow steam to escape. Each diner gets his own pocket to open at the table—truly a novel way to serve a simple fish dish.

You can also cook your parchment-wrapped fish in a microwave oven. For 4 4-ounce fillets (or a 1-pound fillet cut in half and wrapped in one pocket) topped with vegetables and sealed in paper pockets, microwave on high for about 5 to 7 minutes, rearranging pockets once while cooking.

Frozen fish is best thawed before cooking *en papillote* because the enclosure makes it difficult to check for doneness.

Basic recipe for cooking fish en papillote: Sesame Sole in Parchment Hearts with Snow Peas and Ginger, page 255.

Poaching

Poaching is best described as simmering in liquid that's just under a boil—at a point of "shivering," not bubbling. You can poach most types of fish in just about any market form, but the method lends itself best to firm-fleshed fish like halibut, salmon, and swordfish. The ideal market forms are steaks, thicker fillets, and drawn fish. Be sure to try poached scallops, lobster, and crab (usually in the shell), or clams, oysters, and mussels (usually shucked). Some very oily fish, such as mackerel, don't poach as well as others.

The first step is to decide on your poaching medium—it can be milk, wine and water, seasoned and salted water, chicken or fish stock, or any combination thereof. (Beware that milk mixed with wine or lemon juice tends to curdle.) A popular poaching stock, called court bouillon, consists of water simmered for a period of time with herbs and vegetables, such as onion, garlic, celery, carrots, bay leaves, thyme, and peppercorns. Wine or milk may be added, and whole spices can be tied in a cheesecloth sack for easy removal.

Whatever poaching medium you decide upon, make enough to barely cover the fish that's been placed in a single layer in a large shallow pan or dish. If you get hooked on poached fish, you may want to purchase a special fish poacher with a rack that enables you to easily lift the fish out. Otherwise, to remove fish—particularly delicate types—from a pan or dish without having it fall apart on you, just line the dish with foil, leaving some hanging over the edges to use as handles at the ends. You can also wrap the fish in cheesecloth, tying the ends at the top so they don't drape on the burner. For firmer fish, however, you only need a large spatula to lift the fish out.

You can poach on top of the stove by several different methods. For fillets, steaks, shellfish, and small dressed or drawn fish, Sue Faria recommends that the fish be added to liquid that's already simmering—remember that the liquid should barely cover the fish. If simmering stops when the fish is added, raise the heat a little to bring it to a simmer again. Then lower the temperature and immediately start timing.

To avoid overcooking the outside flesh before the inside is done, large drawn or dressed fish should start out in cool liquid that's brought to a simmer. Begin timing when simmering starts.

You can use the 10-minute rule for poaching fish or cook for 8 to 10 minutes per pound of fish. When simmering on top of the stove, you may or may not choose to use a lid. Keep the heat adjusted so the water never boils.

Another way of poaching fish on top of the stove is to bring the poaching liquid to a full boil, add the fish, then turn off the heat. Cover the fish and allow it to remain in the hot liquid for the calculated cooking time. This method works especially well for smaller pieces of fish and fillets.

You can also poach fish in the oven if you place it in a baking dish, cover with boiling poaching liquid, and lay a sheet of foil across the top of the dish. Place it immediately in a preheated 375° to 400° F oven and cook until the fish is done.

Whatever poaching method you choose, remove the fish from the hot liquid as soon as the time is up. Allowing it to sit for a few minutes will firm the fish, but be sure to drain the fish again before saucing. The poaching liquid can be reduced and thickened to make a sauce or used as is for a broth or soup base.

Frozen fish need not be thawed before poaching. *Sunset* magazine offers the following guidelines for poaching frozen fish: very thin fillets should be poached for 4 to 6 minutes; ½- to ¾-inch-thick pieces need 6 to 9 minutes; 1- to 1½-inch portions should go for 13 to 22 minutes; and a 1- to 1¼-pound package of frozen fish requires about 15 to 18 minutes of poaching.

Basic poached fish recipes: Poached Salmon with Lemony Dill Sauce, page 299, and Oven-Poached Halibut with Florentine Sauce, page 310.

Steaming

Like poaching, steaming can enhance the light, natural taste of fish without any added fat. Almost any fish or shellfish can be steamed, but oily types don't work as well as the leaner ones. Steamed fish is cooked inside a large pan holding a rack or basket that suspends the fish over—not in—boiling water. For the rack, you can use a wok steamer or improvise with a roasting rack or a foil pan that has holes poked in it—balance the rack or pan on an inverted coffee cup or two. Another way to steam that retains the fish's juices is to place it directly on a shallow dish or platter—the dish sits in the hot steaming liquid, but keeps it from directly touching the fish.

Aside from just plain water, the steaming liquid can include all kinds of savory herbs and spices. You can also use beer, a mixture of wine and water, or broth.

Get the fish ready by placing it in a single layer on a lightly greased or nonstick-spray-coated rack or dish. Bring the steaming liquid to a boil, lower the fish over it, cover tightly, and start timing according to the 10-minute rule. Never allow the water to touch the fish, and keep it at a gentle boil. (To avoid a steam burn, be sure to open the cover so the steam is released away from you.)

Steaming is an especially nice way to cook drawn and scaled fish. Simply steam as described above for 12 to 15 minutes per pound. For quicker cooking of larger fish, make shallow diagonal slashes through the skin about an inch apart on both sides of the fish's body.

Frozen fish can be steamed without thawing if you allow extra cooking time. Be it fresh or frozen steamed fish, save the steaming liquid for a broth, soup, or sauce. Tasty accompaniments to steamed fish that can be placed on, under, or inside it are grated fresh ginger, garlic, orange peel, lemon slices, onion, and scallions.

Steaming is a favorite way to cook live mussels, clams, and oysters. Once they're cleaned (and those with opened shells are discarded), just add the live shellfish directly to a large pot holding about a half-inch of boiling liquid. To allow shells to open, the shellfish should be in a shallow layer and not overcrowded. Cover tightly and shake the pot once or twice during cooking. Guidelines for timing often say to steam until the shells open, which could only take a minute. But recent evidence suggests that's not long enough to kill viruses that could be present in the bivalves (see chapter 7). A good 4 to 6 minutes of steaming are needed to inactivate viruses. (Start timing after the water returns to a boil.) Any that refuse to open after cooking should be discarded.

Live lobsters can be steamed in a large, heavy, covered kettle containing about an inch of boiling seawater or salted water. In her book *Fish and Shellfish,* Charlotte Walker recommends steaming 8 to 10 minutes for 1 to 1¼ pounds of lobster, 15 to 18 minutes for 1½ to 2 pounds, and 20 to 25 minutes for 2½ to 5 pounds.

Shrimp can be steamed in the shell or cleaned. Use a rack or place a shallow layer of shrimp directly in a small amount of boiling liquid. For a change, try steaming in beer, white wine, or water seasoned with bay leaves and lemon juice. After the liquid returns to a boil, cover, and steam for 2 to 4 minutes, depending on size and until the shrimp turn pink. Then plunge in cold water to stop the cooking process and drain.

Steaming is also recommended for live, hard-shell crabs. All you need is a shallow layer of boiling liquid in the bottom of a large kettle. Add the crabs, cover, and steam until the aprons begin to rise—it could take 30 minutes or more.

Basic steamed fish recipes: Steamed Mango Mako Shark, page 307, and Steamed Mussels Marinara, page 236.

Stir-frying

Although stir-frying is often done in a wok, you can use any large, heavy frying pan. A large nonstick frying pan enables you to use less oil. Stir-frying entails quick cooking and frequent stirring of foods in a small amount of oil over high heat. The method lends itself best to firm-textured fish including monkfish, wolffish, cusk, swordfish, shrimp, and scallops. Vegetables such as broccoli, carrots, pea pods, and scallions are commonly added. Finfish is usually cut in bite-size chunks of similar size or in thin strips. To make cutting into strips easier, freeze the fish for 30 to 60 minutes (depending on thickness) to allow it to firm slightly.

Because everything happens quickly with stir-frying, have all ingredients (as well as the rest of the meal) ready to go when you start. Heat your wok or skillet over high heat (medium-high may work better with an electric stove). When it's nice and hot, add a tablespoon or two of corn, safflower, peanut, or soybean oil and tilt the pan to coat all surfaces. If the recipe calls for minced garlic or ginger root, start by cooking them briefly—don't brown. Then add the remaining ingredients in sequence according to what takes longest to cook. For instance, add carrots in the beginning and quick-cooking bean sprouts toward the end. Small pieces of fish, such as bay scallops, are often added at the very end. As all ingredients are cooking, stir frequently and gently—a wooden spoon works well. At the end, you can leave everything a bit underdone and add a sauce made of ½ to ¾ cup of broth or unsweetened pineapple juice, a tablespoon or two of soy sauce, and a little wine or sherry—all thickened with several teaspoons of cornstarch. Mix in with the fish and vegetables at the last minute and stir until thickened.

I have my own no-oil method which combines stir-frying with steaming techniques. Just make the sauce mixture described above, but don't add the cornstarch. Place several tablespoons of the sauce in a large nonstick skillet and bring to a boil over medium-high heat. Add ingredients in sequence, as described above, covering with a lid after each addition. The steam will do the cooking. Stir periodically and watch closely to avoid overcooking—vegetables should be tender but crisp. At the very end, add cornstarch to the remaining sauce and stir the mixture in with the fish and vegetables until thickened.

Frozen fish should be partially or completely thawed before stir-frying.

Basic stir-fried fish recipes: Sweet 'n' Sour Swordfish, page 293, and Egg-Coated Salmon and Fresh Spinach Stir-Fry, page 274.

AROMA-ENHANCING TECHNIQUES

I purposely did not entitle this section "odor-fighting techniques" because your fish should not have an aversive fishy smell. If it does, you're not buying fresh fish. (See chapter 9 for guidelines on purchasing fresh fish and storing it to prevent smelliness.) If, however, you are very sensitive to the natural scent of fish, there are some steps you can take to enhance its aroma.

For starters, oilier, darker-fleshed fish—which tend to smell the strongest—can be marinated for an hour or two before cooking in an acidic solution containing lemon juice, lime juice, wine, vinegar, or orange juice. This will also lighten the flesh somewhat. You can remove skin and darker sections of flesh before cooking. The scent of fish is also cut if you cook in any of the acidic liquids described above, as well as in tomato juice or sauce.

If the smell of fish tends to linger on your fingers, rub them with lemon juice or dry mustard before and after you handle the catch. After cooking, you can help rid your home of any food odors by boiling lemon slices, cinnamon sticks, whole cloves, or a scented potpourri in water. To freshen the garbage disposal, grind a piece of lemon after cleaning up a fish meal. Fish drippings on counters, in the refrigerator, or on cutting boards should be washed up well then followed by a lemon-juice wiping. Be sure to discard any fish trimmings or cooked wastes in a tightly closed plastic bag.

A FINAL WORD ABOUT SEASONING YOUR CATCH

Seasoning fish with savory herbs, spices, and vegetables expands all of the basic cooking methods I've described, giving you even more variety in your fish meals. Seasonings also add tastiness to dishes that cut back on fat and salt. It's important, however, to use seasonings judiciously—they're meant to complement the lightness of fish, not hide its taste. When experimenting with herbs and spices, start with just a quarter-teaspoon added to each pound of fish or pint of sauce or soup. (Use even less for hot or strong ingredients like cayenne pepper or garlic powder.) To avoid muddying the flavors, don't add any more than two herbs or spices to a new dish at once. And if you aim to have less sodium in your diet, be sure to use vegetable powders, not salts.

There really is nothing like a fresh herb for flavoring fish. And many markets now stock fresh dill, basil, and chives, as well as the old standby parsley. You may also choose to have your own windowsill herb garden all year round. To keep cut herbs fresh, store them with stems in a glass of water in the refrigerator. Of course, fresh herbs are not always handy. When that's the case, in a recipe calling for fresh herbs, use about ⅓ teaspoon powdered or ½ to ¾ teaspoon crushed dried herb for every tablespoon of fresh, chopped herb.

Following are some of the seasonings that are meant for fish and shellfish. (See also "Stocking Your Kitchen," on pages 226–29.)

Basil. A must for dishes including any form of tomatoes.

Celery seed. Add to cold seafood salads and to boiling water for crustaceans.

Chives. They bring out the flavor of almost any fish dish, hot or cold.

Coriander. Enhances shrimp's flavor and is great in yogurt sauces and rice dishes that include fish.

Cumin. One of my favorite herbs for fish casseroles and stuffings.

Curry powder. Good mixed in cold seafood salads, as well as yogurt and tomato sauces.

Dill weed. A natural for salmon and just about any white finfish or shrimp. Can't be beat in a cucumber-yogurt sauce or hot lemon sauce.

Garlic. If, like me, you tend to go heavy on this favorite flavoring, go easy when you have guests. A must for tomatoey and stir-fried seafood dishes. You can substitute ¼ teaspoon garlic powder for a small, whole clove.

Ginger root. Add grated to marinades, orange sauces, and stir-fry dishes.

Horseradish. Adds zest to cold fish salads, dips, and cocktail and tartar sauces.

Lemon, lime. It almost goes without saying that lemon enhances the flavor of any type of fish or shellfish. Be sure to try lime juice for a change of pace—directly on plain fish or in sauces and marinades.

Mint flakes. Add to poaching or steaming liquids along with carrots and onions. Also good in cold seafood salads and hot lemon sauces.

Mustard. In dry powdered form, mustard complements almost any seafood sauce, casserole, or stuffing. Dry and Dijon-style mustard are good in cold seafood salads and dips. Dijon mustard also makes a tasty topping for broiled, oily types of fish.

Nutmeg. Essential to any fish dish that also includes broccoli or spinach.

Onions, scallions, and leeks. These complement almost any fish in any form—be it plain, sauced, or in a casserole. I use the three interchangeably. Minced shallots are also wonderful with fish—you can substitute 3 or 4 for 1 medium onion. (If in a hurry, use ¾ teaspoon onion powder for one small onion.)

Oregano. Another natural for tomato-based dishes. Also tasty in marinades that include olive oil.

Paprika. Not only flavorful, paprika adds color when serving too many "whites" in a meal.

Parsley. You name the fish recipe, and I'll add parsley to it—as you'll see in the recipe section.

Tarragon. Nice with broiled and baked fish, as well as in marinades containing white wine. Try it in a light white sauce.

Thyme. Use in fish salads, stuffings, or baked fish recipes. Especially good with oily fish.

CHAPTER ELEVEN

Working from Your Own Recipes

IT'S FUNNY HOW the very same friends and relatives who would never dream of cooking with ingredients other than the "real things"—butter, sour cream, cheddar cheese, heavy cream, and the like—always rave about the food I serve. Unbeknownst to them, my cuisine (which I immodestly admit they often refer to as "gourmet") typically has less than half the fat and far fewer calories than traditional versions of recipes.

In fact, my motivation for writing *Eat Fish, Live Better* was triggered largely by my frustration with the many seafood cookbooks on the market—how could I tell people to eat fish three to seven times a week when the recipes available to them were laden with butter, cheese, and cream? Imagine Coquilles St. Jacques with ½ cup heavy cream and 5 tablespoons of butter—my version (on page 304) employs half a cup of evaporated skim milk and a tablespoon of reduced-calorie margarine, cutting the fat by close to three-quarters. How about Tilefish à l'Orange with half a cup of butter plus another tablespoon? The *Eat Fish* version—Tilefish Medallions in Sherried Orange Sauce on page 314—uses just the one tablespoon of butter, saving you 800 calories.

So if my encouragement to eat healthfully prepared fish has you thinking your lips will never again touch your favorite coquilles, Newburg, or scampi dishes, take heart—this chapter will show you how to adapt your own recipes to meet your lower-fat and fewer-calorie goals. Soon, the healthful substitution ingredients and preparation techniques will become second nature. Contrary to popular opinion, cooking low-fat will take up no more of your time than any other type of cooking.

I do suggest that you be willing to experiment and be prepared to encounter some flops along the way, as you would when learning any new art. Yes, low-fat cooking is an art that involves trial, error, and a bit of patience. To avoid frustration, be sure to document your successes—write down your new recipe versions so you remember what you should (and shouldn't) do the next time around.

I'd also advise that you don't tell guests or family members about your kitchen chemistry until they're about halfway through a meal— the words "low-calorie" and "low-fat" carry a stigma that can taint perception of what they're eating. Allow these choosy gourmands to think they're downing the "real thing"; then greet them with the healthful news of what they're really eating. Your regular diners will soon become so accustomed to a lighter, more natural taste that they'll feel uncomfortably weighted down when they eat richly prepared fish elsewhere.

GETTING THE FAT OUT

Since fat has more than double the calories of protein and carbohydrate on an ounce-for-ounce basis, removing fat from recipes will automatically reduce their calorie content. Therefore, the number-one goal in adapting recipes to make them more healthful is to get rid of as much fat as possible—start hacking away at the greasy stuff by cutting the recommended amount in half. If a casserole calls for half a cup of margarine, for instance, use a quarter cup;[1] when pan-frying, use two tablespoons of oil rather than four. With many recipes, you'll find that you can get away with a single tablespoon of fat or leave it out altogether.

Table 9 lists foods that nutritionists consider as fats—note that even the more healthful fats, such as unsaturated vegetable oils and margarine, contain the same number of calories per tablespoon as butter. Every tablespoon of any of the three that you omit from recipes saves approximately 100 calories and about 12 grams of fat. (Vegetable shortening is also a fat with 100 calories per tablespoon. Because it's hydrogenated, it's more saturated than the fats in the "unsaturated" category. Like olive oil, peanut oil is considered monounsaturated. But peanut oil has not been shown to have the beneficial effects that olive oil appears to have [see page 14].)

Let's face it—butter can't be beat on lobster, cream was meant for Newburg sauce, and scampi isn't scampi without the olive oil. Exactly what is it about all of these fats that makes food so mouth-watering? How can we make up for what we're cutting out?

NOTE: The footnote numbers refer to table 11 beginning on page 218. Refer to this table to determine the amount of calories and fat you'll save by making the recommended substitutions throughout the chapter.

TABLE 9. Approximate Amount of Fats Equivalent to 100 Calories

Unsaturated fats	Amount
Avocado (4″ diameter)	¼
Margarine (regular)	1 tablespoon
Mayonnaise (regular)	1 tablespoon
Nuts[a] (almonds, cashews, peanuts, walnuts)	⅔ ounce
Oil (corn, cottonseed, olive, safflower, sesame, soybean, sunflower)	1 tablespoon
Olives	
small	20
large	10
Salad dressing (regular blue cheese, French, Italian, Russian)	1½ tablespoons
Seeds (sesame, sunflower)	2 tablespoons

Saturated fats	Amount
Bacon	2-2½ slices
Butter	1 tablespoon
Coffee creamer (nondairy)[b]	
liquid	5 tablespoons
powder	3 tablespoons
Cream	
light (table or coffee)	3½ tablespoons
heavy	2 tablespoons
Cream cheese	1 ounce
Lard	1 tablespoon
Sour cream	3 tablespoons

[a] Although nuts contain a fair amount of protein, they're about half fat by weight.
[b] There are some unsaturated nondairy creamers on the market. Check product ingredient listings for unsaturated fats.

For one thing, fats add *flavor*—flavor that you'll need to make up for when you cut the butter, cream, oil, and mayonnaise. But remember that the idea is to enhance—not hide—the light, natural taste of fish. For starters, enrich low-fat fish recipes by using the freshest ingredients available—fresh rather than dried herbs, whole onions and garlic instead of flakes and powders, just-squeezed lemon or lime juice, and, of course, the freshest fish you can get your hands on.

Experiment with low-calorie flavor enhancers such as Dijon mustard, horseradish, chopped green peppers, and seasonings like tarragon, curry powder, dill, and dry mustard. (See chapter 10, page 204, for more seasoning ideas.)

In everyday cooking, I recommend that the small amounts of fat that you do use come from the unsaturated family—get in the habit of using unsaturated oils and margarines in place of butter and shortening. For occasional dishes, however, I think the taste of small amounts of less-healthful fats is worth it for the little bit that winds up in each serving. Sometimes, all you need in a recipe is a teaspoon or tablespoon of a flavorful fat such as butter or even bacon fat. Aromatic vegetables like onions, peppers, celery, and garlic will pick up the flavors of small amounts of these fats and carry them throughout an entire dish. You'll see, for instance, that in some *Eat Fish* Recipes I use a tablespoon of real butter. In Sole Aux Fines Herbes, I even use some half-and-half, but it's in place of the much richer heavy cream the original recipe called for.[2] By the time you divide the recipe among four people, the amount of saturated fat isn't worth quibbling about (as long as the rest of the ingredients in the dish are low in fat).

Don't be afraid to use lavish amounts of lemon or lime juice and parsley to enhance your fish dishes—they'll add flavor, as well as *moisturizing power,* another function of fats in cooking. You can also moisten fish recipes with marinades, broths (be sure to chill first so you can skim any fat off the top), chopped or sliced vegetables, and alcoholic beverages. The alcohol in white wine and sherry will evaporate during cooking, leaving their meant-for-fish flavors behind.

Fats also serve to *lubricate* foods, resulting in that familiar, hard-to-resist smooth and creamy texture. You can get similar results by using smaller amounts of fats, "reduced-fat fats," low-fat milk products, and low-fat sauces. Most people don't realize that making a white sauce requires no butter, margarine, or oil—ingredients typically used to separate flour or cornstarch granules so they don't clump together. You can just as easily accomplish a lump-free sauce by slowly whisking cold liquid, such as low-fat milk or evaporated skim milk, into the flour or cornstarch. (The liquid must be cold to separate the starch granules.) Bypass the addition of fat, and stir the sauce constantly over medium to medium-high heat until it comes to a boil.[3] Then add herbs and spices, salt and pepper, mushrooms, low-fat cheese, or lemon juice.

By now, you're familiar with the cooking methods that work best to get the fat out—poaching, steaming, and microwaving, as well as baking, grilling, or broiling on a rack. As far as utensils are concerned, I think a worthwhile investment is a large, nonstick skillet with a lid, which will allow you to get away with using little or no fat, yet your fish won't stick.

Another way to get the fat out of your diet is to substitute fish in meat recipes—Sweet 'n' Sour Swordfish, for example, on page 293, is an adaptation of traditional sweet-and-sour pork.[4] You can also save fat and calories (not to mention money) by using less fish than the amount called for in many recipes—two pounds of fillets just aren't necessary for four people.[5] (See page 172 for amounts of fish to buy per person.) Stretch the fish you use with lots of vegetables, pasta, and low-fat sauces. Most fish is quite lean as it is, but it's leaner still if you remove the skin and any dark portions of flesh before you serve it.

CHOOSING THE BEST FATS AND USING "REDUCED-FAT FATS"

You already know which fats are better for you, but how do you apply that knowledge when faced with blended products ranging from regular and diet margarine to vegetable-oil spreads, butter-margarine blends, imitation cream cheese, no-cholesterol sour cream, and the like? You need to cultivate the fine art of label reading—a feat that challenges even experienced nutritionists, who can hardly keep up with the new products in supermarkets.

It makes sense to start by comparing *ingredient listings,* which spell out the contents of most packaged products in descending order of predominance (by weight). In other words, the most prevalent ingredients are itemized early on in the listing. In selecting a margarine, you want to choose one that *first* lists a *liquid* version of one of the unsaturated oils (on page 14). In general, tub margarines and soft stick margarines tend to be the most healthful. If the oil that appears first in the ingredient listing is *hydrogenated* or *partially hydrogenated,* it's more saturated and therefore less desirable than a liquid version. You also want to avoid products that list any of the following saturated fats in an ingredient listing: *beef fat, butter, cream, lard, cocoa butter, coconut oil,* and *palm oil.*

Ingredient listings can be somewhat deceiving since they don't reveal absolute amounts. In comparing a stick of reduced-calorie margarine with a brand of regular margarine in the example below, you can see that both list a liquid vegetable oil, partially hydrogenated vegetable oil, and water as their first three ingredients. Does this suggest that they both have the same number of calories and amount of fat? Not if you look at the *nutrition labels* that list the amounts of calories, protein, carbohydrate, and fat in a single serving of a product. You can see that the reduced-calorie stick margarine has one-third less calories and fat than the regular. Indeed, the nutrition information can be very helpful in comparing similar products. But be careful to note what the label lists as a serving size so you're comparing like portions.

Regular margarine

Ingredients: Liquid sunflower oil, partially hydrogenated soybean oil, water, partially hydrogenated cottonseed oil, salt, sweet dairy whey, vegetable mono- and diglycerides (plus additives that I won't bother to enumerate)

Nutrition information per serving:
Serving size . . . . 14 g (1 tablespoon)
Servings per container 32
Calories 90
Protein . . . . 0 g
Carbohydrate . . . . 0 g
Fat . . . . 10 g

Reduced-calorie margarine

Ingredients: Liquid soybean oil, partially hydrogenated soybean oil, water, salt, vegetable mono- and diglycerides (plus additives)

Nutrition information per serving:
Serving size . . . . 14 g (1 tablespoon)
Servings per container 32
Calories 60
Protein . . . . 0 g
Carbohydrate . . . . 0 g
Fat . . . . 7 g

Nutrition labels—now featured on many, but not all, products—also list amounts of sodium, as well as give percentages of the US RDA for seven vitamins and minerals. In addition, they sometimes list amounts of unsaturated fat, saturated fat, and cholesterol.

Ingredient listings and nutrition labels can come in handy when purchasing any of the "reduced-fat fats" on the market. Be careful about products that boast "nondairy," "cholesterol-free," or "no butterfat." Check their ingredient listings to see if the fats within are healthful since products can get away with any of these claims yet still contain highly saturated coconut or palm oil. Use nutrition labels to tell you if, compared to regular versions of products, the reduced-fat counterparts are substantially different—say, at least 25 percent lower in fat and calories. Regular cream cheese, for instance, has anywhere from 9 to 11 grams of fat per ounce, while similar-tasting Neufchâtel has a more healthful level of around 7 grams. Better yet, Kraft has come out with a tasty "Light Philadelphia Brand" cream-cheese product that has just 5 grams of fat per ounce.[6] (Many people are surprised to learn that cream cheese is considered a fat—it has very little protein and proportionately more fat than most other cheeses.)

You may be hesitant to try reduced-fat fats and other low-fat products, because of bad experiences in years past with bland-tasting products once relegated to the "diet" section of the grocery store. But thanks to our fitness-conscious society, manufacturers have been spurred to develop better-tasting low-fat foods—a job now so well done that low-fat dairy products compete with higher-fat fare, and reduced-calorie salad dressings and mayonnaise are displayed right beside the regular condiments.

Some of the better-tasting reduced-fat fats on the market today include reduced-calorie mayonnaise and tub margarine—with half the calories of their regular counterparts—and diet salad dressings. (Compare calorie values for salad dressings carefully since they vary greatly.) I haven't bought regular mayonnaise in years, and no one who eats at my house knows the difference.[7] There are also several excellent "light" sour-cream products on the market that offer only two-thirds the calories and half the fat of regular sour cream.[8]

You'll see that the *Eat Fish* Recipes frequently call for a tablespoon of reduced-calorie margarine to grease casseroles—I prefer it to nonstick sprays because it adds some flavor and seems to better prevent sticking. (Nonstick sprays that are practically calorie-free are fine to use, too.) A tablespoon or two of the low-fat margarine also works well for sautéing vegetables.[9] Sometimes it works better if you grease a cold, nonstick pan with the stuff; add your food, then place the pan on a preheated burner set at medium.

It's important to give reduced-fat fats more than one chance—some are much better than others. You might find that you can't stomach one type of low-fat sour cream, but relish another. You also have to experiment when you cook with low-fat fats because they aren't successful in all types of products. Reduced-calorie margarine, for example, doesn't work well in baked goods because of its high water content. And reduced-fat cream cheese tends to be softer than regular —in cooked dishes you can add an egg white as a thickener. You may find that a mixture consisting of reduced-fat fats and regular fats works well in some recipes.[10]

Finally, don't think that because a product has been pared down in fat and calories it's okay to use it indiscriminately. Reduced-calorie margarine and mayonnaise still contain fat (even if it is the good kind) and calories that few of us need more of. And so-called "light" sour creams and cream cheeses still contain some saturated fat. So the rule about always trying to use less fat than a recipe calls for still holds, even with reduced-fat fats.

COOKING WITH LOW-FAT MILK PRODUCTS

The difference between 3.3 percent and 1 percent fat sure doesn't sound like much. But it's enough of a difference between regular milk and 1-percent-fat milk to save you about 50 calories and more than 5 grams of fat for each cup that you drink or use in cooking. That's why you should make the switch to low-fat milk products whenever you can.

A small amount of fat, however, can make a big difference in taste —you may find your family more likely to accept dairy products that aren't stripped of all their fat. That's why I recommend using low-fat milk over skim milk, which is virtually fat-free—the 15 calories you save with skim milk just isn't worth the watery taste in fish cookery as far as I'm concerned.

In adapting fish recipes, simply use one-percent-fat milk any time whole milk is suggested.[11] For a creamier taste and somewhat thicker texture, I sometimes use evaporated skim milk in place of part of the low-fat milk. If a recipe calls for cream, I up the proportion of evaporated skim milk,[12] which gives you the bonus of double the calcium since only water is taken out when milk is evaporated. Try using half low-fat milk and half evaporated skim milk in place of light cream or whole milk for a rich-tasting white sauce.[13] If you go for a sour flavor, you can also use buttermilk—contrary to its greasy-sounding name, buttermilk is usually just one percent fat. Buttermilk can be used in place of sour cream in some recipes,[14] but you'll probably need to decrease other liquid ingredients.

A versatile substitute for sour cream[15] and mayonnaise[16] is plain, low-fat yogurt—half a cup has about 70 calories compared to 240 for the same amount of sour cream and 800 for mayonnaise! In cold seafood salads, plain yogurt is also great for stretching reduced-fat sour cream (which, as mentioned earlier, still has some saturated fat and more than double the calories of plain, low-fat yogurt) and reduced-calorie mayonnaise at 400 calories per half-cup.[17]

Since low-fat yogurt tends to thin out too much when it's heated for a sauce, you can whisk a tablespoon of flour into it while it's still cold. (See Crab and Mushroom Stroganoff on page 280.) Another strategy is to barely warm—rather than boil—a yogurt sauce (see Broiled Sole with Sour and Creamy Cucumber Sauce on page 279).

Low-fat yogurt is also often recommended for dips, but I prefer what's commonly called "mock" sour cream. It's basically a blenderized mix of low-fat cottage cheese with several tablespoons of plain yogurt or lemon juice. If you whirl the mixture in a blender until smooth, it comes out thick and creamy and works well in place of sour cream in both dips and cooked foods.[18] (See Zesty Seafood Dip on page 232.)

When it comes to cheese, some special words are in order. While it's a delicious, versatile food that's high in protein and calcium, most regular cheese is also loaded with fat—sometimes containing a third to two times more fat than the same-size portion of meat. Indeed, many cheeses fall into the high-fat category of 9 to 11 grams of fat per ounce. Popular examples include American, brick, cheddar, colby, Gruyère, Roquefort, and Brie. Swiss has about 8 grams of fat per ounce. The problem is that people tend to use cheese as a snack food and quite freely in recipes—it's nothing to sit down and eat several ounces when munching before dinner or to use half a pound in a casserole. But at around 100 calories per ounce—with more than 70 percent of calories contributed by fat (most of it saturated)—for most types, cheese is something that really adds up.

I advise that you get in the habit of using regular cheese more as a condiment and experimenting with some of the lower-fat cheeses in cooking. Start adapting your recipes by cutting the recommended amount of regular cheese in half.[19] Even though they're not low-fat, you can get a lot of mileage out of small amounts of grated Parmesan and Romano cheese. Because of their strong flavor, a tablespoon or even a teaspoon per serving is often adequate.[20] A small amount of blue cheese goes a long way, too. For example, the original version of Shark with Crumbly Blue Cheese Topping called for 4 ounces of blue cheese and ½ cup of grated Parmesan cheese. But 1½ ounces of blue cheese and 2 tablespoons of Parmesan cheese were all the *Eat Fish* version needed for a rich, cheesy taste. (See page 254.)

You have to be careful when trying out special "diet" cheeses with labels boasting that they're lower in fat and/or cholesterol. Some reduced-fat cheeses have only a gram or two less fat than regular cheese. And low-cholesterol "imitation" cheeses made from skim milk with added vegetable oil can be just as high in fat and calories as regular cheese. As long as it's not coconut or palm oil, the vegetable oil in imitation cheeses is certainly more healthful than whole-milk fat in regular cheese. The cholesterol content of imitation cheeses is much lower, too.

According to the American Heart Association, the best cheeses for everyday use contain no more than 2 grams of fat per ounce. In this category are cottage cheese (low-fat and regular), Borden Lite-Line slices, and Weight Watchers® cheese slices. (Laughing Cow Reduced Calories Cheese and part-skim ricotta come close at less than 3 grams of fat per ounce.) Try using the low-fat cheese slices in place of regular cheese in your fish recipes.[21] They don't always melt as well, so you may resort to a mix of low-fat and regular cheese.[22]

If low-fat and regular cottage cheese, as well as part-skim ricotta, all fall into the recommended 2-grams-fat-per-ounce category, why would you ever use the 1-percent fat version over the others? Because cottage cheese is more commonly eaten in 4-ounce portions. As you can see in comparing the products below, the calorie difference in 4-ounce servings isn't that great, particularly for the cottage cheeses. But fat content varies considerably. (Certainly if you're just using a small amount in a recipe, the difference becomes less significant.)

If you replace whole-milk ricotta cheese with the part-skim version, you'll only lose about 80 calories per 8 ounces. But using low-fat cottage cheese instead of whole-milk ricotta will save you more than 200 calories.[23] If you don't care for the taste, combine low-fat cottage cheese with part-skim ricotta.[24]

Cheeses that fall in the range of 3 to 5 grams of fat per ounce are recommended by the Heart Association as lean-meat substitutes. Some reduced-fat cheeses made from part-skim milk fall into this category. A particularly tasty example that works well as a substitute for ched-

TABLE 10. Fat and Calorie Content of 4-Ounce Portions of Cottage and Ricotta Cheeses

	Calories	Fat (grams)
1-percent fat cottage cheese	80	1
2-percent fat cottage cheese	90	3
Regular cottage cheese (4-percent fat minimum)	110	5
Part-skim ricotta cheese	156	9
Whole-milk ricotta cheese	197	15

dar, Monterey Jack, or Swiss cheese in fish recipes is Weight Watchers® Natural Part-Skim Milk Cheese that comes in a block.[25] And few people can tell the difference between part-skim mozzarella cheese (5 grams fat per ounce) and the whole-milk version (6 or 7 grams fat per ounce) when it's used in cooking.[26] When using these lower-fat cheeses in fish recipes, you can cut back on the amount of fish you'd normally allow for each person since the cheeses can serve as replacements for lean protein foods.

As I mentioned earlier, even the most savvy of dietitians has trouble keeping up with the array of new products in the dairy case. To really get a handle on all the low-fat products out there, I suggest you take a few notes from this chapter, then head for the supermarket and employ your label-reading skills. Go without your kids if possible and allow about a half-hour to scan the dairy cases. That's exactly what I did (no one paid any attention to me) before writing this chapter. I came home with several new reduced-fat cheeses that were surprisingly good.

I haven't said much about adapting your recipes specifically to lower cholesterol because the tips I've outlined for reducing fats and selecting more healthful fats will automatically subtract cholesterol from your diet as well. The only high-cholesterol recipe ingredient that I haven't mentioned is eggs. Since one large egg provides close to the daily recommendation for cholesterol, it's wise to cut back when often-used recipes call for more than a few eggs. You can substitute two egg whites—which are cholesterol-free—for one whole egg. Or you can use cholesterol-free egg substitutes available in supermarkets.

But if only a few of your dishes call for eggs, and you don't eat eggs very often, I wouldn't worry too much about tossing them out of your fish recipes—particularly if a couple of eggs will be divided among four people. (If you know you have high blood cholesterol, more detailed guidelines than I've laid out are in order from a registered dietitian.)

CUTTING BACK ON SALT

Although I think that most of us could do with a lot less salt than we eat, I'm not as obsessed with getting salt out of my recipes as some other health-conscious cooks. The reason is that your palate can only withstand so much change. And I believe that, for the vast majority of people, it's more important to cut fat intake. I suspect that many a well-intentioned cook abandons healthful cuisine because of attempts to do too much at once—a drastic cut in salt can be more difficult to get used to than sacrificing fat in recipes. (As with cholesterol, you may need more specific guidelines from a dietitian if you've been told to cut back because of hypertension or some other problem that necessitates restricting sodium intake.)

I'm not saying that you shouldn't make an effort to cut back on salt added in cooking and at the table. Remember that salt is about 40 percent sodium and provides 2,300 milligrams of sodium per teaspoon. Some high-sodium condiments are soy and steak sauces, catsup, and pickles. Likewise, canned tomato products (such as sauce and juice), bacon bits, olives, low-fat and processed cheese slices, canned soups and broths, and bouillon are all considered to be high in sodium.

I don't feel that most people need to go to the extremes of using low-sodium tomato products, salt substitutes, and the like. But I do think that it's a good idea to get in the habit of using half the amount of salt that receipes call for—guests can always add more salt at the table, but they can't take it out once the chef adds it in cooking. You can also try cutting back on the amounts of salty condiments you use, too. If a recipe contains high-sodium condiments or prepared foods, plus added salt, you can probably cut salt substantially or leave it out. Before cutting the sodium, however, ask yourself if the taste sacrifice is worth it by the time a recipe is divided among four people.

You'll find that little or no added salt is needed in fish recipes containing fair amounts of high-sodium ingredients such as imitation shellfish and low-fat cheese slices. Salt becomes less of a necessity, too, if you make liberal use of lemon and lime juice, herbs and spices, and savory vegetables such as green peppers and onions. Make sure that, in seasoning recipes, you use onion and garlic *powders* instead of *salts*.

Fortunately, by lowering your sodium intake you will probably learn to like less of it, for the desire for sodium is acquired—basically, the more you use, the more you want. But after several months of cutting back, your taste buds get used to less salt.

TABLE 11. Saving Calories and Fat with Low-Fat Substitutions

For	Substitute	Calorie Savings	Fat Savings (grams)
1 ½ c. butter, margarine, or oil	¼ c. butter, margarine, or oil	406	46
2 ½ c. heavy cream	½ c. half-and-half	253	30
3 White sauce made with 1 c. whole milk, 2 T. magarine, 2 T. flour	White sauce made with 1 c. 1%-fat milk, 2 T. flour	250	28
4 1 lb. pork shoulder roast (raw, lean only)	1 lb. swordfish (raw)	147	20
5 2 lb. haddock (raw)	1⅓ lb. haddock (raw)	268	2
6 4 oz. regular cream cheese	4 oz. reduced-fat cream cheese (5 g. fat/oz.)	160	20
7 ½ c. regular mayonnaise	½ c. reduced-calorie mayonnaise	390	48
8 ½ c. regular sour cream	½ c. reduced-fat sour cream (3 g. fat/2 T.)	80	12
9 2 T. regular stick margarine, butter, or oil	2 T. reduced-calorie tub margarine	102	11
10 4 T. butter	2 T. reduced-calorie margarine plus 2 T. butter	104	11
11 1 c. whole milk	1 c. 1%-fat milk	48	5.5
12 ½ c. heavy cream	½ c. evaporated skim milk	310	44
13 1 c. light cream	½ c. evaporated skim milk plus ½ c. 1%-fat milk	318	45
14 1 c. sour cream	1 c. buttermilk	381	46
15 ⅔ c. sour cream	⅔ c. plain, low-fat yogurt	222	29
16 ⅔ c. mayonnaise	⅔ c. plain yogurt	949	113
17 ⅔ c. reduced-calorie mayonnaise	⅓ c. plain yogurt plus ⅓ c. reduced-calorie mayonnaise	216	25
18 1 c. sour cream	1 c. "mock" sour cream (made with 1%-fat cottage cheese)	320	46

19	8 oz. Swiss cheese	4 oz. Swiss cheese	432	32
20	1 c. shredded cheddar cheese	3 T. grated Parmesan cheese	369	31
21	4 oz. cheddar cheese	4 oz. reduced-calorie cheese slices (2 g. fat/oz.)	256	30
22	4 oz. Swiss cheese	3 oz. reduced-calorie cheese slices plus 1 oz. Swiss cheese	174	18
23	8 oz. whole-milk ricotta cheese	8 oz. 1%-fat cottage cheese	233	27
24	8 oz. whole-milk ricotta cheese	4 oz. 1%-fat cottage cheese plus 4 oz. part-skim ricotta	157	19
25	4 oz. Monterey Jack cheese	4 oz. part-skim-milk cheese (5 g. fat/oz.)	108	15
26	4 oz. whole-milk mozzarella cheese	4 oz. part-skim mozzarella cheese (5 g. fat/oz.)	40	8

Note: Values are approximate and vary according to brand. Numbers correspond to references throughout the chapter.

A WALK THROUGH SOME RECIPES

To give you hands-on experience with adapting recipes, I'm going to walk you through some of the *Eat Fish* Recipes that were adapted from high-fat, high-calorie versions. When you see how easy it is to become more healthful in the kitchen, you'll have no problem tackling your own recipes.

Curried Hot Crab Spread

Makes approximately 1½ cups or 6 quarter-cup servings

Adapted recipe	Original version
nonstick vegetable spray	none
½ cup reduced-fat cream cheese (7 grams fat or fewer per ounce), at room temperature	¾ cup regular cream cheese
2 tablespoons reduced-calorie mayonnaise	2 tablespoons regular mayonnaise
2 tablespoons lemon juice	1½ tablespoons
1 tablespoon dry sherry	same
1 egg white	no egg
¾ to 1 teaspoon curry powder	same
¼ teaspoon salt (omit with imitation crabmeat)	unspecified
grating of black pepper	same
6 ounces imitation or cooked fresh crabmeat, flaked	same
2 tablespoons chopped chives or scallions	1 tablespoon

See page 233 for complete directions.

Calorie savings: 460   Fat savings: 54 grams

Explanation of adaptation: Reduced-fat products were used in place of regular versions. I increased the lemon juice and chives (or scallions) to enhance flavor. Egg white was added as a thickener since reduced-fat cream cheese is softer than regular.

Sole Aux Fines Herbes

Makes 4 to 5 servings

Adapted recipe	Original version
2 tablespoons reduced-calorie margarine	2 tablespoons butter
12-ounce package of fresh mushrooms, washed, trimmed, and sliced	8 ounces
3 tablespoons minced shallots or scallions	2 tablespoons
2 tablespoons lemon juice	½ tablespoon
¼ teaspoon salt	unspecified
grating of black pepper	same
10 or 12 medium sole or flounder fillets (about 2 pounds; you can substitute 5 or 6 long, thin scrod fillets)	same
¾ cup dry white wine	same
¾ cup canned chicken broth or fish stock	same
½ cup cold half-and-half	½ cup heavy cream (plus some to thin sauce)
2 tablespoons plus 1 teaspoon all-purpose flour	same
(The original adds 2 tablespoons butter at this point—I use none.)	
1 tablespoon lemon juice	unspecified
3 tablespoons chopped, fresh parsley	
1 teaspoon dried chervil	2 tablespoons fresh, minced herbs
1 teaspoon dried tarragon	
¼ teaspoon salt	unspecified

See page 301 for complete directions.

Calorie savings: 596   Fat savings: 77 grams

Explanation of adaptation: For extra body, I increased the mushrooms. Smaller quantities of reduced-calorie margarine were used in place of butter for sautéing and greasing. I used more shallots, lemon juice, and herbs than the original to enhance flavor. (Dried chervil and tarragon were used because most people don't have access to fresh.)

  In the original recipe, a roux was made by mixing the flour into 2 tablespoons of melted butter; then the hot, reduced poaching juice was added to the roux, followed by heavy cream. So that the 2 table-spoons of butter could be omitted, I chose to separate the starch granules with cold liquid—in this case, half-and-half, which is much less fatty than heavy cream. The mixture was then added to the hot poaching liquid.

Shark with Crumbly Blue Cheese Topping

Makes 4 servings

Adapted recipe	Original version
1 tablespoon reduced-calorie margarine	3 tablespoons butter
1½ ounces crumbled blue cheese (about ⅓ cup, lightly packed)	4 ounces
2 tablespoons grated Parmesan cheese	½ cup
3 tablespoons unseasoned bread crumbs	½ cup
1 tablespoon finely chopped shallot or onion	none
1 tablespoon lemon juice	same
2 tablespoons chopped, fresh parsley	1 tablespoon
1 teaspoon soy sauce (preferably tamari)	1½ teaspoons
3 tablespoons low-fat milk	4 tablespoons whole milk
nonstick vegetable spray	none
1¼ to 1⅓ pounds shark steaks, ¾ to 1 inch thick	1½ to 2 pounds
2 tablespoons lemon juice	none

See page 254 for complete directions.

Calorie savings: 1,228   Fat savings: 75 grams

(Calculations are based on 1⅓ lb. shark for the adapted recipe and 2 lb. for the original version.)

Explanation of adaptation: Instead of butter, I substituted reduced-calorie margarine, using ⅓ the amount. Because blue cheese and Parmesan cheese are so flavorful, I was able to use much less than the original recipe, yet still maintain the taste of the topping. I cut the bread crumbs because the topping had plenty of body with just 3 tablespoons. (Less milk was needed to moisten the bread crumbs.) For extra flavor, I added shallots and upped the lemon juice and parsley. Sodium was lowered a bit by using less soy sauce. Since the topping is quite rich-tasting and filling, I saw no need for 1½ to 2 pounds of shark for 4 people.

CHAPTER TWELVE

The *Eat Fish* Recipes

I KNOW, I KNOW—the thought of healthfully prepared fish conjures up images of dried-out broiled or baked fillets that someone has unsuccessfully attempted to mask with a soaking of lemon juice and bread crumbs so few in number you can scarcely see them. Not any more! From simple to fancy fare, the *Eat Fish* Recipes provide you with 79 scrumptious choices to drown out your memories of "diet" fish.

Start with "To Whet the Palate—Appetizers and Accompaniments" for dips, spreads, canapés, and cold sauces. Move on to "Light Fare—Soups, Salads, and Sandwiches" when you're in the mood for a hot soup, cold salad, or unusual sandwich. You'll likely spend most of your cooking time with "Quick-and-Easy Recipes" which cover a multitude of different types of fish and simple preparation methods. The next section, "Pasta, Casseroles, and Sauced Dishes," offers hearty recipes that vary in complexity and make great family fare. Finally, the "Especially for Company" recipes are just that—recipes that are worth a bit more effort when someone special is coming to dinner. (Of course, many of the other recipes are perfectly appropriate for guests, too.)

The *Eat Fish* Recipes are much lower in calories, fat, and cholesterol than many traditional seafood recipes. The majority of *Eat Fish* Recipes are also moderately low in sodium. (If sodium concerns you, reduce the amount in recipes by lowering quantities of added salt, rinsing canned fish, using fresh crabmeat instead of imitation, and by using reduced-sodium soy sauce, as well as tomato products with no added salt.) Before you dig in to the *Eat Fish* Recipes, however, I suggest that you skim chapter 11—"Working from Your Own Recipes"—for general guidelines about healthful cookery and ingredient selection. If you're on a special diet—say, to lower blood cholesterol or your blood pressure—chapter 11 offers ideas for further limiting cholesterol and sodium in recipes. (People with special dietary needs should consult with a registered dietitian and their physician to see if specific recipes are appropriate for them.)

You'll find that the portion sizes are substantial (about 4 ounces of fish, cooked)—but not huge—in keeping with the American Heart Association's advice to eat no more than 6 ounces of meat, poultry, or fish *each day*. Most *Eat Fish* Recipes have suggestions for starch, salad, and vegetable accompaniments that will round out your meals. (The "Especially for Company" recipes tend to provide larger portion sizes so you have plenty to offer guests.)

Chapter 10, "Cook It Right," will refresh your memory about general fish-cooking methods and how to assess when fish is done. Cooking times for all *Eat Fish* Recipes are approximate and will differ from one stove and one piece of fish to the next. (Times are particularly variable for dishes cooked in a microwave oven or on a grill.) For some recipes, you may not be able to purchase fish that's exactly of the thickness I specify—use the fish that's available and scale the time up or down according to its thickness, roughly applying the 10-minute rule described in chapter 10. The message: it's up to you to determine when your fish is done. Remember how important it is to watch fish closely so it's not overcooked.

For each *Eat Fish* Recipe, pay close attention to the suggested "fish trade-offs." They give ideas about other types of fish that should work in a given recipe. Learning about trade-offs will provide you the flexibility to shop with a particular recipe—not a specific type of fish —in mind. Unless otherwise specified, assume the form (fillet, steak, etc.) of the trade-off is the same as that called for in the original recipe. In some cases, thick fillets can substitute for steaks. (Since salmon and mackerel fillets are usually purchased skin-on and with pin bones, purchase about 10 percent more fish when substituting either one for skinless, boneless fillets.) Again, it's up to you to adjust cooking times for trade-offs according to the type of fish and its thickness. (Because cooking time may be different when you substitute a "new" fish in an *Eat Fish* Recipe, refer to cooking guidelines for the specific fish in chapter 8 any time you make such an alteration.)

Note that a number of *Eat Fish* Recipes include wine or sherry. If you can't or don't want to use alcoholic beverages, you can substitute broth, water, or fruit juice.

NUTRITIONAL ANALYSES OF RECIPES

Each *Eat Fish* Recipe is followed by per-serving values for calories, fat, sodium, and cholesterol. Recipes that are outstanding sources of other nutrients are called to your attention in the introductions.

Note that when an ingredient option occurs in a recipe—for example, "shallots or onions"—the first option was used for the nutritional analysis. Likewise, when a choice exists for the amount of fish, the first option was analyzed. Sodium values assume that any canned products used in recipes have added salt, unless otherwise noted. Be aware that sodium values for commercial products, such as canned tomato goods, are quite variable.

In some cases, published nutritional data for fish and shellfish (as well as certain other products) are unclear or incomplete. In these instances, estimates have been made for nutritional values. Nutritional data for all recipes are considered approximate. (Nutritional information does not necessarily apply to "fish trade-offs.")

STOCKING YOUR KITCHEN

There's nothing more frustrating than having your mouth watering for something to eat, only to find that you're missing a key ingredient for a recipe when you go to prepare it. So assemble your ingredients ahead of time, and check to see which, if any, require a small amount of preparation beforehand—for example, you may have to parboil or chop some vegetables. Don't wait until you're in the middle of a recipe to do these preliminaries.

Eat Fish Recipes require everyday cooking utensils and common ingredients that most people have on hand. You may choose to buy special cooking devices, such as fish-grilling baskets and poaching pans (see chapter 10). But you really can make do with what you have on hand. About the only item I'd suggest you purchase if you don't already have one is a large, nonstick frying pan with a lid. A food scale is also a worthwhile investment. (Remember that you should use a glass or plastic dish rather than aluminum for marinating because certain foods react with metal.)

Very few unusual foods are needed to make the recipes. But there are some items that you should regularly stock if you intend the *Eat Fish* Recipes to become part of your life. Following is a list of ingredients that regularly appear in the recipes. The items in italics should be ever-present in your kitchen; the foods listed in regular type appear with some frequency, but it's only necessary to keep small amounts on hand or to purchase them as needed. (In keeping with the preventive guidelines discussed throughout the book, it's important not to "cheat" with regular versions of ingredients when low-fat items are called for.)

Milk and dairy products

Low-fat milk—preferably 1 percent fat

Evaporated skim milk

Plain, low-fat yogurt

Grated Parmesan cheese

Low-fat cheese—5 grams fat or less per ounce (I recommend Weight Watchers® Natural Part-Skim Milk Cheese that comes in a block. Other possibilities are part-skim mozzarella and low-fat cheese slices.)

Large eggs (2 egg whites can be used for each whole egg in recipes, such as fish patties, that use eggs as a binder.

Cholesterol-free egg substitutes will work better in recipes that call for egg yolks or that use eggs as thickeners in sauces.)

Low-fat cottage cheese—1 or 2 percent fat

Swiss cheese

Reduced-fat cream cheese—7 grams fat or less per ounce (Examples: Neufchâtel and Kraft Light Philadelphia)

Reduced-fat sour cream—1½ grams fat or less per tablespoon (Examples: Hood Light Sour Cream and Land O'Lakes Lean Cream)

Fruits and vegetables

Lemons, limes (Fresh-squeezed juice is the only way to go with fish recipes, as far as I'm concerned.)

Onions

Scallions

Garlic cloves

Celery

Canned mushrooms—small and large sizes

Fresh mushrooms

Green and red peppers

Fresh tomatoes

Canned tomatoes: plum, stewed, crushed, and paste

Vegetable juice cocktail

Fresh ginger root (To delay mold growth on cut ends, dip them in vinegar, then refrigerate.)

Frozen, chopped spinach

Orange juice

Fish

Canned salmon
Canned tuna
Imitation crabmeat
Canned mackerel
Canned clams, minced
Canned tiny shrimp

Frozen fish blocks (These are particularly handy if your access to fresh fish is poor. See chapter 9, page 177, and chapter 10, page 185, for guidelines on storing and preparing.)

Fats and substitutes

Reduced-calorie mayonnaise
Reduced-calorie margarine—
    reduced-calorie tub margarine
    at 50 calories per tablespoon
Olive oil
Vegetable oil—corn, cottonseed,
    safflower, soybean, or sunflower

Nonstick vegetable spray
Sesame oil—dark
Peanut oil
Regular margarine
Butter
Sesame seeds
Slivered almonds

Condiments/baking supplies

Bottled horseradish
Worcestershire sauce
Dijon-style mustard
Sweet green relish
Soy sauce (preferably tamari)
All-purpose flour
Dry white wine
Dry or semidry sherry
Dry white vermouth

Catsup
Vinegar: cider, white, and
    wine
Bottled salsa
Bottled chili sauce
Tabasco sauce
Granulated cane sugar
Brown sugar
Cornstarch
Honey

Herbs and spices

Salt
Black peppercorns and pepper mill
Fresh parsley
Paprika
Fresh chives
Dried, flaked:
  dill weed
  basil
  chervil
  tarragon
  onion
  parsley
  thyme
  oregano
  marjoram

Ground:
  dry mustard
  coriander
  cumin
  nutmeg
  ginger
Curry powder
Chili powder
Bay leaves
Celery seed
Cayenne pepper
Onion powder
Garlic powder
Cinnamon

Miscellaneous canned goods/packaged foods

Chicken broth—skim fat off the top
Unseasoned bread crumbs
Flake-type cereal
Low-fat crackers—such as stoned-wheat crackers or saltines

White and brown rice
Pimientos
Bottled clam juice
Black olives

A DIRECTORY FOR SAUCES, DRESSINGS, STUFFINGS, AND MARINADES

The following are lists of *Eat Fish* Recipes that offer accompaniments which can be used for other purposes—for other forms and types of fish, and, in some cases, for vegetables, lean meats, and skinless poultry. Experiment!

Sauces

Slimmed-Down Tartar—
    p. 237
Cocktail—p. 237
Debby's Barbecue—p. 270
Marinara—p. 283
Tomato-Basil-Mint—p. 285
Anne's Meatless Spaghetti—
    p. 287

Slim White—p. 291
Lemony Dill—p. 300
Sour and Creamy Cucumber—
    p. 279
Florentine—p. 310

Dressings/stuffings

Chervil-Dill Dressing—
    p. 244
Savory Stuffing—p. 297

Marinades

Sesame-Soy—p. 262
Honey-Lime with Tarragon—
    p. 265
Minty Lime—p. 275
Broiled Bluefish—p. 273
    (step 1)
Mom's Teriyaki—p. 313
Wine-Dill—p. 313

Smoky Salmon Spread

Makes approximately 1½ cups or 6 quarter-cup servings

This is always a hit—with children and adults alike. Based on a recipe calling for loads of high-fat cream cheese, this version substitutes cottage cheese and reduced-fat cream cheese. Serve on crisp crackers, soft rye bread squares, or cucumber rounds.

Fish trade-off: canned tuna

⅓ cup low-fat cottage cheese
2 tablespoons plain yogurt
⅓ cup reduced-fat cream
   cheese (7 grams fat or fewer
   per ounce), at room
   temperature
6- to 7-ounce can of skinless,
   boneless salmon, drained

1 tablespoon lemon juice
1 teaspoon bottled
   horseradish
¾ teaspoon liquid smoke
2 tablespoons minced
   scallions

1. In blender, blend the cottage cheese, yogurt, and cream cheese just until smooth. You'll probably need to scrape the sides several times. (Don't overblend or cream cheese will become runny.) Set aside.

2. In a medium-size bowl, finely mash the salmon with a fork. Add the cottage-cheese mixture, lemon juice, horseradish, liquid smoke, and scallions. Mix thoroughly.

3. Chill several hours or overnight. (If desired, garnish with a sprinkling of chopped parsley or sliced scallions just before serving.)

*Per serving: Calories: 73   Fat: 4 gm.   Cholesterol: 19 mg.
Sodium: 230 mg.*

Zesty Seafood Dip

Makes 4½ to 5 cups

A delightful *and* healthful change from your typical sour-cream-based dips, this rendition gets its thick, creamy texture from blenderized cottage cheese. The radishes and horseradish add a pleasant bite. Serve with fresh, raw carrots, broccoli, cucumbers, cauliflower, green peppers, or any vegetable you like. The large quantity makes this dip an ideal crowd-pleaser.

Fish trade-offs: shredded crabmeat (canned, imitation, or cooked, fresh); canned tuna or salmon (flaked); chopped, cooked squid

¼ cup plain, low-fat yogurt
2 cups low-fat cottage cheese
2 tablespoons lemon juice
1 teaspoon Worcestershire sauce
½ teaspoon salt
6 medium scallions (include bulb plus several inches of green section), cut into one-inch segments

2 6½- to 7-ounce cans minced clams, drained well
1 6½- to 7-ounce can tiny shrimp, drained well
3 tablespoons bottled horseradish
4 medium radishes, minced

1. Place the yogurt, cottage cheese, lemon juice, Worcestershire sauce, and salt in a blender and blend until smooth. (You may have to scrape the sides several times.) Add the scallions and blend until finely chopped.

2. Transfer the cottage-cheese mixture to a medium-size serving bowl or large plastic container. Add the clams, shrimp, horseradish, and radishes. Thoroughly combine.

3. Cover and refrigerate for at least several hours (better still, overnight) to allow the flavors to combine.

Per serving (approximately ½ cup): Calories: 85   Fat: 1 gm. Cholesterol: 36 mg.   Sodium: 346 mg.

Curried Hot Crab Spread

Makes approximately 1½ cups or 6 quarter-cup servings

An appetizer with zip, this spread can be served right in the baking dish and guests can spread their own on crackers or chunks of pita bread.

Fish trade-offs: cooked lobster or skate; tuna or salmon, canned or cooked, fresh

Nonstick vegetable spray
½ cup reduced-fat cream cheese (7 grams fat or less per ounce), at room temperature
2 tablespoons reduced-calorie mayonnaise
2 tablespoons lemon juice
1 tablespoon dry or semidry sherry
1 egg white

¾ to 1 teaspoon curry powder, depending on how spicy you like it
¼ teaspoon salt (omit with imitation crabmeat)
Grating of black pepper
6 ounces imitation or cooked fresh crabmeat, flaked
2 tablespoons chopped chives or scallions

1. Preheat the oven to 375° F. Coat a shallow 1-quart casserole with nonstick vegetable spray.

2. In a medium-size mixing bowl, beat together the cream cheese, mayonnaise, lemon juice, sherry, egg white, curry powder, salt, and pepper. Beat until the mixture just becomes smooth.

3. Stir in the crabmeat and pour the mixture into the prepared baking dish.

4. Bake, uncovered, for 20 to 25 minutes or until firm in the middle. Serve hot with a sprinkling of chives or scallions.

Per serving (based on imitation crabmeat): Calories: 100   Fat: 6 gm. Cholesterol: 22 mg.   Sodium: 360 mg.

Smoked Oyster Canapés

Makes 4 servings

It can't get much easier than shellfish on crackers with a dollop of sauce. This combination makes an unusual hors d'oeuvre *and* provides loads of iron and zinc.

Fish trade-offs: smoked clams or mussels, sardines

2 3⅔ oz. cans smoked oysters
¼ cup plain, low-fat yogurt
¼ cup reduced-fat sour cream
  (1½ grams fat per
  tablespoon)

Melba toast rounds
  (approximately 18)
Paprika

1. Thoroughly drain the oysters, then blot them well on both sides with paper towels.

2. Mix the yogurt and sour cream.

3. Place one or two oysters (depending on size) on a Melba round. Top with a well-rounded teaspoonful of the yogurt mixture. Repeat until all oysters are used.

4. Top each canapé with a light sprinkling of paprika.

Per serving (values are rough—since no reliable nutritional data are available for smoked oysters, adjustments were made using regular, canned oysters): Calories: 148   Fat: 6 gm.   Cholesterol: 57 mg. Sodium: 246 mg.

Dilled Tuna-Salmon Mousse

Makes approximately 4 cups or 8 half-cup servings

Sans the heavy cream of traditional mousse recipes, this light version makes a tasty spread for crackers, small bread squares, or cucumber slices. As a salad alternative, you can also serve mousse slices on a bed of crisp greens. (If you don't have both kinds of fish on hand, you can use all of one kind.)

Fish trade-off: cooked weakfish

1 envelope unflavored gelatin
½ cup cold vegetable-juice cocktail
¾ cup boiling vegetable-juice cocktail
¼ cup reduced-calorie mayonnaise
1 cup regular cottage cheese
3 tablespoons lemon juice
1 teaspoon dried dill weed
½ teaspoon Worcestershire sauce
6½- to 7-ounce can water-packed tuna, drained and flaked
½ cup flaked canned salmon (drain and remove skin before measuring)
2 teaspoons vegetable oil

1. In a small bowl, soften the gelatin in the cold vegetable-juice cocktail for about 5 minutes. Add the boiling vegetable juice and stir until the gelatin is dissolved.

2. When the gelatin–vegetable-juice mixture is cool, add it to a blender along with the mayonnaise, cottage cheese, lemon juice, dill, and Worcestershire sauce. Blend until smooth.

3. Add the tuna and salmon. Combine by turning the blender on and off quickly in order to avoid overblending the fish.

4. Coat a 4½- to 5-cup mold with the oil. (Drain off excess oil.) Pour in the fish mixture. Chill until set, 2½ to 3 hours. Unmold.

*Per serving: Calories: 105   Fat: 5 gm.   Cholesterol: 19 mg.
Sodium: 427 mg.*

Steamed Mussels Marinara

Makes 4 servings

A savory tomato-and-white-wine broth complements the light, delicate taste of mussels in this iron-rich recipe. No need for butter-dunking here! Serve as an appetizer—in soup bowls, with mussels swimming in their own broth, or on top of small pasta portions. (For a main dish, this recipe can be doubled and served over linguine with crusty bread and a romaine lettuce salad.)

Fish trade-offs: clams, crawfish, oysters, shrimp, squid rings or strips

1 tablespoon olive oil
2 large garlic cloves, pressed
   or minced (use one if you
   like a more subtle taste)
2 tablespoons thinly sliced
   scallion or chopped onion
1 large, ripe tomato, peeled *
   and chopped (or the
   equivalent amount of
   canned, whole plum
   tomatoes)

½ teaspoon salt
½ cup dry white wine
⅓ cup hot water
2 dozen large live mussels
   (buy a few extra, in case
   some don't make it),
   cleaned
1 tablespoon lemon juice
2 to 3 tablespoons chopped,
   fresh parsley

1. In a kettle large enough to accommodate the mussels in a shallow layer, heat the olive oil over medium heat. Add the garlic and scallion (or onion). Sauté for about 1 minute, avoiding browning.

2. Add the tomato and sauté for another 2 to 3 minutes, stirring occasionally.

3. Add the salt, wine, and water. Bring to a boil, then lower heat, cover, and simmer for 10 to 15 minutes (until the tomato is soft).

4. Add the mussels, lemon juice, and parsley. Toss lightly to combine. Cover and bring to a boil over medium-high heat. Steam for 6 to 7 minutes. Shake the kettle once or twice during cooking. (Discard any mussels that remain closed after cooking.)

Per serving: Calories: 124   Fat: 5 gm.   Cholesterol: 20 mg. Sodium: 404 mg.

* To peel easily, plunge into boiling water for a minute or two, then rinse in cold water.

Slimmed-Down Tartar Sauce

Makes approximately 1¼ cups

You can fool anyone with this version of tartar sauce that sacrifices calories, but not taste. Reduced-calorie mayonnaise and plain yogurt cut the calories of traditional tartar sauce by more than 1,100!

½ cup reduced-calorie
  mayonnaise
½ cup plain, low-fat yogurt
1 teaspoon prepared mustard
3 tablespoons sweet green
  relish

1 tablespoon wine vinegar
1½ tablespoons minced fresh
  onion

Mix all ingredients well. If time permits, refrigerate for at least an hour before serving to allow flavors to blend.

Per serving (2 tablespoons): Calories: 45   Fat: 3.5 gm.   Cholesterol: 4 mg. Sodium: 129 mg.

Cocktail Sauce

Makes approximately 1 cup

Chili sauce, salsa, and celery seed make this cocktail sauce different from the usual. Much more healthful than butter for your favorite shellfish, cocktail sauce provides barely a smidgen of fat. Serve with cold or hot cooked shrimp, lobster, crawfish, clams, mussels, or oysters.

⅓ cup catsup
⅓ cup mild or medium-hot
  bottled salsa
⅓ cup prepared chili sauce
2 tablespoons bottled
  horseradish

½ teaspoon Worcestershire
  sauce
½ teaspoon celery seed
1 tablespoon lemon juice

Combine all ingredients. If time permits, refrigerate overnight to allow flavors to blend.

Per serving (¼ cup): Calories: 38   Fat: 0.5 mg.   Cholesterol: 0 mg. Sodium: 259 mg.

Hearty Scallop-Vegetable Soup

Makes 8 servings

A wonderful, light medley of mild vegetables that doesn't smother the scallops' taste. Bacon adds a nice, smoky accent, but the amount is small (and the other ingredients are practically fat-free) so you don't have to worry about its extra fat and calories. Be sure not to overcook the scallops as they'll continue to cook in the hot liquid after you remove the pan from the burner. (One serving meets the US RDA for vitamin A.)

Fish trade-offs: small chunks of crawfish, lobster, monkfish, skate, tilefish, cusk, wolffish, eel, or drum; mussel or oyster meats; squid rings or strips

3 slices bacon, diced
1 large onion, chopped
1 medium green or yellow
  pepper, cut into thin strips
  which are then halved
35-ounce can Italian peeled
  tomatoes
1 cup bottled clam juice
13- to 14-ounce can chicken
  broth, fat skimmed off top
2 bay leaves
¼ teaspoon Tabasco sauce (or
  to taste; use less if you
  prefer a milder flavor)

1 teaspoon dried tarragon
¼ teaspoon salt
Generous grating of black
  pepper
2-3 tablespoons chopped,
  fresh parsley
2 carrots, sliced
2 medium potatoes, peeled
  and cut into ½-inch cubes
1 pound scallops (if sea
  scallops, cut into quarters)

1. In a large soup pan, sauté the diced bacon over medium heat until almost crisp (stir frequently to keep from sticking).

2. Add the onion and pepper. Sauté 5 to 7 minutes, stirring occasionally (until the vegetables just start to soften).

3. Add the juice from the tomatoes, then the tomatoes—one at a time, cutting them in ½-inch slices as you place in the pan. Add the clam juice, chicken broth, bay leaves, Tabasco sauce, tarragon, salt, pepper, and parsley. Cover. Bring to a boil, then reduce the heat and simmer for 20 to 25 minutes.

4. Add the carrots and potatoes. Cover, raise the heat to medium, and cook for another 20 to 25 minutes, until the potatoes and carrots are done. Remove the bay leaves.

5. Stir in the scallops and cook for another 2 to 3 minutes.

Per serving: Calories: 175   Fat: 6 gm.   Cholesterol: 27 mg. Sodium: 716 mg.

Shrimp and Salmon Gumbo

Makes 6 servings

A takeoff on Southern chicken gumbo, this hearty, thick soup is a meal in itself. The list of ingredients looks forbidding, but the directions are simple if you assemble everything before cooking. You can save time by using a food processor to chop the green pepper, onion, celery, and parsley ahead of time. (A single serving provides the US RDA for vitamin C.)

Fish trade-offs: leftover, cooked white-fleshed fish; flaked crabmeat (canned, imitation, or cooked, fresh); steamed crawfish or lobster chunks; canned or steamed clams, oysters, or mussels; chopped, cooked squid; tuna or mackerel (canned or cooked, fresh)

1 tablespoon olive oil
1 medium green pepper, chopped
½ cup chopped onion
2 cups canned crushed tomatoes
15- to 16-ounce can stewed tomatoes
1 cup canned chicken broth, fat skimmed off top
1 tablespoon Worcestershire sauce
2 teaspoons bottled horseradish
2 tablespoons lemon juice
¼ teaspoon paprika
Generous grating of black pepper

¼ cup chopped, fresh parsley
1 medium stalk celery with leaves, chopped
⅓ cup uncooked white rice
2 tablespoons chopped pimiento
10-ounce package frozen cut okra, cooked according to package directions and undrained (if okra is whole, cook, cool slightly, then cut in ½-inch sections)
6- to 7-ounce can skinless, boneless pink salmon, drained and flaked
6- to 7-ounce can tiny shrimp, drained

1. In a large, heavy soup pan, heat the olive oil over medium heat. Add the green pepper and onion. Sauté, stirring frequently, for 3 to 4 minutes; don't brown.

2. Stir in the crushed and stewed tomatoes, chicken broth, Worcestershire sauce, horseradish, lemon juice, paprika, black pepper, parsley, and celery. Bring to a boil, then reduce heat and simmer, covered, for 20 to 25 minutes.

3. Stir in the rice. Cover and cook another 20 to 25 minutes or until the rice is done.

4. Stir in the pimiento and okra. Cook 5 minutes.

5. Remove the pan from the heat. Gently stir in the salmon and shrimp.

Per serving: Calories: 189   Fat: 4.5 gm.   Cholesterol: 42 mg. Sodium: 655 mg.

Chunky Clam Chowder

Makes 5 large servings

Traditional clam chowder takes on a healthful flair in this very low-fat rendition that doesn't spare the clams or potatoes. (It's an excellent source of calcium, iron, and zinc.) I serve this chowder with a large tossed salad and bagels that have been wrapped in foil and heated whole. (To spare yourself the butter, put manners aside and dip bagels in the soup before you take a bite.)

Fish trade-offs: canned oysters or shrimp; chopped, steamed squid; cooked wolffish or cusk chunks (for all but the oysters, you'll need to add more broth)

1 cup chopped onion
1 large clove garlic, pressed or minced
2 medium-large potatoes, peeled and cut in ½-inch cubes (about 2 cups)
1 cup canned chicken broth, fat skimmed off top
⅓ cup packed chopped, fresh parsley

2 cups cold, low-fat milk
¼ cup flour (use ⅓ cup if you prefer thicker soup)
3 6½- to 7-ounce cans minced clams or whole baby clams, with broth
1 cup evaporated skim milk
¼ teaspoon ground cumin
½ teaspoon salt
Grating of black pepper

1. In a large soup kettle, combine the onion, garlic, potatoes, and chicken broth. Cover and bring to a boil. Then reduce the heat and simmer for 10 minutes.

2. Stir in the parsley and simmer for another 5 minutes or until the potatoes become soft—not mushy.

3. While the broth and vegetables are simmering, slowly whisk the low-fat milk into the flour in a small bowl. Stir into the broth-vegetable mixture when the potatoes are soft.

4. Increase the heat to medium. Add the clams with broth, evaporated skim milk, cumin, salt, and pepper. Bring to a boil, stirring often.

Per serving: Calories: 284   Fat: 3 gm.   Cholesterol: 50 mg. Sodium: 770 mg.

Crab Slaw

Makes 4 to 5 servings

This crunchy, colorful, summery salad can be served as a side dish on a bed of fresh greens or as a main course with corn on the cob and fresh fruit wedges.

Fish trade-offs: canned tuna or salmon; cooked and shredded skate or tilefish

8 ounces imitation crabmeat or cooked fresh crabmeat, flaked

½ large green pepper, chopped medium-fine

2 large stalks celery, chopped medium-fine

1 small onion, chopped medium-fine

¼ cup chopped, fresh parsley

¾ cup low-fat cottage cheese

2 tablespoons reduced-calorie mayonnaise

¼ teaspoon salt (omit with imitation crabmeat)

Paprika

Thoroughly combine all the ingredients (except the paprika) in a large bowl. Sprinkle with paprika and serve cold.

Per serving (based on 4 servings, made with imitation crabmeat): Calories: 124   Fat: 3.5 gm.   Cholesterol: 16 mg.   Sodium: 725 mg.

Mustardy Marinated Scallop Salad

Makes 4 servings

This is a fancy salad loaded with eye appeal and a special, tangy taste. Although it requires a bit of effort, the scallops can be marinated and the dressing made ahead of time. Delightful as an appetizer or served with any light fish or chicken entrée.

Fish trade-offs: cusk, wolffish, monkfish, skate, or salmon cut in small chunks; lobster; crawfish; shrimp; mussel meats; squid rings or strips

TO COOK AND MARINATE SCALLOPS

1 cup water
2 tablespoons lemon juice
½ teaspoon salt
3 peppercorns
2 slices of medium-size onion

scallops, cut in quarters),
rinsed with cool water and
drained
¼ cup lime juice
1 tablespoon vegetable oil

1. In a large frying pan, combine the water, lemon juice, salt, peppercorns, and onion. Bring to a boil. Reduce the heat and simmer for 5 to 10 minutes.

2. Raise the heat to medium. Distribute the scallops over the onions, cover, and cook for 3 to 4 minutes, until the scallops are just done.

3. Remove the scallops from the heat, drain well, and place in a medium-size bowl. Pick out the onions and peppercorns.

4. While still warm, cover the scallops with the lime juice and oil. Stir gently to distribute the marinade. Refrigerate for 2 to 3 hours, stirring occasionally. Drain the scallops, reserving the marinade for dressing (below).

SALAD DRESSING AND REMAINING INGREDIENTS

¼ cup lime juice–oil mixture
 drained from scallops
1 tablespoon white vinegar
2 tablespoons vegetable oil
2 teaspoons Dijon mustard
¼ medium onion, coarsely
 chopped
2-3 sprigs parsley, stems
 removed
1 teaspoon sugar
1 small clove garlic, sliced
¼ teaspoon salt

4 servings of dark green and/
 or red curly lettuce leaves,
 rinsed well and dried
20 snow peas (caps and
 strings removed), blanched
 for 1 minute in boiling
 water
6 3- to 4-inch sections of
 hearts of palm, sliced
 lengthwise in quarters
 (optional ingredient)

1. In a blender, combine the lime-juice mixture, vinegar, oil, mustard, onion, parsley, sugar, garlic, and salt. Blend 45 to 60 seconds, until frothy and no large chunks of onion or garlic remain. Set aside.

2. Arrange the lettuce on 4 salad plates. Place the scallops in the centers of the lettuce. Surround with alternating snow peas and strips of hearts of palm.

3. Drizzle the blended dressing over all, distributing evenly among the 4 plates.

Per serving (without hearts of palm): Calories: 204   Fat: 10.5 gm. Cholesterol: 38 mg.   Sodium: 416 mg.

Shrimp-Tortellini Salad

Makes 4 servings

This substantial salad—rich in iron, zinc, and calcium—can stand alone as a main course accompanied by fresh-sliced tomatoes and scoops of shredded carrots with seasonings. It also makes a nice side dish for a buffet luncheon or brunch. The dressing offers a refreshing blend of chervil and dill with tangy yogurt and sour cream.

Fish trade-offs: mussel meats, crawfish, lobster chunks, bay or calico scallops, squid rings or strips, crabmeat

½ pound medium raw shrimp, thawed, peeled, deveined, and tails removed
2 cups cooked and drained cheese tortellini

½ cup Chervil-Dill Dressing (recipe below)
Fresh lettuce greens (4 servings), rinsed and dried

1. Bring a medium-size potful of water to a boil. Add the shrimp, reduce the heat to low, and cook for about 3 minutes (uncovered), until done. Drain, rinse with cold water, and drain again.

2. Cut the shrimp in thirds and place in a medium-size bowl. Add the tortellini and ½ cup Chervil-Dill Dressing. Gently toss. Chill for one hour.

3. Arrange the lettuce on 4 salad plates. Distribute the shrimp-tortellini salad equally among plates.

Per serving: Calories: 311   Fat: 12 gm.   Cholesterol: 134 mg. Sodium: 465 mg.

CHERVIL-DILL DRESSING

Makes a little more than 1 cup

½ cup plain, low-fat yogurt
⅓ cup reduced-fat sour cream
  (1½ grams fat per
  tablespoon)
¼ cup reduced-calorie
  mayonnaise

½ teaspoon salt
Grating of black pepper
½ teaspoon dried chervil
½ teaspoon dried dill weed
Juice of one lime

Thoroughly combine all the ingredients. Serve on cold seafood salads, hot or cold poached fish, or fresh vegetables.

Tuna-Pasta Toss

Makes 4 meal-size servings or 6 side-dish servings

When it's your turn to bring a salad to a picnic or covered dish supper, Tuna-Pasta Toss offers a change of pace from common potato or macaroni salad. At home, serve on a bed of dark greens as the main dish for a light supper or as an accompaniment to a meal.

Fish trade-offs: shrimp—canned (drained), frozen (cooked), or steamed (fresh); cooked crab or lobster meat; cooked, fresh mackerel; steamed squid rings, strips, or chopped pieces; salmon (canned or cooked, fresh); cooked eel meat

1 tablespoon Dijon mustard
1 medium clove garlic,
  pressed or minced
2 tablespoons olive oil
3 tablespoons wine vinegar
½ teaspoon salt
Grating of black pepper
4 cups cooked (al dente)
  corkscrew-shaped pasta
¼ cup sliced scallions

⅓ cup sliced black olives
  (about 12 medium, pitted
  olives)
¼ cup packed chopped, fresh
  parsley
6½-ounce can water-packed
  tuna, drained and flaked
½ cup drained, canned
  chickpeas (garbanzo beans)

1. To make the dressing, thoroughly combine the mustard, garlic, olive oil, vinegar, salt, and pepper.

2. Place the pasta in a large bowl and pour the dressing over it.

3. Add the remaining ingredients and toss lightly to combine. Refrigerate until serving time. (If time permits, chill for several hours to allow flavors to blend.)

Per serving (based on 4 servings): Calories: 299   Fat: 11 gm. Cholesterol: 18 mg.   Sodium: 658 mg.

Whipped Tuna Salad

Makes enough for 6 to 8 sandwiches (approximately 3⅓ cups)

You really need a food processor to achieve the whipped, spreadlike texture of this low-calorie alternative to traditional tuna salad. The relish adds a special taste—even if you mix the ingredients by hand. (But you'll wind up with a much moister version if you use a food processor.) The recipe makes a large quantity which lasts for several days. You can use light or albacore tuna—I prefer the heartier taste of light in this recipe, but albacore has more omega-3s. Serve on whole-wheat, rye, or pumpernickel bread.

Fish Trade-offs: canned salmon or mackerel

1 small onion, quartered	3 tablespoons sweet green
3 stalks celery (peel outer	relish
layers if especially tough),	⅓ cup reduced-calorie
cut in 1½-inch sections	mayonnaise
3 6½-ounce cans water-	3 tablespoons cider vinegar
packed tuna, drained	

1. Using the steel blade of a food processor, chop the onion and celery until they're medium-fine.

2. Remove the steel blade and insert the plastic mixing blade. Add the tuna, relish, mayonnaise, and vinegar. Process for about 2 minutes or until well combined and a "whipped" texture is achieved. (Scrape the sides occasionally.)

Per serving (⅐ of recipe): Calories: 146   Fat: 5 gm.   Cholesterol: 35 mg. Sodium: 434 mg.

Seafood Salad

Makes 4 servings

You can use just about any cooked fish or shellfish in this creamy blend of mayonnaise, yogurt, and tasty seasonings. Serve on a bed of lettuce, as a sandwich, or on a hard roll.

Fish trade-offs: (any combination of the following can replace the lobster, the imitation crabmeat, or both) cooked meat of any white-fleshed fish; cooked eel or monkfish; steamed mussels or squid; cooked and shredded skate; steamed shrimp, lobster, or crawfish chunks

½ pound cooked, shredded
  lobster meat
½ pound imitation crabmeat,
  flaked
2 stalks celery, finely chopped
¼ cup plain, low-fat yogurt
⅓ cup reduced-calorie
  mayonnaise
2 teaspoons sweet green relish

1 teaspoon Dijon mustard
2 tablespoons chopped, fresh
  chives
2 tablespoons chopped, fresh
  parsley
1 teaspoon bottled
  horseradish
2 tablespoons lemon juice

Combine all the ingredients. Chill until ready to serve.

Per serving: Calories: 186   Fat: 6.5 gm.   Cholesterol: 60 mg. Sodium: 903 mg.   (To lower sodium, substitute fresh crabmeat for imitation.)

Tuna Tacos

Makes 10 tacos

When I first served tuna tacos to my family, I didn't dare tell them that I had used tuna instead of hamburger. But after half of the tacos were gone, I surprised everyone with my confession, which didn't keep anyone from polishing off the remaining tacos. In this recipe, I use several reduced-sodium ingredients because the taco mix alone is so salty. For a complete meal, serve with an endive salad and a large bowl of steamed summer squash with sliced green peppers.

Fish trade-offs: canned salmon; cooked, flaked weakfish; canned baby shrimp

4 tablespoons packaged taco seasoning mix
8-ounce can tomato sauce, with no added salt
²⁄₃ cup water
2 6½-ounce cans water-packed "less salt" or no-added-salt tuna, drained and flaked

10 taco shells
3 ounces shredded low-fat cheese (5 grams fat or less per ounce)
½ cup plus 2 tablespoons bottled salsa
½ cup chopped onion
2½ cups shredded lettuce

1. Preheat the oven to 350° F. In a large skillet, combine the taco seasoning mix, tomato sauce, and water. Bring to a boil, reduce heat, and simmer (uncovered) for 5 to 7 minutes. Stir occasionally. Remove from the heat.

2. Stir the tuna into the tomato-sauce mixture. Divide the sauce evenly among the 10 taco shells. Top with the shredded cheese and place the tacos on a baking sheet. Bake for 5 to 7 minutes.

3. Serve each taco with a tablespoon of salsa, a sprinkling of onions, and shredded lettuce. Guests can do this step themselves at the table.

*Per taco: Calories: 154   Fat: 5 gm.   Cholesterol: 15 mg.
Sodium: 311 mg.*

Crab-Meringue Toasties

Makes 4 servings

Perfect for a brunch or luncheon, these warm "toasties" are topped with a creamy mix of crabmeat and cheese. The meringue topping adds some panache. Serve with fresh-sliced tomatoes and cucumber quarters.

Fish trade-offs: tuna or salmon (canned or fresh, cooked); cooked lobster, shrimp, or crawfish; cooked, flaked, white-fleshed fish

8 ounces imitation crabmeat, cooked fresh crabmeat, or drained, canned crabmeat —flaked

1½ ounces low-fat block cheese (5 grams fat or less per ounce), shredded

2 tablespoons reduced-calorie mayonnaise

2 tablespoons plain yogurt

1 tablespoon chopped, fresh chives

¼ teaspoon salt (omit with imitation crabmeat)

Grating of black pepper

½ teaspoon dry mustard

1 tablespoon lemon juice

4 English muffins, split and lightly toasted

1 egg white beaten to soft peaks with ¼ teaspoon salt

1. Preheat the broiler. In a medium-size bowl, combine the crab-meat, cheese, mayonnaise, yogurt, chives, salt, pepper, mustard, and lemon juice.

2. Divide the crab mixture evenly among the 8 English-muffin halves, spreading to the edges.

3. Broil 6 to 8 inches from the heating element for 1½ to 2 minutes or until lightly browned.

4. Remove from the oven and spread the beaten egg white over the top of each muffin half. Return to the oven and broil for another minute or so, until the meringue browns. Watch very closely.

Per serving (based on imitation crabmeat): Calories: 265   Fat: 6 gm. Cholesterol: 14 mg.   Sodium: 1,146 mg.   (To reduce sodium, substitute fresh crabmeat for imitation and omit salt.)

Cheesy Fish Fillets

Makes 4 servings

These puffy fillets never fail to bring rave reviews—from youngsters and old folks alike. Serve with fresh or frozen peas and pickled beets.

Fish trade-offs: thin cod, haddock, or hake fillets; catfish; ocean perch; rockfish; orange roughy; pout; red snapper; tilapia; turbot; weakfish; whiting fillets

1 tablespoon reduced-calorie margarine
1¼ pounds flounder or sole fillets
⅓ cup reduced-calorie mayonnaise
2 scallions, sliced once lengthwise, then thinly sliced crosswise (include bulb plus an inch of green)
2 tablespoons grated Parmesan cheese
2 tablespoons chopped, fresh parsley
1 egg white, beaten until soft peaks form
Paprika

1. Preheat the oven to 450° F. (Place the oven rack about 6 to 8 inches from the broiler element.) Lightly grease a shallow baking pan with the reduced-calorie margarine; add the fish fillets in one layer.

2. In a small bowl, combine the mayonnaise, scallions, Parmesan cheese, and parsley. Fold the mixture into the beaten egg white.

3. Spread the mayonnaise mixture over the fish fillets, covering all surfaces. Sprinkle with paprika.

4. Bake for 5 or 6 minutes (until fish is almost done); then turn on the broiler and cook for another minute or two, until lightly browned and puffy on top. (Watch closely to avoid burning the topping.)

Per serving: Calories: 228   Fat: 9.5 gm.   Cholesterol: 93 mg. Sodium: 359 mg.

Mexicano Catfish Fillets

Makes 4 servings

Tomatoes, cheese, onions, and salsa smother tender catfish fillets, but not to the point where the topping overpowers the unique taste of catfish. Serve with sliced, steamed zucchini and a baked potato topped with herbed plain yogurt.

Fish trade-offs: thin, cod, haddock, or hake fillets; sole or flounder; pout; ocean perch; rockfish; mackerel; yellow perch; orange roughy; tilapia; weakfish

1 tablespoon reduced-calorie margarine
1 to 1¼ pounds catfish fillets (you need four fillets of similar size)
¾ teaspoon chili powder
¼ teaspoon salt
½ cup chopped onion

2 ounces shredded part-skim mozzarella cheese (5 grams fat or less per ounce)
1 large tomato, cut into 8 thin slices
½ cup mild-flavored bottled salsa, at room temperature

1. Grease a 13- x 9-inch shallow microwaveable baking dish with the reduced-calorie margarine. Add the catfish fillets, lining them up side by side. Sprinkle with the chili powder, salt, and chopped onion.

2. Cover with plastic wrap, leaving a corner open for venting. Microwave at full power for 2 to 3 minutes. Give the dish a half-turn once while cooking. Remove from the oven.

3. Evenly divide the cheese among the 4 fillets. Then top each with 2 slices of tomato. Cover and vent again. Microwave at full power for another 4 to 5 minutes or until the fish is barely done. (Again, give dish a turn while cooking.) Let stand a minute or two before removing the plastic wrap. Check to make sure fish is done.

4. Place the cooked fillets on individual plates and top each with a share of salsa.

Per serving: Calories: 202   Fat: 9 gm.   Cholesterol: 74 mg. Sodium: 308 mg.

Southern Slim-Fried Catfish

Makes 4 servings

When it comes to calories and fat, this catfish recipe is a far cry from the traditional fried version. But you're not spared crunchiness or good taste. Serve with cole slaw (made low-calorie, of course) and a dark green vegetable.

Fish trade-offs: cusk, hake, ocean perch, rockfish, pout, tilapia, wolffish

1 tablespoon plus 2 teaspoons vegetable oil	Grating of black pepper
	¼ teaspoon onion powder
1 egg	¼ teaspoon paprika
2 tablespoons milk	½ teaspoon sugar
Several dashes of Tabasco sauce	½ teaspoon salt
	1¼ to 1⅓ pounds catfish
⅓ cup cornmeal	fillets

1. Preheat the oven to 450° F. Spread the oil evenly in the bottom of a 1½- to 2-quart rectangular casserole.

2. In a shallow bowl, whisk together the egg, milk, and Tabasco. Set aside.

3. In a separate bowl, thoroughly mix the cornmeal, pepper, onion powder, paprika, sugar, and salt. Spread on a flat plate or paper plate.

4. Dip each fish fillet in the egg mixture. Then thoroughly coat the fillets with the cornmeal mixture.

5. Place the fillets in the casserole, overlapping slightly. After you've placed the last fillet, turn each fillet over, starting with the one placed in the casserole first. (This allows both sides of the fillets to receive some of the oil.) Tuck under any thin ends of fish.

6. Bake for 12 to 17 minutes (until the fish is almost done), depending on fillet thickness. Then set the oven for broiling. Broil until the tops of the fillets are golden brown and the fish is done. Watch closely to avoid overbrowning.

Per serving: Calories: 278   Fat: 14 gm.   Cholesterol: 152 mg. Sodium: 377 mg.

Karen's Breaded Pollock with
Straw Mushrooms

Makes 4 servings

For a quick—but different—weeknight supper, breaded pollock is lightly sautéed, then baked in a lemony broth and topped with straw mushrooms and herbs.

Fish trade-offs: catfish, cusk, drum, grouper, pout, dogfish, skate, tilefish, wolffish, cod, haddock, hake

13- to 14-ounce can chicken broth, fat skimmed off top
¼ cup all-purpose flour
¼ cup unseasoned bread crumbs
1¼ pounds skinless pollock fillets, ½- to ¾-inch thick
1 egg, lightly beaten in a shallow bowl
1 tablespoon regular margarine

2-3 tablespoons fresh, chopped parsley
½ teaspoon dried basil
15-ounce can straw mushrooms, drained (if unavailable, regular mushrooms will do)
Juice of 1 freshly squeezed lemon

1. Preheat the oven to 450° F. While preparing the fish, bring the chicken broth to a boil and keep it piping hot.

2. Evenly spread the flour on a paper plate. Spread the bread crumbs on another paper plate. Lightly dredge both sides of the fillets in the flour, then the egg. (You'll only need to use 1 to 2 tablespoons of the flour and part of the egg.) Then dredge the fish in the bread crumbs, trying to use them up.

3. Heat the margarine over medium-high heat in a large nonstick frying pan. Tilt the pan to coat evenly with margarine. Add the breaded fish and sauté for about 2 minutes on each side, until golden brown. (Don't overcook.)

4. Place the fillets in a 13- x 9-inch baking dish. Tuck under the thinner "tails" of fish so the fillets are of uniform thickness. Pour the hot broth over the fish.

5. Top with the parsley, basil, and mushrooms. Drizzle lemon juice over all. Bake for 8 to 12 minutes, depending on the thickness of the fish. Remove individual portions from the pan with a slotted spoon and serve topped with mushrooms.

Per serving: Calories: 229   Fat: 6 gm.   Cholesterol: 147 mg. Sodium: 524 mg.

Broiled Basil Swordfish

Makes 4 servings

Basil and mayonnaise offer a pleasant change of pace from simple swordfish broiled in butter. You'll find the perfect accompaniment in cooked pasta mixed with steamed vegetables and a sprinkling of Parmesan cheese.

Fish trade-offs: croaker, mackerel, mahimahi, mullet, sablefish, mako shark, fresh tuna, whitefish, halibut, bluefish, salmon

3 tablespoons reduced-calorie mayonnaise	½ teaspoon onion powder
1 tablespoon lemon juice	1⅓ to 1½ pounds swordfish
1 teaspoon dried basil leaves	Nonstick vegetable spray

1. Preheat the broiler. With a wire whisk, thoroughly combine the mayonnaise, lemon juice, basil, and onion powder in a small bowl. Set aside.

2. Place the swordfish on the broiler pan coated with nonstick spray. Blot the side of fish facing up with a paper towel to remove moisture. Spread evenly with half of the mayonnaise mixture. Broil 6 to 8 inches from the heating element for 5 to 6 minutes. Watch closely to keep the topping from turning black.

3. Remove the fish from the oven, turn, and blot again with a paper towel. Coat with remaining mayonnaise mixture. Broil for another 4 to 6 minutes depending on the thickness of the fish.

Per serving: Calories: 206   Fat: 9 gm.   Cholesterol: 59 mg. Sodium: 212 mg.

Shark with Crumbly Blue Cheese Topping

Makes 4 servings

For blue cheese aficionados, this fancy-tasting topping is easy to make and adds a unique touch to simple, broiled fish. Serve with fresh corn on the cob, a bright green vegetable, and shredded carrot salad.

Fish trade-offs: Spanish mackerel, mahimahi fillets, fresh tuna, whitefish, halibut, salmon steaks or fillets, bluefish steaks or fillets

1 tablespoon reduced-calorie margarine
1½ ounces crumbled blue cheese (about ⅓ cup, lightly packed)
2 tablespoons grated Parmesan cheese
3 tablespoons unseasoned bread crumbs
1 tablespoon finely chopped shallot or onion
1 tablespoon lemon juice
2 tablespoons chopped, fresh parsley
1 teaspoon soy sauce (preferably tamari)
3 tablespoons low-fat milk
Nonstick vegetable spray
1¼ to 1⅓ pounds shark steaks, ¾ to 1 inch thick
2 tablespoons lemon juice

1. In a medium-size bowl, with an electric mixer, beat together the reduced-calorie margarine, blue cheese, Parmesan cheese, bread crumbs, shallot or onion, 1 tablespoon lemon juice, parsley, soy sauce, and milk. The mixture will be lumpy. Set aside.

2. Preheat the broiler. Spray the broiler pan with the nonstick spray. Add the fish and top with the remaining 2 tablespoons lemon juice. Broil 6 to 7 inches from the heating element for 7 to 8 minutes.

3. Remove the fish from the oven and turn over. Thoroughly blot the side facing up with a paper towel. Then spread evenly with the blue-cheese mixture.

4. Broil for another 3 to 4 minutes. Watch closely to make sure the topping doesn't blacken. Make a small cut to be certain the fish is done. If not, shut off the broiler and leave the fish in the hot oven until it's done.

Per serving: Calories: 280   Fat: 13 gm.   Cholesterol: 83 mg. Sodium: 435 mg.

Sesame Sole in Parchment Hearts
with Snow Peas and Ginger

Makes 4 servings

Sole takes on a Chinese flair in this recipe with crunchy sesame seeds, soy sauce, pea pods, and ginger. The parchment pockets make a very easy recipe seem like gourmet fare. For a complete meal, all you need is a baked potato with herbed plain yogurt and a large tossed salad.

Fish trade-offs: thin cod, haddock, or hake fillets; pout; pompano; red snapper; catfish; whiting fillets; ocean perch; rockfish; orange roughy; tilapia; weakfish

1 tablespoon plus 1 teaspoon sesame seeds
2 tablespoons dry or semidry sherry
2 tablespoons lime juice
2 teaspoons soy sauce
1 tablespoon sesame oil
¾ teaspoon grated fresh ginger root
4 large squares of parchment paper, each 3 to 4 inches

more than double the size of a fish fillet
4 large sole or flounder fillets, about ½ inch thick (4 to 5 ounces apiece)
20 snow peas, washed, with caps and strings removed
4 scallions (include bulb plus an inch or two of green), cut into slivers lengthwise

1. Preheat the oven to 350° F. Spread the sesame seeds evenly on a baking sheet. Bake for 10 to 12 minutes, shaking once or twice to prevent burning. Remove from the oven and save until serving time. Raise the oven temperature to 425° F.

2. In a small bowl, make the sauce by combining the sherry, lime juice, soy sauce, sesame oil, and ginger. Set aside.

3. To make the hearts, fold the parchment squares in half. Beginning at the fold, cut out a large half-heart. Open the hearts and place one fish fillet inside each, right next to the crease.

4. Spread the sauce over the 4 fillets, dividing it evenly among them. Then top each fillet with 5 pea pods and slivered scallions.

5. Fold the top halves of the hearts over the sides with the fish fillets. Crimp the edges tightly closed by folding over twice every 1½ to 2 inches. (See chapter 10, page 198, for more details.)

6. Place the pockets on a cookie sheet and bake for 7 to 8 minutes. Allow people to open their own pockets and top with a teaspoon of sesame seeds.

Per serving: Calories: 171   Fat: 6 gm.   Cholesterol: 54 mg. Sodium: 267 mg.

Salmon Burgers

Makes 4 large burgers

Served on a bun with a little catsup, this hamburger alternative appeals to kids in a big way. Or make a main meal of salmon burgers, broccoli mixed with cauliflower, and a no-sugar Jell-O and fruit salad. Try salmon burgers with Slimmed-Down Tartar Sauce (page 237), Lemony Dill Sauce (page 299), or lemon wedges.

Fish trade-offs: canned mackerel or tuna

15½-ounce can salmon, drained, skin removed, and flaked
¼ cup uncooked oatmeal
½ cup slightly crushed flake cereal, such as cornflakes
2 tablespoons reduced-calorie mayonnaise

⅓ cup chopped onion
1 egg
2 tablespoons lemon juice
2 teaspoons bottled horseradish
1 tablespoon reduced-calorie margarine

1. Mix all the ingredients except the reduced-calorie margarine until just combined. Shape into 4 burgers. (The mixture may be somewhat crumbly.)

2. Coat the bottom of a large nonstick skillet with the reduced-calorie margarine. Add the burgers.

3. Preheat a burner to medium-high. Place the pan with the burgers on the burner. Cook for 7 to 8 minutes, until the burgers form a nice, brown crust. Carefully flip the burgers, being certain to take up the brown crust when you turn them. Reduce the heat to medium and cook for another 5 to 6 minutes, until that side forms a crust, too.

Per serving: Calories: 238   Fat: 11 gm.   Cholesterol: 112 mg. Sodium: 660 mg.

Tarragon Skate Wings Sautéed in Bread Crumbs and Lemon Butter

Makes 4 servings

Since my family wasn't adventuresome enough to try skate wings when I was writing this book, I tried this simple recipe one night when I was on my own for dinner. The lightly breaded skate wings and lemon butter are a melt-in-your-mouth combination. For this one, I vote for the taste of butter since the amount is so small for 4 people. Serve with stewed tomatoes and a spinach salad with croutons.

Fish trade-offs: croaker, smelt, shad, eel, tilefish, or any ½- to ¾-inch-thick white-fleshed fish fillets, such as cod, haddock, hake, or pollock

2 tablespoons all-purpose flour
¼ cup unseasoned bread crumbs
1 teaspoon dried tarragon
2 tablespoons grated Parmesan cheese
¼ teaspoon onion powder
¼ teaspoon salt
1¼ pounds skinless skate-wing fillets, in 4 serving size pieces (see page 148 for directions on preparing skate fillets)
1 egg beaten with 2 tablespoons low-fat milk
1½ tablespoons butter or margarine
3 tablespoons lemon juice
2 tablespoons chopped, fresh parsley

1. Evenly spread the flour on a paper plate. Then in a large, shallow bowl, mix together the bread crumbs, tarragon, Parmesan cheese, onion powder, and salt.

2. Dredge both sides of each fillet first in the flour, next in the egg and milk, and then in the bread-crumb mix. Set aside.

3. In a large nonstick skillet, heat the butter and lemon juice over medium-high heat until the butter is melted and the mixture starts to sizzle. Add the parsley. Tilt the pan to evenly coat with the lemon-butter mixture. Lower the heat to medium.

4. Add the fillets and sauté on one side for 4 to 5 minutes, until lightly browned. Turn the fillets and cook for another 4 to 5 minutes or until the fish is done. Watch closely—turn more often if the fillets get too brown. (If the wings were partially cooked beforehand—as described on page 148—cooking time may be shorter.)

Per serving: Calories: 294   Fat: 13 gm.   Cholesterol: 132 mg. Sodium: 397 mg.

Spanish Mackerel Steaks
Grilled with Mustardy Topping

Makes 4 servings

Mackerel steaks were meant for grilling, and this light topping really complements the oiliness of the fish. Serve with a colorful vegetable or two and sliced red-skinned potatoes marinated in low-calorie Italian dressing.

Fish trade-offs: (any of the following in steak or fillet form) bluefish, salmon, eel, tuna, swordfish, pompano, striped bass, mahimahi, mullet, sablefish, mako shark, whitefish

3 tablespoons reduced-calorie mayonnaise	1 tablespoon lemon juice
1 tablespoon Dijon mustard	Grating of black pepper
2 tablespoons finely chopped, fresh parsley	1⅓ to 1½ pounds Spanish mackerel steaks, ¾ to 1 inch thick
1½ tablespoons finely chopped scallion or shallot	

1. Start a charcoal fire or preheat a gas grill.

2. In a small bowl, make the sauce by combining the mayonnaise, mustard, parsley, scallion or shallot, lemon juice, and pepper. Set aside.

3. When the coals are ready, grease the grill rack well (or use foil with holes poked in it—see page 191). Then preheat it over hot coals.

4. Blot the fish with a paper towel. Using half of the sauce, spread a light coating on one side of the fillets. Placing that side down, grill 4 to 5 minutes. Then blot the side of the fish facing up and spread with the remaining sauce. Carefully turn the steaks and cook for another 4 to 5 minutes or until the fish is done.

Per serving: Calories: 184   Fat: 9 gm.   Cholesterol: 72 mg. Sodium: 195 mg.

Spicy Tomato-Cod Curry

Makes 4 servings

Spicy—but not hot—this recipe give a real dressing-up to cod or any white-fleshed fish. Serve over white or brown rice with a Waldorf salad and steamed, fresh broccoli.

Fish trade-offs: haddock, hake, cusk, drum, turbot, grouper, mackerel, monkfish, pollock, pout, dogfish, skate, tilefish, wolffish

1 tablespoon olive oil
¼ cup chopped onion
1 medium clove garlic, pressed or minced
2 teaspoons ground coriander
2 teaspoons ground cumin
1½ teaspoons curry powder
¼ teaspoon each of ground ginger, cinnamon, and dry mustard
Grating of black pepper
canned Italian plum tomatoes (removed from canning juices before chopping and measuring)
½ cup juice from canned tomatoes (above)
1 tablespoon tomato paste
½ teaspoon salt
1 pound cod fillets, cut in 1- to 1½-inch chunks
1 tablespoon lemon juice

1. In a large nonstick skillet, heat the olive oil over medium heat. Add the onion and garlic. Sauté until they just start to brown, 3 to 4 minutes.

2. Add the coriander, cumin, curry, ginger, cinnamon, mustard, and pepper. Heat for another minute, stirring constantly.

3. Stir in the chopped tomatoes, tomato juice, tomato paste, and salt. Bring to a boil, then reduce the heat, cover, and simmer for 10 to 15 minutes, stirring occasionally.

4. Gently stir in the fish chunks and lemon juice. Increase the heat slightly. Cover the skillet and simmer for 7 to 8 minutes or until the fish is done. Do not stir again, but shake the pan gently 2 or 3 times.

Per serving: Calories: 167   Fat: 5 gm.   Cholesterol: 49 mg. Sodium: 559 mg.

Stovetop Scallops with Garlic, Snow Peas, and Water Chestnuts

Makes 4 servings

Bay scallops, snow peas, and water chestnuts are naturals for an easy stovetop supper—and there's no cutting involved. Here, they're accented with garlic, scallions, and sherry. Heap over a bed of white rice.

Fish trade-offs: shrimp; crawfish; croaker strips or chunks; chunks of monkfish, skate, or lobster

- 2 tablespoons soy sauce
- 3 tablespoons dry or semidry sherry
- 2 tablespoons dry white wine
- 2 tablespoons lemon juice
- 1 tablespoon cornstarch
- 2 tablespoons peanut oil
- 2 medium garlic cloves, finely grated
- ½ teaspoon grated fresh ginger root
- 8-ounce can sliced water chestnuts, drained
- 6 large scallions (include bulb plus 3 inches of green), sliced once lengthwise, then cut in 1-inch sections
- 4 to 5 ounces snow peas, caps and strings removed
- 1¼ to 1⅓ pounds bay scallops, rinsed and drained well (if sea scallops are used, cut in quarters or halves, depending on size)

1. In a small bowl, combine the soy sauce, sherry, wine, lemon juice, and cornstarch into a sauce. Set aside.

2. In a large nonstick skillet or wok, heat the peanut oil over medium-high heat. Add the garlic and ginger. Cook for about 1 minute, until the garlic just barely starts to brown.

3. Stir in the water chestnuts, scallions, and snow peas. Cover and steam for about 2 minutes. Stir once while cooking.

4. Stir in the scallops. Cover and steam for another 2 to 3 minutes. Stir once while cooking.

5. Thoroughly mix the sauce ingredients again and pour over the scallop-vegetable mixture. Heat just until the sauce thickens, stirring gently and constantly.

Per serving: Calories: 266   Fat: 8 gm.   Cholesterol: 47 mg. Sodium: 751 mg.

Cod Fillets with Lemon-Herb Butter

Makes 4 servings

A simple summery dish, this pleasant alternative to "plain-baked" cod has a light herb-butter sauce that complements the delicate flavor of the fish. Serve with steamed asparagus and a mixed fresh fruit and yogurt salad.

Fish trade-offs: haddock, hake, pollock, pout, red snapper, drum, grouper, whiting, mullet, dogfish, skate, tilefish, whitefish

1 tablespoon reduced-calorie margarine

2 tablespoons regular margarine or butter (I use one of each)

2 tablespoons minced, fresh parsley

2 tablespoons minced shallots

(use several tablespoons fresh, chopped dill if you have it)

½ teaspoon salt

Grating of black pepper

2 tablespoons lemon juice

1⅓ pounds thick cod fillets, 1 to 1½ inches thick

1. Preheat the oven to 450° F. Use the reduced-calorie margarine to grease a baking dish that's just large enough to accommodate the fish in a single layer.

2. To make the sauce, combine the margarine and/or butter, parsley, shallots, dill, salt, and pepper in a small saucepan. Heat over low heat, stirring occasionally, until the margarine and/or butter is melted. Remove from the heat and stir in the lemon juice.

3. Place the fish in the casserole in a single layer and cover with the sauce. Bake for 13 to 18 minutes (or until the fish is done), covered for half of the time, then uncovered. When served, spoon some sauce over each portion.

Per serving: Calories: 170   Fat: 6 gm.   Cholesterol: 70 mg.
Sodium: 317 mg.

Sesame-Soy Halibut Steaks

Makes 4 servings

Some diners won't even know they're eating fish when they eat this version of halibut, adapted from a recipe in Sonja and William Connor's *The New American Diet*. A sesame-soy marinade complements the meaty texture of halibut, which also lends itself to the grill; toasted sesame seeds add some crunchiness.

Fish trade-offs: swordfish, tuna, salmon, bluefish, mako or blue shark, striped bass, grouper, mahimahi, mullet, sablefish

¼ cup orange-juice
   concentrate
3 tablespoons water
2 tablespoons catsup
1 tablespoon plus 2 teaspoons
   soy sauce
2 tablespoons cider vinegar
1 tablespoon sesame oil

2 packed tablespoons brown
   sugar
1½ pounds halibut steaks,
   ¾ to 1 inch thick
Nonstick vegetable spray
1½ tablespoons toasted
   sesame seeds (see page 255
   for directions)

1. Thoroughly combine the orange-juice concentrate, water, catsup, soy sauce, vinegar, sesame oil, and brown sugar. Pour over the fish.

2. Marinate the fish in the refrigerator for 2 to 3 hours, turning several times and spooning the sauce over the top of the fish.

3. Preheat the broiler. Coat the broiler-pan rack with the nonstick spray. Broil the fish about 6 inches from the heating element for 4 to 5 minutes on each side. (Baste the fish with marinade before turning.)

4. Divide the fish into 4 servings and sprinkle with the sesame seeds.

*Per serving: Calories: 202   Fat: 6 gm.   Cholesterol: 44 mg.
Sodium: 267 mg.*

Simple Cod Fillets
with Buttery Crumb Topping

Makes 4 servings

This is one of my favorite ways to serve thick white-fish fillets—and a cinch to prepare. The milk keeps the fish moist, while the crumbs add a crunchy topping. Serve with a fresh fruit salad and baked tomato halves topped with a sprinkling of Parmesan cheese and basil. (If you use thinner fillets, scale down the cooking time.)

Fish trade-offs: haddock, hake, pollock, cusk, drum, grouper, orange roughy, pout, dogfish, skate, tilefish, weakfish, whitefish, wolf-fish

⅓ cup low-fat milk
1⅓ pounds thick cod fillets,
   1 to 1½ inches thick
⅓ cup low-fat cracker crumbs
   (you can use unsalted
   saltines or stoned-wheat
   crackers)

1 teaspoon dried parsley flakes
¼ teaspoon salt
1½ tablespoons melted
   margarine or butter

1. Preheat the oven to 450° F. Pour the milk into a 1½-quart shallow baking dish. Add the fish.

2. Combine the cracker crumbs, parsley, and salt. Evenly distribute across the top of the fish.

3. Drizzle the margarine or butter over the crumbs. Place the fish in the preheated oven and bake for 12 to 17 minutes or until the fish is done.

Per serving: Calories: 190   Fat: 6 gm.   Cholesterol: 66 mg.
Sodium: 326 mg.

Easy Oven-Fried Cusk Fillets

Makes 4 servings

For the fried-fish lover in you, this recipe for crisp-coated fish has about two-thirds the calories of a deep-fried version. Superb with Slimmed-Down Tartar Sauce, page 237, or just plain lemon juice. Kids go for oven-fried fish with catsup. (When using less-firm fish, you may need to shorten the cooking time.)

Fish trade-offs: cod, haddock, hake, pollock, catfish, pout, dogfish, tilapia, wolffish

2 teaspoons regular margarine	flake-type cereal (about
2 tablespoons low-fat milk	3 cups before crushing)
1 egg	1¼ pounds cusk fillets, ½ to
3 tablespoons plain yogurt	⅝ inch thick, cut into
½ teaspoon onion powder	4 portions
½ teaspoon salt	2 tablespoons melted
	margarine

1. Place the oven rack in the upper third of the oven. Preheat the oven to 550° F. Grease a cookie sheet with the 2 teaspoons of margarine.

2. In a large, shallow bowl, whisk together the milk, egg, yogurt, onion powder, and salt. Set aside. Spread the crushed cereal crumbs on a large, flat plate or paper plate.

3. Pat the fish dry. Dip each fillet in the egg-yogurt mixture, assuring that all spots are coated. Let the excess drip off, then press the fish into the crushed cereal, evenly coating all surfaces.

4. Place the coated fillets on the greased cookie sheet. Drizzle the melted margarine across the tops of the fish, distributing evenly. Bake for 8 to 10 minutes or until the fish is done.

Per serving: Calories: 297   Fat: 10 gm.   Cholesterol: 130 mg. Sodium: 724 mg.

Broiled Honey-Lime Salmon
with Tarragon

Makes 4 servings

Salmon's special flavor is highlighted by Dijon mustard, lime juice, and tarragon. Honey adds a slightly sweet accent. Serve the fish with fresh lime wedges.

Fish trade-offs: mako shark, swordfish, bluefish, tuna, pompano, freshwater trout, mahimahi, sablefish, whitefish

2 tablespoons Dijon mustard
Juice of one freshly squeezed
   lime
2 teaspoons olive oil
1 tablespoon honey
1½ teaspoons dried tarragon

2 tablespoons dry or semidry
   sherry
¼ teaspoon salt
1¼ to 1⅓ pounds salmon
   fillets, ½ to ⅝ inch thick
Nonstick vegetable spray

1. To make the marinade, thoroughly combine the first 7 ingredients.

2. Place the salmon fillets in a shallow, nonmetal dish and top with the marinade. Turn to coat the other side. Marinate in the refrigerator for about an hour, turning once or twice.

3. Preheat the broiler. Coat the broiler-pan rack with the nonstick spray.

4. Place the salmon on the rack, skin side down. Spoon the marinade over the fish.

5. Broil the fish 4 to 6 inches from the heating element for 5 to 6 minutes or until the fish is done. (No need to turn.)

Per serving: Calories: 259   Fat: 13 gm.   Cholesterol: 87 mg. Sodium: 208 mg.

Shrimp Scampi

Makes 4 servings

Meant for shrimp and garlic lovers, scampi should be served over white rice or rice pilaf. (This recipe is loaded with iron and is a good source of zinc.) Steamed pea pods and melon wedges make a complete and colorful meal.

Fish trade-offs: crawfish, mussel meats, scallops (use a tablespoon or two less wine)

¼ cup olive oil
4 to 5 good-sized garlic
cloves, pressed or minced
2 pounds raw shrimp thawed,
peeled, deveined, and tails
left intact, drained well
¼ cup minced scallion or
onion

½ teaspoon salt
Grating of black pepper
¼ cup minced, fresh parsley
6 tablespoons dry white wine
2 tablespoons dry or semidry
sherry
4 tablespoons lemon juice

1. Heat the oil over medium-high heat in a large frying pan. Add the garlic and sauté for about 30 seconds (don't brown).

2. Add the shrimp, scallion or onion, salt, pepper, and parsley. Sauté for 4 to 5 minutes, stirring occasionally.

3. When the shrimp is pinkish-white and its translucent look is gone, add the wine, sherry, and lemon juice. Heat for another minute or two.

Per serving: Calories: 350   Fat: 16.5 gm.   Cholesterol: 276 mg. Sodium: 539 mg.

Cheese-Topped Baked Fish Fillets

Makes 4 servings

This simple dish makes a quick supper that's perfect family fare. The uncomplicated tastes of white fish and cheese are especially pleasing to youngsters. Serve with fresh, steamed carrot strips and marinated broccoli.

Fish trade-offs: thin cod, haddock, or hake fillets; pout; yellow perch; catfish; ocean perch; rockfish; orange roughy; tilapia; weakfish

1 tablespoon reduced-calorie margarine
4 large scallions, sliced (include bulb plus several inches of green)
15-ounce can mushrooms, drained
1¼ pounds flatfish fillets, ½ to ⅝ inch thick
¼ cup dry white wine
2 tablespoons lemon juice
½ teaspoon dried, flaked marjoram
Grating of black pepper
4 slices reduced-fat cheese (2 grams fat per ounce), cut in ½-inch strips
2 tablespoons unseasoned bread crumbs

1. Preheat the oven to 400° F. Grease a shallow 2-quart baking dish with the reduced-calorie margarine.

2. Evenly scatter the scallions and mushrooms over the bottom of the baking dish. Place the fish fillets on top in a single layer. (Overlap or tuck under thin ends of the fillets.)

3. Mix the wine and lemon juice together and pour over the fish. Sprinkle with the marjoram and black pepper. Evenly distribute the cheese strips over the fillets.

4. Crumple a large piece of waxed paper and wet it. Shake off excess water and place the paper loosely across the fish. Bake for about 7 minutes.

5. Remove the fish from the oven. Take off the waxed paper. (Remove any stuck cheese and replace it on the fish.) Sprinkle the fish with the bread crumbs. Bake for another 7 to 9 minutes or until the fish is just done.

6. Remove the fish from the oven and heat the broiler. Stick the fish under the broiler just long enough to brown the top—about 1 minute. (Watch closely.)

Per serving: Calories: 258   Fat: 6 gm.   Cholesterol: 76 mg. Sodium: 743 mg.

Easiest-Ever Baked Pollock Fillets

Makes 4 servings

No chopping, cutting, or basting! This simple combination of bread crumbs and Parmesan cheese turns pollock into a mouth-watering treat. Delicious with stewed tomatoes, a green vegetable, and cole slaw.

Fish trade-offs: cod, haddock, hake, cusk, drum, pout, skate, tilefish, whitefish, wolffish

¼ cup unseasoned bread
  crumbs
2 tablespoons grated
  Parmesan cheese
1½ tablespoons lemon juice
1½ tablespoons melted
  margarine

Nonstick vegetable spray
1¼ to 1⅓ pounds pollock
  fillets, ¾ to 1 inch thick
1 tablespoon reduced-calorie
  mayonnaise

1. Preheat the oven to 450° F. In a small bowl or coffee mug, mix the bread crumbs, Parmesan cheese, lemon juice, and melted margarine. (The mixture will be pasty.) Set aside.

2. Coat a baking sheet with the nonstick spray and add the pollock fillets. Blot the tops with paper toweling, then spread with the mayonnaise.

3. Take the crumb mixture and spread it evenly across the tops of the mayonnaise-coated fillets. Bake for 15 to 18 minutes.

Per serving: Calories: 216   Fat: 7.5 gm.   Cholesterol: 104 mg. Sodium: 292 mg.

Spicy Mackerel Patties

Makes 4 servings

This is an ideal recipe for someone who wants to eat more omega-3s but who isn't too enamored of oily fish; and it's easy on the pocketbook since canned mackerel is inexpensive. The savory vegetables and seasonings complement mackerel's hearty taste. (These patties are rich in iron and provide nearly as much calcium as a cup of milk.) Serve with catsup, Worcestershire sauce, lemon wedges, or Slimmed-Down Tartar Sauce (see page 237).

Fish trade-offs: canned salmon or tuna

15-ounce can mackerel, drained, skin removed, and flaked

1 cup whole-wheat bread crumbs (made from 3 slices toasted whole-wheat bread, processed into crumbs in blender or food processor while warm so crumbs remain soft and moist)

⅓ cup chopped, fresh parsley

1 small green pepper, finely chopped (about ⅓ cup, packed)

⅓ cup finely chopped onion

½ teaspoon dried, flaked thyme

½ teaspoon paprika

2 teaspoons bottled horseradish

1 tablespoon prepared mustard (any kind)

1 tablespoon lemon juice

2 tablespoons bottled chili sauce

Dash of cayenne pepper

Grating of black pepper

1 egg plus one egg white, lightly beaten

1 tablespoon reduced-calorie margarine

1. Thoroughly mix all the ingredients except the reduced-calorie margarine in a large bowl. Firmly shape into 4 large patties.

2. Coat the bottom of a large nonstick frying pan with diet margarine. Add the patties.

3. Preheat a burner to medium-high. Place the skillet on the burner. Cook for 7 to 8 minutes, until the patties have a brown crust. Turn very carefully. Reduce the heat to medium and cook for another 5 to 6 minutes.

Per serving: Calories: 234   Fat: 9 gm.   Cholesterol: 140 mg. Sodium: 533 mg.

Debby's Barbecued Fresh Tuna

Makes 4 servings

For the taste of a cookout on a rainy or cold winter's night, try marinating and broiling fresh tuna saturated with this tasty combination of seasonings and juices. Of course, if weather permits, the flavors are also great when grilled. Serve with lemon or lime wedges.

Fish trade-offs: swordfish, mako or blue shark, mahimahi, bluefish, mullet, sablefish, salmon, halibut

3 tablespoons soy sauce
2 large cloves garlic, pressed
  or minced
¼ cup catsup
2 tablespoons lemon juice
2 tablespoons dry vermouth
½ cup orange juice
¼ cup finely chopped parsley

1 teaspoon dried oregano
½ teaspoon paprika
Generous grating of black
  pepper
1¼ to 1⅓ pounds fresh tuna
  steaks, 1 to 1¼ inches thick
Nonstick vegetable spray

1. Combine all the ingredients except the fish and vegetable spray into a barbecue sauce. Pour over the fish and marinate in the refrigerator for about 2 hours, turning several times.

2. Preheat the broiler. Coat the broiler-pan rack with the nonstick vegetable spray and add the fish. Broil about 6 inches from the heating element for 6 to 7 minutes, basting with sauce at the halfway point.

3. Turn the fish and baste with sauce. Broil for another 5 to 6 minutes, again basting at the halfway point.

Per serving: Calories: 237   Fat: 7.5 gm.   Cholesterol: 57 mg. Sodium: 431 mg.

Simple Sole Amandine

Makes 4 servings   (MICROWAVE)

Unlike the traditional butter-drenched recipe, this microwave version of sole amandine offers a savory combination of lemon juice, margarine, and seasonings that render the fish moist and tasty. Serve with golden winter squash and a cucumber and tomato salad.

Fish trade-offs: thin cod, haddock or hake fillets; pout; red snapper; yellow perch; butterfish; freshwater trout; catfish or whiting fillets; skate; tilapia; weakfish; orange roughy

1 tablespoon regular margarine or butter	1¼ to 1⅓ pounds sole or flounder fillets
3 tablespoons lemon juice	Paprika
½ teaspoon dried, flaked thyme	2-3 tablespoons chopped, fresh parsley
¼ teaspoon onion powder	¼ cup toasted slivered almonds*
½ teaspoon salt	

1. In a small microwaveable bowl, place the margarine or butter, lemon juice, thyme, onion powder, and salt. Cover loosely and microwave at full power until the margarine melts (about 1 minute).

2. Place the fish fillets in a single layer (overlap slightly if necessary) in a 12- x 7-inch baking dish. Stir the warm margarine mixture and drizzle it evenly over the fish. Lift the fillets to get some of the juice under the fish. Top the fish with a light sprinkling of paprika and all of the parsley.

3. Cover the baking dish with plastic wrap, leaving a corner open for venting. Microwave at full power for 3½ to 5 minutes, or until the centers of the fillets just start to flake. Give the dish a half-turn once while cooking. (Watch closely to avoid overcooking.) Let stand, covered, for a minute or two.

4. Divide into 4 servings and distribute almonds over each.

Per serving: Calories: 227   Fat: 9 gm.   Cholesterol: 85 mg. Sodium: 433 mg.

* To toast almonds, spread them in a single layer on a baking sheet or foil and bake in a preheated 350° F oven for 10 to 15 minutes. Watch closely.

Savory Pollock with Tomatoes and Green Peppers

Makes 4 servings (MICROWAVE)

Pollock smothered with a vegetable-laden sauce is perfect for a cold winter's night or as a light summer supper. (A serving of this dish will meet your daily vitamin C requirement.) Serve with a sliced cucumber and onion salad dressed with plain yogurt and dill.

Fish trade-offs: You name it—cod, haddock, hake, pout, turbot, catfish, cusk, drum, grouper, mackerel, monkfish, dogfish, skate, tilefish, wolffish

1 tablespoon regular margarine

2 large, firm tomatoes, peeled and coarsely chopped (see page 236n for directions on peeling)

1 medium green pepper, diced

½ cup sliced scallions (6 to 8 large—include bulb plus 2 to 3 inches of green) or diced onion

3 tablespoons chopped, fresh parsley

Juice of 1 freshly squeezed lemon

½ teaspoon salt

Grating of black pepper

3 to 4 dashes Tabasco sauce

½ teaspoon dried basil

1¼ to 1⅓ pounds pollock fillets, ½ to ¾ inch thick

1. In a medium saucepan, melt the margarine over medium heat. Add the tomatoes, green pepper, scallions or onion, and parsley. Cover and cook for 5 to 6 minutes or until the vegetables are barely limp. (Stir once or twice.)

2. Stir in the lemon juice, salt, pepper, Tabasco, and basil. Cover and cook for another minute or two. Drain several tablespoons of liquid from the sauce. Set the sauce aside.

3. Place the fish in a microwave-proof casserole large enough to accommodate the fish in a single layer. Top with the sauce. Cover with waxed paper or vented plastic wrap. Microwave at full power for 7 to 10 minutes (depending on fish thickness) or until the fish is barely done—just slightly translucent in the center. Rotate the dish halfway through the cooking time. (You have to push the sauce aside to test for doneness.) Remove from the oven and let stand, covered, for a minute or two and check again for doneness.

Per serving: Calories: 191   Fat: 4.5 gm.   Cholesterol: 101 mg. Sodium: 432 mg.

Broiled Bluefish à l'Orange

Makes 4 servings

A citrus marinade complements the rich taste of bluefish in this recipe, which goes well with fresh peas and carrot-cabbage slaw with a sweet-and-sour dressing.

Fish trade-offs: swordfish, mako shark, tuna, freshwater trout, black bass, pompano, shad, eel, mackerel, mahimahi, mullet, sablefish, whitefish, halibut

3 tablespoons frozen orange-juice concentrate melted over low heat with 1 tablespoon butter or margarine

Juice of 1 freshly squeezed lime

1 tablespoon plus 2 teaspoons soy sauce

2 teaspoons grated orange rind

1 garlic clove, pressed or minced

½ teaspoon freshly grated ginger

1¼ to 1⅓ pounds skinless bluefish fillets, ⅝ to ¾ inch thick

Nonstick vegetable spray

1. To make the marinade, use a small bowl to combine the orange juice–butter (or margarine)) mixture with the lime juice, soy sauce, orange rind, garlic, and ginger.

2. Pour the marinade into a shallow glass dish just large enough to accommodate the fish. Add the fish and spoon some of the marinade over the top. Marinate in the refrigerator for about 1 hour.

3. Preheat the broiler. Spray the broiler pan with nonstick spray. Add the fish and broil 5 to 6 inches from the heating element for 7 to 9 minutes or until the fish just starts to blacken. (Watch closely to avoid burning the top.) Baste once while cooking.

4. Shut off the oven and leave the fish in until it's done—about another 5 minutes.

Per serving: Calories: 212   Fat: 8 gm.   Cholesterol: 89 mg. Sodium: 391 mg.

Egg-Coated Salmon and
Fresh Spinach Stir-Fry

Makes 4 servings

If you have everything assembled ahead of time, this stir-fry dish is a breeze to prepare. (It's also loaded with iron, plus vitamins A and D.) For years I made it with chicken, and was delighted to find that I like it even better with salmon. In all honesty, my family thought I was serving them chicken the first time that I made this dish with salmon. (But be sure to reserve this recipe for only the freshest of fish.) Serve over Chinese noodles or on a bed of rice and you have a complete meal.

Fish trade-offs: swordfish, mako or blacktip shark, tuna, cusk, wolffish, monkfish

1¼ to 1⅓ pounds salmon
   fillets, skinned and boned
1 beaten egg
2 tablespoons dry white wine
2 tablespoons soy sauce
¾ teaspoon sugar
2 tablespoons dry white wine
2 tablespoons dry or semidry
   sherry

1½ teaspoons cornstarch
2 tablespoons peanut oil
16 to 18 good-sized fresh
   mushrooms, washed,
   trimmed, and sliced
10-ounce package of fresh
   spinach, stemmed, washed,
   dried, and cut into ½-inch
   strips

1. Cut the skinned salmon fillets into strips approximately 2 inches long and ½ inch wide. (You can place the salmon in the freezer for 20 to 30 minutes ahead of time to make slicing easier.) Place in a medium-size bowl.

2. Add the egg, the first 2 tablespoons wine, soy sauce, and sugar to the salmon. Toss gently and refrigerate for 30 to 60 minutes.

3. In a small sauce dish, thoroughly combine the remaining 2 tablespoons wine, sherry, and cornstarch. Set aside.

4. Heat the oil over medium-high heat in a large nonstick skillet or wok. Add the mushrooms and stir-fry for about 2 minutes.

5. Add the salmon mixture (pour in all juices along with the salmon) and gently stir-fry for another 3 to 3½ minutes or until the fish is not quite done. (Try not to break up the salmon.)

6. Quickly stir the wine-cornstarch mixture (from step 3) again. Add to the fish and mushrooms. Stir for 20 to 30 seconds.

7. Gently mix in the spinach, cover tightly, and steam for another 1½ to 2 minutes or until the spinach is just wilted. Serve immediately.

Per serving: Calories: 361   Fat: 19.5 gm.   Cholesterol: 148 mg. Sodium: 652 mg.

Minty-Lime Grilled Mahimahi

Makes 4 servings

What a pleasant surprise this combination was for my first taste of mahimahi. Lime and mint flavors grace a meaty fish that simply melts in your mouth.

Fish trade-offs: swordfish, halibut, mako shark, bluefish, salmon, mackerel, tautog, tilefish, tuna, mullet, sablefish, whitefish

Juice of 2 freshly squeezed medium limes
1 tablespoon olive oil
2 tablespoons soy sauce
2 medium cloves garlic, pressed or minced
¼ cup dry white wine

2 tablespoons minced fresh mint leaves
1⅓ to 1½ pounds thick mahimahi fillets (with skin), 1¼ to 1½ inches thick

1. To make the marinade, combine all the ingredients except the fish in a small bowl. Momentarily set aside.

2. Score the fish skin several times (don't do any scoring if you substitute skinless fillets) and place the fillets in a shallow dish just large enough to accommodate them.

3. Pour the marinade over the fish and turn it to coat both sides. Marinate in the refrigerator for 1½ to 2 hours, turning several times and spooning marinade over the tops of the fillets.

4. Toward the end of the marinating time, start a charcoal fire or preheat a gas grill. While the coals are heating, take a large sheet of heavy-duty foil and poke holes in it. (The holes should be small enough to keep the fish from sticking to the grill, but large and plentiful enough to allow the smoky taste to come through.)

5. Just before cooking the fish, place the foil on the preheated grill and spoon some of the marinade over it. (Try as best you can to miss the holes.) Add the fish and grill for 8 to 10 minutes per side, basting before you turn it.

Per serving: Calories: 161   Fat: 3.5 gm.   Cholesterol: 105 mg. Sodium: 469 mg.

Breaded Monkfish Medallions

Makes 4 servings

The firm texture of monkfish is complemented by a tasty bread-crumb mix. Based on an idea from the Massachusetts Division of Marine Fisheries, this simple recipe works well with a small serving of reduced-fat frozen French fries, green beans, and a large helping of slimmed-down cole slaw.

Fish trade-offs: tilefish, or any of the following, cut in 2- x 2-inch pieces: pout, cusk, wolffish, tilapia

1 tablespoon vegetable oil	Grating of black pepper
⅓ cup plus 2 tablespoons unseasoned bread crumbs	1¼ pounds monkfish fillet (remove membrane if
3 tablespoons grated Parmesan cheese	present—see page 128)
½ teaspoon dried basil	⅓ cup plus 2 tablespoons reduced-calorie Italian salad
½ teaspoon paprika	dressing

1. Place a rack in the upper third of the oven. Preheat the oven to 500° F. Grease a cookie sheet with the oil. (Absorb excess with a paper towel.)

2. In a small bowl, combine the bread crumbs, cheese, basil, paprika, and pepper. Mix well and set aside.

3. Slice the fish into ¼-inch medallions (cross sections of the thick fillet). Dip each one in dressing, allowing the excess to drip off. Then lightly press both sides of each medallion into the bread-crumb mixture.

4. Place the coated medallions on the greased cookie sheet. Bake for 6 to 7 minutes. (If you like a crispy topping, you can decrease baking time by a minute or two and broil the medallions for a few minutes at the end—watch closely.)

*Per serving: Calories: 220   Fat: 9 gm.   Cholesterol: 41 mg.
Sodium: 397 mg.*

Cajun-Style Grilled Mackerel

Makes 4 servings

In another recipe inspired by the Massachusetts Division of Marine Fisheries, grilled mackerel is complemented by the spicy mix typically used for "blackened redfish." Serve with corn on the cob and fresh, sliced tomatoes. (Mackerel's high omega-3-fatty-acid level is reflected in a higher fat value for this recipe.)

Fish trade-offs: butterfish, sablefish, salmon, bluefish

1⅓ pounds mackerel fillets (weight is with skin and pin bones)	Prudhomme's basic seasoning mix—page 197 (use 1½ teaspoons salt instead of 2½)

1. Start a charcoal fire or preheat a gas grill.

2. When the grill is ready, prepare the fillets by placing them side by side on a cookie sheet, skin side down. Then evenly sprinkle the seasoning mix over the tops of the fillets.

3. Place the fillets on a well-oiled preheated grill (you can top the grill with greased foil with holes), skin side down. Cook for about 4 minutes. Turn with care (don't worry if the skin sticks and is left behind) and cook for another 2 to 3 minutes. When done, carefully remove from the grill and serve skin side down. (Warn people about bones.)

Per serving: Calories: 282   Fat: 19 gm.   Cholesterol: 80 mg. Sodium: 328 mg.

Cod Fillets with Fettuccine and Broccoli

Makes 4 hearty servings

A bit higher in calories than some of the other recipes, this is a one-dish supper. A serving provides you with fish, a starch, a vegetable, milk, and cheese. (This dish is particularly high in calcium.) Accompany with a large wedge of lettuce and tomato slices.

Fish trade-offs: haddock, pollock, hake, tilefish, drum, grouper, pout, dogfish, skate

1 tablespoon reduced-calorie margarine	2 cups fettuccine, cooked al dente and drained (about
3 tablespoons all-purpose flour	4 ounces, dry)
1 teaspoon dry mustard	10-ounce package frozen, chopped broccoli, cooked
2 cups cold low-fat milk	according to package
3 tablespoons lemon juice	directions and drained
¼ teaspoon salt	(don't overcook—you want
3 tablespoons chopped, fresh parsley	the bright green color to remain)
¼ teaspoon ground nutmeg	1 pound cod fillets
½ teaspoon cumin	1½ ounces shredded low-fat
Grating of black pepper	cheese (5 grams fat or less
⅓ cup grated Parmesan cheese	per ounce)

1. Preheat the oven to 400° F. Grease a deep 2½-quart casserole with the reduced-calorie margarine.

2. In a medium-size bowl, combine the flour and mustard. Slowly whisk in the milk until smooth. Pour into a medium-size saucepan. Stir constantly over medium heat until the sauce just comes to a boil.

3. Add the lemon juice, salt, parsley, nutmeg, cumin, pepper, and Parmesan cheese. Stir until blended. Cover and remove from heat. Set aside.

4. Place the fettuccine in the bottom of the baking dish. Evenly layer the broccoli on top of the fettuccine. Cover with half of the sauce. Top with a single layer of cod. Cover evenly with the remaining sauce. Sprinkle with the low-fat cheese.

5. Bake, covered, for 15 minutes. Uncover and bake another 10 to 15 minutes or until the fish is done.

Per serving: Calories: 385   Fat: 9.5 gm.   Cholesterol: 60 mg. Sodium: 535 mg.

Broiled Sole with Sour and Creamy Cucumber Sauce

Makes 4 servings

This dish is best described as refreshing and light. A subtle creamy cucumber sauce highlights marinated sole. Serve with a colorful fresh fruit salad and steamed broccoli seasoned with nutmeg and lemon juice.

Fish trade-offs: thin cod, haddock, or hake fillets; catfish; mackerel; whiting fillets; ocean perch; rockfish; orange roughy; pout; tilapia; weakfish; yellow perch; pompano; red snapper; freshwater trout

1 tablespoon olive oil	seeded, and chopped
2 tablespoons wine vinegar	medium-fine
3 tablespoons dry white wine	⅓ cup reduced-fat sour cream
2 tablespoons minced chives	(1½ grams fat per
1 teaspoon grated lemon peel	tablespoon)
1¼ to 1⅓ pounds sole fillets,	½ cup plain, low-fat yogurt
⅓ to ½ inch thick	¼ teaspoon dried, flaked
1 tablespoon reduced-calorie	thyme
margarine	1 tablespoon lime juice
2 scallions, minced (include	½ teaspoon salt
bulb plus two inches of	Grating of black pepper
green)	Nonstick vegetable spray

1. In a small bowl, make the marinade by mixing the oil, vinegar, wine, chives, and lemon peel. Place the sole in a large, shallow, non-metal dish and top with the marinade. Turn to coat the other side of the fish. Marinate in the refrigerator for 30 to 40 minutes, turning once or twice.

2. When about 10 minutes of marinating time remains, preheat the broiler and make the cucumber sauce by spreading the reduced-calorie margarine over the bottom of a large nonstick frying pan. Place over a burner that's preheated to medium. Add the scallions and cucumber. Cook, uncovered, for 6 to 7 minutes (until the vegetables just start to get limp), stirring occasionally.

3. Add the sour cream, yogurt, and thyme. Cook for about 2 minutes —stirring gently and frequently—until warmed through. Do not boil. Remove from the heat and stir in the lime juice, salt, and pepper. Set aside, covered.

(continued)

4. Coat the broiler-pan rack with nonstick spray. Add the fish in a single layer with edges slightly overlapping (so they don't dry out). Top with any remaining marinade. Broil approximately 4 inches from the heating element for 4 to 5 minutes or until done. (Don't turn the fish.)

5. Divide the fish among 4 serving dishes and top with equal portions of sauce.

Per serving: Calories: 235   Fat: 9.5 gm.   Cholesterol: 86 mg. Sodium: 450 mg.

Crab and Mushroom Stoganoff

Makes 4 servings

Yogurt in place of sour cream makes for a heart-healthy, low-calorie stroganoff that's a great source of zinc. It's simple, yet elegant enough to serve to company—and a unique way to stretch crabmeat. Serve over a bed of green spinach noodles for a nice contrast with the white and red colors of the stroganoff. For a complete meal, serve with steamed julienne carrots, crusty bread, and a salad of tossed greens and tomatoes. (Be sure to have all your cutting and chopping done ahead of time for this one.)

Fish trade-offs: cooked and shredded skate, lobster, or crawfish; shrimp (canned or cooked, fresh or frozen); steamed squid strips

1 tablespoon regular margarine	¼ teaspoon salt (omit with imitation crabmeat)
½ cup finely chopped onion	Grating of black pepper
16 to 18 good-sized fresh mushrooms, washed, trimmed, and sliced	3 tablespoons dry or semidry sherry
2 to 3 tablespoons chopped, fresh parsley	3 tablespoons chopped pimiento
1 tablespoon all-purpose flour	8 ounces cooked fresh crabmeat or imitation
1½ cups plain, low-fat yogurt	crabmeat, flaked

1. Melt the margarine in a large nonstick frying pan over medium heat. Add the onion and mushrooms, cover, and cook for about 3 minutes, stirring once. Stir in the parsley and cook for another minute or two, covered—until the vegetables are just tender.

2. Quickly whisk the flour into the cold yogurt in a small bowl. Stir into the onion-mushroom mixture. Add the salt (if used) and pepper.

3. Stirring constantly, cook until heated through and the yogurt just starts to bubble. (Don't overheat or the yogurt may separate.)

4. Add the sherry, pimiento, and crabmeat. Mix gently until just combined. Heat for another minute or two, stirring constantly.

Per serving (based on fresh crabmeat): Calories: 189   Fat: 5.5 gm. Cholesterol: 62 mg.   Sodium: 391 mg.

Mackerel in Creamy Garlic Sauce

Makes 4 servings

A colorful medley of fish and vegetables in a light, garlicky sauce. Ladle over curly noodles or linguine and serve with a Bibb lettuce salad and sourdough bread. I again engaged in duplicity when I served this dish to a family none too keen on mackerel. I didn't announce what it was when I served it, and the dish was eaten with relish! For the extra calories in this dish, you get high amounts of zinc, iron, and vitamin D—not to mention omega-3s! (Mackerel is tricky to skin— since it's inexpensive to begin with, I think it's worth it to pay a bit more to have your fish dealer skin it for you.)

Fish trade-offs: fresh tuna slices, squid rings or strips, shrimp or crawfish meat, eel (parboil ahead of time), pout

1 tablespoon olive oil
1 large clove garlic, pressed or minced
16 to 18 good-sized fresh mushrooms, washed, trimmed, and sliced
½ large sweet red pepper, cut in thin strips and then halved
2 tablespoons all-purpose flour
¾ cup evaporated skim milk
½ cup low-fat milk
⅓ cup dry white wine
½ teaspoon salt
Grating of black pepper
⅓ cup tiny frozen peas
1¼ pounds skinned mackerel fillets (weight is with pin bones), bones removed and cut in 1- to 1½-inch pieces

1. In a large nonstick frying pan, heat the oil over medium heat. Add the garlic and cook for 1 to 2 minutes. (Don't brown.) Stir in the mushrooms and red pepper. Cover and cook for 4 to 5 minutes or until the vegetables just start to wilt. (Stir once or twice.)

2. Sprinkle the flour over the vegetables and stir to combine. Slowly add both types of milk. Bring to a boil, stirring constantly.

3. Stir in the wine, salt, pepper, and peas. Reduce the heat to low. Cover and cook for 3 to 4 minutes.

(continued)

4. Raise the heat to medium and add the mackerel. Stirring gently and frequently, cook for another 4 to 5 minutes or until the fish is just done.

Per serving: Calories: 419   Fat: 23 gm.   Cholesterol: 97 mg. Sodium: 477 mg.

Fillet of Pollock Parmigiana

Makes 4 servings

Even the non-fish-lovers in your family will go for this dish—the pollock could pass for chicken or tender veal. (Also higher in calories than many of the other recipes, this one contains 3 of the major food groups and is rich in calcium.) For each diner, serve a portion of fish on a bed of pasta and top with plenty of sauce. The short list of ingredients is a clue that you can prepare this dish in just minutes.

Fish trade-offs: haddock, cod, cusk, drum, grouper, hake, pout, dogfish, skate, tilefish, tuna, wolffish

3 cups meatless spaghetti
  sauce (bottled or your own
  recipe—see Anne's
  Meatless Spaghetti Sauce on
  page 287)
1¼ pounds pollock fillets,
  ½ to ¾ inch thick

3 ounces shredded part-skim
  mozzarella cheese
3 tablespoons grated
  Parmesan cheese

1. Preheat the oven to 400° F. In a medium-size saucepan, bring the spaghetti sauce to a boil over medium heat.

2. Distribute about half of the hot sauce over the bottom of a 9- x 13-inch baking dish. Lay the pollock over the sauce in a single layer.

3. Evenly distribute the remaining sauce, then the mozzarella cheese over the fillets.

4. Sprinkle with the Parmesan cheese. Bake, uncovered, for 13 to 16 minutes, or until the fish is done.

Per serving: Calories: 405   Fat: 15 gm.   Cholesterol: 116 mg. Sodium: 1,217 mg.   (To reduce sodium, make your own sauce using tomato products with no added salt.)

Squid Rings Marinara

Makes 4 servings

Nothing complements squid like a savory marinara sauce—red wine gives this version extra fullness. (This is another good source of iron and zinc.) Serve over linguine or spaghetti with a dusting of freshly grated Romano or Parmesan cheese. A large romaine lettuce salad and Italian bread will complete the meal.

Fish trade-offs: mussel or clam meats (cook a minute or two longer); shrimp, lobster, or crawfish meat; eel (cook much longer)

2 tablespoons olive oil
½ cup chopped onion
2 cloves pressed or minced
   garlic
¼ cup finely chopped green
   pepper
2 cups sliced canned plum
   tomatoes (remove from
   canning juices before
   slicing)
1 cup juice from canned
   tomatoes (above)
⅓ cup dry red wine

⅓ cup tomato paste
1 teaspoon sugar
1 teaspoon dried basil
1 teaspoon dried oregano
Grating of black pepper
1¼ to 1⅓ pounds cleaned
   squid (double the amount if
   you purchase whole squid;
   see page 151 for cleaning
   directions), cut into rings
   (rings can be halved to
   make strips, or they can be
   chopped)

1. In a large nonstick frying pan, heat the oil over medium-high heat. Add the onion, garlic, and green pepper. Cook until barely tender, stirring frequently.

2. Stir in all the remaining ingredients, except the squid. Bring to a boil, then reduce the heat and simmer for 10 minutes, uncovered. Cover and simmer for another 10 to 15 minutes.

3. Add the squid, cover, and simmer for 3 to 4 minutes. Serve at once.

Per serving: Calories: 276   Fat: 9.5 gm.   Cholesterol: 331 mg. Sodium: 531 mg.

Spinach-Ricotta–Stuffed Calamari

Makes 6 servings

A great way to introduce newcomers to squid, this vitamin A- and calcium-rich dish can be served with spaghetti or linguine. (For those leery of squid, try using less squid and substituting some cooked pasta shells or manicotti stuffed with the spinach-ricotta mixture.) Complement with lightly sautéed zucchini slices and a salad of dark greens, red onions, and tomatoes.

10-ounce package of frozen, chopped spinach, cooked and drained (press out some of the water)
1 cup part-skim ricotta cheese
1 cup low-fat cottage cheese
⅓ cup grated Parmesan cheese
¼ teaspoon ground nutmeg
Grating of black pepper

1 egg, slightly beaten
32-ounce jar of meatless spaghetti sauce (bottled or your own recipe—see Anne's Meatless Spaghetti Sauce on page 287)
12 large or 18 small squid, cleaned and drained (about 18 ounces of meat)

1. In a large bowl, thoroughly mix the spinach, all three cheeses, nutmeg, pepper, and egg. Preheat the oven to 350° F.

2. Spread 1 cup of the spaghetti sauce over the bottom of a 13- x 9-inch baking dish.

3. Using a small spoon or your fingers, fill each squid with stuffing. Place in the baking dish.

4. When all the squid have been added to the baking pan, top with the remaining spaghetti sauce.

5. Cover with foil and bake for 30 to 35 minutes. Remove the foil and bake for another 15 minutes or until the squid is tender.

Per serving: Calories: 376   Fat 14.5 gm.   Cholesterol: 263 mg. Sodium: 1,137 mg.   (To lower the sodium level, make your own spaghetti sauce with canned tomato products containing no added salt.)

Grilled Tuna in Tomato-Basil-Mint Sauce

Makes 4 servings

Fresh basil and mint are musts for this savory—yet easy—tomato sauce. Serve with any type of pasta, a curly-leaf lettuce salad, and broiled eggplant slices.

Fish trade-offs: swordfish, halibut, whitefish, mackerel steaks or fillets, mahimahi, mako shark, eel (parboil first)

16-ounce can of stewed tomatoes, drained of excess juice	Generous grating of black pepper
1 medium garlic clove	1 tablespoon olive oil
¼ cup whole basil leaves (about 20 good-sized leaves)	2 tablespoons dry or semidry sherry
10 large mint leaves	1¼ to 1⅓ pounds fresh tuna steaks, ¾ to 1 inch thick

1. In a blender, blend the stewed tomatoes and garlic for 20 to 30 seconds—until frothy and fine. Add the basil and mint and blend another 10 seconds (not too fine).

2. Pour the tomato-sauce mixture into a medium-size saucepan. Add the pepper and oil. Bring to a boil. Reduce the heat and simmer, uncovered, for 20 to 25 minutes. At the end of that time, stir in the sherry.

3. While the sauce is simmering, start a charcoal fire or preheat a gas grill. When the coals are ready, grease the grill rack well. Then preheat it over the hot coals.

4. Blot the fish well with a paper towel. Spread a coating of sauce on one side of the fish and place it on the preheated grill, sauce side down. Grill for 5 to 7 minutes.

5. Blot the side of the fish facing up and spread with a coating of sauce. (Keep the remaining sauce warm in the pan.) Turn the fish and grill for another 5 to 7 minutes or until it's done.

6. Divide into 4 portions and top with the remaining sauce.

Per serving: Calories: 280   Fat: 10.5 gm.   Cholesterol: 57 mg. Sodium: 318 mg.

Saucy Monkfish and Scallops

Makes 4 servings

This hot and spicy combination of lobsterlike monkfish, scallops, tomatoes, and seasonings is best served over spaghetti or linguine.

Fish trade-offs: (for either type of fish) cusk, croaker, mackerel, mussel meats, pollock, skate, squid rings, tilefish, wolffish, crawfish, shrimp or lobster meat, oysters

2 tablespoons olive oil	¾ cup dry white wine
3 cloves garlic, pressed or minced	1 teaspoon dried basil
¼ teaspoon crushed, hot red pepper flakes	½ teaspoon ground cumin
	¼ teaspoon salt
¾ cup finely chopped onion	Grating of black pepper
5 or 6 thinly sliced medium scallions (include bulb plus several inches of green)	3 to 4 tablespoons chopped fresh parsley
1 large stalk celery, finely chopped	¾ pound skinless monkfish fillet, cut in bite-size pieces (remove membrane if present—see page 128)
2 cups canned, crushed tomatoes	½ pound sea scallops (cut to about the same size as the monkfish)
Several dashes Tabasco sauce	

1. Heat the oil in a large skillet over medium heat. Add the garlic and cook for about 1 minute. (Do not brown.) Stir in the pepper flakes, onion, scallions, and celery. Cook several minutes, stirring frequently, until the vegetables just start to become limp.

2. Add the tomatoes, Tabasco, wine, basil, cumin, salt, pepper, and parsley. Thoroughly combine and bring to a boil. Lower the heat, cover, and simmer for 15 to 20 minutes, stirring periodically.

3. Increase the heat to medium and stir in the monkfish. Cover and cook for 3 to 4 minutes. Add the scallops, cover again, and heat for another 2 to 3 minutes—until the fish is done.

Per serving: Calories: 260   Fat: 9 gm.   Cholesterol: 40 mg. Sodium: 465 mg.

Anne's Meatless Spaghetti Sauce

Makes approximately 4 quarts

Since some *Eat Fish* Recipes call for already-made spaghetti sauce, I thought I'd offer my easy homemade version. I like the taste and texture best when the vegetables are finely chopped in a food processor —start by mincing the garlic. Then, all at once, add the pepper, onion, and celery leaves and chop away. A range of seasonings is offered so you can prepare the sauce according to taste.

2 28-ounce cans crushed tomatoes

2 28-ounce cans tomato purée

3 to 5 cloves garlic, pressed or minced

1 medium green pepper, finely chopped

2 large onions, finely chopped

⅓ cup celery leaves, finely chopped

1 tablespoon sugar

2 to 3 tablespoons dried basil

2 to 3 tablespoons dried oregano

⅓ cup chopped, fresh parsley

Salt and pepper to taste (optional)

1 small can tomato paste (or less), added toward the end for thickening (optional)

1. In a large kettle, combine all the ingredients. Cover and bring to a boil over medium heat, stirring occasionally.

2. Reduce the heat and simmer for 2 to 3 hours.

Per serving: (1 cup with no added salt "to taste"): Calories: 87 Fat: 0.5gm. Cholesterol: 0 mg. Sodium: 601 mg. (To lower sodium, use tomato products with no added salt.)

Crab Frittata with Zucchini

Makes 4 servings

A delight for garlic and onion lovers, this omelettelike dish is perfect for lunch or supper. During the last 15 to 20 minutes of cooking, pop some fresh tomato halves sprinkled with basil into the oven. Serve the frittata with the baked tomatoes and spinach salad. The frittata also succeeds as a leftover, warmed in a microwave oven.

Fish trade-offs: cooked skate, weakfish, crawfish, or lobster; shrimp (cooked pieces or canned baby shrimp)

1 tablespoon reduced-calorie margarine	¼ teaspoon salt (omit if using imitation crabmeat)
1 medium clove garlic, pressed or minced	Grating of black pepper
⅔ cup sliced scallion or chopped leek	1 tablespoon plus 1 teaspoon all-purpose flour
1 cup lightly packed shredded zucchini	½ cup low-fat milk
1 small can sliced mushrooms, drained (about 4 ounces, drained weight)	⅓ cup grated Parmesan or Romano cheese
3 eggs	8 ounces imitation or cooked fresh crabmeat, flaked
	1 tablespoon reduced-calorie margarine

1. Preheat the oven to 375° F. Spread 1 tablespoon of the reduced-calorie margarine over the bottom of a large nonstick frying pan; heat over moderate heat for a minute or two. Add the garlic, scallion or leek, zucchini, and mushrooms. Cover and cook for 4 to 5 minutes, until the vegetables just start to get limp, stirring once or twice. Remove from the heat and set aside.

2. In a large bowl, beat together the eggs, salt, pepper, flour, milk, and cheese for 1 to 2 minutes. Stir in the crabmeat.

3. Add the vegetable mixture to the egg mixture and gently combine.

4. Grease the bottom and sides of a 1½-quart soufflé dish or round casserole with the other tablespoon of reduced-calorie margarine. Pour in the vegetable-egg mixture. Bake uncovered for 45 to 50 minutes or until firm in the center.

5. When done, remove from the oven and let stand for 5 minutes. Loosen the sides with a sharp knife and cut into 4 wedges.

Per serving (based on imitation crabmeat): Calories: 222
Fat: 12 gm.   Cholesterol: 223 mg.   Sodium: 861 mg.
(To lower sodium, substitute fresh crabmeat for imitation.)

Escalloped Scallops

Makes 4 servings

A rendition of a traditional butter-rich scallop casserole, this more healthful version is made thick and hearty by low-fat crackers and cheese. Sliced, cooked beets and a shredded-carrot and raisin salad make colorful accompaniments.

Fish trade-offs: oysters, skate chunks

1 tablespoon reduced-calorie margarine

1 cup (10 to 12) coarsely crumbled unsalted saltines or stoned-wheat crackers

2 ounces shredded, low-fat cheese (5 grams fat or less per ounce)

1 small can sliced mushrooms, drained (about 4 ounces, drained weight)

3 to 4 tablespoons chopped, fresh parsley

Grating of black pepper

1 pound scallops, drained well (if sea scallops are used, cut into quarters)

2 tablespoons dry or semidry sherry

2 tablespoons lemon juice

½ cup evaporated skim milk

1. Preheat the oven to 375° F. Grease a round, deep 1½-quart casserole with the reduced-calorie margarine.

2. In a large bowl, gently toss ⅔ cup of the crackers with the cheese, mushrooms, parsley, and pepper. Add the scallops, sherry, and lemon juice and gently toss again.

3. Pour the mixture into the greased baking dish. Top with the remaining ⅓ cup of crackers. Pour the evaporated milk over all.

4. Bake, covered, for 15 minutes. Uncover and bake for another 25 to 30 minutes or until the scallops in the middle are done.

Per serving: Calories: 233   Fat: 6 gm.   Cholesterol: 40 mg. Sodium: 527 mg.

Curried Salmon-Rice Ramekins

Makes 4 servings

This most palatable way to get your omega-3s was inspired by a recipe from *Seafood: A Collection of Heart-Healthy Recipes* by Janis Harsila, R.D., and Evie Hansen. (This is a good source of calcium and iron.) Serve with steamed broccoli and fresh pineapple slices.

Fish trade-offs: canned tuna or mackerel

1 tablespoon reduced-calorie margarine

15½-ounce can salmon, drained, skin removed, and flaked

2 cups cooked white or brown rice

2 tablespoons minced celery leaves

1 stalk celery, chopped medium-fine

2 scallions, sliced once lengthwise, then chopped crosswise (include bulb plus an inch of green)

3 tablespoons chopped pimiento

3 tablespoons chopped, fresh parsley

1 egg, slightly beaten

¼ cup reduced-calorie mayonnaise

⅓ cup plain, low-fat yogurt

¼ teaspoon salt

3 tablespoons lemon juice

1 tablespoon curry powder

Paprika

1. Preheat the oven to 400° F. Lightly grease 4 individual 8-ounce ramekins, custard cups, or large clamshells with the reduced-calorie margarine.

2. In a medium-size bowl, combine all the remaining ingredients except the paprika, and mix lightly.

3. Divide the mixture among the ramekins. Sprinkle with paprika.

4. Bake 10 minutes, covered lightly with foil. Remove the foil, and bake another 8 to 10 minutes or until piping hot in the middle.

Per serving: Calories: 358   Fat: 15 gm.   Cholesterol: 115 mg.
Sodium: 821 mg.   (To lower sodium, omit the salt and rinse the salmon well.)

Spinach-Topped Flounder
in Slim White Sauce

Makes 4 to 5 servings

This dish provides your "meat" and vegetable all in one. All you need to add are boiled, parslied red-skinned potatoes. (This is a good way to stretch flatfish when prices are high.) A single serving provides as much calcium as a cup of milk and will meet the daily vitamin A recommendation for an adult.

Fish trade-offs: thin cod, haddock or hake fillets; pout; catfish; yellow perch; whiting fillets; ocean perch; rockfish; orange roughy; tilapia; weakfish

3 tablespoons all-purpose flour	2 tablespoons lemon juice
¾ teaspoon salt	1 tablespoon reduced-calorie margarine
½ teaspoon dry mustard	1¼ pounds sole fillets
¾ teaspoon onion powder	10-ounce package frozen, chopped spinach, cooked according to package directions and thoroughly drained
¼ teaspoon ground nutmeg	
¾ cup cold low-fat milk	
¾ cup evaporated skim milk	
2 tablespoons chopped, fresh parsley	Paprika
½ teaspoon Worcestershire sauce	

1. Preheat the oven to 425° F. In a medium saucepan, combine the flour, salt, mustard, onion powder, and nutmeg. Slowly whisk in the low-fat milk and combine until smooth.

2. Add the evaporated milk, parsley, and Worcestershire sauce. Cook over medium heat, stirring constantly, until the mixture comes to a boil. Stir in the lemon juice, remove from the heat, cover, and set aside.

3. Grease the bottom and sides of a 9- x 13-inch baking dish with the reduced-calorie margarine. Spread ½ cup of the sauce over the bottom of the baking dish, in a thin layer.

4. Add the fish in a single layer, but with edges overlapping slightly. (Tuck under any skimpy ends so they don't overcook.) Evenly spread the spinach over the fish and pat down lightly.

(continued)

5. Top with the remaining sauce, spreading it so all surfaces are covered. Sprinkle with paprika and bake, uncovered, for 12 to 15 minutes or until the fish is done.

Per serving (based on 4 servings): Calories: 250   Fat: 5 gm. Cholesterol: 72 mg.   Sodium: 684 mg.

Crab-Mushroom Supreme

Makes 4 to 5 servings

This rich-tasting combination of crab and mushrooms in a creamy sauce is topped with Swiss cheese and bread crumbs. It sounds health-threatening, but it's not because of the low-fat dairy products and small amount of cheese. To boot, a single serving is loaded with iron, zinc, and calcium. Serve with broiled tomatoes and steamed spinach topped with nutmeg and lemon juice.

Fish trade-offs: canned salmon, white tuna, or baby shrimp; cooked and shredded skate; cooked weakfish

1 tablespoon reduced-calorie margarine
20 to 22 good-sized mushrooms, washed, trimmed, and sliced
¾ cup cold low-fat milk
⅓ cup all-purpose flour
¾ cup evaporated skim milk
1 tablespoon dried, flaked onion
½ teaspoon salt (use ¼ teaspoon if using imitation crab)
¼ cup dry or semidry sherry
¼ cup lemon juice

½ teaspoon Worcestershire sauce
½ teaspoon ground cumin
¼ teaspoon dry mustard
3 dashes Tabasco sauce
1 pound cooked, fresh crabmeat or imitation crabmeat, flaked
1 tablespoon reduced-calorie margarine
1½ ounces shredded Swiss cheese
3 tablespoons unseasoned bread crumbs

1. Preheat the oven to 350° F. Grease a large nonstick frying pan with 1 tablespoon of the reduced-calorie margarine. Add the mushrooms, cover, and cook over medium-high heat until limp.

2. While the mushrooms are cooking, slowly whisk the low-fat milk into the flour in a small bowl. Whisk until smooth. Add the evaporated skim milk.

3. When the mushrooms are ready, decrease the heat to medium and add the milk mixture to the skillet. Bring to a boil, stirring constantly.

4. Stir in the dried onion, salt, sherry, lemon juice, Worcestershire sauce, cumin, mustard, and Tabasco. Cook another minute or two— until heated through. Add the crabmeat and stir until just combined. Remove from the heat.

5. Grease a deep, round 1½-quart casserole with the remaining tablespoon of reduced-calorie margarine. Pour in the crab mixture. Evenly distribute the cheese across the top. Then sprinkle with the bread crumbs. Bake for 25 to 30 minutes. (Optional: turn on the broiler at the very end to brown the crumbs. Watch closely.)

Per serving (based on 4 servings, made with fresh crabmeat):
Calories: 349   Fat: 9 gm.   Cholesterol: 127 mg.
Sodium: 776 mg.

Sweet 'n' Sour Swordfish

Makes 4 servings

This sweet-and-sour dish will certainly provide you with more omega-3s than chicken or pork versions. It will also more than meet your daily need for vitamins A and C, plus provide plenty of iron and zinc. Serve over a generous helping of steamed white rice, along with a mandarin orange and shredded cabbage salad.

Fish trade-offs: tuna, blacktip or mako shark, cusk, wolffish, croaker, grouper, mackerel, mahimahi, tilefish, squid rings, monkfish

20-ounce can unsweetened, crushed pineapple	12 to 15 large fresh mushrooms, washed, trimmed, and sliced
2 tablespoons vegetable oil	2 tablespoons cider vinegar
1¼ pounds swordfish steak, cut in 1-inch cubes (remove skin)	2 tablespoons soy sauce
	1 tablespoon cornstarch
2 medium carrots, sliced thinly on an angle	½ teaspoon grated fresh ginger root
1 large green pepper, cut in bite-size cubes	3 tablespoons plum or other seedless jam
5 scallions, sliced (include bulb plus 2 inches of green)	

1. Thoroughly drain the pineapple. Set aside the juice and 1 cup of the pineapple in separate containers. (Save the remaining pineapple for another use.)

(continued)

2. In a large nonstick skillet or wok, heat the oil over medium-high heat. Turn the pan to coat evenly with oil. Add the swordfish and brown for 4 to 5 minutes, turning the cubes frequently. Remove the swordfish with a slotted spoon and drain on several layers of paper towels.

3. Reduce the heat to medium and return the pan to the burner. Add the carrots, green pepper, scallions, and mushrooms. Cover and cook for 5 to 6 minutes, stirring occasionally. Remove the vegetables and place in a large bowl.

4. In a small, separate bowl, thoroughly blend the pineapple juice, vinegar, soy sauce, cornstarch, and ginger. Add to the hot pan and cook, stirring constantly until the mixture thickens. Add the jam and stir until it melts into the sauce. Add the cup of pineapple (from step 1) and heat until the mixture just returns to a boil.

5. Add the fish and vegetables and stir until just heated through.

Per serving: Calories: 347   Fat: 13 gm.   Cholesterol: 53 mg. Sodium: 652 mg.

Mackerel with Creamy Cucumber-Dill Sauce

Makes 4 servings

Inspired by a suggestion from the Massachusetts Divison of Marine Fisheries, this subtle herbed yogurt sauce enhances the rich taste of mackerel. (This is another mackerel recipe that's a little higher in calories—but it's a good source of vitamin D; iron, and omega-3 fatty acids.) Serve with egg noodles, steamed spinach, and sliced summer squash.

Fish trade-offs: salmon, pompano, butterfish, rockfish, ocean perch, orange roughy, pout, tilapia, freshwater trout

1 tablespoon reduced-calorie
  margarine
1½ pounds mackerel fillets
  (weight is with skin and
  pin bones)
⅓ cup finely chopped onion
1 medium clove garlic,
  pressed or minced

½ cucumber, peeled, seeded,
  and coarsely chopped
1 cup plain, low-fat yogurt
¾ teaspoon dried dill weed
¼ teaspoon salt
Grating of black pepper

1. Preheat the oven to 400° F. Grease the bottom of a 13- x 9-inch baking dish with the reduced-calorie margarine. Add the fillets, placing them with skin on the bottom of the dish.

2. Mix the onion, garlic, and cucumber. Sprinkle evenly over the fish.

3. Place a layer of waxed paper over the fish and bake for 7 to 8 minutes. While the fish is cooking, mix the yogurt with the dill, salt, and pepper.

4. Remove the fish from the oven and take off the waxed paper. Pour the yogurt mixture evenly over the fish. Return to the oven and bake for another 5 to 6 minutes, until the yogurt is warm and the fish is done. (Warn people about bones when you serve this dish.)

Per serving: Calories: 371   Fat: 23.5 gm.   Cholesterol: 111 mg. Sodium: 333 mg.

Pout Fillets with Spinach and Wheat Germ Stuffing

Makes 4 servings

White pout, green spinach, and tomatoes make for a colorful combination. Toasted wheat germ adds body to the stuffing and boosts the zinc content of this recipe. As the stuffed fish bakes, it generates its own sea-green sauce that can be spooned over the finished product. For smaller fillets, this recipe can be used to make fish roll-ups—just spread the fish with stuffing, roll up, and secure with toothpicks. (Baking time may be less.)

Fish trade-offs: flatfish; thin cod, haddock, or hake fillets; ocean perch; rockfish; tilapia; catfish; whiting fillets

⅔ cup frozen, chopped spinach, cooked according to package directions, drained well (press out water before measuring)
1 egg, slightly beaten
⅓ cup toasted wheat germ
2 tablespoons grated Parmesan cheese
⅛ teaspoon ground nutmeg

1 teaspoon dried, flaked onion
¼ teaspoon garlic powder
¼ teaspoon salt
4 good-sized pout fillets (1 to 1¼ pounds total)
2 teaspoons olive oil
1 medium tomato, cut in 4 slices
1 tablespoon lime juice
1 tablespoon olive oil

1. Preheat the oven to 400° F. To make the stuffing, combine the spinach, egg, wheat germ, Parmesan cheese, nutmeg, onion flakes, garlic powder, and salt.

2. Evenly divide the stuffing and spread on *half* of each fillet. Fold over the top half of each fillet. (If the ends look skimpy, tuck them under the fish "packet.")

(continued)

3. Coat the bottom of a shallow 1½-quart casserole with the 2 teaspoons of olive oil. Add the fillets. Top each with a tomato slice. Drizzle with the lime juice and remaining oil. Bake uncovered for 20 to 25 minutes.

Per serving: Calories: 222   Fat: 10 gm.   Cholesterol: 129 mg. Sodium: 289 mg.

Lemony Curried Creamed Tuna with Almonds

Makes 4 to 5 servings (about 4 cups)

A low-fat, high-calcium cream sauce is enriched with the taste of lemon and curry powder. Serve over a bed of white or brown rice with a steamed medley of broccoli flowerets and sliced carrots.

Fish trade-offs: salmon (canned or cooked, fresh), crabmeat (canned, imitation, or cooked, fresh), shrimp (canned or cooked, fresh or frozen)

3 tablespoons all-purpose flour	15-ounce can sliced mushrooms, drained
2 teaspoons curry powder	¼ cup lemon juice
¼ teaspoon dry mustard	¼ teaspoon salt
1 cup cold low-fat milk	Grating of black pepper
1 cup evaporated skim milk	3 tablespoons toasted, slivered
1 tablespoon dried, flaked onion	almonds (see page 271n for almond-toasting directions)
1½ 6½-ounce cans water-packed tuna, drained and flaked	Paprika

1. In a medium-size bowl, combine the flour, curry powder, and dry mustard. Slowly whisk the low-fat milk into the flour mixture until smooth.

2. Mix in the evaporated milk and onion flakes. Pour the mixture into a large saucepan and bring to a boil over medium-high heat, stirring constantly.

3. Stir in tuna, mushrooms, lemon juice, salt, and pepper. Cook for another minute or two, stirring frequently.

4. Divide the sauce into 4 or 5 servings and top with almonds. Serve with a sprinkling of paprika.

Per serving (based on 4 servings): Calories: 250   Fat: 6 gm. Cholesterol: 32 mg.   Sodium: 755 mg.

Savory Stuffed Sole

Makes 4 to 5 servings

A food processor cuts the time for this seafood stuffing that's loaded with finely chopped vegetables. Once stuffed, the fish bakes in a lemony butter sauce and will melt in your mouth. (This stuffed sole will boost your iron and zinc intake for the day.) Endive salad with a warm sweet-and-sour dressing plus julienne zucchini with carrots make colorful accompaniments.

Fish trade-offs: thin cod, haddock, or hake fillets; pout; red snapper; rockfish; ocean perch; tilapia

STUFFING

1 tablespoon reduced-calorie margarine
½ cup finely chopped onion
⅓ cup finely chopped celery
⅓ cup finely chopped celery leaves
½ cup thinly sliced scallions
⅓ cup finely chopped red pepper
1 cup chopped fresh mushrooms
1 garlic clove, pressed or minced
½ cup cold low-fat milk
1½ tablespoons all-purpose flour

½ cup dry white wine
6 ounces cooked shrimp meat, chopped medium-fine (or 6-ounce can baby shrimp, rinsed and drained)
6 ounces fresh cooked crabmeat or imitation crabmeat, flaked
⅓ cup unseasoned bread crumbs
¼ cup chopped, fresh parsley
1 egg, lightly beaten
¼ teaspoon salt
Grating of black pepper
Dash of cayenne pepper
½ teaspoon ground cumin

1. Spread the reduced-calorie margarine over the bottom of a large nonstick frying pan. Place over medium heat. Add the onion, celery, celery leaves, scallions, red pepper, mushrooms, and garlic. Stir, cover, and allow steam to cook the vegetables for about 3 minutes or until just tender. Remove from the heat, and uncover to allow the steam to escape. Set aside momentarily.

2. Slowly whisk the milk into the flour until smooth. Add the milk-flour mixture to the cooked vegetables. Return to medium-high heat, and stir constantly until thickened. Remove from the heat.

(continued)

3. Add the wine, shrimp, crabmeat, bread crumbs, parsley, egg, salt, black pepper, cayenne, and cumin. Toss lightly to combine. Set aside.

ASSEMBLY OF FISH

1 tablespoon reduced-calorie
  margarine
1 tablespoon butter (or
  regular margarine)
1 tablespoon reduced-calorie
  margarine

Juice of 1 large, fresh lemon
10 or 12 medium sole fillets
  (about 2 pounds)
¼ teaspoon salt
Paprika

1. Preheat the oven to 375° F. Grease a 13- x 9-inch rectangular casserole with 1 tablespoon of the reduced-calorie margarine.

2. Heat the butter, the remaining tablespoon of reduced-calorie margarine, and the lemon juice in a small saucepan over medium heat until the butter and reduced-calorie margarine are melted. Set aside.

3. Place half of the fillets in the bottom of the casserole. Divide the stuffing evenly over all the fillets, leaving about ½ inch from the edges of the fish free of stuffing. Top with the remaining fillets and press the edges to seal.

4. Pour the melted butter–lemon mixture over the stuffed fillets. Sprinkle with salt and paprika. Cover with foil and bake for 20 minutes. Uncover and bake another 5 to 10 minutes or until the fish is done. Spoon some of the juice over each serving.

*Per serving (based on 5 servings): Calories: 365   Fat: 9 gm.
Cholesterol: 248 mg.   Sodium: 675 mg.*

Poached Salmon with Lemony Dill Sauce

Makes 4 servings

First you poach it in a court bouillon, then you smother the salmon with a light, lemony sauce. Serve with fresh Brussels sprouts with slivered almonds and a red cabbage and chopped apple salad.

Fish trade-offs: tuna, bluefish, halibut, pompano, striped bass, freshwater trout, cusk, drum, mahimahi, sablefish, skate, whitefish

TO POACH SALMON

2½ cups water	½ teaspoon salt
½ cup dry white wine	2 tablespoons slivered shallots
2 teaspoons white vinegar	or onions
4 to 5 sprigs parsley	3 peppercorns
1 large stalk celery with	1⅓ to 1½ pounds salmon
leaves, cut in 1-inch chunks	fillets, ½ to ⅝ inch thick

1. Combine all the ingredients except the salmon in a medium saucepan. Cover and bring to a boil. Reduce the heat and simmer for 30 minutes.

2. Pour the liquid through a strainer into a large skillet. Return to a boil over medium heat.

3. Add the salmon, skin side down. (If the fillets are large, you may have to cut the fish to fit the pan.) Cover, and turn off the burner. Allow to sit there for 6 to 10 minutes, depending on the thickness of the fish. (Test to make sure the fish is done; if you use a thicker cut of fish, you may need to leave the burner on low to cook it adequately.)

4. When the fish is done, carefully move it to a serving dish with a slotted spatula (you may need to use two), placing it skin side up. Save ¾ cup of the poaching liquid for sauce (below). Gently pull back the skin to remove. Cover the fish and keep it warm.

SAUCE

Makes approximately 2 cups

¾ cup cold evaporated skim milk	¾ cup poaching liquid (from above) *
2 tablespoons all-purpose flour	1 beaten egg yolk
	½ teaspoon salt
2 to 3 tablespoons chopped, fresh dill weed (or 1 to 1½ teaspoons dried)	Juice of 1 lemon
	⅓ cup plain, low-fat yogurt
	Paprika

(continued)

1. In a medium saucepan, slowly whisk the milk into the flour until smooth. Add the dill and poaching liquid. Stir constantly over medium heat until the mixture comes to a boil.

2. Remove from the heat, but leave the burner on. Quickly whisk a small amount (¼ to ⅓ cup) of the hot mixture into the beaten egg yolk. Then whisk the yolk-milk mixture back into the remaining sauce in the pan. Return to the burner and stir constantly for 1 minute.

3. Remove from the heat. Whisk in the salt, lemon juice, and yogurt.

4. Drain the poached fish again, and pour 1¼ cups of sauce over it. Sprinkle with paprika. (Save the remaining sauce for vegetables, poached eggs, or salmon burgers later in the week.)

Per serving: Calories: 285   Fat: 13 gm.   Cholesterol: 129 mg. Sodium: 366 mg.

* If making this sauce for another recipe, you can substitute fish stock or bottled clam juice for poaching liquid.

Sole Aux Fines Herbes

Makes 4 to 5 servings

When I first served this recipe to a guest he commented that the sauce had "that taste and richness so typical of French cuisine." But he knew it couldn't be rich because I—the nutritionist—had made it. Indeed, he was right. I pared down the original recipe by replacing 900 calories' worth of butter and heavy cream with reduced-calorie margarine and half-and-half (amounting to just 260 calories). Yes, half-and-half does have some cream in it, but using evaporated skim milk instead would only save 15 calories per serving. I figured the small trade-off in calories wasn't worth the difference in taste. Serve with brown and wild rice, plus fresh green beans tossed with dill and a tablespoon or two of Dijon mustard.

Fish trade-offs: thin cod, haddock, or hake fillets; pout; catfish; tilapia

2 tablespoons reduced-calorie margarine
12-ounce package of fresh mushrooms, washed, trimmed, and sliced
3 tablespoons minced shallots or scallions
2 tablespoons lemon juice
¼ teaspoon salt
Grating of black pepper
10 or 12 medium flounder or sole fillets (about 2 pounds; you can substitute 5 or 6 long, thin scrod fillets)

¾ cup dry white wine
¾ cup canned chicken broth or fish stock (or clam broth)
½ cup cold half-and-half
2 tablespoons plus 1 teaspoon all-purpose flour
1 tablespoon lemon juice
3 tablespoons chopped, fresh parsley
1 teaspoon dried chervil
1 teaspoon dried tarragon
¼ teaspoon salt

1. Preheat the oven to 400° F. Evenly spread 1 tablespoon of the reduced-calorie margarine in the bottom of a large nonstick frying pan. Add the mushrooms and shallots or scallions. Cover and cook over medium-high heat until the mushrooms just start to become limp. (Stir once or twice while cooking.) Remove from the heat, add the 2 tablespoons of lemon juice, and sprinkle with ¼ teaspoon of the salt and the pepper. Set aside momentarily.

2. Grease a 13- x 9-inch baking dish (one that can withstand direct heat from a burner—I use a glass Pyrex casserole, then in step 5 place it on a wire ring normally used on the burner under my glass coffeepot) with the remaining tablespoon of reduced-calorie margarine.

(continued)

3. Place half of the fish fillets side by side in the dish. With a slotted spoon remove the mushrooms and shallots or scallions from the frying pan and evenly distribute them over the fillets. (Save the juice from the mushrooms for step 4.) Top each mushroom-covered fillet with the remaining fillets—like a sandwich. (If using long scrod fillets, line them up in the baking dish, spread half of each with mushrooms, and fold over the remaining half.)

4. Pour the wine, chicken broth or fish stock, and reserved mushroom juice over the stuffed fillets. The liquid should just barely cover the fish. (Add a bit of water if necessary.)

5. Loosely lay a piece of foil across the top of the baking dish. On the top of the stove, bring the fish and poaching juices just to a simmer over medium heat. (To distribute the heat, move the liquid around by carefully tilting the dish back and forth several times.)

6. Set the loosely covered baking dish in the middle of the oven and bake for 8 to 10 minutes or until the fish is just done. With a large slotted spoon or metal turner, gently transfer the fish to a serving dish. Cover and keep the fish warm.

7. Transfer the poaching liquid to the skillet and rapidly boil it down to 1 cup. While that's boiling, slowly whisk the half-and-half into the flour in a small bowl until smooth. (Reduce the heat under the poaching liquid to medium and wait a minute or two before going on to step 8.)

8. Add the half-and-half mixture to the reduced poaching liquid along with the remaining tablespoon of lemon juice, the parsley, chervil, tarragon, and the remaining ¼ teaspoon of salt. Stir constantly over medium heat until the sauce comes to a boil.

9. Drain the fish of any remaining liquid and evenly distribute the sauce over each packet of fillets.

Per serving (based on 5 servings): Calories: 284   Fat: 7.5 gm. Cholesterol: 96 mg.   Sodium: 526 mg.

Grilled Rainbow Trout with
Orange-Almond Brown Rice Stuffing

Makes 4 servings

Marinated rainbow trout is stuffed with a savory rice stuffing and enhanced by the smoky taste of charcoal grilling. You can make the rice ahead of time, but heat it well and add the almonds just before stuffing the fish. (You'll have leftover rice—serve it as a side dish in case people want seconds.)

Fish trade-offs: brook trout or lake trout, striped bass, shad, drum, whiting, mackerel, mullet, porgy, whitefish

1 cup dry white wine
Juice of 1 medium fresh
   lemon
½ cup orange juice
4 drawn rainbow trout, scaled
   with heads and tails intact
   (about 2½ pounds)
1 cup uncooked brown rice
1¼ cups water
¾ cup orange juice
1 cup finely chopped celery
   with leaves

¼ cup chopped, fresh parsley
⅓ cup chopped onion
1 tablespoon margarine
1 tablespoon grated orange
   rind
½ teaspoon salt
⅓ cup toasted, slivered
   almonds (see page 271n for
   almond-toasting directions)

1. Prepare the marinade by combining the wine, lemon juice, and ½ cup of orange juice. Pour the mixture over the fish in a shallow glass baking dish. Expose all sides of the fish to the marinade. Marinate for 1 hour in the refrigerator, turning several times. Light the charcoal 30 to 40 minutes before you're ready to cook the stuffed fish or preheat a gas grill.

2. Place the rice in a strainer, rinse with cold water, and drain.

3. Bring the water and ¾ cup of orange juice to a boil. (Watch closely so it doesn't boil over.) Add the rinsed rice, stir, and turn the heat to low. Cover tightly. Check in 5 minutes to make sure the rice is simmering, but don't stir again. (Rice becomes gummy when stirred too often.) Simmer the covered rice for another 20 minutes.

4. Add the celery, parsley, onion, margarine, orange rind, and salt to the rice. Stir just until combined. Cover. (If the rice stops boiling, increase the heat to bring it to a simmer again; then lower the heat.) Simmer for another 25 to 30 minutes or until the liquid is absorbed
(continued)

and the rice is tender (but still firm). Remove from the heat and gently stir in the almonds.

5. Drain the fish and place on a large cookie sheet or plastic cutting board. Stuff each trout with about ½ cup of rice stuffing, pressing it into the head and gut cavity. Press the opening closed as best you can.

6. Place the stuffed fish on a greased sheet of heavy-duty foil that has holes poked in it. Place on the grill and cook 5 to 7 minutes on each side or until done in the fleshy part just behind the head. (Turn very carefully with a large spatula and watch closely because timing is difficult to predict with grilling.)

Per serving (figured without leftover rice): Calories: 340   Fat: 10.5 gm. Cholesterol: 81 mg.   Sodium: 233 mg.

Coquilles St. Jacques

Makes 4 to 5 servings

This pared-down rendition of the classic French recipe spares you fat and calories but not the creamy texture and taste. Where butter is called for, the *Eat Fish* version uses none. And evaporated milk supplants heavy cream. I've served this to guests countless times and never tire of the compliments! Accompany with fresh peas and carrots, sourdough rolls, and a spinach salad.

Fish trade-offs: monkfish or skate chunks

⅔ cup dry white wine	¼ cup all-purpose flour
⅓ cup dry white vermouth	1 egg
½ teaspoon salt	½ cup evaporated skim milk
2 bay leaves	½ teaspoon salt
3 tablespoons minced scallions or shallots	Grating of black pepper
1¼ pounds bay or calico scallops (if sea scallops are used, cut in quarters)	Juice of 1 medium fresh lemon
12-ounce package of fresh mushrooms, washed, trimmed, and sliced, then steamed for 3 to 4 minutes	3 tablespoons chopped, fresh parsley
	1 tablespoon reduced-calorie margarine
	1½ ounces shredded Swiss cheese
¾ cup cold, low-fat milk	Paprika

1. In a large skillet, combine the wine, vermouth, ½ teaspoon of the salt, bay leaves, and scallions or shallots. Bring to a boil. Lower the heat and simmer for 2 to 3 minutes.

2. Add the scallops and steamed mushrooms. Cover. Quickly bring to a boil. Then immediately remove from the heat and let sit undisturbed for 4 to 5 minutes.

3. With a slotted spoon, remove the scallops and mushrooms and set aside in a covered bowl. Remove and discard the two bay leaves. Save 1 cup of the scallops' cooking liquid.

4. Preheat the oven to 350° F. In a medium-size saucepan, slowly whisk the low-fat milk into the flour until smooth. Add the cup of the scallops' cooking liquid. Bring the mixture to a boil over medium heat, stirring constantly. Continue cooking for 1 more minute. Remove from the heat, cover, and set aside momentarily.

5. With an electric beater, mix the egg and evaporated milk in a medium-size bowl for about 1 minute. With the beaters going the whole time, slowly pour the hot milk mixture (from step 4) into the egg mixture. Beat for another minute after the hot sauce is added. Stir in the remaining salt and the pepper, lemon juice, and parsley. Cover and set aside.

6. Grease a shallow 1½- to 2-quart baking dish with the reduced-calorie margarine. Drain the scallops and mushrooms well and add to the baking dish. Top with all of the sauce.

7. Evenly distribute the cheese over the top of the casserole. Sprinkle lightly with paprika. Bake for 25 to 30 minutes. (Note: You can make this dish ahead of time and refrigerate it after the paprika is added. If you do, increase baking time to about 45 minutes.)

8. (This step is optional.) Remove the casserole from the oven. Preheat the broiler. Broil 6 to 8 inches from the broiler element until the top is browned. Watch closely.

Per serving (based on 5 servings): Calories: 263   Fat: 6 gm. Cholesterol: 102 mg.   Sodium: 608 mg.

Shrimp à la Grecque

Makes 4 servings

One of my favorites, this combination of shrimp, tomatoes, black olives, and feta cheese is best served over a bed of steamed rice or vermicelli. It's a good way to stretch expensive shrimp when you want to serve it to guests. (This recipe is another one that scores high for iron and zinc.) Great with Mustardy Marinated Scallop Salad (page 242) and crusty French bread.

Fish trade-offs: shelled lobster or crawfish, mussels, scallops, squid rings

1¼ to 1⅓ pounds medium raw shrimp thawed, peeled, deveined, and tails left intact
2 tablespoons lemon juice
3 medium-large tomatoes
2 tablespoons olive oil
¼ cup sliced scallions (include bulb plus an inch or two of green)
1 large clove garlic, pressed or minced

3 tablespoons tomato paste
⅓ cup dry white wine
¾ teaspoon dried basil
2 tablespoons minced, fresh parsley
¼ teaspoon salt
Grating of black pepper
2 ounces feta cheese, crumbled in fairly large chunks
⅓ cup whole black olives, pitted

1. Place the shrimp in a medium bowl and cover with the lemon juice, turning the shrimp to coat all pieces. Set aside.

2. Blanch the tomatoes for about 2 minutes in a pot of boiling water. Drain and rinse with cold water. Then peel, remove the seeds, and coarsely chop. Set aside.

3. Heat the oil over medium-high heat in a large skillet. Add the scallions and garlic and sauté for a minute or so, stirring to prevent browning. Add the tomatoes, tomato paste, wine, basil, parsley, salt, and pepper. Cover and bring to a boil. Then reduce the heat and simmer until the tomatoes are soft, for about 15 minutes.

4. Raise the heat to medium. Add the shrimp with lemon juice. Stir, cover, and cook for 4 to 5 minutes or until the shrimp are pink and just firm.

5. Add the feta cheese and olives and toss lightly.

Per serving: Calories: 284   Fat: 14.5 gm.   Cholesterol: 185 mg. Sodium: 649 mg.

Steamed Mango Mako Shark

Makes 4 servings

This is a summery, light dish that's great for a hot night or to brighten a dreary winter's evening. The colors of fresh mango, red pepper strips, and kiwi fruit brighten this unusual dish. Serve with steamed rice and a dark green vegetable.

Fish trade-offs: tuna, swordfish, bluefish, black bass, grouper, mahimahi, sablefish, skate, whitefish

2 tablespoons dry or semidry
   sherry
1 tablespoon soy sauce
1 teaspoon grated fresh ginger
   root
1 medium clove garlic,
   pressed or minced
1 teaspoon sesame oil
3 tablespoons lime juice
1⅓ to 1½ pounds shark
   steaks, about 1 inch thick

Nonstick vegetable spray
½ ripe (but not overripe)
   mango, peeled and cut in
   ½-inch strips away from
   central pit
¼ large red pepper, cut into
   thin strips (use green
   pepper if red is unavailable)
1 kiwi fruit, peeled and cut
   into ⅛-inch-thick slices

1. Combine the sherry, soy sauce, ginger root, garlic, sesame oil, and lime juice into a sauce. Place the fish in a shallow dish and pour the sauce over it, turning to coat both sides. Refrigerate for 45 to 60 minutes.

2. Place the marinated fish on a steamer rack that's been coated with nonstick spray. Top with any remaining sauce. Place the steamer rack with the fish over boiling water. Cover and steam for about 8 minutes.

3. Quickly and artistically arrange the mango, red pepper, and kiwi across the top of the fish. (It will be crowded.) Cover and steam for another 6 to 7 minutes or until the fish is done.

*Per serving: Calories: 256   Fat: 8 gm.   Cholesterol: 77 mg.
Sodium: 379 mg.*

Zucchini-Carrot Fish Roll-Ups á la Diable

Makes 4 servings

One of my recipe-testers rated this dish in the top ten of the *Eat Fish* Recipes. Dijon mustard lends its spicy hand to the yogurt sauce. Carrots and zucchini let a touch of color peek through and help boost the vitamin A value in a serving to more than the US RDA. Serve with lima beans and a leaf lettuce salad with tangerine sections and green grapes.

Fish trade-offs: thin cod, haddock, or hake fillets; pout; catfish; rockfish; ocean perch; tilapia

2 large carrots, peeled, cut in half crosswise, then cut in thin strips lengthwise
10 to 12 large, fresh mushrooms, washed, trimmed, and sliced
1 long, thin zucchini (about 8 inches), cut into thin 4-inch-long strips
1 cup plain, low-fat yogurt
3 tablespoons Dijon mustard

1¼ to 1⅓ pounds flatfish fillets or thin scrod fillets (allow one good-sized fillet per person)
Nonstick vegetable spray
2 teaspoons all-purpose flour
¼ cup cold low-fat milk
½ teaspoon dried dill weed
⅛ teaspoon salt
Grating of black pepper

1. Preheat the oven to 450° F. Steam the carrots for 3 minutes. Add the mushrooms and steam for 3 more minutes. Then add the zucchini and steam for another 2 to 3 minutes or until the vegetables are just tender. Remove from the heat and uncover to allow the steam to escape. Set aside.

2. Mix together the yogurt and mustard in a small bowl. Set aside ⅔ cup for sauce in step 6. Brush about *half* of the remaining ⅓ cup of the yogurt mixture on one side of each fillet. (Save the rest for step 4.)

3. Go back to the steamed vegetables and evenly divide the drained carrots and zucchini among the 4 fillets, placing the vegetables at one end of the yogurt-coated side of each fillet. (Save the mushrooms for step 6.) Roll up the fillets firmly around the vegetables, starting at the vegetable end. (If you wind up with extra vegetables, scatter them around the pan in step 4 and serve alongside the sauced fish at the end.)

4. Spray a square baking pan (about 1½ quarts) with nonstick spray. Add the fish roll-ups, placing them seam side down. Brush with the remainder of the ⅓ cup of the yogurt mixture.

5. Bake, uncovered, for about 20 minutes or until the fish is done. Carefully drain off excess juice.

6. While the fish is cooking, in a medium-size saucepan whisk the flour and milk into the leftover ⅔ cup of the yogurt mixture. Add the mushrooms, dill, salt, and pepper. Cook over medium heat, stirring constantly, until the sauce just starts to bubble. Pour the sauce over the fish roll-ups after they're finished baking.

Per serving: Calories: 213   Fat: 3.5 gm.   Cholesterol: 79 mg. Sodium: 395 mg.

Oven-Poached Halibut with Florentine Sauce

Makes 4 servings

Make sure you have all ingredients in order ahead of time since the timing is a little tricky for this one—you have to juggle making the sauce and poaching the fish at the same time. The extra effort is worth it for the unique creamy and dark sauce that contrasts beautifully with white halibut. (The sauce can be made ahead of time, but its color will be less pleasing; be sure to warm it slowly, just until hot.) Serve with egg noodles, steamed carrot strips, and fresh or frozen peas. (You can spoon the extra sauce over noodles; it's also superb for both poached eggs on English muffins and chicken.)

Fish trade-offs: salmon, tuna, swordfish, mako or blue shark, striped bass, skate, cusk, grouper, mahimahi, pollock, wolffish, whitefish

POACHING LIQUID

¾ cup dry white wine
1½ cups canned chicken
   broth
½ cup coarsely chopped
   celery

¼ cup chopped, fresh parsley
½ teaspoon Old Bay
   Seasoning or dried, flaked
   thyme
Grating of black pepper

FISH

1⅓ to 1½ pounds halibut
   steaks, ¾ to 1 inch thick

SAUCE

Makes about 2¼ cups

10-ounce package frozen
   spinach (chopped or leaf),
   cooked according to
   package directions (don't
   overcook), drained slightly
½ cup chopped onion

1 tablespoon all-purpose flour
¾ teaspoon salt
Generous grating of black
   pepper
¼ teaspoon ground nutmeg
1¼ cups plain, low-fat yogurt

1. Combine all the poaching-liquid ingredients in a medium saucepan, cover, and set aside.

2. Preheat the oven to 400° F. Place the fish in a baking dish just large enough to accommodate the fish and poaching liquid. Set aside.

3. Start the sauce by puréeing the spinach, onion, flour, salt, pepper, and nutmeg in a blender or food processor.

4. Pour the purée into a medium saucepan and heat over medium heat—stirring constantly, scraping the sides and bottom frequently —until the mixture just comes to a boil. (It will be thick.)

5. While the sauce is heating, bring the covered poaching ingredients to a boil. Reduce the heat and simmer for 8 to 10 minutes.

6. When the spinach mixture is bubbly, whisk in the yogurt. Stir constantly over medium heat for another 2 to 3 minutes. Remove from the heat. Cover and set aside. (I like the sauce thick; if you prefer a thinner sauce, whisk in several tablespoons of milk.)

7. Pour the piping hot poaching liquid over the fish. (The liquid should barely cover the fish—add boiling water or chicken broth, if necessary.) Lay a sheet of foil loosely across the top of the dish and place in the preheated oven. Bake for 12 to 15 minutes or until the fish is done.

8. Remove the fish from the poaching liquid. Divide into 4 equal portions. Top each with about ⅓ cup of spinach sauce.

Per serving: Calories: 178   Fat: 3.5 gm.   Cholesterol: 41 mg. Sodium: 369 mg.

Scallop-Shrimp Kebabs

Makes 4 servings

Two marinades—one for shrimp and mushrooms, the other for scallops and zucchini—make these kebabs something special. Once the marinades are made (which you can do ahead of time), the skewered shellfish and vegetables are a breeze to prepare. You can also assemble your kebabs well in advance as long as you refrigerate them. (These kebabs are another excellent source of iron and zinc.) Serve with low-fat potato salad and a large tossed salad.

Fish trade-offs: (for both types of fish, in either marinade) chunks of cusk, wolffish, monkfish, sablefish, mako shark, tuna, crawfish, salmon, swordfish

Mom's Teriyaki Sauce (recipe
page 313—use oil)
1 pound medium raw shrimp,
thawed, peeled, and
deveined
18 to 20 fresh medium-size
mushrooms, washed and
trimmed
Wine-Dill Marinade (recipe
page 313—use oil)

1 pound sea scallops (cut in
half if very large)
2 thin 7- or 8-inch zucchinis,
sliced crosswise in ¾-inch
chunks and parboiled for 3
to 4 minutes
16 to 18 cherry tomatoes

1. Pour hot Teriyaki Sauce over the shrimp and mushrooms. Marinate in the refrigerator for ¾ to 1 hour.

2. Pour Wine-Dill Marinade over the scallops and parboiled zucchini. Marinate in the refrigerator for ¾ to 1 hour.

3. Start a charcoal fire or preheat a gas grill. Skewer alternating pieces of marinated shrimp, mushrooms, scallops, and zucchini, and the tomatoes.

4. Grease the grill rack and preheat it. Add the kebabs and cook over hot coals for 5 to 7 minutes (or until the fish is done), turning 2 to 3 times.

*Per serving: Calories: 246   Fat: 3.5 gm.   Cholesterol: 193 mg.
Sodium: 390 mg.*

MOM'S TERIYAKI SAUCE

This marinade is especially good for shrimp and firm-fleshed fish cooked over the coals. Try it with flank steak or London broil, as well.

½ cup unsweetened pineapple juice (I usually drain it from a can of unsweetened pineapple)
⅓ cup cider vinegar
¼ cup soy sauce

3 tablespoons packed brown sugar
¼ teaspoon garlic powder
1 tablespoon vegetable oil (optional)

In a small saucepan, combine all the ingredients. Bring just to a boil, uncovered. (Watch carefully because the marinade boils over easily.) Pour over fish while the marinade is still hot or reheat it just before using.

WINE-DILL MARINADE

A tasty marinade for any type of fish—whitefish, shellfish, or oily fish.

½ cup dry white wine
½ cup canned chicken broth
3 tablespoons lemon juice
1 teaspoon dried dill weed

¼ teaspoon dry mustard
1 tablespoon vegetable oil (optional)

Combine all the ingredients into a marinade and pour over fish.

Tilefish Medallions in
Sherried Orange Sauce

Makes 4 servings   (MICROWAVE)

An elegant combination of orange juice and sherry accents a delicate
lobsterlike fish. Just one tablespoon of real butter gives the low-calorie
sauce a rich, full flavor. Rice pilaf or a wild- and brown-rice combination make perfect accompaniments for the sauced medallions. These
are also good served over broad noodles with a dark green vegetable.

Fish trade-offs: (if fillets are too thin for medallions, cut them in 2-
by 2-inch pieces) pollock, tuna, drum, monkfish, mahimahi, orange
roughy, skate

1⅓ to 1½ pounds skinless tilefish fillets	2 tablespoons cider vinegar
3 tablespoons dry or semidry sherry	1 tablespoon plus 2 teaspoons cornstarch
¾ cup orange juice	1 tablespoon sugar
½ cup canned chicken broth	½ teaspoon grated fresh ginger root
¼ teaspoon salt	1 tablespoon butter (or margarine)
1 teaspoon grated orange rind	Parsley sprigs
1 medium orange (from above), peeled and sectioned	

1. Prepare the tilefish medallions by slicing the fillets at 2½- to 3-
inch intervals, with the "grain" or striations of the fish at an angle.
Set aside.

2. In an 8-inch square microwaveable baking dish, combine the
sherry, orange juice, chicken broth, and salt. Cover, vent, and microwave at full power for 4 to 5 minutes, until the liquid comes to a
boil.

3. Add the tilefish medallions to the hot liquid, overlapping somewhat. Cover, vent, and microwave at full power for 3 to 4 minutes or
until the center of the fish medallions just start to flake. Give the dish
a half-turn once while cooking. (Watch closely to avoid overcooking.)
Let stand, covered, for 2 to 3 minutes. Check again for doneness.

4. Transfer the fish to a serving dish with a slotted spoon. Save the
poaching liquid. Garnish the fish with the orange sections. Cover and
keep warm.

5. To prepare the sauce, mix the vinegar with the cornstarch until smooth. Stir the vinegar-cornstarch mixture into the fish poaching liquid. Add the sugar, orange rind, ginger, and butter. Cover, vent, and microwave at full power until the sauce thickens and bubbles (about 3 minutes). Whisk several times while cooking.

6. Immediately pour 1¼ cups of hot sauce over the fish and garnish with parsley. (Save the remaining sauce and serve over broccoli, carrots, or poached chicken another day.)

Per serving: Calories: 224   Fat: 5.5 gm.   Cholesterol: (no data available for tilefish)   Sodium: 259 mg.

Poached Sole and Broccoli Roll-Ups
in Wine Sauce

Makes 4 servings

Sole is rolled around small broccoli sprigs, smothered with a light herb and wine sauce, and topped with Swiss cheese. (It all adds up to plenty of calcium, zinc, and vitamin C.) Serve with steamed baby carrots and a Bibb lettuce, tomato, and red onion salad.

Fish trade-offs: thin cod, haddock, or hake fillets; pout; catfish; rockfish; ocean perch; tilapia

POACHING LIQUID

1 cup dry white wine
2 cups water
3 tablespoons chopped, fresh parsley
¼ cup sliced scallions (include

bulb plus an inch or two of green)
½ teaspoon salt
Grating of black pepper

FISH AND SAUCE

20 fresh broccoli sprigs, about 3 inches long with thin stem sections, steamed for 3 minutes and cooled
10 small sole or flounder fillets (1⅓ to 1½ pounds total)
Toothpicks
½ cup cold low-fat milk

2 tablespoons all-purpose flour
½ cup evaporated skim milk
½ teaspoon salt
2 tablespoons lemon juice
½ teaspoon dried, flaked marjoram
1½ ounces shredded Swiss cheese

1. Combine the wine, water, parsley, scallions, salt, and pepper in a large frying pan. Cover. Bring to a boil, lower the heat, and simmer for 5 minutes.

2. While the poaching liquid is cooking, place two broccoli sprigs—with ends close together and flower portions facing outward, in opposite directions—at one end of each fillet. Roll each fillet up from that end to the no-broccoli end and secure with toothpicks.

3. When the poaching liquid is done simmering, add the fish roll-ups, placing them seam side down. Cover and quickly return to a gentle boil. Immediately lower the heat and simmer for 4 to 6 minutes or until the fish is done. (Watch closely to avoid overcooking.)

4. With a slotted spoon or spatula, gently transfer the fish roll-ups to a large rectangular baking dish. Cover and set aside. Save the poaching liquid for the next step.

5. Quickly boil down the poaching liquid, uncovered, for 10 minutes. Use this time to preheat the broiler.

6. While the poaching liquid is boiling, take a medium saucepan and slowly whisk the low-fat milk into the flour until the mixture is smooth. Add the evaporated skim milk and salt. Bring to a boil over medium heat, stirring constantly.

7. When the poaching liquid has boiled for 10 minutes, stir ½ cup of it (no need to strain) into the milk sauce. Add the lemon juice and marjoram. Return the milk sauce to a boil, stirring constantly.

8. Carefully drain the fish roll-ups of any excess juice. Evenly cover with the sauce and shredded cheese.

9. Place under the broiler about 8 inches from the heating element just until the cheese is lightly browned. Watch closely. Carefully remove the toothpicks before serving or warn guests about them.

Per serving: Calories: 281   Fat: 5.5 gm.   Cholesterol: 85 mg. Sodium: 549 mg.

PART III

A Program for Weight-Loss and Nutrition

The *Eat Fish* Diet

THERE ARE TWO ways to think of a diet. One is more a way of living —how you eat *most* of the time. The majority of people, however, think of a diet as a short-lived plan for losing weight. The problem with the second type of diet is that "going on" one implies you'll eventually "go off" it. Much of this chapter, therefore, is devoted to the way-of-life type of diet that will help you make your fish-eating habits *permanent* ones. But I won't disappoint those of you who can't wait to get your hands on a new plan for losing weight—the chapter concludes with the two-week *Eat Fish* Launching Diet and the *Eat Fish* Mix-and-Match Diet.

WHAT'S THIS WELL-BALANCED DIET NUTRITIONISTS KEEP TALKING ABOUT?

Throughout this book I've been telling you that your efforts to bring more fish into your life will be most beneficial if you incorporate fish into a diet low in total fat. And your newfound fish fancy should also be made part of a varied eating plan containing adequate amounts of other nutrients such as carbohydrate, protein, vitamins, and minerals.

This probably isn't the first time you've heard a nutritionist chant terms like "balance" and "moderation." And you're probably wondering if, all by yourself, it's possible to plan a nutritious diet without calculating grams of this nutrient and that nutrient. Can you implement a diet with no more than 30 percent fat calories without spending hours in deep consultation with a dietitian? I think you can with some basic guidelines provided in this chapter, a little patience, and willingness to change—but make those changes gradually without the kind of diet fanatacism that invariably wears off.

For starters, consider some common-sense guidelines meant to steer the U.S. population as a whole toward a nutritious, preventive-type diet. Put together by the U.S. Department of Agriculture and the Department of Health and Human Services, the "Dietary Guidelines for Americans" are as follows.

Eat a variety of foods to obtain the 40-some nutrients needed for good health. It's important to choose your daily foods from each of the major food groups (see the "Making a Low-Fat Diet Part of Your Life" chart on page 326 for specifics) and to select different foods within the groups. "You will rarely need to take vitamin or mineral supplements if you eat a variety of foods," state the guidelines, with a few exceptions that apply to adults. (Infants have special needs that I won't get into.) Premenopausal women may need an iron supplement to replace losses from menstrual bleeding; pregnant and breast-feeding women may need a supplement of several nutrients; and elderly people who don't eat a varied diet and/or who are on medications that alter nutrient needs could require nutrient supplements. I'd add chronic dieters to the list of those who might benefit from a multivitamin-mineral pill—particularly those who consistently consume 1,200 calories or less a day. (In all four cases, people should consult with a physician and/or registered dietitian about the possible need to take a supplement.)

Maintain desirable weight by eating more fruits and vegetables, as well as whole grains; by consuming less fat, fatty foods, sugar, sweets, and alcoholic beverages; and by increasing your physical activity. (A discussion of "desirable weight" begins on page 336.)

Avoid too much fat, saturated fat, and cholesterol. The chart on page 326 gives you the "how-to" details.

Eat foods with adequate starch and fiber by consuming more whole-grain breads and cereals, fruits, vegetables, starchy vegetables (like potatoes), and dry beans and peas. These items should be substituted for foods loaded with fat and sugar.

Avoid too much sugar by using less white sugar, brown sugar, raw sugar, honey, and syrups. Go easy on sugar-containing soft drinks, candies, cakes, cookies, and syrup-packed fruits.

Avoid too much sodium by using less salt at the table and in cooking, reading labels carefully, and limiting foods that have large amounts of added sodium. Specifically, go easy on salty snack foods, pickled items, cured meats, certain canned vegetables and soups, and salty cheeses, as well as high-sodium condiments like soy sauce and steak sauce.

If you drink alcoholic beverages, do so in moderation by having no more than one or two daily drinks. A "drink" is considered to be a 12-ounce beer, 5 ounces of wine, or 1½ ounces of distilled spirits. (Many health professionals advise that pregnant women abstain from alcohol altogether.)

ARE YOU EATING TOO MUCH FAT?

By now you know that fat should amount to no more than 30 percent of your calorie intake. And the National Heart, Lung, and Blood Institute (of the National Institutes of Health) advises that saturated fats should take up a maximum of 10 percent of the total calories you eat. For cholesterol, the recommendation is no more than 250 to 300 milligrams a day.

If you're someone who requires 2,000 daily calories to maintain your weight, 30 percent fat calories would amount to 67 grams of fat —that's the level of fat in about 6 tablespoons of oil or margarine. Indeed, it would be easy to keep track of your intake if all your fat came from obvious sources like margarine; but recall the "invisible" fats (discussed in chapter 2) dispersed throughout foods like cheese, meats, and baked goods. It's these not-so-obvious sources of fat that are difficult to keep tabs on.

So how can you determine whether your intake of fat is too high? Rather than keep a running record of the number of grams of fat in various foods, you can get a rough idea by taking the following quiz from the Human Nutrition Information Service of the U.S. Department of Agriculture.

HOW DO YOU SCORE ON FAT?

Do the foods you eat provide more fat than is good for you? Answer the questions below, then see how your diet stacks up.

How often do you eat:

	Seldom or never	1 or 2 times a week	3 to 5 times a week	Almost daily
1. Fried, deep-fat fried, or breaded foods?	☐	☐	☐	☐
2. Fatty meats such as bacon, sausage, luncheon meats, and heavily marbled steaks and roasts?	☐	☐	☐	☐
3. Whole milk, high-fat cheeses, and ice cream?	☐	☐	☐	☐
4. High-fat desserts such as pies, pastries, and rich cakes?	☐	☐	☐	☐
5. Rich sauces and gravies?	☐	☐	☐	☐
6. Oily salad dressings or mayonnaise?	☐	☐	☐	☐
7. Whipped cream, and table cream, sour cream, and cream cheese?	☐	☐	☐	☐
8. Butter or margarine on vegetables, dinner rolls, and toast?	☐	☐	☐	☐

Take a look at your answers. Several responses in the last two columns means you may have a high fat intake.*

* Home and Garden Bulletin Number 232–3
April 1986

PUTTING A LOW-FAT DIET TO WORK FOR YOU

If you're like most Americans, you probably scored on the high side
—now what can you do about it? The chart on pages 326 lays out the
basics of what it takes to implement a well-balanced, low-fat diet. To
the far right, you'll see the major food groups and a recommendation
for the *minimum* number of daily servings that can provide you with
the balance of nutrients you need to stay healthy.* These servings only
supply about 1,200 calories. Therefore, most people eat greater
amounts of food—I suggest you get the majority of your extras from
fruits, vegetables, and grain products. (The American Heart Association encourages at least 3 daily servings of fruit, as well as at least 3
servings of vegetables.)

The second column lists "First-Choice Foods," the lowest-fat bets
which most of your daily choices should come from. "Second-Choice
Foods," in the next column, are meant to be used in small amounts
or when the "First-Choice" counterparts are totally unacceptable.
(Two-percent-fat milk, for instance, is better than whole milk if your
family won't tolerate skim or 1-percent-fat milk.)

"Make-It-Scarce Foods" should be eaten no more than once in a
while—just a couple of servings from the whole group a week (not
counting the three egg yolks). It would be ideal if we could completely
do without "Make-It-Scarce Foods," but—realistically speaking—
most of us really enjoy these rich foods and can afford to eat them
occasionally. So if you've stuck with "First-Choice Foods" most of the
week and you want to have ice cream on Saturday night or a few strips
of bacon on Sunday morning, go ahead—and don't feel guilty! (Turn
to chapter 10, "Cook It Right," and chapter 11, "Working from
Your Own Recipes," for specifics about low-fat cooking and label
reading.)

The chart may seem overwhelming at first, but when you consider
the millions of foods that life has to offer, there really isn't all that
much to learn. Of course, committing some dos and don'ts to memory

---

* Iron is one nutrient that's likely to be in short supply for premenopausal women who eat
the minimum number of servings from the major food groups, particularly when they cut
back on iron-rich red meats. To make up for the shortage, women of childbearing age should
be certain to regularly consume iron-rich shellfish, such as oysters and clams (see page 70).
Some nonanimal iron sources are dark green vegetables, enriched and whole-grain breads and
cereals, iron-fortified cereals, beans and peas, wheat germ, tofu, and dried fruits. The body
more readily uses the iron in plant foods if they're eaten along with a good vitamin C source
(such as citrus fruit) and/or a small amount of meat, poultry, or fish. Despite all these efforts,
some still need to take an iron supplement, so it's wise for women to check with their
physicians.

TABLE 12. MAKING A LOW-FAT DIET PART OF YOUR LIFE

Food Group and Minimum Recommended Amount for Adults	First-Choice Foods	Second-Choice Foods	Make-It-Scarce Foods
Milk products: 2 daily servings 1 serving: 1 cup milk / 1 cup yogurt / 1½ oz. cheese / 2 cups cottage cheese[a] / 1¾ cups ice cream[a] *Milk products supply calcium, riboflavin, and protein.*	skim or 1%-fat milk, fortified with vitamins A and D (regular, evaporated, powdered, buttermilk) skim or low-fat yogurt (preferably with little or no added sugar; plain, vanilla, lemon) low-fat cheeses (no more than 2 g fat/oz.; Borden Lite-Line, Weight Watchers® cheese slices) 1%- to 2%-fat cottage cheese low-fat frozen yogurt	2%-fat milk cheeses in the 3 to 5 g fat/oz. range (part-skim mozzarella) regular cottage cheese part-skim ricotta cheese ice milk	whole milk half-and-half whole-milk yogurt regular cheeses (American, cheddar, Swiss) whole-milk ricotta cheese ice cream
Protein foods: 2 to 3 daily servings 2 oz. cooked fish, poultry or meat (2 oz. cheese can also be counted as a protein serving) 1 serving: 2 eggs / 1 cup cooked, dried beans or peas / 4 tablespoons peanut butter[a] *Protein foods supply protein, B-vitamins, iron, and zinc.*	most fresh, frozen, canned-in-water fish 3 to 7 times a week (a mix of high-, medium-, and low-fat fish) skinless chicken, turkey very lean, fat-trimmed beef, veal, pork, lamb egg whites or cholesterol-free egg substitutes dried beans, peas (cooked without fat; used in place of some meat) tofu (soybean curd) low-fat cold cuts (no more than 2 g fat/oz.; turkey breast, lean boiled ham, turkey pastrami) skinless, fat-trimmed wild game	shrimp, lobster, squid, crayfish (all are low in total fat but higher in cholesterol than other fish) eel canned-in-oil and drained fish ground beef (containing no more than 15% fat by weight) peanut butter	fish roe, caviar chicken with skin, turkey with skin highly marbled, fatty beef, veal, pork, lamb regular ground beef organ meats (liver, intestines) egg yolks (no more than 3/ week) hot dogs sausage, bacon high-fat cold cuts (bologna, pastrami, salami) domestic duck
Fruits and vegetables: 4 daily servings 1 serving: ½ cup juice / ½ cup cooked vegetable or fruit / 1 cup raw vegetable or fruit / 1 medium fresh fruit *Fruits and vegetables supply vitamins A and C, potassium, and fiber.*	all plain fresh, frozen fruits and vegetables (canned vegetables are low-fat but higher in sodium; note that avocados and olives are considered fats; for vitamin A intake, have dark green or orange vegetables at least 3 to 4 times a week; use fruits without added sugar; for vitamin C intake, have citrus fruits, strawberries, cantaloupe, tomatoes, green peppers, broccoli, cabbage, dark greens at least 1 time a day)	fruits and vegetables with small amounts of "First-Choice" fats	fruits and vegetables with added butter, sour cream, cream, sauces, cheese

[a]These choices provide more calories than others in the same group. For example, you would have to eat about 400 calories worth of low-fat cottage cheese to get the same amount of calcium contained in a 100-calorie cup of low-fat milk.
[b]These products vary widely in calorie content—read labels to select a portion size that provides between 70 and 100 calories.

Food Group and Minimum Recommended Amount for Adults	First-Choice Foods	Second-Choice Foods	Make-It-Scarce Foods
Grain products: 4 daily servings (whole grain or enriched) 1 serving: 1 slice bread / 4 to 6 crackers[b] / 1 cup flake-type cereal[b] / ½ cup cooked cereal / ½ cup cooked pasta, rice or bulgar *Grain products supply B-vitamins, iron, and fiber.*	plain bread (whole wheat, rye, oatmeal, bran, white) low-fat rolls (hamburger rolls, hot dog rolls, English muffins, Syrian bread, water bagels) low-fat crackers (saltines, melba toast, matzoh, oyster crackers, flatbread, graham crackers, enriched pretzels, rice cakes) hot and cold cereals (preferably with little sugar) pasta, rice, bulgar (without added fat) low-fat cookies (ginger snaps, animal crackers, vanilla wafers, fig bars) angel food cake	egg breads, egg noodles, egg bagels quick-breads made with "First-Choice" fats and milk products (muffins, biscuits, pancakes, waffles) "First-Choice" grain products with small amounts of "First-Choice" fats	butter rolls, cheese breads, croissants, doughnuts pies, cakes, cookies, other baked goods made with "Make-It-Scarce" fats high-fat crackers (with cheese, butter, palm oil or coconut oil) potato chips, corn chips granola-type cereals made with coconut or coconut oil "First-Choice" grain products made with "Make-It-Scarce" fats, sauces, regular cheese
Calorie-booster foods (fats,* sugars, alcoholic beverages): there is no recommended amount; try to eat as few as possible *Calorie-booster foods supply calories and fat.* *The American Heart Association recommends no more than 5 to 8 servings of polyunsaturated fats per day (count olive oil in this total). One serving equals 1 teaspoon vegetable oil or margarine, 2 teaspoons reduced-calorie margarine, regular mayonnaise or salad dressing.	margarine, mayonnaise, and salad dressings that are reduced calorie vegetable oils (olive, canola, corn, cottonseed, safflower, sesame, soybean, sunflower) regular margarine (with a *liquid* "First-Choice" oil listed as the first ingredient) regular mayonnaise and salad dressings made with "First-Choice" oils avocados, olives nuts, seeds non-dairy creamers made with "First-Choice" oils	peanut oil partially hydrogenated "First-Choice" oils reduced-fat sour cream, reduced-fat cream cheese	butter, lard, bacon fat, shortening cream, sour cream, cream cheese non-dairy creamers and dessert toppings made with coconut oil or palm oil palm oil, palm kernel oil, coconut oil chocolate coconut

[a]These choices provide more calories than others in the same group. For example, you would have to eat about 400 calories worth of low-fat cottage cheese to get the same amount of calcium contained in a 100-calorie cup of low-fat milk.
[b]These products vary widely in calorie content—read labels to select a portion size that provides between 70 and 100 calories.

isn't the same as actually implementing 30-percent-fat guidelines in your everyday diet. But you really can do it if you take things slowly and don't overwhelm yourself—or your family—with too many changes at once. To be sure, a family accustomed to whole milk, cheddar cheese, bacon, and steaks is not likely to adjust to skim milk, low-fat cottage cheese, and broiled fish overnight.

To make the transition easier, start by making your grocery-shopping list from the chart so you have plenty of well-liked healthful foods on hand. As you use up higher-fat items on your shelves, try not to replace them (if you do, buy small quantities) so you're not faced with constant temptation. (If corn chips and sour cream dips aren't around, people will go for low-fat snacks including pretzels and popcorn, as well as veggies and cottage-cheese-based dips, like Zesty Seafood Dip on page 232.)

Another idea is to work on single categories of foods for two-week blocks of time. The first two weeks, for instance, you could experiment with low-fat dairy products. Set up a family taste panel to sample various low-fat cheeses; you may decide that some would work best in cooked foods, while others are great for snacking. Or see how many different ways you can use low-fat milk and yogurt in cooking. Youngsters love to be involved in planning and cooking recipes for puddings, soups, dips, and the like. For another two-week period, you could try introducing one new fruit or vegetable each day, experimenting with different preparation methods—say a grated carrot and pineapple salad, steamed broccoli with a low-fat cheese sauce, or baked Hubbard squash with cinnamon and nutmeg topping.

DOES IT REALLY WORK?

If you follow the guidelines on the chart, will you really wind up with a diet that has 30 percent or less fat calories? Compare a typical American's daily intake with one that primarily includes "First-Choice Foods," but also incorporates a number of "Second-Choice" items.

Typical American High-Fat Day

Breakfast: 1 cup cornflakes with 1 teaspoon sugar and ¾ cup whole milk
1 cup coffee with 1 ounce half-and-half

Coffee
break: Plain doughnut
1 cup coffee with 1 ounce half-and-half

Lunch: Cheeseburger
12-ounce can diet cola
3 chocolate chip cookies

Snack: 6 ounces dry white wine
1 ounce cheddar cheese
4 Triscuit crackers

Supper: Broiled lamb chop
             Baked potato with 1 tablespoon sour cream
             ½ cup cole slaw (with regular mayonnaise)
             ½ cup cooked spinach with 1 pat butter
             Iced tea sweetened with sugar

Dessert: ¾ cup vanilla ice cream

Total calories: 2,037   Percentage of calories from fat: 43%   Percentage of fat calories from saturated fat: 15%   Cholesterol: 273 mg.

A Low-Fat Alternative

Breakfast: 1 cup bran flakes with ¾ cup 1%-fat milk; ½ banana
             1 cup coffee with 1 ounce evaporated skim milk

Coffee
break: 1 English muffin with 2 teaspoons reduce-calorie margarine
             6 ounces grapefruit juice

Lunch: 2 ounces turkey breast on 2 slices rye bread with Dijon mustard and lettuce
             Iced coffee with ½ cup 1%-fat milk and low-calorie sweetener
             Apple, sliced and spread with 1 tablespoon peanut butter
             2 gingersnaps

Snack: 4 ounces seltzer water mixed with 4 ounces orange juice
             8 Ry Krisp crackers spread with ¼ cup part-skim ricotta cheese

Supper: 4 ounces swordfish, broiled with 1 tablespoon reduced-calorie mayonnaise and lemon juice
             Baked potato with 1 tablespoon reduced-fat sour cream
             Large Romaine lettuce salad with sliced red onion and 2 tablespoons reduced-calorie Italian dressing
             1 cup cooked spinach with lemon juice and nutmeg
             1 cup 1%-fat milk

Dessert: ⅛ honeydew melon with ½ cup vanilla ice milk

Total calories: 2,057   Percentage of calories from fat: 21%   Percentage of fat calories from saturated fat: 6%   Cholesterol: 169 mg.

To me, the low-fat day looks pretty appetizing—with just 21 percent fat calories to boot! And for someone with a good appetite, you get to eat more food for the same number of calories when you go the low-fat way.

If you're really serious about adopting a low-fat lifestyle, I suggest you pick up some additional references to help you plan and cook your meals. Three excellent possibilities are *The New American Diet* by Sonja L. and William E. Connor (New York: Simon and Schuster, 1986), *Jane Brody's Good Food Book: Living the High Carbohydrate Way* (New York: Norton, 1985), and *The American Heart Association Cookbook*, 4th Edition (New York: Ballantine, 1984).

WORKING MORE FISH INTO YOUR DIET

At the end of the chapter, I give you plenty of menus that incorporate lots of fish. But it's important for you to learn to do the job yourself so you can plan according to your taste, have plenty of variety, and make fish eating a lifelong habit.

As with other healthful changes suggested previously, it's important to take things slowly when making the move toward more fish. If your family is used to eating fish every two weeks, for instance, start out by serving it just once a week for the first month. Gradually work up to having fish two or three times a week for supper; then add another fish meal or two at lunchtime.

Remember that lunches *do* count—if your family gets sick of fish at supper, work in noontime meals such as *Salmon Burgers, Whipped Tuna Salad, Crab Slaw, Hearty Scallop-Vegetable Soup,* or *Tuna Tacos.**
Leftovers from fish suppers are also good reheated at lunchtime. Another way to get more fish into your diet routine is to substitute it for meat or cheese in certain dishes or add it to some of your regular recipes, such as pepper steak, cheese omelette, noodle casserole, pasta or rice salads, stuffed peppers, chili, and vegetable soup. (See pages 166–74 in chapter 9 for tips on shopping and planning fish meals.)

If your family basically likes fish, but isn't used to eating a lot of it, start out with familiar types like swordfish, scrod, and canned tuna. Stick to simple recipes such as *Broiled Basil Swordfish* and *Simple Cod Fillets with Buttery Crumb Topping.* It also helps to serve dishes similar to familiar fare—*Easy Oven-Fried Cusk Fillets* for fried-fish lovers, for instance. You may find that big meat-eaters will go for firmer, more meaty fish including fresh tuna, shark, and mahimahi, as well as more traditional swordfish and halibut. Non-fish fans may also like fish better if it's doctored up in a sauce or casserole. And don't hesitate to serve your fish-eaters *Slimmed-Down Tartar Sauce,* catsup, or lots of lemon juice to ease the transition.

* Recipe titles in italics are *Eat Fish* Recipes. To locate them, see the recipe index on page 365.

I wouldn't necessarily lie about it (although I must confess to a few deceptions in developing the *Eat Fish* Recipes), but when serving a new or unusual type of fish, don't go out of your way to announce what you're having until after everyone has had a chance to taste it. In addition, I'd certainly advise against serving newcomers fish with heads and tails. Another turnoff for many is bones—ask your fish dealer for boneless fillets and steaks or learn how to remove bones yourself (see page 182 for some guidelines).

As far as getting children to try new types of fish is concerned, it depends on the individual—after my preschooler got an aquarium for his room, he seemed to view eating new types of fish as an adventure and wanted to know what the different kinds look like. Other kids are better off not knowing it's shark, catfish, or the like. "What are we having for dinner, Mom?" can be handled with a response like "Seafood and pasta with tomatoes and cheese."

For your first attempts at making more fish part of your life, keep it simple. Since most of us tend to cook the same few recipes over and over, it may be unrealistic to think you'll add a slew of fancy new fish dishes to your everyday fare. Try selecting five to ten easy *Eat Fish* Recipes to call your own. (Remember that your goal is to eat a mix of high-, medium-, and low-fat fish.) Following are some basic, easy-to-like dishes.

FIFTEEN STANDBY *EAT FISH* RECIPES

Broiled Basil Swordfish
Broiled Honey-Lime Salmon
  with Tarragon
Cheesy Fish Fillets
Chunky Clam Chowder
Cod Fillets with Fettuccine
  and Broccoli
Cod Fillets with Lemon-Herb
  Butter
Fillet of Pollock Parmigiana
Mackerel with Creamy
  Cucumber-Dill Sauce

Salmon Burgers
Seafood Salad
Sesame-Soy Halibut Steaks
Simple Cod Fillets with
  Buttery Crumb Topping
Stovetop Scallops with Garlic,
  Snow Peas, and Water
  Chestnuts
Tuna Tacos
Whipped Tuna Salad

After a repertoire of uncomplicated fish recipes is under your belt and to your family's liking, work up to the more sophisticated tastes of combinations like *Shark with Crumbly Blue Cheese Topping* or *Tilefish Medallions in Sherried Orange Sauce*. If you anticipate some resistance, initially serve such recipes as side dishes (you may choose to make half the amount) along with familiar foods like a rice or pasta casserole.

THE INLAND FISH-EATER

How can you meet the challenge to eat more fish if you live in Nebraska, Colorado, Kansas, or any other inland state? You could turn to upscale water-to-door mail-order services that ship fresh fish to your home, an expensive solution proposed by ads in such sophisticated dailies as the *New York Times* and the *Wall Street Journal*. On the other hand, if your budget is tight, you may feel locked in to frozen, breaded fillets and fish sticks.

The good news is that, according to industry trade journals, affordable, top-quality fresh fish is increasingly on the move to interior sections of the country. According to *Restaurants and Institutions,* fish are now commonly gutted and iced within minutes of catching, then layered in shipping boxes and not touched again until they reach distributors; "the results, especially for inland markets, are superior." Linda Foley—who is vice president of a top-quality seafood processing plant, the M. F. Foley Company of New Bedford, Massachusetts— maintains that "the best piece of scrod can be had at the Cape Cod Room at the Drake in Chicago because the freshest fish gets sent to the heartland of the country."

True, when you move outside of major cities like Chicago, fresh fish is more difficult to come by in inland areas. But all indicators are that markets are expanding to smaller towns. In fact, a 1987 nationwide *Seafood Business* survey of more than 2,000 supermarkets and specialty stores indicates that the demand for fresh seafood is rising in stereotypical beef-eating interior regions. And a number of fish distributors are responding by giving top priority to further market penetration in the Midwest. In part, it's up to you, the consumer, to keep the momentum rolling by repeatedly asking local retailers for more fresh fish.

In the meantime, inland dwellers who don't have easy access to unfrozen fresh seafood have a number of options for making more fish part of their lives. One is frozen fish (uncooked and unbreaded). Correspondence with the Alaska Seafood Marketing Institute made clear their position that frozen seafood is often "fresher" than unfrozen —"modern freezing techniques lock in flavor at the peak of freshness when fish are caught, whereas fresh seafood is in a constant state of decline from the moment it is removed from the water." As a consumer you have to be careful to purchase quality frozen fish—the details are laid out on pages 176–77 of chapter 9.

Review chapter 10's rules for frozen-fish cookery and its discussion of the pros, cons, and how-tos of thawing frozen fish. In addition, guidelines for cooking frozen fish are described at the ends of most of the specific cooking-method descriptions in that chapter.

So go ahead and experiment with frozen fish in the *Eat Fish* Recipes. Don't hesitate to try frozen fish blocks in dishes calling for other kinds of fish—for example, *Sweet 'n' Sour Swordfish, Egg-Coated Salmon and Fresh Spinach Stir-Fry* (partially or completely thaw fish beforehand for these two), *Fillet of Pollock Parmigiana,* and *Cod Fillets with Lemon-Herb Butter.* You can also thaw frozen fish blocks for 20 to 30 minutes or until they can be cut into bite-size chunks with a sharp knife; add to soups, stews, omelettes, and casseroles.

Inland dwellers may also want to rely on frozen-fish entrées, which —according to *Seafood Business*—represent one of the fastest-growing seafood categories. So many come and go in the frozen-food case, however, that it would be futile to attempt to review individual products here. But an evaluation of the nutritional adequacy of more than 350 frozen dinners which I conducted for the *Tufts University Diet & Nutrition Letter* made it clear that health-conscious consumers need to be aware of wide disparities in products.

Considering that dinner should represent about a third of your day's intake, some useful guidelines to apply when selecting a frozen entrée are to select one that offers at least 15 to 19 grams of protein (about a third of the RDA for women and men), no more than 30 percent fat calories (see page 57 in chapter 6 for calculations), a maximum of 1,000 milligrams sodium (700 milligrams or less for people on sodium-restricted diets), and approximately one-third of your day's caloric intake (many provide 300 calories or less). People with hearty appetites may find the portions to be small and can add a large salad with reduced-calorie dressing, a vegetable or two, plus a low-fat grain product if the dinner doesn't come with one.

Those who live in noncoastal areas should come to rely on canned products, too. Just look at all the *Eat Fish* Recipes developed with you in mind—*Dilled Tuna-Salmon Mousse, Shrimp and Salmon Gumbo, Chunky Clam Chowder, Tuna Tacos, Salmon Burgers, Spicy Mackerel Patties, Lemony Curried Creamed Tuna with Almonds,* and *Curried Salmon-Rice Ramekins,* to name just some. By all means be sure to stock a regular supply of canned tuna, salmon, mackerel, baby shrimp, oysters, and clams. Try any one in your favorite soufflé or omelette, scalloped potato, soup, stew, or pizza recipe. (As mentioned earlier, rinsing with water will help to lower sodium content of canned fish.)

Inland dwellers also commonly have access to imitation shellfish products made from surimi. They're certainly low-fat choices, but can't be relied on for omega-3 fatty acids, which are largely lost in processing. Furthermore, salt watchers need to be aware of the high sodium level of imitation seafoods. (Most *Eat Fish* Recipes for shellfish can be adapted for surimi-based products.)

THE *EAT FISH* RESTAURANT DINER

Whether you live inland or "outland," most restaurants carry at least a few fish options on their menus. In reviewing *Seafood Business*'s 1987 restaurant survey of more than 40 seafood chains, I was struck by the number that now offer entrées mesquite-grilled, broiled, baked, and even poached or steamed. At a national conference on the health benefits of fish, columnist and author Jane Brody even described a restaurant that serves *all* fish broiled, poached, or steamed; in tiny print on the menu appears "Fish entrees may be fried upon request"!!

Nevertheless, *Seafood Business* quotes the president of Washington State–based Sea Galley Stores, Inc., as saying, "Despite what they *say* they want, people still order fried." So it's up to you to issue the low-fat call in restaurants—request that fish be cooked by the methods mentioned above rather than fried or smothered in rich sauces. (Be certain, however, to ask if your low-fat-cooked fish is subsequently topped with the infamous ladleful of melted butter.)

Restaurants *will* respond, as evidenced in a National Restaurant Association survey of more than 500 establishments—nearly 75 percent will alter preparation methods upon request. And about 8 out of 10 of these will cook with unsaturated fats rather than butter, lard, or shortening; as many will broil or bake an item instead of fry it. (If you simply cannot part with your butter for lobster, crab, or steamers, ask for lots of lemon wedges. Squeeze them into a bowl, then add a small amount of melted butter and enjoy.)

When it comes to fast-food restaurants, many people kid themselves that they're eating healthfully when they order a fried-fish sandwich. The reality is that fish burgers typically provide more than 400 calories (in the same vicinity as McDonald's Quarter Pounders and Wendy's double hamburgers) and 40 to 50 percent fat calories. If it's fast food you're after, better stick with broiled offerings, which are growing in numbers at places like Long John Silver's and Arthur Treacher's Fish & Chips.

IF YOU WANT TO LOSE WEIGHT

Simply eating more fish is unlikely to make you lose weight, but it *can* help since fish is generally so low in fat. And curtailing fat intake is the name of the game when it comes to losing weight since fat has more calories per ounce than any other nutrient. In addition, mounting evidence suggests that the body has more trouble getting rid of fat calories than carbohydrate calories. While some calories are expended when the body processes any nutrient eaten, it seems that it burns off fewer in metabolizing fat than in handling carbohydrate.

People who want to lose anywhere from 5 to 20 pounds can typically accomplish their goal by simply following the guidelines on the "Making a Low-Fat Diet Part of Your Life" chart on page 326. If you're skeptical, think about the fact that cutting back by 100 calories a day (below the calories required to maintain your current weight) can result in a 10-pound weight loss in a year's time. That means if you use a tablespoon less of mayonnaise and one less of oil or butter each day (recall that each tablespoon of fat provides 100 calories) you could be 20 pounds lighter a year from now!

Individuals who want to lose larger amounts of weight and who choose to do something more aggressive can benefit from a low-calorie diet. The two-week *Eat Fish* Launching Diet gets you off to a safe start by providing fish each day in the context of well-balanced meals that add up to a total of approximately 1,000 daily calories for women and 1,500 calories for men. I've purposely made this diet quite limited because, in my experience, many dieters get off to the most successful start (that is, a fairly quick one) when given specific daily guidelines detailing exactly what they should eat. The meals and *Eat Fish* Recipes included in the Launching Diet are quite simple so you don't have to spend a lot of time in the kitchen.

Many women can expect to lose four or five pounds on the two-week Launching Diet; very active individuals and men may lose even more. As with any diet, it's important to check with your physician before embarking, particularly if you have any medical problems.

I set stringent standards for only two weeks because I want to avoid dieter's doldrums—the boredom that so often brings weight-loss efforts to a screeching halt. Another reason for not staying on a strict diet for too long is that your metabolic rate—the speed with which your body burns off calories—tends to drop when food intake is restricted. Moreover, I believe it's important to be able to make your own decisions about what to eat to help you maintain your weight loss in the long run.

For all of these reasons, I've planned the *Eat Fish* Mix-and-Match Diet—a diet providing ten breakfasts in the 300- to 350-calorie range, ten lunches of approximately 450 calories, ten 550-calorie suppers, and ten 150-calorie snacks; men get 500 daily bonus calories. The idea is for you to take responsibility for selecting each of your meals from the ten possibilities. Many people can expect to lose another pound each week on the Mix-and-Match Diet. (Even nondieters can use the two diets to get ideas about how to plan nutritious meals and how to incorporate more fish into their daily menus.)

WHO NEEDS TO LOSE WEIGHT?

To determine whether you're carrying too much fat, you could turn to insurance-company charts that spell out desirable weights for given heights and body-frame sizes. But for some people—namely those who've had a lifelong weight battle—it's nearly impossible to attain what the chart spells out. Yet many much thinner individuals fear they'd be "fat" if they weighed in at the number of pounds dictated by the charts. (It's true that individuals who have a weight-related medical problem such as hypertension or diabetes may be healthier weighing less than the charts say.)

In recent years, a National Institutes of Health panel on the health implications of obesity decided that a "hazardous" weight is one that's 20 percent or more above Metropolitan Life Insurance Company chart values so commonly seen in doctors' offices. For obesity is associated with high blood pressure, the adult form of diabetes, high blood cholesterol, and certain forms of cancer. But the jury is still out on the risks of being mildly to moderately overweight when you have no other medical problems.

Since "ideal" weight is such an individual matter, my personal feeling is that you should try to reach and maintain the weight at which you feel good about yourself and at which you have no major medical problems. It should also be a value that you can maintain without undue psychological suffering—if a healthy woman can comfortably stay at 130 pounds, but she constantly struggles to weigh 125, I'd say she's better off with the extra 5 pounds.

KEEPING THE WEIGHT OFF

It's nothing new, but I'll repeat what women's magazines and diet programs have been saying for some time now—to lose weight permanently, you've got to change the habits (or behaviors) that made you chubby in the first place. If not, you may join the 95 percent of all people who lose weight only to gain it back within 5 years.

A full-scale course on behavior modification is beyond the scope of this book, but the kinds of habits you need to change include your buying patterns—if fattening foods aren't around the house, you can't eat them. When tempting items are available, keep them out of sight rather than on countertops, coffee tables, and desks. Don't set yourself up for purchasing volumes of snack foods by going grocery shopping when you're hungry. And avoid waiting so long between meals that you're ravenous enough to eat anything that comes your way.

It helps some people to eat more slowly so they appreciate what they're eating and feel more control over food. Others benefit by making eating a "pure" activity—that is, by not doing other things like reading or walking around at the same time.

Social situations can be dealt with by preplanning what you'll eat, saving up some of your calories for special foods. It's important to allow yourself occasional treats so you don't feel deprived, predisposing you to binge eating. Establish realistic goals which set the stage for accomplishment rather than failure. After all, isn't it more likely that someone who's accustomed to eating ice cream every night will succeed at having ice cream once or twice a week rather than an unreasonable "never again"?

People who overeat in response to anxiety, unhappiness, or work-related pressure can benefit by generating lists of alternate activities that really will make them feel better. (Eating invariably offers only a temporary way to soothe the soul.) More appropriate ways of comforting yourself include going for a bike ride or walk, calling a supportive friend or relative, buying yourself a new article of clothing, or reading a good book.

THE IMPORTANCE OF EXERCISE

The last-place position of the subject of exercise in no way captures the importance I place on physical activity as a means of weight control. In fact, the longer I worked with obese people, the more convinced I became of the benefits of regular exercise. For just as cutting back on calories here and there can lead to substantial weight loss with time, so can manageable amounts of exercise.

Consider that a brisk half-hour walk just 4 times a week could result in a loss of about 20 pounds a year for a 150-pound person—and that's without dieting (assuming he doesn't eat as many extra calories as his walk is burning off). Exercise may also counteract the drop in metabolic rate that occurs when calorie intake is restricted. Still another way to look at exercise is that you get to eat more food if you simply want to maintain your weight—a several-mile run equals a dish of ice cream! Exercise also tends to lift your spirits and can alleviate stress that could lead to overeating.

Exercise doesn't have to be strenuous to be of value—walking is an excellent form of exercise that most anyone can do. If you choose something more aggressive—like jogging, swimming, or aerobic classes—be sure that you like the activity and can fit it into your lifestyle or you'll never stay with it. As with food-related goals, be realistic about exercise—start out slowly and plan to give yourself at least two days off each week. (I recommend checking with your physician before starting an exercise program, especially if you've been sedentary for years.)

You can also benefit by working more physical activity into your daily routine. Take stairs instead of elevators and escalators, for instance. And walk rather than ride anytime you have the opportunity. Park your car at the far sides of parking lots. At work, try to take frequent "move-around" breaks, particularly if you have a desk-type job.

TWO FULL-OF-FISH DIETS

Following are the two-week *Eat Fish* Launching Diet and the *Eat Fish* Mix-and-Match Diet. Stay on the Launching Diet for the first two weeks, then switch over to the Mix-and-Match Diet. It's perfectly fine to stay on the Mix-and-Match Diet until you reach your weight goal, provided you consume breakfast, lunch, dinner, and a snack each day *and* you select a wide variety of meals from the different possibilities.

If you find that you lose too slowly or not at all on the Mix-and-Match Diet, it's okay to switch back to the Launching Diet for another two weeks provided you've previously had a full two weeks on the Mix-and-Match Diet. You can keep alternating the two diets for two-week periods until your goal is reached. Women who stay on the diets for longer than a month should be aware, however, that they may need extra iron and zinc, particularly if the meals containing liver and oysters aren't consumed. In these cases, it's wise to take a multi-vitamin-mineral supplement.

In general, men and women who diet for any length of time (say, more than a month or two) may benefit from a combination multi-vitamin-mineral product. A good supplement provides levels *no higher than US RDA levels* for the following nutrients: vitamins A, C, D, E, B_6, and B_{12}; and thiamine, riboflavin, niacin, folic acid, iron, calcium, iodine, magnesium, copper, and zinc. It may also include vitamin K, biotin, pantothenic acid, phosphorus, chromium, selenium, molybdenum, manganese, potassium, and chloride. There's no need for an expensive product—a store brand will do, and you probably only need to take a pill every other day. (I don't recommend taking supplements of single nutrients.)

Once you weigh what you'd like, gradually add more "First-Choice Foods" (from the chart on page 326) until your weight stabilizes. You can start by adding an extra 200 to 300 calories to your total day's intake. Do that for about a week, but if you're still losing, add another 100 to 200 daily calories each 4 to 7 days until you're at a standstill. (Some small women will find that they maintain their weight on not much more than 1,500 calories per day.)

It's not a bad idea to pick up a pocket calorie-counter book to help familiarize yourself with calorie values of foods. Table 13 offers some general guidelines.

Some generalities

If certain fruits or vegetables on the diet menu plans are unavailable, it's acceptable to occasionally substitute a serving of another item from the same general food group. When strawberries are not in season, for instance, you may have an orange instead. In selecting fruits, try to stick with fresh ones (of medium size) as much as possible—if they're unavailable, you may substitute products canned in water or unsweetened fruit juice, as well as frozen fruits (without added sugar). Unless stated otherwise, assume that cooked vegetables are fresh, frozen (without salt), or canned (without salt), and are steamed or boiled for a short time in a covered pan with a small amount of water. Salad dressings should contain no more than 30 calories per tablespoon.

TABLE 13. Approximate Calorie Content of the Major Food Groups

Food Group	Approximate Calorie Content
Milk products:	
1%-fat milk, 1 cup	100
plain, low-fat yogurt, 1 cup	150
low-fat cheese, 1½ ounces (2 grams fat per ounce)	75
low-fat cottage cheese, 1 cup	200
Low-fat protein foods, 1 ounce cooked:	
very low-fat fish	30
skinless poultry	45
lean meat	55
Fruits—½ cup cooked, 1 cup raw, 1 medium fresh fruit, or ½ cup juice	60 to 80
Vegetables (nonstarchy)—½ cup cooked or 1 cup raw	25 to 30
Grain products (see chart on page 326 for serving sizes)	70 to 100

As they're described on the menus, all foods are prepared without added fats, salt, and sugar unless specified differently or unless they're part of a standard recipe. It's okay for most people to use small amounts of salt in cooking or at the table—but remember that each half-teaspoon you add contains about 1,200 milligrams of sodium. Your goal should be to stay below 3,300 milligrams of sodium each day. (The Launching Diet contains an average of about 2,000 milligrams of daily sodium, while the Mix-and-Match Diet has an average of approximately 2,300 milligrams. Note that these values do not account for the additional foods for men nor for salt that you add.) When you use salt, be certain to choose the iodized type—check product labels; "sea salt" does not contain substantial amounts of iodine.

Since it's very difficult to meet the RDAs for calcium and vitamin D if you don't drink milk, both diets incorporate plenty of milk as a beverage and in cooked foods. Don't forget to "count" milk that you add to coffee and tea—each quarter-cup of 1%-fat milk has 25 calories. If you use more than a quarter-cup a day in hot beverages, you should take it from your daily allotment for milk. If you can't drink milk, it would be a good idea to check with your physician and/or a dietitian about how to meet your calcium and vitamin D needs. Skim milk can be substituted for 1%-fat milk and will save you about 15 calories per cup.

Both the Launching Diet and the Mix-and-Match Diet are designed to meet the nutritional needs of the average healthy adult; they're not geared for pregnant or breast-feeding women, teenagers, children, or sick people. Therefore, if you have any health problems or if you're on a special diet for a medical reason, be especially careful to check with your doctor before following the diets in this chapter.

The only beverages planned with meals are milk and fruit juice. But there are plenty of additional ideas on the "Free Foods" list at the end of the Mix-and-Match Diet. Be sure to drink plenty of water or other liquids throughout the day.

When meals call for bread, select loaves with average-size slices (60 to 70 calories per slice). Those extra-large slices you can now buy have more calories and will bring you over the diets' limits. It is acceptable to substitute another kind of bread for the one specified. If you choose to use regular margarine instead of reduced-calorie margarine, add 17 calories per teaspoon.

Anytime you're on a diet, it helps to plan ahead for each meal (better still, a whole day in advance) and to keep track of everything you eat by writing down each item in a food diary. I also advise weighing and measuring foods for at least a few days to familiarize yourself with portion sizes. Cooked foods should be weighed after they're done. Remember that you need to buy a bit more raw fish, poultry, or meat than a menu plan calls for because you may lose 20 to 30 percent of the weight in cooking. Thus, to wind up with a 3-ounce portion of *cooked* fish or meat, you may need to purchase between 4 and 4½ ounces *raw*.

Items in italics on the two diets are *Eat Fish* Recipes—to locate them, see the recipe index on page 365. Menus in the diets that include *Eat Fish* Recipes are based on one serving of each recipe.

For men only

Men should consume an extra 500 calories per day on both the Launching Diet and the Mix-and-Match Diet. To stay in keeping with healthful guidelines, the extra foods should come primarily from "First-Choice Foods" listed on page 326. Selections should come from a variety of food groups. A reasonable combination of "extras" that would amount to about 500 calories is as follows: 2 grain products, 2 fruits, 2 ounces of protein, and 1 tablespoon of "First-Choice" fats. To put this plan to work, you could add a slice of whole-wheat toast with a teaspoon of margarine at breakfast, make a lunchtime open-faced sandwich a closed one and add 2 teaspoons of reduced-calorie mayonnaise, increase the protein-food serving size by 1 ounce both at lunch and at supper, and add a full cup of fruit juice to a snack. (See table 13 on page 339 for an idea of how many calories are in each of the major food groups.)

THE *EAT FISH* LAUNCHING DIET

The *Eat Fish* Launching Diet provides you with menu plans for two weeks. Before starting, carefully read through the diet and stock up on the foods called for in the menu plans. Some items involving preparation are used several times during the same week so you only have to make them once. For convenience's sake and economizing, some foods are leftovers from the day before. If you need ideas for carrying a lunch to work, see the "Brown-Bag Tips" intermingled with the Mix-and-Match lunches starting on page 353. Be sure to check out the "Free Foods" list on page 363.

The 14 daily menu plans can be eaten in any order you choose—if you can't get fresh catfish, for instance, the Day 7 plan can be eaten on Day 9. The important thing is to follow each menu plan—eating all of the day's foods in the designated amounts—once during the 14 days. Although days can be switched on the diet, try not to switch single meals—don't swap one day's lunch for another's, for instance, unless you really dislike a given meal. You may, however, save some items listed for a given day as between-meal snacks—for example, on Day 14 the orange gelatin dessert and gingersnaps from supper can be saved for later in the evening. The amounts of vegetables in salads are approximate—you don't have to be fanatic about measuring them. Remember that fruits can be substituted when not in season. When the 14 days are up, advance to the *Eat Fish* Mix-and-Match Diet.

Day 1

Breakfast: 1 small bran muffin (1½ ounces)
1 cup 1%-fat milk
½ grapefruit

Lunch: 4 halved apricots stuffed with ½ cup low-fat cottage cheese, served on bed of leaf lettuce
1 cup beef-vegetable soup (canned is okay)
6 Ry Krisp (2 triple crackers)

Supper: 3 ounces broiled salmon with lemon juice and tarragon
½ cup cooked curly pasta (packed), mixed with ½ cup each of steamed, chopped broccoli, cauliflower, and red pepper, sprinkled with 1 tablespoon grated Parmesan cheese
Spinach salad:
1½ cups chopped spinach
⅓ cup sliced mushrooms
½ medium tomato
2 tablespoons reduced-calorie Thousand Island dressing
¾-inch slice watermelon

Day 2

Breakfast: 1 ounce Special K cereal
¾ cup 1%-fat milk
½ cup strawberries, sliced

Lunch: 2 ounces lean roast beef on 1 slice rye bread with dark green lettuce leaves and 2 teaspoons Dijon mustard
¾ cup each of raw cauliflower and broccoli flowerets with ¼ cup plain yogurt seasoned with dill weed or curry powder
1 apple

Supper: 1 serving *Spicy Mackerel Patties*
1 cup steamed spinach with lemon juice
Large tossed salad:
    2 cups shredded romaine lettuce
    ½ carrot, sliced
    1 medium tomato, sliced
    2 tablespoons reduced-calorie French dressing
1 cup 1%-fat milk
½ cup sugar-free orange (or any other flavor) gelatin with ⅓ cup crushed pineapple

Day 3

Breakfast: ½ cup low-fat cottage cheese with ½ sliced banana and ¼ cup crushed pineapple
½ whole-wheat bagel with 1 teaspoon reduced-calorie margarine

Lunch: 2 ounces skinless turkey breast on 1 slice oatmeal bread with 2 teaspoons reduced-calorie mayonnaise and dark green lettuce leaves
8 cherry tomatoes
⅛ honeydew melon

Supper: Steamed vegetable-cheese medley:
    Steam or microwave-cook until just crunchy-tender:
    ¾ cup broccoli flowerets
    ¾ cup cauliflower
    12 mushrooms, cleaned and trimmed
    1 medium red pepper, cut in strips
    Top steamed vegetables with 2 slices low-fat cheese
    (about 1⅓ ounces, 2 grams fat per ounce) and re-
    cover, allowing steam to melt the cheese
1 serving *Dilled Tuna-Salmon Mousse* on bed of dark greens
1 small, enriched hard roll with 1 teaspoon reduced-calorie margarine
½ cup sugar-free vanilla pudding

Day 4

Breakfast: Poached egg on ½ whole wheat English muffin and topped
with 1 slice low-fat cheese—broil until melted
4 ounces orange juice

Lunch: 1 serving *Dilled Tuna-Salmon Mousse* on dark greens
(leftover from Day 3)
6 rye Melba toast rounds
½ cup lemon low-fat yogurt with ½ cup green grapes

Supper: 3 ounces poached cod or haddock topped with ¼ cup salsa
1½ cups steamed zucchini and carrot coins
1 small baked potato, 2 tablespoons plain low-fat yogurt,
and chives
1 cup 1%-fat milk
3 Vanilla Wafers

Day 5

Breakfast: 1 ounce Cheerios cereal
½ cup blueberries
¾ cup 1%-fat milk

Lunch: ½ cup *Whipped Tuna Salad*
Iceberg lettuce wedge (or any other type) with 1
tablespoon reduced-calorie Russian dressing
1 carrot, cut in sticks
1 large plum

Supper: Steamed beef and vegetables:
In a large, nonstick skillet combine, cover, and steam
the following, stirring occasionally:
3 ounces lean beef (e.g., top round), cut in strips
½ red pepper, cut in strips
1 cup broccoli flowerets
¾ cup trimmed pea pods
1 tablespoon soy sauce
2 tablespoons dry sherry
½ cup cooked enriched white rice
1½ cups tossed greens with lemon juice and 1 tablespoon
grated Parmesan cheese
½ cup vanilla low-fat yogurt with 10 pitted black cherries

Day 6

Breakfast: 1 cup cooked oatmeal (no salt added in cooking) with ½ cup 1%-fat milk and 1 tablespoon raisins
4 ounces orange juice

Lunch: 1 cup tomato soup (made with 1%-fat milk—canned soup is acceptable) topped with 1 ounce shredded part-skim mozzarella cheese and 6 rye or wheat Melba toast rounds, crumbled
½ cucumber, cut in spears
1 cup red or green grapes

Supper: 20 small steamed clams—just over 3 ounces of cooked meats (you can substitute the same weight of drained, canned clams)
1 tomato, halved and broiled with basil
1 slice enriched French bread with 1 teaspoon reduced-calorie margarine
1 cup shredded raw cabbage with caraway or celery seeds and 3 tablespoons plain, low-fat yogurt
¾-inch slice watermelon

Day 7

Breakfast: Mushroom-cheese omelette (made in nonstick skillet with vegetable spray):
2 eggs
2 tablespoons 1%-fat milk
1 ounce shredded low-fat block cheese or part-skim mozzarella cheese (no more than 5 grams fat per ounce)
⅓ cup sliced, steamed mushrooms
½ cup grapefruit juice

Lunch: ½ cup *Whipped Tuna Salad* (left from Day 5) on 1 slice rye or pumpernickel bread with dark green lettuce leaves
Carrot and celery sticks
1 cup 1%-fat milk
1 tangerine

Supper: 1 serving *Mexicano Catfish Fillets* (If you don't have a
            microwave oven, you can substitute *Cheese-Topped Baked
            Fish Fillets* on page 267.)
            1 cup steamed asparagus
            2 cups tossed greens with 2 tablespoons reduced-calorie
            Italian dressing
            1 cup strawberries sprinkled with 1 teaspoon confectioners'
            sugar

Day 8

Breakfast: 1 ounce bran flakes (fortified with iron)
            ½ cup strawberries, sliced
            ¾ cup 1%-fat milk

Lunch: Chef's salad:
                1 ounce low-fat cheese, shredded
                1 ounce lean ham slivers
                2 cups chopped romaine lettuce
                1 medium tomato, sliced
                ¼ cucumber, sliced
                2 tablespoons reduced-calorie Italian dressing
            ½ cup sliced peaches in ¼ cup evaporated skim milk with
            nutmeg

Supper: Garlicky steamed shrimp and vegetables:
                In a large, nonstick skillet, combine, cover, and steam
                    the following, stirring occasionally:
                6 ounces raw shrimp, cleaned—about 4 ounces cooked
                    (you can substitute 4 ounces of rinsed, canned shrimp)
                1 cup broccoli flowerets
                1 cup trimmed pea pods
                ½ cup sliced mushrooms
                1 to 2 minced or pressed garlic cloves
                1 tablespoon soy sauce
                2 tablespoons dry white wine
            ½ cup cooked brown or white rice
            ½ cup sugar-free orange gelatin with ⅓ cup shredded
            carrots and ⅓ cup crushed pineapple—top with ½ cup
            lemon low-fat yogurt

Day 9

Breakfast: 1 slice raisin toast with 1 tablespoon peanut butter
1 cup hot cocoa made with 1%-fat milk and sugar-free cocoa mix

Lunch: 2 ounces lean ham on 1 slice rye bread with 2 teaspoons Dijon mustard
1 cup Manhattan clam chowder (canned is acceptable)
1 pear

Supper: 1 serving *Broiled Basil Swordfish*
Boiled parslied potato slices (1 small potato)
1 cup steamed spinach with nutmeg and lemon juice
1½ cups cantaloupe and honeydew melon balls

Day 10

Breakfast: ½ cup low-fat cottage cheese topped with ⅓ cup unsweetened applesauce sprinkled with cinnamon
1 slice whole wheat toast with 1 teaspoon reduced-calorie margarine

Lunch: Low-calorie oyster stew:
    Thoroughly mix 1 tablespoon flour with 1 cup cold 1%-fat milk
    Stir constantly over medium heat until boiling
    Add 9 medium oysters—just over 2 ounces of cooked meats (the same weight of drained, canned oysters may be substituted for fresh)
    Season to taste with salt, pepper, cumin
10 enriched oyster crackers
Spinach salad:
    1½ cups chopped spinach
    6 cherry tomatoes
    ⅓ cup sliced mushrooms
    2 tablespoons reduced-calorie Italian dressing

Supper: 1 serving *Spicy Tomato-Cod Curry*
½ cup cooked brown rice
1 cup steamed green beans
1 orange, sectioned and mixed in ½ cup plain low-fat yogurt with low-calorie sweetener and sprinkled with nutmeg
1 fig bar

Day 11

Breakfast: Health shake:
Combine in blender until smooth:
1 cup 1%-fat milk
2 tablespoons toasted wheat germ
1 banana
¼ teaspoon vanilla extract
Low-calorie sweetener, to taste
¼ medium cantaloupe

Lunch: Curried mussel-fruit salad:
2 ounces cooked mussel meats (you can substitute the same weight of drained, canned mussels or clams)
1½ cups shredded leaf lettuce
1 sectioned tangerine
⅓ cup green grapes, halved
3 tablespoons curried yogurt dressing (add ⅛ teaspoon curry powder to low-fat plain yogurt)
1 small whole-wheat roll (or 1 slice whole-wheat bread) with 1 teaspoon reduced-calorie margarine

Supper: 3 ounces sautéed calves' liver (with 2 teaspoons regular margarine and 1 small, sliced onion) Note: Liver is recommended for its iron content, but lean beef, such as top round, may be substituted.
1 tomato, halved and broiled with 1 tablespoon grated Parmesan cheese
1 cup steamed carrots with dill
½ cup sugar-free vanilla pudding

Day 12

Breakfast: 1 cup plain low-fat yogurt mixed with ½ sliced banana, ½ cup blueberries, and low-calorie sweetener
1 graham cracker (2 squares)

Lunch: 1 large tomato stuffed with 2 ounces chicken mixed with 3 tablespoons chopped celery, 1 tablespoon reduced-calorie mayonnaise, 2 tablespoons plain yogurt, and seasonings of your choice
4 saltines
1 cup 1%-fat milk (optional: with ¼ teaspoon vanilla, nutmeg, and low-calorie sweetener)

Supper: 1 serving *Simple Sole Amandine* (If you don't have a microwave oven, you may substitute *Cheesy Fish Fillets* on page 249.)
1 cup steamed broccoli with 1 slice low-fat cheese (about ⅔ ounce)—after broccoli is done, top with cheese and replace cover until cheese is melted by steam
½ sliced cucumber in ¼ cup plain yogurt with chives and 1 tablespoon chopped red onion

Day 13

Breakfast: 1 small corn muffin
1 cup 1%-fat milk
½ grapefruit

Lunch: Fruit salad:
    ½ sliced apple
    ½ cup halved red or green grapes
    ½ cup pineapple chunks
    ½ medium orange
    Serve on bed of greens and top with ½ cup low-fat cottage cheese
1 graham cracker (2 squares)

Supper: 3 ounces baked pollock prepared with 1 slice low-fat cheese and 1 tablespoon unseasoned bread crumbs
1 cup shredded carrots with 1 tablespoon raisins, 1 tablespoon reduced-calorie mayonnaise, and 2 tablespoons plain yogurt
1 cup steamed Brussels sprouts with ¼ cup sliced water chestnuts

Day 14

Breakfast: 1 cup strawberries (or 1 cup mixed fruit left from Day 13's lunch) topped with ⅓ cup part-skim ricotta cheese
1 slice whole-wheat or oatmeal toast with 1 teaspoon reduced-calorie margarine

Lunch: 3 ounces canned salmon mixed with 1 cup shredded iceberg or leaf lettuce, ½ chopped green pepper, and 2 tablespoons reduced-calorie French dressing
6 sesame or rye Melba toast rounds
1 medium orange

Supper:
> 3-ounce pork chop, broiled and trimmed of fat
> 1 cup boiled cabbage with caraway seeds
> ½ cup sliced beets
> ½ cup sugar-free orange gelatin with ½ cup lemon low-fat yogurt
> 2 gingersnaps

THE *EAT FISH* MIX-AND-MATCH DIET

The *Eat Fish* Mix-and-Match Diet allows you a choice of 10 breakfasts, 10 lunches, 10 suppers, and 10 snacks; select one of each on a daily basis. It's important to consume all of the foods in a given meal or snack, but some of the items may be saved for between meals. Try to select a variety of meals from within the options to assure a well-balanced diet—use the recommended number of servings from each of the major food groups described on page 326 to guide you. For example, if you don't select a breakfast with a good vitamin C source, make sure one of your other meals provides citrus fruit, strawberries, broccoli, or the like. Remember, too, to consume 3 to 7 fish meals a week, selecting a mix of high-, medium-, and low-fat types.

The total diet is designed to be nutritionally adequate and, on average, provide less than 300 mg. of cholesterol per day and less than 30 percent of total calories from fat. For each meal, you'll see values listed for calories, percentage of calories from fat, cholesterol, and sodium. (Nutrition information is approximate.) You can use these values to guide your total day's selections—for example, try not to have two or more of the higher-sodium meals in one day. If sodium concerns you, page 71 has suggestions for decreasing your intake. Again, be sure to see the "Free Foods" list on page 363.

Mix-and-Match Breakfasts

Select any one of the following as your morning meal. Most of the breakfasts are quick and easy to prepare, and they consist of readily available foods.

Breakfast 1

Fruit crunch:
½ cup *each* of fresh sliced peaches, blueberries, and raspberries (or any other fresh fruit), topped with ¼ cup Grape-Nuts cereal
Pour over all ½ cup evaporated skim milk mixed with ⅛ teaspoon almond extract and low-calorie sweetener, to taste

Calories: 309   Percentage of calories from fat: 3%   Cholesterol: 5 mg. Sodium: 349 mg.

Breakfast 2

2 whole-wheat pancakes (4-inch)
2 tablespoons reduced-calorie maple syrup
½ grapefruit
1 cup 1%-fat milk

Calories: 316   Percentage of calories from fat: 16%   Cholesterol: 50 mg. Sodium: 443 mg.

Breakfast 3

1 cup sliced strawberries, topped with ⅓ cup part-skim ricotta cheese
1 slice whole-wheat toast with 1 teaspoon reduced-calorie margarine and 1 teaspoon cinnamon sugar
⅓ cup prune juice or apricot nectar

Calories: 352   Percentage of calories from fat: 26%   Cholesterol: 25 mg. Sodium: 305 mg.

Breakfast 4

1 cup bran flakes (fortified with iron) with ½ sliced banana and 1 tablespoon raisins
¾ cup 1%-fat milk
1 tangerine or small orange

Calories: 347   Percentage of calories from fat: 8%   Cholesterol: 7.5 mg. Sodium: 525 mg.

Breakfast 5

1 slice raisin toast spread with 1 tablespoon peanut butter
½ grapefruit with 1 teaspoon honey
1 cup hot cocoa made with 1%-fat milk and sugar-free
cocoa mix

*Calories: 343   Percentage of calories from fat: 31%   Cholesterol: 10 mg.
Sodium: 332 mg.*

Breakfast 6

2 whole shredded-wheat biscuits topped with ½ cup
blueberries (if blueberries are unavailable, substitute sliced
strawberries or ½ banana) and 1 teaspoon brown sugar
1 cup 1%-fat milk

*Calories: 326   Percentage of calories from fat: 9%   Cholesterol: 10 mg.
Sodium: 129 mg.*

Breakfast 7

1 cup cooked oatmeal (no salt added in cooking) with ½
cup 1%-fat milk and 1 tablespoon chopped dates
⅛ medium honeydew melon (or ¼ cantaloupe)
½ cup apple cider or juice

*Calories: 344   Percentage of calories from fat: 10%   Cholesterol: 5 mg.
Sodium: 83 mg.*

Breakfast 8

½ cup low-fat cottage cheese topped with ⅓ cup
unsweetened applesauce and cinnamon
1 whole-wheat English muffin with 2 teaspoons reduced-
calorie margarine
½ cup grapefruit juice

*Calories: 355   Percentage of calories from fat: 16%   Cholesterol: 5 mg.
Sodium: 962 mg.*

Breakfast 9

Health shake:
Combine ingredients in blender until smooth:
1 cup 1%-fat milk
2 tablespoons toasted wheat germ
1 banana
¼ teaspoon vanilla extract
Low-calorie sweetener, to taste
¼ medium cantaloupe

Calories: 350   Percentage of calories from fat: 13%   Cholesterol: 10 mg.
Sodium: 145 mg.

Breakfast 10

1 egg, scrambled with a splash of low-fat milk and 1
tablespoon grated Parmesan cheese (cooked in a nonstick
skillet)
1 medium corn muffin (about 2 ounces)
4 ounces orange juice

Calories: 358   Percentage of calories from fat: 34%   Cholesterol: 309 mg.
Sodium: 549 mg.

Mix-and-Match Lunches

Select any one of the following for a noontime meal. The lunches are
designed for eating at home or at work. Since nutritious lunches pose
a problem for brown-baggers, tips are included for most meals.
(Again, amounts of vegetables in salads are approximate.)

Lunch 1

Yogurt-fruit salad:
½ sectioned orange
½ cup green grapes
½ sliced banana
1 cup plain low-fat yogurt
Low-calorie sweetener, to taste
2 tablespoons slivered almonds (for topping)
1 small bran muffin

Brown-bag tips: The salad can be made ahead of time at home, but add the almonds at work. If you don't have refrigeration where you work, pack the salad with a commercial ice pack. (One of those tiny one-person coolers is ideal.)

Calories: 455   Percentage of calories from fat: 31%   Cholesterol: 35 mg. Sodium: 330 mg.

Lunch 2

1½ cups *Chunky Clam Chowder*
15 enriched oyster crackers
Romaine lettuce salad:
    1½ cups shredded romaine lettuce
    6 cherry tomatoes
    ½ carrot, sliced
    2 tablespoons reduced-calorie Thousand Island dressing
1 large plum

Brown-bag tips: Clam chowder can be heated at home and carried in a thermos. The salad could be left over from the night before. (If you make a large salad after work—drying the lettuce well and storing the assembled salad loosely in a large, covered plastic container or bowl—it will keep for days. All you have to do when you pack your lunch is grab a handful and plop it in a smaller plastic container.) Carry the salad dressing in a separate tiny jar and add it at work.

Calories: 443   Percentage of calories from fat: 15%   Cholesterol: 54 mg. Sodium: 1,182 mg.

Lunch 3

½ cup *Whipped Tuna Salad* on 2 slices whole-wheat bread
½ cucumber, cut in spears
1 cup 1%-fat milk
10 black cherries

Brown-bag tips: Carry tuna separately from bread to avoid a soggy sandwich. See Lunch 1 for ideas about keeping food cold. If you can't purchase low-fat milk at work, take it in a small thermos.

Calories: 439   Percentage of calories from fat: 21%   Cholesterol: 45 mg. Sodium: 878 mg.

Lunch 4

Omelette:
1 egg, beaten with 1 egg white and several tablespoons
  1%-fat milk
1 ounce shredded crabmeat
1 ounce shredded low-fat cheese (no more than 5 grams
  fat per ounce)
2 tablespoons chopped green pepper
2 teaspoons reduced-calorie margarine (to grease pan)
1 sliced tomato (to top omelette)

Spinach salad:
1½ cups chopped spinach
¼ cup shredded carrot
2 tablespoons reduced-calorie French dressing
4 crumbled Melba toast rounds (to top salad)

1 medium orange

(Because it has to be cooked right before eating, this meal is best saved for weekends—it would make a super brunch.)

Calories: 446   Percentage of calories from fat: 35%   Cholesterol: 303 mg. Sodium: 959 mg.

Lunch 5

Open-faced *Salmon Burger* on ½ enriched hard roll
8 cherry tomatoes
1 cup 1%-fat milk
¼ cantaloupe

Brown-bag tips: Salmon burgers have to be made ahead for this one. You can make a batch, use one the next day, refrigerate another for several days later, and freeze the remaining two. For work, keep things cold as suggested for Lunch 1. You can either eat the burger cold or —if your workplace has a hot plate or microwave—warm it.

Calories: 500   Percentage of calories from fat: 27%   Cholesterol: 122 mg. Sodium: 963 mg.

Lunch 6

Tuna melt:
  Top 1 split and toasted whole-wheat English muffin
  with 2 ounces flaked white canned tuna, 2 slices low-
  fat cheese (no more than 2 grams fat per ounce), and 2
  large tomato slices
  Broil until cheese melts
Cauliflower and broccoli flowerets
1 pear

Brown-bag tips: Tuna melts require a toaster oven, which many workplaces have. Pack ingredients in separate containers and keep them cold until ready to assemble. If your workplace has no toaster oven, you can enjoy this sandwich cold.

Calories: 436   Percentage of calories from fat: 12%   Cholesterol: 33 mg. Sodium: 1,235 mg.

Lunch 7

½ large whole-wheat (or regular) pita bread stuffed with
½ cup regular cottage cheese mixed with chives and
microwaved at full power until cottage cheese is hot (Trust
me—it's delicious! You can use low-fat cottage cheese, but
the consistency of it melted isn't as good.)
1 carrot cut into sticks
½ cup pineapple chunks mixed with ⅔ cup lemon low-fat
yogurt

Brown-bag tips: Again, pack foods in separate containers and keep them cold until ready to eat. If your workplace doesn't have a microwave, the sandwich will still be good cold.

Calories: 459   Percentage of calories from fat: 15%   Cholesterol: 17 mg. Sodium: 789 mg.

Lunch 8

Spinach-shrimp salad:
  2 cups chopped spinach
  2 ounces cleaned, cooked shrimp (or canned, rinsed
  shrimp)
  ½ cup canned chickpeas
  2 tablespoons reduced-calorie Italian dressing
¾ cup sugar-free vanilla pudding with 1 sliced nectarine

Brown-bag tips: For a fresh-tasting salad, don't toss ingredients until just before your meal.

Calories: 424   Percentage of calories from fat: 20%   Cholesterol: 112 mg. Sodium: 1,532 mg.

Lunch 9

> 3 ounces broiled swordfish (cooked with 1 teaspoon melted reduced-calorie margarine, lemon juice, and parsley)
> 1½ cups tossed salad with 2 tablespoons reduced-calorie French dressing
> 1 small baked potato, 1 teaspoon reduced-calorie margarine, and 1 tablespoon grated Parmesan cheese
> 1 cup fresh strawberries sprinkled with 2 teaspoons confectioners' sugar

(This lunch is designed for restaurant dining. Many restaurants can accommodate the simple special requests involved for this meal.)

Calories: 453   Percentage of calories from fat: 32%   Cholesterol: 50 mg. Sodium: 539 mg.

Lunch 10

> Chicken-grape salad:
>> 2 ounces skinless cooked chicken breast, chopped
>> 1 tablespoon reduced-calorie mayonnaise
>> 2 tablespoons plain yogurt
>> 2 tablespoons chopped celery
>> ⅓ cup green grapes, halved
>> Pinch of curry powder (optional)
>> Large bed of Bibb lettuce leaves
> 1 slice rye bread
> 1 cup 1%-fat milk
> 1 apple

Brown-bag tips: You can double the salad ingredients to make enough for 2 days' lunches. Keep things cold by following Lunch 1's instructions.

Calories: 431   Percentage of calories from fat: 11%   Cholesterol: 65 mg. Sodium: 366 mg.

Mix-and-Match Suppers

Pick any one of the meals below for supper. For the suppers that suggest *Eat Fish* Recipes, I intentionally chose easy-to-prepare selections to save you time.

Supper 1

> 1 serving *Broiled Honey-Lime Salmon with Tarragon*
> 1 cup sliced carrots with *petits-pois* (small peas)
> Parslied potato slices (1 small potato)
> ½ cup lime (or any other flavor) sugar-free gelatin with 1 sectioned tangerine and topped with ¼ cup lemon yogurt

Calories: 539   Percentage of calories from fat: 23%   Cholesterol: 87 mg. Sodium: 436 mg.

Supper 2

> 1 serving *Cheesy Fish Fillets*
> ½ cup stewed tomatoes (regular canned is acceptable)
> 1 cup green beans marinated in wine vinegar, dill weed, and 2 teaspoons vegetable oil
> 1 small baked potato, topped with 2 tablespoons plain yogurt with chives
> ¾-inch slice watermelon

Calories: 564   Percentage of calories from fat: 31%   Cholesterol: 95 mg. Sodium: 717 mg.

Supper 3

> 1 serving *Broiled Basil Swordfish*
> ½ cup cooked curly pasta (packed), mixed with ⅓ cup each of steamed, chopped broccoli and red pepper, sprinkled with 1 tablespoon grated Parmesan cheese
> 1½ cups chopped romaine lettuce with 6 cherry tomatoes and 2 tablespoons reduced-calorie French dressing
> ½ cup vanilla ice milk

Calories: 521   Percentage of calories from fat: 29%   Cholesterol: 74 mg. Sodium: 657 mg.

Supper 4

1 serving *Spanish Mackerel Steaks Grilled with Mustardy Topping*
1 cup steamed asparagus
1 ear corn (or ½ cup frozen)
Slim slaw:
    1 cup shredded cabbage
    ⅓ cup shredded carrot
    1 tablespoon reduced-calorie mayonnaise
    2 tablespoons plain yogurt
    Seasonings to taste (e.g., lemon juice, pepper, celery seed)
1 cup 1%-fat milk

Calories: 543   Percentage of calories from fat: 28%   Cholesterol: 88 mg. Sodium: 380 mg.

Supper 5

1 serving *Escalloped Scallops*
1 cup cooked, sliced beets
Carrot-raisin salad:
    ¾ cup shredded carrot
    1 tablespoon raisins
    1 tablespoon reduced-calorie mayonnaise
    2 tablespoons plain yogurt
1½ cups cantaloupe and honeydew melon balls
1 cup 1%-fat milk

Calories: 566   Percentage of calories from fat: 22%   Cholesterol: 56 mg. Sodium: 798 mg.

Supper 6

1 serving *Steamed Mango Mako Shark*
1 cup steamed broccoli flowerets with nutmeg and lemon juice
¾ cup cooked brown rice with fresh mushrooms
1 cup tomato juice

Calories: 535   Percentage of calories from fat: 16%   Cholesterol: 77 mg. Sodium: 1,272 mg.

Supper 7

2 *Tuna Tacos*

1 cup chopped endive with mushrooms and 2 tablespoons reduced-calorie Italian dressing

1 cup steamed summer squash with ½ green pepper, sliced

½ cup crushed pineapple

1 cup 1%-fat milk

Calories: 535   Percentage of calories from fat: 28%   Cholesterol: 41 mg. Sodium: 997 mg.

Supper 8

3 ounces sautéed calves' liver* (cooked with 2 teaspoons regular margarine and 1 small, sliced onion)

1 serving *Crab Slaw* on dark greens

½ cup mashed Hubbard squash with nutmeg and 1 teaspoon reduced-calorie margarine

Baked apple, cored and stuffed with 1 tablespoon raisins, 1 tablespoon brown sugar, and cinnamon

Calories: 533   Percentage of calories from fat: 21%   Cholesterol: 425 mg. Sodium: 873 mg.

Supper 9

1 skinless chicken breast baked with 1 tablespoon Dijon mustard, tarragon or thyme, and paprika

½ cup steamed spinach with lemon juice

Fruit salad on dark lettuce greens: ½ sliced pear, ½ cup each sliced peaches and red grapes

1 baking-powder biscuit with 1 teaspoon reduced-calorie margarine

Calories: 562   Percentage of calories from fat: 23%   Cholesterol: 146 mg. Sodium: 617 mg.

* Although liver is high in cholesterol, the American Heart Association advises having a small serving about once a month because it's also loaded with iron and vitamins. If you really dislike liver, you may substitute 3 ounces of cooked lean beef, such as top round or hamburger that's no more than 15% fat by weight in the raw state.

Supper 10

Stir-fried beef and vegetables:
In a large nonstick skillet, combine and stir-fry over medium-high heat:
1 tablespoon vegetable oil
3 ounces lean beef (e.g., top round), cut in strips
½ red pepper, cut in strips
½ cup broccoli flowerets
¾ cup trimmed pea pods
1 tablespoon soy sauce
2 tablespoons dry sherry
½ cup cooked enriched white (or brown) rice
½ cup grated red cabbage with ½ apple, chopped, and 2 tablespoons plain yogurt
2 apricots

Calories: 568   Percentage of calories from fat: 29%   Cholesterol: 55 mg. Sodium: 1,095 mg.

Mix-and-Match Snacks

Choose one snack each day from the following. You can have it any time you like. As with meals, vary your snack intake.

Snack 1

3 cups popcorn, popped with a small amount of oil and salted, if desired
¼ cup grape juice in seltzer water on ice

Calories: 158   Percentage of calories from fat: 33%   Cholesterol: 0 mg. Sodium: 523 mg.

Snack 2

½ cup *Zesty Seafood Dip*
1 carrot, cut into sticks
½ cup raw cauliflower
½ cup raw broccoli

Calories: 139   Percentage of calories from fat: 10%   Cholesterol: 36 mg. Sodium: 390 mg.

Snack 3

¼ cup *Smoky Salmon Spread*
8 rye Melba toast rounds

*Calories: 164   Percentage of calories from fat: 30%   Cholesterol: 19 mg.
Sodium: 468 mg.*

Snack 4

2 gingersnaps
¾ cup orange juice

*Calories: 152   Percentage of calories from fat: 19%   Cholesterol: 0 mg.
Sodium: 41 mg.*

Snack 5

1 fig bar
1 cup 1%-fat milk (optional: add ¼ teaspoon vanilla
extract, nutmeg, and low-calorie sweetener to taste)

*Calories: 154   Percentage of calories from fat: 21%   Cholesterol: 10 mg.
Sodium: 167 mg.*

Snack 6

¹⁄₁₂ angel food cake
½ cup strawberries, sliced

*Calories: 164   Percentage of calories from fat: 2%   Cholesterol: 0 mg.
Sodium: 143 mg.*

Snack 7

1 cup hot cocoa made with 1%-fat milk and sugar-free
cocoa mix
25 enriched thin pretzel sticks (about 2 inches long)

*Calories: 149   Percentage of calories from fat: 20%   Cholesterol 10 mg.
Sodium: 283 mg.*

Snack 8

> 9 steamed oysters—just over 2 ounces of cooked meats
> (the same weight of drained, canned oysters may be
> substituted for fresh)
> 4 ounces dry white wine (or orange juice)

Calories: 164   Percentage of calories from fat: 17%   Cholesterol: 69 mg.
Sodium: 146 mg.

Snack 9

> 1 apple, halved and spread with 2 teaspoons peanut butter

Calories: 144   Percentage of calories from fat: 34%   Cholesterol: 0 mg.
Sodium: 51 mg.

Snack 10

> ⅓ cup low-fat cottage cheese, seasoned with herbs and
> spread on 1 slice rye bread, topped with sliced cucumber
> ¼ cup apricot nectar in seltzer water on ice

Calories: 158   Percentage of calories from fat: 10%   Cholesterol: 3 mg.
Sodium: 479 mg.

FREE FOODS

Free Foods may be eaten as desired on the *Eat Fish* Launching Diet
and the Mix-and-Match Diet.

Beverages

> Coffee, black
> Tea, black
> Seltzer water or club soda
> Sugar-free carbonated beverages
> Sugar-free drink mixes
> Bouillon* or fat-free broth
> Sugar-free gelatin—no more than 2 cups per day

* Very high in sodium

Condiments/seasonings

> Equal sweetener
> Saccharin
> Lemon and lime juice
> Herbs
> Spices
> Prepared mustard
> Horseradish
> Nonstick vegetable spray
> Vinegar
> Fresh garlic
> Hot pepper sauce (e.g., Tabasco)
> Soy sauce*
> Worcestershire sauce

Raw vegetables

> Lettuce, all types
> Spinach
> Endive, escarole
> Celery
> Mushrooms
> Cucumbers
> Radishes
> Unsweetened pickles*

* Very high in sodium

Index

Page numbers in italics refer to tables.

Cardiovascular disease (CVD) *(cont.)*
    Eskimo study, 17–20
    and fat intake, 7–8; effect of lowering, 16
    fish diet, effect on, 5
    heart attack, prevention of, 24
    and high saturated fat in the diet, 13–14
    and lipids, 13
    omega-3 fatty acids, role of, 35
    and platelet aggregation, 35
    prostaglandins, role of, 35
    risk factors for developing, 23–24
Carp, about, 108
Castelli, William, M.D., 10, 15, 23, 24, 28
Catfish
    about, 108–109
    Fillets, Mexicano, 250
    Southern Slim-Fried, 251
Ceviche, risks of eating, 92–95
Channel bass. *See* Drum
Channel catfish. *See* Catfish
Cheese
    about, 214–16, *215*
    Fish Fillets, Cheesy, 249
    Pollock Fillet Parmigiana, 282
    Spinach-Ricotta-Stuffed Calamari, 284
    -Topped Baked Fish Fillets, 267
Cheesy Fish Fillets, 249
Chemicals, industrial, as fish contaminants, 76–81
Chinook salmon. *See* Salmon
Cholesterol, 13. *See also* Blood cholesterol level
    content of fish roe, caviar, lobster tomalley, 69
    content of shellfish, 67; effect of body's absorption of, 67–68
    in the diet, 14
    and fat content of fish, 68–69
    and fish-oil supplements, 49
    good vs. bad, 26
    values for finfish or shellfish, 69
Chowder, Clam, Chunky, 240
Chum salmon. *See* Salmon
Ciguatera fish poisoning, 86–87
Circulatory system, benefits of fish oils on, 5

Clam(s)
    about, 109–10
    Chowder, Chunky, 240
    cleaning, 183–84
    raw, risks of eating, 89–95
    shucked, storing, 176
    viral contamination, 90; steaming to prevent, 90
Cleaning finfish, 180–82
Cleaning shellfish, 183–84
Clotting, blood. *See* Blood clotting
Cocktail Sauce, 237
Cod(fish), about, 110–11
Cod Fillets
    with Fettuccine and Broccoli, 278
    with Lemon-Herb Butter, 261
    Simple, with Buttery Crumb Topping, 263
Cod-liver oil as supplement, 49
Cod-Tomato, Curry, Spicy, 259
Coho (silver) salmon. *See* Salmon
Columbia river smelt. *See* Smelt
Condiments, stocking your kitchen with, 228
Conger eel. *See* Pout
Connor, William, M.D., 45, 68
Contaminants of fish, 75–83
    environmental, 76
    minimizing exposure to, 82
Cooking fish, 185–205. *See also individual recipes*
    aroma-enhancing techniques, 203
    doneness, 185–86
    methods of, 188–202; baking, 189–90; broiling, 190–91; *en papillote,* 198; grilling, 191–93; marinating, 193; microwave, 193–95; oven-frying, 195–96; pan-frying, 196–97; poaching, 199–200; steaming, 200–201; stir-frying, 202
    parasites and, 186–88
    seasonings, 203–205
    thawing and, 188–89
Coquilles St. Jacques, 304
Cost of fish, 172–74
Crab
    about, 111–13
    cooked, storing, 176
    Frittata with Zucchini, 288

Fat(s) and oils. *See also* Omega-3 fatty acid
  about, 13–15
  blood (triglycerides), 13
  body (adipose tissue), 13
  cholesterol (dietary), 14; in fish, 69
  content of fish, 7–8, 58–65;
      comparison of, 64–65
  content in foods, 56 , 57
  dietary, 12; importance of, 12
  in food (oil, butter, etc.), 12–13
  intake, about lowering, 16; benefits of,
      16
  invisible, 12
  low-fat substitutions for, *218–19*
  monounsaturated, 14
  100 calorie equivalents, *208*
  percent calories from, 57
  polyunsaturated, 15
  questionnaire (U.S. Department of
      Agriculture), 324
  reducing, in diet, 210–16
  reducing, in recipes, 206–210
  role of, 209
  saturated, 13
  stocking your kitchen with, 228
Fettucine, Cod Fillets with Broccoli and,
    278
Filleting fish, 182–83
Fillets. *See also name of fish*
  about, 169
  Cheese-Topped Baked Fish, 267
  Cheesy Fish, 248
  Roll-Ups á la Diable, Zucchini-Carrot
      Fish, 308
Finfish. *See also* Fish, *name of finfish,*
    Shellfish
  breading and frying, effect of, 66
  categories of, 168–69; flatfish, 168;
      roundfish, 168
  cleaning, 180
  fat content of, *59–61, 63*
  filleting, 182–83; sharp knife for, 180
  fish slime, removing, 180–81
  raw, risks of eating, 92–95
  steaking, 182
  whole, drawing and dressing, 180–82
Fish, 103–62. *See also* Finfish, *name of
    fish,* Shellfish
  bacterial growth in, 165–66

Fish *(cont.)*
  benefit to circulatory system, 5
  benefit to immune system, 5
  calcium content of, 70
  calories in, 7–8
  (canned) eating in inland states, 333
  cholesterol content of, 54–55
  consumption of, and incidence of CVD
      (Dutch study), 21–23
  contaminants of, 75–83; minimizing
      exposure to, 82
  cost of, 11, 172–74
  dehydration of, 166, 177
  as a dietary mainstay, 4
  digestibility of, 54
  dishes, basic, easy, 331
  eating in restaurants, 334
  fact or fallacy (questionnaire), 53–73
  fat content of, *59–61, 63*; compared to
      meat, 55–57
  fat (fatty acid) content of, 64–65; and
      cholesterol, 69
  fats, about, 58–65
  fish oil effect on blood lipids, 27–28
  "Fishy" smell of, 10, 166–68, 203
  frozen. *See* Frozen fish
  how to buy, *170–72*
  how to prepare, 9–11, 185–205
  increase in diet, 8–9, 330–31
  iron content of, 70
  new varieties, 99–102
  omega-3 fatty acids in, 66. *See also*
      Omega-3 fatty acid
  overcooking, 185
  parasites, destroying, 186–87
  proper display and handling (in shops),
      166–67
  proper temperature, importance of,
      165–66
  protein, quality of, 7, 53–54
  quality control of, 163–71; controlling
      spoilage, 165–66
  recipes, fat reduction in, 206–210
  -rich diet, importance of, 24
  seasoning, 203–205
  sodium content of, 71–74
  stocking your kitchen with, 228
  "trade-offs" (substitutions). *See
      individual recipes*

Grouper, about, 119
Guidelines for storing shellfish, 175–76
Gumbo Shrimp and Salmon, 239

Haddock, about, 120
Hake (white, red), about, 121
Halibut
    about, 122
    with Florentine Sauce, Oven-Poached,
        310
    Steaks, Sesame-Soy, 262
Hard-shell clams. See Clams
Harmful effects of fish-oil supplements,
    48–50
Headaches, migraine, 6, 42–43
Heart attack. See Cardiovascular disease
Hepatitis from viral contamination of
        mollusks, 90
Herb(s,-ed)
    about, 203–205
    -Lemon Butter, Cod Fillets with, 261
    Sole Aux Fines Herbes, 221, 301
    stocking your kitchen with, 229
Herring/sardines, about, 122–23
High blood cholesterol. See Blood
        cholesterol level
High-density lipoproteins (HDL) (good
        cholesterol), 26
    effect of fish oils on, 29
Home freezing, about, 178–79
Honey-Lime Salmon, Broiled, with
        Tarragon, 265
"Hydrogenated" fats, 15
Hypertension, effect of fish oil on, 31

Immune system, effect of fish (oils) on,
    5–6, 36, 44
Inflammatory diseases, effect of fish (oils)
    on, 5–6, 44
Inkfish. See Squid
Inland states, eating fish in, 332–34
Insecticides (DDT), fish contaminants,
    79
Inspection of fish, for quality control,
    163–65
Iron content of fish, 70

Japanese
    diabetes in, 41

Japanese (cont.)
    level of omega-3 in, 20
    study, 20; diet comparisons, 20
John Dory. See Tilipia
Jonah and rock crabs. See Crab

Kepone as fish contaminant, 79
Kidney disease, influence of fish oil on,
    43
King crab. See Crab
"King Krab." See Surimi products
Kitchen, stocking, 226–29
Kromhout, Daan, Ph.D., M.P.H., 21,
    22, 27, 32

Lake perch. See Perch, freshwater
Lake trout. See Trout
Lands, William, Ph.D., 3, 6, 40, 44
LDL. See Low-density lipoproteins
Leeks, about, 205
Lemon(y)
    Butter, Tarragon Skate Wings Sautéed
        in Bread Crumbs and, 257
    Curried Creamed Tuna with Almonds,
        296
    Dill Sauce, Poached Salmon with, 299
    -Herb Butter, Cod Fillets with, 261
Lemon sole. See Flounder and sole
Leukotrienes
    and arthritis, 39–40
    and asthma, 40
    effect of fish oil, 34–36
Lime
    -Honey Salmon, Broiled, with
        Tarragon, 265
    Minty-, Grilled Mahimahi, 275
Linolenic acid, 65
Lipid risk factors, 24; about lowering,
    27
Lipids (triglyceride and cholesterol), 13;
    and CVD, 13
Lisa. See Mullet
Lobster
    American, about, 124–25
    cooked, storing, 176
    spiny, about, 125–26
Lotte. See Monkfish
Loup de mer. See Wolffish
Low-cholesterol diets and shellfish, 68

Low-density lipoproteins (LDL) (bad
cholesterol), 26
Low-fat milk products, cooking with,
213–16
Low-fat substitutions, *218–19*
Low-fat, well-balanced diet, *326*
Lupus, effect of fish oil on, 43

Mackerel
about, 126–27
Cajun-Style Grilled, 277
with Creamy Cucumber-Dill Sauce,
294
in Creamy Garlic Sauce, 281
Patties, Spicy, 269
Steaks, Spanish, Grilled with Mustardy
Topping, 258
Mahimahi, about, 127–28
"Making a low-fat diet part of your life,"
326
Mako shark. *See also* Shark
Steamed Mango, 307
Margarine, cooking with, 211; reduced
calorie, 211–12
Marinade(s)
for Broiled Sole, 279
Honey-Lime, 265
Minty-Lime, 275
Sesame-Soy, 262
Teriyaki Sauce, 313
Wine-Dill, 313
Marinara
Squid Rings, 283
Steamed Mussels, 236
Marinated Scallop Salad, Mustardy, 242
Marinating fish, 193
Massachusetts Division of Marine
Fisheries, 197, 276
McClane, A. J., 105, 122, 125, 135,
145
Meatless Spaghetti Sauce, Anne's, 287
Mercury, as fish contaminant, 80
Metals, heavy, as fish contaminant, 80
Mexicano Catfish Fillets, 250
Microwave cooking, 193–95
Microwave dishes
Mexicano Catfish Fillets, 250
Pollock with Tomatoes and Green
Peppers, Savory, 272

Microwave dishes *(cont.)*
Sole Amandine, Simple, 270
Tilefish Medallions in Sherried Orange
Sauce, 314
Migraine headaches, effect of fish (oils)
on, 6, 42–43
Milk products
low-fat, cooking with, 213–16
stocking your kitchen with, 227
Minerals and vitamins in fish, 69–74
Mint(y)
-Basil-Tomato Sauce, Grilled Tuna in,
285
-Lime Grilled Mahimahi, 275
Mirex as fish contaminant, 79
Mollusks and crustaceans. *See also* Shellfish
bacterial contamination of, 91
raw, risks of eating, 89–92; viral
contamination, 90
as source of zinc, 70
Monkfish
about, 128–29
Medallions, Breaded, 276
and Scallops, Saucy, 286
Monktail. *See* Monkfish
Monocytes, affected by fish oil, 30
Monounsaturated fatty acids, 13; effect
on cholesterol, 14
Moules. *See* Mussels
Mousse, Dilled Tuna-Salmon, 235
Mullet (black, silver, striped), about, 129
Multiple sclerosis (MS), influence of fish
oil on, 42
Mushroom(s)
and Crab Strogánoff, 280
-Crab Supreme, 292
Straw, Karen's Breaded Pollock with,
252
Mussels
about, 130–31
cleaning, 183–84
Marinara, Steamed, 236
raw, risks of eating, 89–92; viral
contamination, 90; steaming to
prevent, 90
shucked, storing, 176
Mustard(y)
about, 204
Marinated Scallop Salad, 242

Mustard(y) *(cont.)*
  Topping, Spanish Mackerel Steaks
    Grilled with, 258
Muttonfish. *See* Pout

National Academy of Sciences,
    endorsement of fish, 7
National Cancer Institute (NCI) study,
    37
National Heart, Lung, and Blood
    Institute (NHLBI), 25–26
National Institutes of Health (NIH), 3;
    panel on triglycerides, 27
National Marine Fisheries Service, 103
National Seafood Inspection Program,
    163
National Shellfish Sanitation Program
    (NSSP), 89, 164
Nettleton, Joyce, D.Sc., R.D., 3, 61,
    71, 84, 158, 168
The New England Journal of Medicine, 5;
    report, 27
Noncholesterol sterols, 67–68
Northern Lobster. *See* Lobster, American
Nutritional analysis of recipes, about,
    226

Ocean catfish. *See* Wolffish
Ocean perch and Pacific rockfish, 131–32
Oil-packed fish omega-3 fatty acids in,
    65
Olive oil in the diet, 14–15
Omega-6 fatty acids (vegetable oil), 5
Omega-3 fatty acid(s) (fish oil), 4–5, 30–
    35. *See also* Fat(s), Fish oil(s)
  and blood clotting, 30
  consumption during pregnancy, 45
  DHA (docosahexaenoic acid), 15; effect
    on CVD, 5, 44
  EPA (eicosapentaenoic acid), 15; and
    thromboxane, 35
  in fatty fish, 64–65
  fish processing (smoking, canning,
    etc.) effect on, 66
  frying fish, affecting, 66
  immune system, effects on, 5–6, 36
  levels in Eskimos, 19; and CVD, 19
  levels in Japanese, 20
  in oil-packed fish, 65

Omega-3 fatty acid(s) (fish oil) *(cont.)*
  and prevention of CVD, 51–52; taking
    supplements for, 31–32
  rich in polyunsaturates, 15
  in surimi products, 66
  therapeutic effect of, 5–6
Onions, about, 205
Orange
  -Almond Brown Rice Stuffing, Grilled
    Rainbow Trout with, 303
  Sauce, Sherried, Tilefish Medallions in,
    314
Orange roughy, about, 132–33
Oregon Health Sciences University,
    study, 27–30, 45
Organic chemicals, as fish contaminants,
    76
Oven-frying fish, 195–96
Overcooking fish, 185
Oxidation of frozen fish, 166
Oyster(s)
  Canapés, Smoked, 234
  cleaning, 183–84
  Eastern, about, 133–34
  raw, bacterial contamination of, 91;
    risks of eating, 89–92; viral
    contamination, 90
  shucked, storing, 176
  source of zinc, 69–70

Pacific Ocean perch. *See* Ocean perch
Pacific pompano. *See* Butterfish
"Packed Under Federal Inspection,"
    (PUFI), 163–64
Pan-frying fish, 196–97
Pantry, stocking, 226–30
Paralytic shellfish poisoning (PSP), 85;
    red tide, 85
Parasites (flukes, roundworms,
    tapeworms), destroying, 186–
    87
Parasitic infections from eating raw fish,
    93–95
Pasta
  Cod Fillets with Broccoli and
    Fettucine, 278
  Shrimp-Tortellini Salad, 243
  -Tuna Toss, 244
Paugie. *See* Porgy